BEYOND THE LINES

BEYOND THE LINES

Social Networks and Palestinian Militant Organizations in Wartime Lebanon

Sarah E. Parkinson

CORNELL UNIVERSITY PRESS   ITHACA AND LONDON

Copyright © 2022 by Sarah E. Parkinson

This book is freely available in an open access edition thanks to TOME (Toward an Open Monograph Ecosystem)—a collaboration of the Association of American Universities, the Association of University Presses, and the Association of Research Libraries—and the generous support of Johns Hopkins University. Learn more at the TOME website, available at: openmonographs.org.

The text of this book is licensed under a Creative Commons Attribution-NonCommercial-NoDerivatives 4.0 International (CC BY-NC-ND 4.0) license: https://creativecommons.org/licenses/by-nd/4.0/legalcode. To use this book, or parts of this book, in any way not covered by the license, please contact Cornell University Press, Sage House, 512 East State Street, Ithaca, New York 14850. Visit our website at cornellpress.cornell.edu.

First published 2022 by Cornell University Press

Library of Congress Cataloging-in-Publication Data

Names: Parkinson, Sarah E., 1981– author.
Title: Beyond the lines : social networks and Palestinian militant organizations in wartime Lebanon / Sarah E. Parkinson.
Description: Ithaca [New York] : Cornell University Press, [2021] | Includes bibliographical references and index.
Identifiers: LCCN 2022010738 (print) | LCCN 2022010739 (ebook) | ISBN 9781501766299 (hardcover) | ISBN 9781501767142 (paperback) | ISBN 9781501766305 (pdf) | ISBN 9781501766312 (epub)
Subjects: LCSH: Palestinian Arabs—Social networks—Lebanon—History—20th century. | Religious militants—Social networks—Lebanon—History—20th century. | Palestinian Arabs—Lebanon—History—20th century. | Palestinian Arabs—Lebanon—Politics and government—20th century. | Lebanon—History—Civil War, 1975-1990. | Lebanon—Politics and government—1975–1990.
Classification: LCC DS80.55.P34 P37 2021 (print) | LCC DS80.55.P34 (ebook) | DDC 305.892/7405692—dc23/eng/20220815
LC record available at https://lccn.loc.gov/2022010738
LC ebook record available at https://lccn.loc.gov/2022010739

In memory of my father and of Lee Ann Fujii

Contents

Acknowledgments	ix
List of Abbreviations	xiii
Note on Transliteration and Translation	xv
Maps	xvii
Introduction: Backstage Labor and Organizational Adaptation	1
1. Memories and Mythologies of Militancy: An Ethnographic Approach to Studying Militant Organizations	15
2. Building a Social Infrastructure: The Palestine Liberation Organization and the Guerrilla Factions in Lebanon	30
3. Social Networks and Wartime Violence: Comparing Repertoires during the 1982 Israeli Invasion	52
4. Beyond the Lines: Gendered Mobilization and Organizational Resilience in Militant Groups	71
5. Crossing Collaborators: Emotion, Informing, and Civilian Mobilization in Occupied South Lebanon	92
6. The Face of the Camps: Leadership and Loyalty in Combat Units	114
7. "Every Faction for Itself": Personalized Militias and Fragmented Battle Lines	135
Conclusion: Echoes of Organizations	155
Appendix A: Methodological Approach and Ethical Considerations	169
Appendix B: Archival Materials and Methods	187
Appendix C: Palestinian Refugee Camps in Lebanon	193
Notes	195
References	217
Index	239

Acknowledgments

Perhaps it is fitting to start a book that is fundamentally about resistance with the recognition that the success of this project rested on people who encouraged me to push boundaries. My deepest appreciation goes to my Palestinian and Lebanese interlocutors. Without their kindness, generosity, patience, hospitality, and engagement, this project would have gone nowhere. I regret that many of them—particularly in light of their personal dedication to preserving Palestinian history and to empowering the refugee community—have asked to remain anonymous. I would, however, like to thank the members of Fatah's Women's Office, who invited me to spend hours with them, who shared their lives and perspectives with me, and who protected me as though I were their sister. Officers in Fatah and representatives from the Palestine Liberation Organization in Lebanon invited me to meetings, vouched for me, reflected on their memories, and provided copies of video archives from the Sabra and Shatila massacre and the War of the Camps. Members of the al-Khatib family, as well as Umm Umar, Umm Yusif, Umm Tariq, Umm Muhammad, Umm Khaled, and Umm Ibrahim, opened their homes to me and treated me as if I were one of their own children. Members of countless social associations, a number of employees of the United Nations Relief and Works Agency for Palestine Refugees in the Near East (UNRWA), and affiliates of several political factions went out of their way to grant me interviews, to facilitate introductions, and to broaden my understanding of Palestinian communities and histories in Lebanon and beyond. Omar al-Ghannoum, Raji Abdul Salaam, and Salah Hamzeh have acted as my sounding boards for years, and they deserve special recognition.

This project began as a dissertation at the University of Chicago. My PhD adviser, John Padgett, was an unwavering source of support and intellectual inspiration. John's absolute disdain for disciplinary boundaries and pursuit of big, meaningful questions are the best models I could have as a scholar. Lisa Wedeen pushed me to do creative, challenging work and to foreground power and ethics. Despite their not being on my committee, Paul Staniland and Dan Slater were kind and encouraging mentors. Paul, in particular, organized a formative writing group focused on networks and armed organizations that included Jonathan Obert and Eric Hundman; it has been a privilege to continue thinking and discussing with them over the years. My committee members at Yale University were equally invaluable. Elisabeth Jean Wood's incisive, generous comments helped me to think through the social, political, and emotional intricacies of both militant organizations and research methodology. Steven Wilkinson was a grounding force whose comments pushed me to become sovereign over my methodological choices. During my time as a predoctoral fellow at the Program on Order Conflict and Violence at Yale's MacMillan Center, Stathis Kalyvis's relentless critiques forced me to clarify my theoretical and ontological approach, vastly improving the project. Time spent in the OCV offices on Prospect Street also introduced me to Eugene Finkel and to Janet Lewis; their own scholarly contributions and comments have profoundly shaped my work.

The communities anchored by George Washington University's Institute for Middle East Studies, where I spent a year as a post-doc, and the Project on Middle East Political Science (POMEPS) have had a transformative effect on my thinking over the years. I am particularly grateful to Marc Lynch and Jillian Schwedler, who have given me endless feedback, guidance, and emotional support. POMEPS generously hosted an early book workshop that included Amaney Jamal and Roger Petersen; this book and my own thinking are clearer thanks to them. Amaney, in particular, has been extraordinary in her mentorship and encouragement throughout the years. I have also benefited from the advice and friendship of brilliant people in these networks, including Nermin Allam, Melani Cammett, Laryssa Chomiak, Janine Clark, Adria Lawrence, Rabab al-Mahdi, Rima Majed, Lama Mourad, Curtis Ryan, and Stacey Philbrick Yadav.

My colleagues from the University of Chicago's PhD program have continued to be a source of intellectual inspiration, support, and accountability. Christopher Graziul and Chad Levinson remain my amazing friends and collaborators. Throughout my graduate career, I was also lucky to be part of conversations, support networks, and reading groups that included Ahsan Butt, Sofia Fenner, Morgan Kaplan, Diana Kim, Yasmeen Mekawy, Lindsey O'Rourke, Dina Rashed, Erica Simmons, and Nicholas Rush Smith. While at Yale, my conversations with Beth Iams Wellman, Julia Choucair-Vizoso, Regina Bateson, Josh Goodman, and Francesca Grandi consistently influenced my opinions on research methods, the Middle East, and political violence.

Funding from the National Science Foundation's Graduate Research Fellowship, the Social Science Research Council's Dissertation Proposal Development Fellowship and International Dissertation Research Fellowship programs, the Palestinian American Research Center (PARC), a POMEPS Travel Research and Engagement Grant, and Johns Hopkins University made it possible for me to conduct two years of research on the ground in Lebanon. The Issam Fares Institute for Public Policy and International Affairs at the American University of Beirut hosted me in 2009–2010 and again in 2018. For giving me this home away from home, I thank Rami Khoury, Sari Hanafi, Tarek Mitri, and Rayan el-Amine.

A fellowship at the University of Minnesota's Institute for Advanced Study gave me space to think and write for a semester. I am grateful to all these programs, and to their staff.

Archivists and librarians at the American University of Beirut (AUB), the Institute for Palestine Studies (IPS), *al-Safir,* the Institut français du Proche Orient, PARC's Ramallah office, and the American Friends Service Committee (AFSC) Archives provided innumerable hours of assistance and shared invaluable knowledge. I would especially like to thank Kaoukab Chebaro, Donald Davis, and Perla Issa for their gracious assistance over the years. Video interviews from the Palestinian Oral History Archive (POHA), archival materials from the AFSC, and translated portions of Mahmoud Zeidan's memoir (published by IPS) have been excerpted with permission; I extend my heartfelt thanks to the institutions that manage these collections or facilitated materials' creation.

Over the years, I received invaluable feedback on chapters or concepts in this manuscript from Christopher Ansell, Emily Kalah Gade, Amelia Hoover Green, Margaret Keck, Zachariah Mampilly, Theodore McLauchlin, Timothy Pachirat, Wendy Pearlman, Jonah Schulhofer-Wohl, Anastasia Shesterinina, and Michael Weintraub. I am especially indebted to Faten Ghosn and Sean Lee, both of whom read the entire manuscript and contemplated the finer points of Lebanese and Palestinian history with me. Orkideh Behrouzan, Kanisha Bond, Milli Lake, and Sherry Zaks have repeatedly talked through the most minute details of this work with me and reminded me of the importance of practicing empathy and humanity when writing about violence. Before her passing, Lee Ann Fujii organized a writing group that included myself and Devorah Manekin; both read multiple early drafts of this work and provided indispensable suggestions. Helen Kinsella, Samantha Majic, Peregrine Schwartz-Shea, Joe Soss, Scott Straus, and Dvora Yanow have all been touchstones for me as I thought through my methodological approach to this work as well as the ethical commitments it entailed. My colleagues at Johns Hopkins University and the University of Minnesota have provided lively, intellectually generative environments in which I have been privileged to work. I am also grateful for feedback received during workshops at George Washington University, Princeton University, the Radcliffe Institute for Advanced Study, the University of Chicago, the University of Minnesota, the University of Virginia, the University of Washington–Seattle, Uppsala University, and Yale University. Portions of this book were previously published in *The American Political Science Review;* in *Perspectives on Politics;* and in *World Politics.* They have been included with permission from Cambridge University Press.

I have benefited immensely from the labor, wisdom, and wit of many research assistants over the years: Salah and Rima in Lebanon; Eslam Bedawy, Kelsey Fogt, Thomas Vargas, and Sean Williams at the University of Minnesota; Ayesha

Durrani, Sofia Smith, and Raied Haj Yahya at Johns Hopkins University. David Meyer, also of Johns Hopkins, worked tirelessly with me to piece together historical data for the four maps included in this volume. This project would not be nearly as rich without their contributions. I am also indebted to the editing skills of Evan Ramzipoor and Audra J. Wolfe, who made this book far more readable than I could have done alone. I also wish to extend my appreciation to Roger Malcolm Haydon, who brought this project to its home at Cornell University Press, as well as to Jim Lance and to Clare Jones, who brought it to press.

Over the years, Beirut has hosted some of the most intense, skilled, and dedicated journalists I have ever encountered. Annasofie Flamand, in particular, introduced me to Lebanon's Palestinian refugee camps during the summer of 2007, inviting me to tag along for a series of interviews in Ain al-Hilweh that are described at the beginning of chapter 1. She, along with Gabriela Keller and Abigail Fielding-Smith, were confidantes, sounding boards, and close friends throughout my time in Lebanon.

Anyone who has been through the process of writing a book knows that having compassionate friends to cheer you on and force you to go outside for some fresh air now and then is absolutely essential. Sarah Crawford, Laura Davulis, Eric Jabert, Janna Johnson, Alexandra Krensky, Racha Mouawia, Scot Myers, Yoda Patta, and Becca and Andrew Yates have been incredible in this regard. I am also immensely privileged to have a supportive family that has encouraged my career choices. First among them is my mother, whose early skepticism about this research transformed into full-throated encouragement (in part thanks to my interlocutors themselves). Finally, Evann Smith was unexpectedly around for the beginning, middle, and end of this project. They are proof that taking the long road is often the most rewarding path.

Abbreviations

ALF	Arab Liberation Front
ANM	Arab Nationalist Movement
DFLP	Democratic Front for the Liberation of Palestine
GUPS	General Union of Palestinian Students
GUPW	General Union of Palestinian Women
IDF	Israel Defense Forces
LAF	Lebanese Armed Forces
LCP	Lebanese Communist Party
LF	Lebanese Forces
LNM	Lebanese National Movement
NLP	National Liberal Party
PCP	Palestinian Communist Party
PFLP	Popular Front for the Liberation of Palestine
PLA	Palestine Liberation Army
PLF	Palestine Liberation Front
PLO	Palestine Liberation Organization
PNG	Palestinian National Guard
PNO	Popular Nasserite Organization
PNSF	Palestinian National Salvation Front
PPSF	Palestinian Popular Struggle Front
PRCS	Palestinian Red Crescent Society
PSP	Progressive Socialist Party
SLA	South Lebanon Army

Note on Transliteration and Translation

I use a simplified version of the *International Journal of Middle East Studies* (IJMES) transliteration rules. The medial ʿayn, and the *hamza* are marked, but I do not include other diacritical markings (such as the dots to distinguish *da* and *dawd* or the macrons used to mark long vowels). I employ the IJMES Word List as a reference for common Arabic terms and some proper names, including Hizbullah, Yasir Arafat, kaffiyeh, Bekaa, and Salafi.

For the greatest accessibility, I give location names in Lebanon using common colloquial transliterations rather than employing IJMES rules; the same approach applies to maps. "Beirut" is written in English, whereas I use the Arabic names for Saida, Sur, and Trablous (Sidon, Tyre, and Tripoli, as they are rendered in English). I use the transliterated spelling "Sur" rather than "Sour" for clarity of pronunciation in English. Names of historical figures and living individuals are written either as they spell them or according to resources such as the PASSIA guide. Short interview excerpts are reproduced according to colloquial conventions for transliteration.

Translations for conversations and interviews with my interlocutors, as well as those for the Palestinian Oral History Archives interviews that I accessed, are my own. As detailed in appendix B, translations from Arabic-language memoirs, from archival documents, and from other source material are either my own or the work of research assistants who are fluent Arabic speakers. Perla Issa of the Institute for Palestine Studies in Beirut lightly edited the translations of quotes from Mahmoud Zeidan's memoir for accuracy and to ensure that the text conforms with a forthcoming English edition of the work.

MAP 1. Lebanon

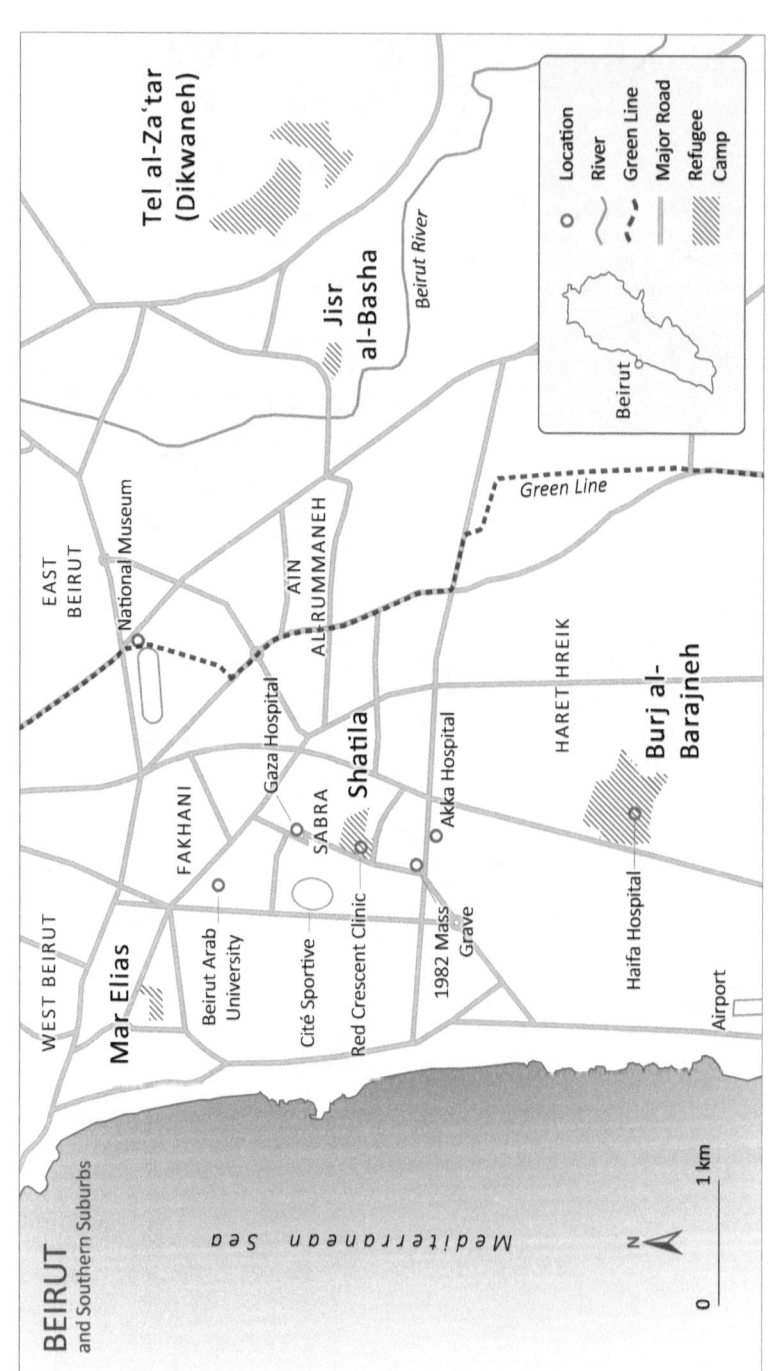

MAP 2. Beirut and Southern Suburbs

MAP 3. Saida

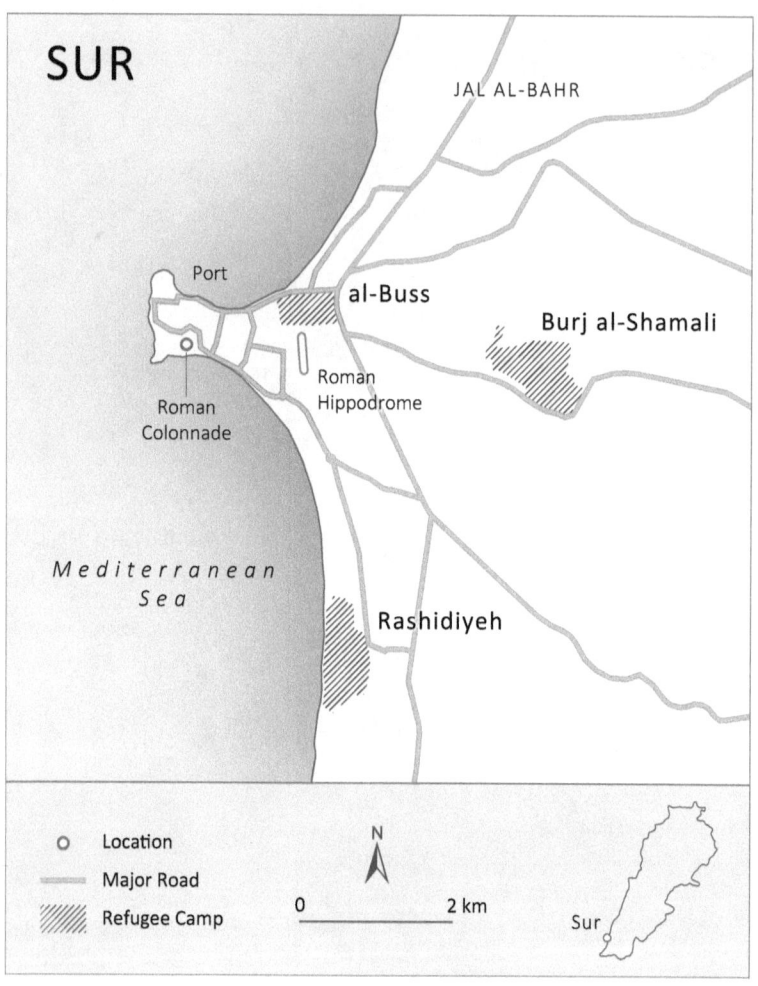

MAP 4. Sur

BEYOND THE LINES

Introduction

BACKSTAGE LABOR AND ORGANIZATIONAL ADAPTATION

Munadileh was deployed just behind the Palestinian guerrilla lines in Saida, a major coastal city in South Lebanon, as she watched the Israeli army approach. It was June of 1982, and the teenager had been well trained to use the AK-47 slung around her back. On that day, however, it wasn't her job to use it. Munadileh was a nurse, and she saw the fighters' positions primarily in terms of their distance from the sterile operating rooms of the hospital. Instead of training her sights on the approaching Israeli forces, she scanned for Palestinian casualties to transfer into an ambulance for the jaw-clenching, rubber-to-the-road ride to a medical facility.

When Munadileh drew the fighters' positions for me in the spring of 2011, she sketched them as a semicircle to the south of a dot representing the hospital; her puzzle was how to get injured guerrillas from the semicircle to the dot without being obliterated by the Israel Defense Forces' (IDF's) ongoing bombardment. Back and forth, back and forth until the Palestinian lines collapsed, at which point Munadileh retreated to the hospital. She was treating patients when bombs started falling around the medical facility itself. With each shuddering impact, the medical workers paused their suturing, withdrew a syringe, or pulled a little more tightly on an unsecured bandage. Those in charge decided to evacuate. In the chaos, anyone who was still physically capable grabbed stretchers, wheelchairs, or gurneys as wounded civilians and soldiers streamed out of the hospital. Munadileh believes that there were still people in the building when a gas tank received a direct hit, creating an explosion that engulfed the facility in flames. Then the arrests began, Munadileh told me, and "*sar al-dunya sawda*"—the world became black.

Raised in a family associated with the leftist Arab Nationalist Movement (ANM), Munadileh knew her way around weapons and had served in frontline combat positions. But, when she described her career trajectory to me, Munadileh emphasized the other roles she had played: as battlefield medic, trauma nurse, ambulance driver, social worker, even logistician. When she told me her story, Munadileh emphasized how much skill went into these different forms of labor, how much education and training they required, and the degree to which taking on these assignments required her to trust and be trusted. She asked me to call her *Munadileh*—which translates from Arabic as "a struggler"—rather than to identify her as a *muqatila,* meaning a fighter. She wasn't, and had never been, "just" a fighter. Another veteran asked me to call her "*Zahra,*" or "flower." This seemingly delicate choice harks back to a specific role in the resistance: the girls' wing of the military scouting unit of Fatah, a leading Palestinian faction, was called the *Zaharat,* the plural of *zahra.* Each woman wanted her experiences understood in terms of her individual story as well as representing the complicated realities associated with participating in an armed national project.

This book highlights people like Munadileh: militants who take on ostensibly "backstage" roles in asymmetric wars. Every armed conflict involves backstage labor—that is, logistic, intelligence, medical, finance, and human resources work that facilitates organizational continuity, resilience, and survival, but that may not involve using a weapon. Indeed, most experienced militants with whom I spoke did not consider the physical labor of *killing* the most important aspect of armed conflict. Rather, these militants approached unconventional warfare as a series of challenges focused on information, logistics, and coordination. They needed to keep mobile forces supplied, identify collaborators, disrupt rival belligerents' operations, and provide essential services such as healthcare to their cadres and to the populations on whose support they depended. Militant organizations that persist do so because they have found ways to negotiate these challenges. Understanding the importance of noncombat roles and the people who serve in them offers essential insights into why militant organizations behave the way they do.

I trace the backstage labor that made it possible for Palestinian resistance groups to adapt and survive in Lebanon in the 1980s, despite repeated military campaigns by Lebanese, Israeli, and Syrian forces. In the pages that follow, I take these roles as being essential to understanding mobilization, political violence, resistance to occupation, organizational adaptation, and armed conflict in general. My commitment to this approach reflects an ambition to engage with the role of individual and collective actors as drivers of expressly organizational outcomes. In no case is a militant "simply" a militant. Rather, the relational perspective that I adopt sees individuals as simultaneously playing multiple roles in distinct social networks. I take seriously Munadileh's insistence that she must be understood as not merely a fighter, but also a nurse, a spouse, a sister, a friend, a coworker, a classmate, a teammate, and a community member.[1] This social complexity, and specifically the way that it interacts with militant organizations' formal hierarchies, is essential to understanding organizations' capacity to adapt and evolve.

Going beyond the Lines in Intrastate War

Zahra, like Munadileh and many other militants, started off her political and military career as a scout at a fairly young age. As a teenager, she survived the months-long 1976 siege of the Tel al-Zaʿtar Palestinian refugee camp in East Beirut's suburbs. Right-wing Lebanese militias blockaded the camp in January 1976, as the Lebanese Civil War escalated. They besieged the population throughout the summer before eventually massacring survivors following the camp's surrender in August 1976. Zahra and her family fled to a village outside Beirut, where Zahra became a military instructor, drilling dozens of other young women eager to fight as guerrillas for the Palestinian resistance. They moved again and were living in South Beirut in September 1982, when militiamen affiliated with the Lebanese Kataʾib, the South Lebanon Army (SLA), and other predominantly Christian militias entered the Greater Shatila district, disappearing and killing between two and three thousand predominantly Palestinian civilians.[2] Zahra again escaped, but she returned forty days later for demonstrations that memorialized the victims.[3] Worried about being arrested, she concealed the Palestinian flag that she had brought along in tribute to the victims in her clothing. At the last moment, standing over the mass grave south of the camp, she pulled it out and laid it gently on the dirt.

Throughout the 1980s, Zahra served in both social service and intelligence positions. Though she was targeted by rival factions and by the Syrian *mukhabarat* (intelligence services), Zahra continued to travel incognito to a blockaded camp to teach in an informal school that the residents organized. People, she underscored to me, did not want their children to fall behind in their education. Zahra also used her position as cover to smuggle messages and supplies into the camp for the guerrilla faction. At one point, a childhood friend from Tel al-Zaʿtar who was affiliated with a rival, Syrian-allied Palestinian faction saved Zahra from a prison sentence by destroying her intelligence file. Her luck ran out about a year later, when the Syrian *mukhabarat* captured and incarcerated her in a notorious prison under the Beau Rivage Hotel in Beirut. Upon her release, she went straight back to political work. This time, she moved into a subunit focused on social aid, becoming an active member of the General Union of Palestinian Women (GUPW).

Over the course of her career as a militant, Zahra survived multiple camp sieges, several massacres, imprisonment, torture, and constant surveillance by rival Palestinian factions, Lebanese militias, the Lebanese Armed Forces (LAF), and the *mukhabarat*. At one point during the 1990s, the Syrians installed a checkpoint in front of her building in an attempt to rearrest her. Zahra responded by sleeping at friends' houses—shoes on, in her street clothes—for the better part of the decade. Despite intense violence, repression, and, at times, the faction's unpopularity within the refugee camps, she remained loyal to Fatah. She remains frustrated that, as a woman, she is currently barred from serving in the organization's military wing despite her long years of service.

When I asked Zahra why she remained active, even after being tortured, she told me: "I didn't train [to fight] because I love war, I trained [to fight] because I love life (*Ma darabt ashan bhib al-harb, darabt ashan bhib al-hayat*)." While anthropomorphizing organizations has its limits, one might ask similar questions of Fatah, the Popular Front, or any of the other Palestinian factions that one wants to ask of Zahra: Why did you remain active? What made you resilient? How did you adapt?

A major takeaway of my research is that both women's and men's militant careers tended to include various roles over time. Only one of my interlocutors portrayed his guerrilla activities solely in terms of violent participation. Now a high-ranking officer in Fatah, Ibrahim joined his refugee camp's defensive front in the mid-1980s at the age of fifteen, was arrested shortly thereafter by Syrian *mukhabarat*, and spent the rest of the war in a military prison in Syria. He described his teenage self as "an idiot spraying bullets [*rash al-rasas*] at anything that moved." He acknowledged that this was not a particularly helpful contribution to the organization. As our conversation progressed, he explained that he did not become valuable to the organization until he was imprisoned with hundreds of other cadres in Syria, at which point Fatah members educated him politically.[4] Not coincidentally, teenage Ibrahim had far less preparation than most Palestinian militants, who tended to move through distinct combat and noncombat roles in the Palestine Liberation Organization (PLO) or the guerrilla parties over time.[5] This pattern of transitioning through various forms of violent and nonviolent participation is true for both men and women militants. The practice allowed them to carry skill sets across multiple roles and subdivisions, which in turn contributed to organizational learning.[6]

In this book, I specifically examine how processes of network adaptation, driven by the hidden labor of quotidian social networks, led to the formation of logistics and smuggling apparatuses, intelligence and counterintelligence units, personalized militias, tactical teams, and, eventually, the emergence of local community defensive fronts among military Palestinian factions operating in Lebanon. I argue that militant adaptation and resilience operate as a continual feedback loop between belligerents engaged in asymmetric conflict as they deploy repertoires of violence—that is, "that set of practices that a group routinely engages in as it makes claims on other political or social actors" (E. J. Wood 2009, 133)—that in turn reshape social networks.[7]

I identify three levels of organizational adaptation in response to external pressure. First, when militants use everyday relationships to reroute organizational communications and resources—for example, orders, intelligence, weaponry, or payments—without altering their fundamental organizational structure, they are engaged in *repurposing*.[8] In a second stage, when these adaptations become systematic across an organization—that is, routinized and institutionalized to the extent that actors rely upon them, rather than on the top-down, formal hierarchies described "on paper"—*remapping* occurs.[9] The third and final step of this adaptive process, *emergence*, only occurs when an organization incorporates new rules, skills, and practices into network ties, thereby creating new constitutive understandings of collective membership and goals (Padgett and McLean 2006; Padgett and Powell 2012; Obert 2014, 2018; R. Gould 1995). In effect, emergence brings about both new structures and organizational identities via endogenous network processes. Building an understanding of organizational adaptation, emergence, and evolution through the interaction of social networks with repertoires of violence facilitates a more complete, better grounded, and representative understanding of conflict dynamics.

Violence, Quotidian Social Networks, and Organizational Resilience

In the contemporary era, multiparty and intrastate conflicts similar to the ones in 1980s Lebanon—for example, those in Yemen, the Democratic Republic of the Congo, and Libya—annually account for millions of civilian casualties and displaced persons. In 2019, 11.7 million refugees, which accounts for 57 percent of the total global refugee population, originated from just three countries experiencing such conflicts: Syria, Afghanistan, and South Sudan (UN High Commissioner for Refugees 2020). These complex intrastate wars often involve diverse state and nonstate armed actors, including rebel and militant groups, paramilitaries, local militias and community civil defense committees, state armed forces, mercenaries, and sometimes foreign military advisers.[10] Foreign governments and corporate entities may fund or otherwise materially support belligerents; regional organizations such as the African Union or the United Nations may send observers or peacekeepers in the hopes of enforcing treaties and stemming violence.

Conventional, front-based combat does not generally characterize these types of "civil" wars; they often feature irregular warfare (Kalyvas and Balcells 2010), varying in both the strategies and tactics that military organizations use as well as in the intensity of hostilities over time. A conflict of this sort may feature aerial bombardment some months, hit-and-run guerrilla engagement during others, and periods of ostensible "calm" punctuated by kidnappings and disappearances. Belligerents and civilians alike must constantly update their survival strategies. These conflicts reach directly into people's neighborhoods and homes via tactics such as informing and siege, with a massive human cost. For example, the 1,417-day Siege of Sarajevo (1992–1995) killed nearly 19,000 people; infrastructural damage to the city totaled US$18.5 billion (Sito-Sucic 2006). Experts have estimated that between 2011 and 2019, the Syrian regime incarcerated approximately 1.2 million of its citizens; in that last year, the Syrian Network for Human Rights reported that government agents had tortured more than 14,000 people to death since the civil war's beginning (Black 2014; Safi 2019). Yet war also affects people's everyday lives by infusing daily activities such as going to work, shopping for food, and attending school with potentially mortal risks. Organizational adaptability and resilience shape how parties to the conflict, as well as civilians, experience wartime violence beyond its public and the spectacular instantiations that garner media attention (Hermez 2017, 9; Parkinson 2015), including in their homes, in prison camps, and on the run. They can mean the difference between a state's fighting isolated, inexperienced, fragmented armed cells or a robust, multiparty insurgent front with a professionalized advocacy wing. They can also affect whether civilians living in rebel-controlled areas have access to food, healthcare, protection, and education.

The repertoires of violence and repression deployed against nonstate armed organizations affect militants' organizational and social networks, shaping the potential for and patterns of repurposing, remapping, and emergence. The first section below discusses the material and social consequences that violence has on militants' networks. The second asks how these groups respond to these material and meaning-based effects. In the face of challenging circumstances and unpredictable futures, the content and structure of militant groups' social network ties evolve, creating new procedures, resource flows, and practices that may ultimately produce additional organizational units.

Experiences of Repression

Violence and repression affect militants' quotidian social networks both via "material" changes to network structure—that is, by disrupting nodes (people) and ties (relationships)—and via shifts in the collective meanings embedded within social relations. For example, when an individual is arrested or is killed, a network has been disrupted; a node in the network has disappeared. Alternatively, when a person joins an organization, marries into a family, takes a new job, or starts worshipping with a new congregation, a new node with fresh ties is created in the relevant network. When a group replaces someone who has been arrested, or redistributes tasks previously assigned to a person who has died, or initiates new lines of communication within prisons, we are witnessing the first level of organizational adaptation: repurposing.

Other transformations within organizations' social infrastructure may be less obvious. As evinced by both Zahra's and Munadileh's telling of their own stories, people interpret encounters with violence and repression via their roles in multiple networks. They come to understand their positions in new ways, and they recalibrate their roles and relations within social structures accordingly.[11] In Zahra's case, her family's and community's experience of Tel al-Zaʿtar and the Sabra and Shatila massacre shaped her own future understanding of wartime risks to civilian communities. These experiences helped to develop the responsibilities she felt and projected onto her organization, the roles she sought out, and even the way that she leveraged her quotidian relationships to organizational ends.

In much the same manner that this account focuses on the wide variety of roles within and adjacent to militant organizations, it eschews an overly narrow understanding of violence. Instead of counting bodies, it explores how people, communities, and organizations experienced a wide array of violent and repressive tactics. It emphasizes how counterinsurgent states and their nonstate allies (such as local paramilitary organizations and militias) deploy tactics that are both visible and surreptitious, sensational and banal, fast and drawn out, often all simultaneously. The effects of the type of violence and repression I discuss—pressure to collaborate and inform, incarceration and detention, sieges and forced starvation, nonlethal intimidation and harassment—are, admittedly, more difficult to quantify than body counts. Nevertheless, these broader repertoires of violence shape key organizational outcomes by creating feedback loops through social networks that, in turn, influence militant groups' trajectories.

This approach examines, theorizes, and compares the distinct network effects of specific violent and repressive tactics—for example, a combat death via an artillery barrage versus a combat death involving hand-to-hand fighting, or the subsequent desecration of a corpse versus the assassination of a high-ranking commander. In one sense, each death has the same material effect on the network, in that each has removed a single node. Focusing on the *meaning* of those deaths, however, produces new analytical insights into how militant groups persist in the face of repression. A meaning-based approach asks how those in the deceased soldiers' social networks understand these deaths—for example, as "lawful" or "unlawful"—and whether those understandings subsequently influence their social networks. In terms of organizational change and adaptation, a qualitative difference can be seen between different types of deaths, as well as between a death, a capture, and a disappearance. A particularly gruesome murder, for instance, might inject a new sharpness into everyday conversation focused on the enemy's barbarism. Taking this observation a step further, we might then ask how those meanings influence organizational decision-making and behavior. Each of these situations holds implications for how people interpret violence, how those understandings ripple through social networks, and how organizations adapt and mobilize in response to those meanings.[12]

Social Infrastructure and Organizational Change

Everyday relationships shape the ways that militants both experience and fight wars. I use the term *social infrastructure* to refer to patterns of overlap between quotidian networks—that is, everyday kinship, marriage, friendship, and community relationships—and formal organizational hierarchies.[13] These latter structures are best thought of as elements of an organization's "official," institutionalized configuration, including chains of command, subdivisional layouts, and planned task differentiation between bureaus, subunits, and so forth (Sinno 2010; Pearlman 2011; Bakke et al. 2012). Overlays and intersections within the social infrastructure influence which quotidian networks are proximate to which formal, intraorganizational ties. Put more concretely, it matters whether an informant plays soccer with the recruiter's cousin or whether the unit commander is married to the general's son.

The overlaps between the multiple types of networks that constitute social infrastructure also influence how violence reverberates through social systems. A counterinsurgent state military's mass detention of "fighters," for example, might broadly target boys and men as "suspected insurgents" based only upon gender (Mikdashi 2014), but communities might experience it as the disappearance of husbands, fathers, children, and brothers, who are also simultaneously understood as, for example, "breadwinners" or "star athletes." This social infrastructure matters both within and across organizations. In Zahra's case, her friendly, ongoing, everyday relationships to other Tel al-Zaʿtar survivors—who had many different affiliations—facilitated much of her militant work, including the destruction of her intelligence file.

On a deeper conceptual level, both Munadileh's and Zahra's stories reveal how the malleability of social ties, via both agentive choice and collective interpretations, allows militants to reshape their social relationships to organizational ends and vice versa. I call this innate malleability of social relationships "relational plasticity," a term I have modified from "neuroplasticity"—that is, the brain's ability to reconfigure neurons in response to stimuli. Relational plasticity allows for increasingly complex relationships to emerge among militant cadres in wartime environments. Munadileh, for instance, met her husband through her Marxist group, an experience shared by many militant women I interviewed. A professional relationship became a personal one because Munadileh's work made her a more desirable spouse. In part, this was because she and her future husband developed profound trust in and admiration of each other because of the nature of their work. Yet it was also because many factions, including Munadileh's, encourage marriage within organizational boundaries.

Both Munadileh's and Zahra's experiences illustrate how one's quotidian relationships are *repurposed* for organizational ends, a practice facilitated by relational plasticity. In each case, the specific relationships formed a network bridge—that is, a connection between otherwise unconnected or distantly connected maps of social ties, and between formal organizational hierarchies and everyday relations. Munadileh's organization went a step beyond, actively *remapping* organizational roles by systematically repurposing specific types of quotidian relationships to *routinely* perform particular organizational functions. In her case, Munadileh and her husband's faction assigned them as well as other married couples to tactical teams together, an arrangement that leveraged systematic overlap between marriage ties and high-skilled operational divisions within the guerrilla faction. That is, militants actively leveraged one facet of the underlying social infrastructure to create a new and distinct type of mixed-gender guerrilla unit. The militants who participated in it had distinct motivations, expectations, and understandings of their roles, in comparison to the positions they had previously inhabited in the group. The destruction of Zahra's intelligence file, in contrast, was a one-off event based on repurposing but not remapping; there was no systematic, routinized repurposing of Tel al-Zaʿtar survivor relationships to destroy all intelligence files.

Repurposing can be collectively organized without necessarily reaching the threshold of remapping; this dynamic frequently applies in the case of ad hoc, collective responses to a specific event or threat. For example, another of my interviewees, Yusif, formed a rapid-response team with his childhood friends to extract their kidnapped former scout leader from a Lebanese militia's prison in the early 1980s. The group disbanded after the operation, having mobilized around a shared response to an individual's predicament and having accomplished their mission.

In certain situations, however, these quotidian networks and formal organizational hierarchies become so intertwined, so responsive to one another's needs, that new organizations materialize or, sometimes, spin off from existing organizations. This final stage constitutes *emergence*. Some of these emergent organizations gain a degree of semipermanence or permanence, continuing to exist either in whole or as networks that share specific practices even after a war draws to a close. For instance, the emergent camp defensive fronts that I discuss in chapters 6 and 7 created routines that persist today for blood donation along with systems for securing the camps during crises. The following chapters demonstrate how organizational forms evolve by acquiring routines, institutions, and structure based on broader, collective understandings of threats and goals. In doing so, they also underscore the constructions of collective meaning in war (Mampilly 2011; Balcells 2012; Arjona et al. 2015; Shesterinina 2016; Metelits 2018) and the ways that emotions and symbolic processes shape individual-level identities as well as both quotidian and organizational networks' behavior (Swidler 1986; Emirbayer and Goodwin 1996; McLean 2016).

Emergence often occurs even as the official, "on-paper" organizational diagram does not change. Indeed, the cases of remapping and emergence that I describe in this volume were not initially designed, ordered, approved, controlled, or indeed always appreciated by Palestinian factions' elite leaderships, who largely spent the 1980s living in Tunis or Damascus. In some cases, as with the woman-dominated smuggling networks in the early 1980s, foreign leadership recognized, reinforced, and co-opted local innovations to regain top-down control and reassert expressly factional loyalties. In others, as with camp-level, cross-factional guerrilla fronts in the late 1980s, leaders or state patrons ordered members of multiple factions to cease participation and punished disobedience. Emergent organizations became sites of contestation among members of the same militant organizations and engines for engaging in internal critiques of leadership.

Lebanon in the 1980s

This analysis of organizational adaptation and emergence focuses specifically on Palestinian militant organizations in Lebanon between 1982 and 1990, a period that is nested within that of the fifteen-year (1975–1990) Lebanese Civil War. Palestinian militant organizations, such as nationalist Fatah, the Marxist Popular Front for the Liberation of Palestine (PFLP), and the Baʻthist al-Saʻiqa, have been active in Lebanon since the 1960s. These organizations found support both in Palestinian refugee camps and in middle- and upper-class urban Palestinian communities, both products of the 1947–1948 war that resulted in the creation of the state of Israel as well as the dispossession and flight of between 100,000 and 130,000 Palestinian refugees into Lebanon.[14] Palestinians became heavily involved in Lebanese domestic politics, including through their alliances with various Lebanese leftist and sectarian parties. Palestinian military activity in South Lebanon, the Israeli reprisals that it prompted, and political cleavages regarding the appropriate response to Israeli actions all contributed to the Lebanese Civil War.

The specific setting of 1980s Lebanon provides rich ground to explore social and organizational change in war, specifically because of the hyper-localized nature of the various subconflicts that took place and the way that they fed back into the larger national and international context.[15] Following the PLO's withdrawal of its leadership and guerrilla fighters from Beirut in 1982 (see chapter 3), local branches of larger guerrilla parties and of PLO umbrella institutions were shattered. Tens of thousands of their members had fled, been imprisoned, or died; the invasion annihilated Palestinian militant organizations' social and political apparatuses in South Lebanon and Beirut. Soon, however, Palestinian militant organizations began reemerging under conditions that ranged from Israeli military occupation in South Lebanon to Lebanese government control in West Beirut.

This historic moment serves as a starting point for a cross-regional study focused on Palestinian organizational and quotidian networks' adaptation to localized repertoires of violence in three cities: Beirut, Saida, and Sur. From 1982 to 1985, the Israel Defense Forces occupied Saida and Sur; the Lebanese government and right-wing, Christian militias controlled West Beirut until 1984, when a left-wing coalition of Lebanese militias pushed them out. From 1985 to 1988, the predominantly Shi'i Lebanese militia Amal, working with the LAF's 6th Brigade and the Syrian government, tried to expel all members of the PLO and Fatah from camps in each city. Amal drew on a wide variety of repressive techniques, using different repertoires of violent tactics in Saida than were used in either Beirut and Sur—and employing multiple different repertoires within Sur. During these time frames, Palestinian officers at the regional level (meaning each city and its immediate surroundings) coordinated their strategy across each city in tune with predominating conditions.[16]

The Lebanese Civil War, including the concurrent Israeli occupation of South Lebanon and the Syrian occupation of northern and eastern Lebanon, reflects the realities of contemporary and recent intrastate conflicts—such as those in Iraq, the Central African Republic, or the former Yugoslavia—in contrast to the simplified, dyadic state-versus-rebels game-theoretic and quantitative models commonly used in political science. Specifically, this was a heavily internationalized, multiparty intrastate war, fought along intersecting political, socioeconomic, and social cleavages, that was profoundly shaped by foreign funding, military intervention, and diplomatic engagement. Examining how these dynamics played out across time and space thus serves to inform more-detailed, nuanced understandings of contemporary conflict.

Plan of the Book

The rest of this book explores organizational dynamics in Palestinian militant groups in Lebanon between 1982 and 1990—the PLO, guerrilla organizations, and eventually, emergent local actors—across Beirut, Saida, and Sur, three cities in southern and central Lebanon. It identifies how militants made sense of and responded to various forms of violent repression through their social networks. Throughout, I call attention to forms of organizational fluidity, resilience, and adaptation that only become visible by centering the essential labor of militants who are not serving on the front lines.

Chapter 1 further situates the work within the research on political violence, intrastate conflict, and social networks; details my ethnohistorical approach to studying militant organizations; and introduces the concept of "organizational metadata." Chapter 2 provides historical background to contextualize the outcomes of interest in the rest of the volume: organizational adaptation and emergence. Drawing on archival sources, interviews, and secondary literature, I trace the development of the PLO and Palestinian guerrilla organizations in Lebanon between 1948 and 1982. In particular, I pay attention to the ways in which organizational subunits layered onto and drew upon quotidian social ties. This chapter thus provides a foundation from which to evaluate change to organizations' structures, behaviors, and informal practices.

Building on this groundwork, chapter 3 details the regionalized repertoires of violence deployed against Palestinian militant organizations during the Israeli invasion of June 1982, the subsequent Siege of Beirut, the "mopping-up" operations conducted by the LAF that fall, and the Sabra and Shatila massacre in September. While laying out the comparative framework for the remainder of the book, the chapter also reveals how a more nuanced treatment of categories such as "indiscriminate" and "(in)direct" violence can help explain outcomes linked to organizational adaptation, particularly through a deeper understanding of how militants and civilians alike experience and narrate them.

Chapter 4 traces the emergence of clandestine supply and intelligence networks in wartime Lebanon. It examines how militants remapped quotidian relationships into woman-dominated smuggling, logistics, and intelligence networks and how they redesigned mobile guerrilla cells in response to gendered counterinsurgent tactics. Cadres' mixed-gender, trust-based relations—especially kinship, friendship, and marriage ties—provided alternate pathways for organizational resource flows when formal bureaucratic pathways were inaccessible. These networks adopted specific routines and practices, producing semiofficial auxiliary information channels and alternative organizational hierarchies.

Chapter 5 examines how the Israeli forces' mass internment of Palestinian boys and men, alongside widespread Israeli use of collaborators, spurred Palestinian women and youth in South Lebanon to remap ties across political affiliations and between generational cohorts. These processes created community-based advocacy and counterintelligence networks. Narratives of shared fear, resentment, and vulnerability; resistance toolkits; and, eventually, practices of unmasking and anticollaborator violence constituted these emergent networks.

Chapter 6 moves north to Beirut, where it follows processes of network adaptation and emergence from 1982 to 1990. Specifically, it maps the emergence of community-based, cross-faction defensive fronts in Burj al-Barajneh and Shatila camps. While the chapter underscores the development of clandestine communications, logistics, and intelligence networks along similarly gendered lines to those in South Lebanon, it also notes subtle differences in organizational adaptation arising from regionally distinct repertoires of violence that Israeli and Lebanese forces deployed against Palestinian communities. I explore how Beirut-based defensive fronts—in contrast to those in South Lebanon—relied heavily both on quotidian relationships between midlevel officers and on marriage ties between Palestinians and Shiʻa communities in South Beirut. The chapter also delves into cleavages between on-the-ground fighters and their exiled leaderships, exploring how constitutive understandings of community obligations often proved stronger than factional affiliation.

Chapter 7 returns to South Lebanon, presenting a comparison between the War of the Camps in Saida and Sur. Saida was the center of PLO reinfiltration and the site where Palestinians fought a factionally segmented, front-based guerrilla war against Amal. Meanwhile, groups operating out of the camps in Sur demonstrated at least two distinct trajectories based on collective understandings of threat and previous violence: one camp's militants reconsolidated into a shared combat front, while another camp's militants and population collectively declared political neutrality. Throughout the chapter, I show how long-term feedback between violent repertoires, quotidian networks, and organizational structures in Saida resulted in the emergence of an atomized, personalized logic of factional organizing.

In the conclusion, I summarize the book's findings and draw out its implications for theories of civil war, militant organizations, political violence, and postwar transitions. I emphasize one of the book's core, overarching findings: that militant groups with similar social infrastructures adapt in remarkably different ways to localized repertoires of violence and repression. Building on this conclusion, I note potential trajectories for future research, emphasizing approaches that incorporate social network and gender analysis. I conclude with a discussion of the policy implications of the work. I encourage both scholars and policymakers to broaden their analytical focus beyond spectacular modes of wartime violence and participation in armed conflict. Instead, I contend that gaining an understanding of the less-visible dynamics of asymmetric war, the hidden labor of militant organizations, and the social processes that drive organizational change will yield better engagement with both the challenges posed by intrastate conflict and its broader effects on society.

1
MEMORIES AND MYTHOLOGIES OF MILITANCY
An Ethnographic Approach to Studying Militant Organizations

The core chapters of this book trace Palestinian militant organizations' adaptation and evolution across South Lebanon and Beirut during the 1980s by illustrating processes of repurposing, remapping, and emergence. Drawing from approaches pioneered in relational sociology and social network theory (Granovetter 1973, 1985; Padgett and Ansell 1993; Emirbayer and Goodwin 1994; Emirbayer 1997; Padgett and McLean 2006; White 2008; Padgett 2010; Padgett and Powell 2012; McLean 2016), I adopt an ethnohistorical, meaning-centric, and explicitly relational perspective. I examine how the social infrastructure of Palestinian communities interacted with formal militant hierarchies, emphasizing material, practice-based (Bourdieu 1977), and ideational changes to these social structures over time. In doing so, I challenge methodologies grounded by what Philip Howard (2002, 553–54) terms "organizational determinism," which "occurs when the researcher imputes community culture from the formal structure of its networks and hierarchies."[1] Networks, in this study, are not independent variables that influence discrete outcomes. Rather, they are systems of dynamic and complex social relations that shape and are shaped by each other to produce often unexpected and unforeseeable outcomes.

Militant Organizations as Dynamic Social Networks

Focusing on unofficial, highly localized emergent organizational networks and how they overlap and interact with formal group structures complements studies that emphasize the form of and change in official hierarchies and institutions (Sinno 2010; Pearlman 2011; Bakke et al. 2012; P. Krause 2017; Gutiérrez-Sanín 2018). At the same time, this approach expressly challenges scholarly approaches that center exclusively on elite, top-down control of militant behavior (Shapiro 2013) to the exclusion of these informal dynamics. This perspective thus provides a comparatively more nuanced and more grounded view of how militant organizations acquire new capabilities, goals, and recruits throughout the duration of armed conflict.

The micro-level processes that drive militant organizational adaptation in contexts of intrastate armed conflict and asymmetrical war have thus far remained ambiguous. However, a burgeoning body of research on militant organizations and civil war emphasizes the importance of prewar or simply preexisting social networks in shaping organizational structure, mobilization, and actors' behavior (Petersen 2001; E. J. Wood 2003; Staniland 2012, 2014; Metternich et al. 2013; Parkinson 2013; Shesterinina 2016, 2021; Dorff 2017; Lewis 2017, 2020; Larson and Lewis 2018; Hundman and Parkinson 2019; Mazur 2019, 2020). Building on its insights, I argue that ongoing organizational and social change—especially the emergence of new organizations that cope with of-the-moment challenges—must be understood in the context of adaptive network interaction (Lubkemann 2008; E. J. Wood 2008; Fujii 2009; Daly 2016, 2014; Bultmann 2018; Parkinson and Zaks 2018). This approach thus dovetails with perspectives that treat war as an ongoing, iterative, and dialectic process (McGovern 2011; Hermez 2021), rather than as a series of discrete military engagements.

My research reveals that members of militant groups respond to diverse repertoires of violence by leveraging quotidian social networks—the everyday connections of kinship, marriage, friendship, neighborhood, congregation, and co-membership—to perform explicitly organizational labor. Violence and repression affect militants' social networks both through "material" changes to structure—for instance, by changing who is physically available to perform certain tasks—and also by shifting the collective meanings embedded within social relations—for example, what is perceived as an existential threat and which tasks are consequently perceived as necessary for community survival. I argue that resilient militant organizations systematically and continuously adapt to wartime environments by altering the membership, content, or structure of their social ties.

To analytically zero in on these processes, I trace the backstage labor that made it possible for Palestinian resistance groups to adapt and survive in Lebanon in the 1980s, despite repeated military campaigns by Lebanese, Israeli, and Syrian forces. While "fighters"—understood as people who engage directly in armed combat—feature prominently in journalistic coverage of civil war and in conflict scholarship (Gates 2002; Weinstein 2005, 2007; Humphreys and Weinstein 2006, 2008; Fujii 2009; Daly 2012, 2014, 2016; Beber and Blattman 2013; Eck 2014), research has long noted that only a small minority of those who actively participate in civil war use a weapon (E. J. Wood 2003).[2] A related, developing body of scholarship has addressed the complex organization of militant groups and labor divisions within them (Parkinson and Zaks 2018). An especially relevant area of this literature examines rebels' relationships with and governance of civilian populations, focusing on issues such as institutional design, service provision, and taxation (Branch and Mampilly 2005; Beardsley and McQuinn 2009; Mampilly 2009, 2011; Arjona 2014, 2016; Arjona et al. 2015; March and Revkin 2015; Huang 2016a, 2016b; Revkin 2016, 2019; Stewart 2018, 2020; Mampilly and Stewart 2020). Related research highlights the sociopolitical and gender dynamics involved with recruitment, mobilization, and participation, all of which affect network dynamics (Straus 2005; Viterna 2006, 2013; Thomas and Bond 2015; Shesterinina 2016, 2021; Gowrinathan 2017). These studies have helped shift analytic focus from the production of violence to the overarching political projects and relationships that sustain militancy as well as insurgency. Moreover, they provide an important foil to top-down examinations of leadership and elite-level management of militant organizations (Shapiro 2013; Foster and Siegel 2019) by complicating notions of hierarchy and agency within militant organizations. Collectively, these perspectives suggest a more holistic approach to understanding the puzzles surrounding asymmetric and intrastate conflict, based on complex interactions among militant organizational structures, civilian communities, and other armed actors.

Methodological Approach

Studying Palestinian militant organizations in the aftermath of Israel's 1982 invasion of Lebanon provides multiple opportunities to develop comparative, micro-level and meso-level studies[3] of network adaptation, emergence, and resilience within the same overarching context; that is, to abductively collect and assemble network data without prior knowledge of existing relations or structures (Parkinson 2021b). A historical and comparative research design, carried out with an ethnographic sensibility (Pader 2006; Schatz 2009; Simmons and

Smith 2017, 2019) through immersive fieldwork, enables me to examine militant organizations' adaptive processes at both the regional and local levels (including camp and neighborhood), and then to present a deep analysis of the effects of repertoires of violence on militant resilience.

My research process reflects the realities of intrastate conflict by focusing on the diverse forms of day-to-day critical labor that militants perform within nonstate armed organizations. Examples include paying salaries, resolving disputes, coordinating engineering and maintenance divisions, and assembling intelligence, among many others. Years of engagement with current and former members of militant organizations ground this work. Over a period of two years, I spoke to hundreds of current and former Palestinian and Lebanese militants who played a variety of roles during both the Lebanese Civil War (1975–1990) and the Israeli and Syrian occupations of Lebanon (1982–2000 and 1976–2005, respectively).[4] My research includes in-depth and often life-history interviews with 114 current and former militants who were active in Beirut and South Lebanon during the 1970s and 1980s. It also comprises interviews with employees of nongovernmental and community organizations as well as individuals who worked for the United Nations, with some overlap between groups. After the initial background work, most of my interviews occurred in the broader context of my immersive engagement with Palestinian communities, including ten months of organizational ethnography with members of Fatah's Women's Office. I draw upon deep and extensive analysis of primary-source Palestinian texts, mainstream and clandestine Arabic-language newspapers from the periods under study, original documentary film footage from the Palestine Liberation Organization, and a review of relevant memoirs from Palestinian, Lebanese, and limited Israeli sources. Throughout my research, I volunteered with three camp-based, educationally focused Palestinian civil society organizations for periods lasting between two and nine months. The following section outlines core aspects of the ethnographic methodology I deployed to generate historical evidence and explores the role of memory in this research.

Meeting People Where They Are

Cognizant of an increasing trend of "fly-by" and "parachute" research in Palestinian communities in Lebanon,[5] I spent the initial months of my 2009–2010 stay in Lebanon volunteering in a South Beirut refugee camp, engaging in archival research, and slowly building relationships by talking to Palestinian acquaintances both about their everyday lives and about what I was reading in the archives. When they asked what I found, I would tell them about an article that I discovered about a specific battle, or about a youth organization leading a protest, or perhaps about a foreign humanitarian group arriving with aid. Sometimes my interlocutors asked follow-up questions; often they started entire conversations based on the events that I mentioned, by location and date. At times, the conversation moved away from my research entirely. Adopting this method allowed people to approach me about their possible formal participation in the project later, if and when they chose to do so, often after knowing and vetting me for months, sometimes years. People were paying attention; during later group interviews, interlocutors who knew me would sometimes shush someone who tried to explain that the Lebanese Civil War was between Muslims and Christians, arguing that I had read the history and "knew better."[6] The result of this incremental approach to relationship building was that when I was "invited in," so to speak, it was often with extensive, ongoing access, including times when I left Lebanon and returned a few months or even a year later. My travel schedule in many ways came to mimic that of a family member or friend who had emigrated and who visited for holiday breaks and summer vacation; methodologically, it facilitated ongoing revisits of the sites and organizations that interested me (Burawoy 2003) and provoked constant reflection on my own positionality. The fact that I kept returning over several years, when many researchers do not, also increased people's willingness to speak to me in depth for my project.

Shadowing people in their everyday jobs and social lives became one of the most productive ways for me to examine the intersection of multiple social networks, as well as to deduce how they interacted with organizational histories and memory. My technique emerged organically from several initial interviews. After I introduced my project, discussed informed consent, and in some cases also conducted an informal or semistructured interview, someone would often remark that I should "just follow them around for a few days." When I did, they would almost inevitably introduce me and my project to colleagues, friends, and family, many of whom would volunteer to participate in a later interview. Shadowing was also the first step in observing organizational-level phenomena; people invited me to political party events such as rallies and commemorations, encouraged me to attend demonstrations, took me along on recruitment visits, won permission to bring me into closed camp-level meetings, and included me in social events such as group picnics. Speaking to people informally on the way to or from and during such events revealed previously hidden and often unexpected social connections and sites of network overlap. For example, as I walked through the Sabra market with Abu Houli, a member of Fatah and a former member of the ANM, I witnessed him greet several members of ostensibly rival, Syrian-allied factions with a hearty handshake and warm questions about their family, noting afterward that he had played football (soccer) with them in the 1970s or served during the camp sieges with them in the 1980s.

Such practices often revealed historical networks that otherwise would have been invisible to me. For example, chapter 4, which focuses on gendered clandestine logistics and smuggling networks grew out of participant observation alongside a woman named Sawsan, who was involved with curating a Nakba Day (the commemoration of Palestinians' dispossession and expulsion from the present-day state of Israel) exhibit on women in Fatah. Sawsan was one of my earliest contacts in Fatah; I met her in November of 2009 and told her about my research project. She listened with interest and expressed a desire to help; however, given the newness of our relationship, I did not push the matter. On a few occasions in winter 2009 and the following spring, I tagged along on her visits to young women who, as I later learned, Sawsan hoped to recruit to the faction. In April 2010, in what I interpreted as a signal of her trust in me and acceptance of my presence around her office, Sawsan asked me to proofread her weekly professional activities report. I had accompanied her during most of her work activities that week, and she asked me to check whether she had forgotten anything. Shortly thereafter, Sawsan suggested that I assist with her assignment for Nakba Day.

In the lead-up to Nakba Day, I accompanied Sawsan to poster design sessions, to her visits with both camp-level and regional-level Fatah and PLO officials, and to specially scheduled interviews with women cadres and elderly camp residents. This experience introduced me to new social networks, allowed Sawsan to vouch for me with high-ranking officers in both the Women's Office and Fatah, and exposed me to several suborganizational memory cultures (in this case, those associated with the 1980s underground). At each stop, she would introduce me to other party members and casually tell them about my research project. Often, after discussing my research interests with them and getting their consent, I would then conduct a brief interview on the spot. I usually stopped after a few questions so as not to distract from my interlocutors' tasks at hand and so that people did not feel socially obligated to speak to me. In almost every case, I was invited to meet someone again for a more in-depth interview.

When Sawsan and her colleagues were formatting posters and pamphlets, I leveraged my previous, short-lived career in magazine publishing along with my Arabic language training to ask questions about their design and texts. This mode of participation opened numerous conversations about noteworthy types of women's participation in Fatah and the positions women had held over time. For example, a particular poster featured images of women who had served as commandos, pilots, and suicide bombers, in addition to others who had been factional officials and members of the Palestinian National Council. Our searching for certain women's photos was also instructive; it was easy to locate, for instance, a formal portrait of Dalal al-Mughrabi, a Fatah cadre who led a 1978 attack in northern Israel. However, in one case, Sawsan and I spent an entire day visiting various offices in Beirut searching for a decent photo of a high-ranking woman in Fatah's Lebanon branch. We ended up relying on a grainy, undated snapshot; it seemed that no one in the faction had ever taken an official portrait, despite the woman's status. Sawsan explained that it was likely because she had been an important figure during the War of the Camps, when she had achieved her highest rank. The lack of a portrait might have been for security, or it may have simply been neglected, owing to more-pressing matters at the time. These types of moments sensitized me to the limits of official narratives and records, which in turn encouraged me to continue developing contacts through more-informal channels.

Experiences like these continued to shape my interviewing technique. Shadowing others produced unexpected opportunities for me to ask people questions about their past and to explore how their relationships with each other and with various factions had evolved over time. Whenever I accompanied a factional cadre or a UNRWA official in their daily work, they often situated what they were doing in their own history, given the knowledge I shared with them of my research topic. In particular, I noted patterns of social network overlap (i.e., a cadre might have militant siblings or friends who worked in a social association). I also noted some interviewees' previous movements among organizational subdivisions (e.g., from a fighting position to a logistics role). For example, as I accompanied Abu Hadi, a UNRWA employee, a former guerrilla fighter, and an ex-officer in one of the General Unions, back and forth between his formal meetings and *arguileh* cafés, he would explain exactly how he had come to know each party official, NGO worker, or community member and what role he remembered them playing. While his current professional networks only partially overlapped with those associated with his former roles, he revealed that he constantly accessed past organizational networks to get things done around the camps, such as asking someone who had once fought alongside him for a favor. At one point, he "coincidentally" scheduled a visit to a school where he knew that a former officer in the Arab Liberation Front (ALF), who was a veteran of the Magdousheh campaign, would be picking up his sons. Though Abu Hadi only intended to facilitate an introduction, the officer's enthusiasm on meeting me led me to conduct an interview in a secluded corner of the parking lot as the children happily scampered around us.

As a researcher, I was embedded within present-day relations and organizational structures; I was, of course, unable to witness historical processes firsthand. Instead, I was observing contemporary meetings, demonstrations, and practices. These experiences provided countless opportunities to ask people about their recollection of events in the 1970s and 1980s. Seemingly fleeting moments—a complaint, a joke, an offhand comment, the offer of hot sauce for one's lunch—could be leveraged into a question about how things had been in the past. From a network perspective, engaging with the contemporary incarnation of an organization revealed crucial sites of disjuncture with the past, such as discarded practices, gaps in official memory (e.g. when a leader was unaware of how the organization had previously functioned), or marginalized cliques of cadres. For example, many of my interviewees, particularly those with detailed knowledge of the 1980s, had left their previous factions or had withdrawn from leadership roles; current members who maintained friendships with them nevertheless frequently referred them to me. However, these encounters could also lead to tensions and ethical dilemmas. Below, I use an ethnographic interlude to reveal how arguments about historical participation and political authenticity emerged among my interlocutors after I was well into my research on clandestine activism. I use this section to introduce the concept of organizational metadata and to underscore how the acknowledgment of these metadata can inform the historical study of militant groups and other collectivities.

Credit Claiming and Authenticity Debates

Nafisa is sitting on the couch, calm and smiling yet clearly livid; I realize she has been waiting for me to arrive. I am barely across the threshold when she asks, in what feels like a dangerously cheerful tone: "So, what did that liar tell you? Did she tell you that she was in Beirut for the siege? Did she tell you she smuggled food? She didn't, she couldn't, she's afraid of everything! She was in the Gulf the whole time with her husband!"[7]

In order to reconstruct historical militant hierarchies and quotidian social networks, I deliberately interviewed key figures from different strata within the factions, often repeatedly. Long-term engagement with Palestinian organizations and communities allowed me to recognize three relevant dynamics that affected my ongoing research. First, as one might expect, people spoke in increasing detail and depth about their experiences over a series of interviews and conversations, frequently over months or years. Informal, ethnohistorical group interviews, especially when they involved members of different generations and followed an initial, one-on-one semistructured interview, often elicited particularly poignant material, in part because my interlocutors would focus on connecting multiple individuals' experiences or on teaching younger cadres who were present, rather than speaking as they would to a foreign researcher like me. For example, during my second interview with Nafisa at her house in Burj al-Barajneh camp, Sawsan asked her where the community had buried the people who died during the War of the Camps.⁸ Nafisa and her elderly mother gently explained to her that many were buried under the camp alleyways through which we had just walked. This fact pained Sawsan immensely, yet she also expressed that, as a party member, she needed to know this history. Without my long-standing commitment to doing immersive fieldwork, information of this nature would have been largely unavailable to me.

Second, also unsurprisingly, many interlocutors omitted certain types of information in our early interactions. An obvious category for omission related to negative feelings about officers or factions, though numerous people spoke quite candidly about their critiques of the factions (Parkinson 2016). Yet many of my interlocutors, specifically those who had been involved in clandestine work, also didn't want to risk overemphasizing their personal contributions in what they strongly felt had been collective efforts, a practice that several associated with opportunistic politicians. Others worried about the tension between their experiences and factional narratives, especially when it came to present-day reconciliation with Lebanese parties such as Amal.⁹ As people shared different memories over time, I attributed their increasing openness to confidence in my growing ability to appropriately contextualize their experiences as well as to their own exercise of agency in how they wanted to tell their stories, rather than how they imagined their contemporary chains of command wanted them to be told. Third, delicately discerning who had experienced certain historical events or participated in them first-hand, who knew about these occurrences secondhand (but might speak as though they had participated), and who hadn't been aware of them in the first place all became essential to my understanding the structure of past organizational and social ties (e.g., the degree of compartmentalization in underground networks) and how they had evolved.

In the lead-up to Nafisa confronting me, the leadership of her faction had delegated Umm Amir, a high-ranked local officer, to assemble a group of women for me to interview about the sieges during the War of the Camps. Umm Amir, a sweet but somewhat naive woman, was clearly pleased with the responsibility and had gathered several women together for coffee and a chat. But, outside the office, women who were long-term members of the faction seethed; they felt insulted that a senior male officer had appointed Umm Amir as their representative, given that she was in fact a new member who had never engaged in wartime activism or militancy.

The resulting group interview revealed that, despite general familiarity with the workings of the camp's defensive efforts, the women whom Umm Amir assembled had certainly not been core activists. Neither she nor the contemporary leadership knew exactly who *had* been part of the woman-dominated underground in the 1980s. Nevertheless, one of the interviewees Umm Amir selected,

Rana, subsequently bragged to Nafisa that she had been chosen to take part in an interview with a foreign researcher; now, Nafisa was asking me what had been said. I had to negotiate the situation before she confronted Umm Amir.

"Nafisa, you know I have to get the 'official' story. It doesn't matter what she said to me, it matters how and why she said what she said." I assure her that I understand that some people are going to misrepresent history and that I can often tell if they are.

Nafisa storms into the kitchen, where the target of her rage changes to the faction's leadership. She begins furiously scrubbing the stove. I'm welcome to get the official story from the leaders, she says, but they didn't experience the siege like everyone else. People in the camp had been starving and yet "you could find fresh banana peels and candy wrappers outside the political leaders' offices." She yanks back her clothing and, for the first time, shows me several deep scars; she explains that a shell fell directly into her home. I know that she would have had limited access to emergency care during the siege. The camp's field hospital had minimal supplies and would have necessarily prioritized life-threatening injuries before treating wounds like hers, despite their apparent seriousness. Nafisa asks me come to the window by the stove and shows me where exactly fighters had positioned themselves [next to her house, emphasizing her proximity to the battles].[10]

Nafisa was adding nuance to what I already knew of her own story. When she had previously spoken to me about the siege, she, like others, always drove home the point that "everyone" in the camp participated in some way. At this point, Nafisa and I had spoken multiple times over two years about her political activity, and specifically about her life during the War of the Camps. Because she had served on the defensive front, her neighbors from multiple factions viewed her with deep respect, especially in comparison to her newer colleagues. However, when asked whether older members like Nafisa were recognized or promoted for their actions, another woman who had been active in the underground remarked that "now everything is like there was nothing."[11]

Practices of memory sharing and claiming organizational histories offer researchers important insights into long-term organizational structures, expose dynamic processes of organizational change, and reveal politicized divisions in collective memory frameworks. Nafisa and I originally met when I was shadowing Sawsan and another woman, Sabah, during the Nakba Day project. When I described my research, Nafisa sat back thoughtfully and asked me whether I smoked. I produced a pack of Marlboro Golds and offered her one. She laughed and took out her Kents, making sure to tease me for smoking "light" cigarettes. We then spoke briefly about clandestine operations during the 1980s, which is the first time that she told me how important it was to understand that everyone—across factions—had participated in camp defense together. She invited me to her house, where I later conducted a life history interview with her; I returned afterward to conduct a follow-up interview about the camp siege and her role in the underground. Our conversations continued over the course of a decade as I returned repeatedly to Lebanon.

As I conducted more interviews, I was increasingly present at demonstrations and party events alongside members of the Women's Office such as Nafisa. I came to know her and several of her family members as part of an organizational subgroup constituted by past co-membership in the clandestine apparatus and the interfactional defense front during the War of the Camps. As we interacted more at party events and as her children came to know me better, I began visiting them socially, got to know her extended family and friends well, and frequently slept at her house.

By contrast, in 2012, when the party leadership introduced me to Umm Amir, I had decided to try a more formal route to conducting interviews by approaching factional leadership. On paper, the women leaders were all party colleagues and neighbors. Umm Amir herself was a member of the camp community and a current officer. However, as I learned, she had been excluded from the two elite subgroups of which Nafisa was a member.

The group interview that I conducted with Umm Amir and the women she gathered clearly included the inventions, evasions, and silences that Lee Ann Fujii theorizes alongside rumors and denials as metadata, that is, the "spoken and unspoken thoughts and feelings which [interlocutors] do not always articulate in their stories or interview responses, but which emerge in other ways" (Fujii 2010, 231). As Fujii underscores: "Meta-data are as valuable as the testimonies themselves because they indicate how the current social and political landscape is shaping what people might say to a researcher" (Fujii 2010, 232). In the group interview, the outright inventions stood out to me, first because they came in the form of appropriations and exaggerations, and second because they were shared in an official manner on behalf of a political faction. For instance, Umm Amir told me, twice, that she gave birth to her son during the siege, with bombs dropping around her. In reality, the son was born overseas and *after*, not during, the time of the siege, meaning that her statement was an invention. Other women in the camp, whom Umm Amir certainly knew, had in fact given birth during the siege; she had appropriated their experiences and represented them as her own.[12] In another instance, Rana, whom Umm Amir recruited to speak with me, told me that she been one of the women who picked up the faction's money at the bank. Yet, her description of how her bank runs worked did not jibe with my previous interviews. In addition to naming the wrong bank, the way she described carrying the money—strapped to her stomach, to mimic a pregnancy—was known by veteran smugglers as an easy way to get caught by Lebanese militia members. Rana may in fact have smuggled food or money into the camp as a civilian or a supporter of the faction (as another interviewee's husband did), but I doubted her claim that she was one of the trusted lynchpins of the clandestine financial apparatus. The two other women in the room stayed silent during these periods in conversation, neither affirming nor contradicting what Umm Amir and Rana said. This unusual lack of interaction (particularly during a lively conversation), which was characterized by deliberate silences, signaled that something was "off" about Rana's and Umm Amir's stories. I also noted that women who had served as underground activists always requested that I conceal their identities; the implication was that they might have something to fear (particularly as the Syrian Civil War escalated). By contrast, each woman in the "official" interview requested that I use their real names in my writing, and also mentioned to friends and neighbors that they had spoken to me about the siege.

Rather than examining my interlocutors' verbal strategies in a vacuum, I came to recognize the collective and explicitly *organizational* meanings that they embodied, ultimately revealing what I label "organizational metadata." In other words, the variety of metadata linked to the multiple encounters surrounding a specific interview revealed important aspects of organizational networks, collective experiences, and participants' histories. These include several events preceding and following the interview, such as: (1) my asking Farouq, an officer whom I knew well, and who had been part of the underground, if he knew women activists I might interview; (2) Farouq's deferral to his commanding officer (who had not served in the underground); (3) the commanding officer's referral to Umm Amir, a high-ranking officer in the Women's Office; (4) Umm Amir's selection of individuals for my interview; (5) interview-specific metadata, in particular Umm Amir's and Rana's embellishments and appropriations alongside the others' silence; and finally (6) Rana's choice to then brag to Nafisa about being chosen for the interview.

Organizational metadata amplified the importance of factions' contemporary cultures and structures in shaping the material I gained through interviews and participant observation. They also augmented my understanding of the geographic segmentation of contemporary social networks associated with the 1980s Palestinian underground. For instance, as an officer, Farouq interacted with cadres from the Women's Office. However, he was not from one of the camps that had been besieged; he had not had direct contact with women from Shatila, Burj al-Barajneh, or Rashidiyeh during the 1980s. Given a lack of personal connections in this specific realm,[13] he defaulted to contemporary party protocol and referred me to a ranking (male) political officer in the Beirut chain of command. That officer referred me laterally to Umm Amir at the Women's Office. Referring me to her meant one of two things: it could have reflected the officer's lack of knowledge of how the underground had actually operated, or it may have implied that my inquiry had been classified as a "woman question" rather than a "military question" or a "camp question," which would have elicited a different referral.

This starkly gendered divide in contemporary party structures was not representative of the 1980s, when women served in both military and clandestine roles alongside or in cooperation with men. In other words, the gendered referral process reflected *present* structures, not the historical ones I was studying. Alternately, if Farouq knew that many former underground activists had quit or reduced their roles in Fatah owing to disenchantment, he may have wanted to avoid referring an outsider to critical members of the party. Either way, if I had relied solely on the party hierarchy or on my male contacts, I never would have encountered the underground network.

By appropriating siege stories, both Umm Amir and Rana engaged in multiple types of political and memory work. First, they acknowledged the lasting social prestige associated with being a veteran of the 1980s underground. Second, they established ownership of that collective memory for an organization rather than for the camps as communities—in marked contrast to the narrative shared by members of the underground network (see, e.g., chapters 4, 5, and 6). It was, in effect, an act of what sociologist Eviatar Zarubavel (1996, 286) calls "mnemonic socialization," in that it deliberately encouraged me to see the clandestine apparatus as an exclusively factional project. Moreover, by claiming firsthand experience of these events, Umm Amir was appropriating the roles, sacrifices, and suffering of survivors such as Nafisa. As a political officer, she was smoothing over an intra-organizational cleavage by equating herself and her friends with long-term members who were veterans of the underground. By claiming female smugglers' stories for all women in the faction, and by making women's smuggling efforts banal rather than recognizing certain individuals' unique contributions, Umm Amir challenged Nafisa's and similar women's elite status, both discursive and structural, in the faction. Tellingly, Nafisa was not the only individual who sought to correct Umm Amir's narrative. After learning that Umm Amir had been delegated to run the interview, Farouq pointedly and privately told me that while Umm Amir was "with" them and a fundamentally good woman, she nevertheless did not *know* anything; he made it very clear that even *he* knew she was never part of the underground. He said this in a way to indicate that she was excluded from the clique of old-school activists, but also in a way that preserved the faction's reputation.

This situation reveals how memory cultures (Zerubavel 1996; Auyero 1999; Haugbolle 2012) that are associated with the militant organizations I studied emerge from and help to maintain intra-organizational networks.[14] Overlapping network membership in the party and in the underground meant that unlike the male-dominated leadership of Fatah, women like Nafisa had direct access to the camps' populations. The contemporary brokerage role that women like Nafisa play, in part owing to their prior roles as clandestine actors, also highlights their potentially substantial "informal" power as well as their capacity for social innovation (Burt 2005; Papachristos 2006, 105–11); indeed, Nafisa frequently walked a strategic line between organizational stalwart and peripheral critic, depending on whether she needed, for example, financial support from the faction or a job with a nonpartisan NGO. As Nafisa's mention of the banana peels and candy wrappers outside party offices during the siege implied, it also meant that members of her clique had a more contentious relationship with the leadership than the new "9 a.m.–2 p.m." members (referring to the limited office hours they kept). Nafisa's subgroup represented more than a few people with unique local connections; it also represented a clique with a shared understanding of organizational history (which the new leadership had downplayed), common critiques of both the old and the new leaderships, and a membership base that granted mutual respect and authority based on members' past deeds. In many ways, this clique thereby challenged the formal organizational hierarchy.

My interlocutors' past organizational roles often translated into divergent behaviors during our interviews. Former members of the underground, including Nafisa herself, often downplayed the uniqueness of their roles, avoided drawing distinctions between women activists, acknowledged cross-factional cooperation, and eschewed articulating hierarchies of sacrifice between themselves and others. Instead, like many others whom I interviewed, Nafisa insisted they had all sacrificed and that everyone did *something*. Only when women who had not been part of the underground claimed membership did Nafisa condemn them on the grounds of appropriating others' experiences and informal status.[15] In response to Rana's bragging, and in stark contrast to her previous behavior, Nafisa subsequently learned who had been at the interview and broke down exactly how much of a *right* each woman had to speak. One had lost a son in front of her eyes during the siege and was a "good woman" (but not an activist herself). Another's husband had smuggled money for the PLO and was also a "good woman." One was a "gossip and an airhead who knew nothing." And Umm Amir was simply "a liar."

This approach underscores that researchers of political organizations must study not only the formal, "consciously designed entities" (Tsoukas 2001, 8) but also the informal, everyday aspects of organizations' political power. Experiences such as those I relate in this chapter have allowed me to think seriously about how to pursue an ethnographic methodology in ways that would enable me to systematically understand relationships among the factions, broader communities, and historical memory, as well as ultimately to reflexively evaluate my role in them as a researcher.

2

BUILDING A SOCIAL INFRASTRUCTURE

The Palestine Liberation Organization and the Guerrilla Factions in Lebanon

Members of the Lebanese Armed Forces (LAF) routinely warn foreign visitors to Ain al-Hilweh that the Palestinian refugee camp is a veritable war zone. Journalistic coverage reinforces these warnings' undertones; the Lebanese newspaper *al-Safir*'s archive holds several thick binders of Ain al-Hilweh-specific media clippings under the heading of "*ishtibakat*" ("clashes"). Many Palestinians share this view of the camp; a local UNRWA employee told me in 2010: "Ain al-Hilweh, it's like Texas. You anger someone in their car and they might shoot you. What do you call them? Cowboys."[1] A former United Nations Interim Force in Lebanon (UNIFIL) official to whom I spoke referred to the most well-known leader in the camp as "a mafioso."[2] Palestinians from other communities informed me that they were afraid of visiting Ain al-Hilweh. Palestinians from Ain al-Hilweh called it "the capital of the camps" because its population reflected all political tendencies, ranging from Marxism, secular nationalism, and Salafism to apathy.

Militant leaders in Ain al-Hilweh go out of their way to explain that each faction has its own physical, economic, and social "turf" inside the camp. With practiced precision—they have given versions of the speech to dozens of journalists—officers explain that each of the camp's dozen-plus mosques is linked formally or informally to a party or Islamic organization (see also Rougier 2007, 2004).[3] Militia members staff checkpoints that straddle the camp's main access points. When asked in 2007 how policing and security was handled within each neighborhood, the leader of Ansar Allah, a Sunni Islamist group that received funding from Hizbullah, explained: "Each faction has its own security 'square' and protects the families inside it."[4] Ain al-Hilweh's organizations field a Security Committee to manage checkpoint allocation, violent disputes between organizations, relations with the LAF, and boundaries between the camp and Ta'amir, a working-class Lebanese neighborhood to the north known for housing Salafi organizations' offices and members. Belonging to this committee is a reputational goal for armed groups. More recent iterations of the committee, assembled in the mid-2010s, included Salafi groups that it had fought in earlier years.

Leaders cultivate strongman images to match these militarized organizational forms. Interviewing a local Fatah leader in his home in 2007, I was escorted alongside a journalist friend and her fixer through an antechamber with at least a dozen new automatic rifles hanging on the wall, which were protected by a huge, cheerful guard in body armor. We conducted the interview in a trellis-shaded courtyard as the commander's young grandchildren romped around us. The official sported khaki military fatigues and a pistol; in my now fifteen years of traveling to Lebanon, it was the first and only time that I saw a Fatah officer wearing a sidearm during one of my interviews. A brief glance into an adjoining receiving room revealed what looked like a tripod-mounted rocket-propelled grenade. Looking back, I strongly believe it was all for the foreign journalist's benefit; the visible weapons conveyed a particular, media-ready image of militancy. The same day, a leader of Usbat al-Ansar, one of the Salafi groups in the camp, locked me and the journalist in a safe house with metal sheeting over the windows. He wanted privacy while he fought with his public affairs officer about whether he should grant an interview to two women, given the group's fundamentalist ideology. The public affairs officer refused to interact with us on principle, but allowed our male fixer to interview him. Meanwhile, the leader returned to the room, sat down, poured coffee out of a thermos, and offered us dates while chatting animatedly. The leader later insisted on being photographed in full *mujahidin* regalia—that is, an Afghan *salwar kameez*, a turban, and a Kalashnikov rifle strapped to his back—with each of us uncomfortably forcing smiles on either side.

These militarized performances have little to do with most people's everyday lives in Ain al-Hilweh (Khalili 2007b). Indeed, despite the breathless narratives of "a coming war" in the camp, Ain al-Hilweh's large, central market bustles like any other in Lebanon.[5] Children walk to school in matching uniforms. Youth struggle to find green space where they can play; when I conducted my research, a dirt football field on the camp's west side served as one of the only large recreational areas. Unemployment figures are often estimated to be as high as 80 percent; the availability of cheap Syrian labor following the beginning of the Syrian Civil War depressed wages for many unskilled workers. Local NGOs—many headed by former militants who have rechanneled their commitment to the community—find creative ways to fund and run programs that focus on youth, disabled people, the elderly, or gender-based violence. As in other camps, seemingly banal issues, such as the management of the overcrowded local graveyard, morph into wrenching political debates over land, noncitizen rights, and dignity.[6]

This deliberate public relations entrepreneurship on the part of some factions exploits international audiences' appetites for media stories that focus on "Salafi jihadis," and constitutes a form of organizational metadata (see chapter 1). While many media analysts have adopted the narrative that the Salafi organizations were growing in power and set to destabilize the region, scholarship on gang rivalry (Papachristos 2009) suggests that viewing these performances and the violence associated with them is a mode of status competition to which media attention contributes. That is not to say that Ain al-Hilweh isn't a distinct context; both the militarized performances and the frequency of violence among some of the factions—which has periodically included shootouts, grenade-throwing, and car bombings—set it apart from the eleven other refugee camps in Lebanon. But, as this chapter will demonstrate, the consistent emphasis on security-centric narratives with reference to the camp draws on historical and highly politicized fears surrounding Palestinian populations in Lebanon, crowding out more nuanced, contextualized stories and negatively shaping public impressions of the Palestinian camps and the people who live in them.

The significant question, I suggest, is why this specific structure of relations and system of practices evolved in the way that it did. Palestinian factions in Lebanon today are vastly different from those of the 1970s and 1980, even if they share the same names. For example, one DFLP representative in Sur described the Palestinian factions today as "mainly playing an advocacy role" rather than engaging in armed resistance and related projects.[7] It's worth noting, furthermore, that the officers now performing hyperviolent masculinity for journalists in Ain al-Hilweh may or may not have served with the same faction during the war era; Palestinian contacts told me that the Salafi leader who locked me in a safe house had previously belonged to a Marxist organization. Many leaders whom I interviewed had switched allegiances over time, moved between combat and administrative roles, or advanced in status as those above them in the hierarchy quit, immigrated, or died. Some had experienced incarceration or exile; still others had collaborated with Israeli or Syrian forces.

Situating collective organizational performances and individuals such as the khaki- and sidearm-wearing Fatah officer simultaneously within long-term organizational trajectories and the contemporary Lebanese context grounded my ability to generate working relationships with interviewees and to leverage contemporary encounters to inform historical research. Thus, to create a foundation for the analysis that follows, this chapter first highlights critical moments in Palestinian history in Lebanon in order to provide key reference points for the actors, processes, and events that I feature throughout the remainder of the book. The chapter intentionally centers topics that my interlocutors repeatedly mentioned in our interactions both by sketching broad dynamics (such as the suppression of Palestinian freedoms under the Lebanese *Deuxième Bureau* in the period between 1948 and 1969) as well as by detailing specific events (like the siege of Tel al-Zaʿtar camp in East Beirut) so as to historically situate core discursive threads as well as modes of identification that served as collective reference points during the 1980s.

In doing so, this chapter offers a brief chronological view of Palestinian political and military organizations' entry into and developing roles in Lebanon in relation to the country's politics, while recognizing that any hard division between discrete "Palestinian politics" and "Lebanese politics" during this period is at least partially artificial. It seeks to situate these organizations in the social, political, and economic realities of Palestinian refugee life, which drove decisions by Lebanese as well as Palestinians to participate in resistance activities. In doing so, this section provides an organizational and social topography of Palestinian communities in Lebanon while underscoring key points of institutional overlap between the PLO, guerrilla parties, and other actors in society. Finally, this chapter highlights key points of intersection between Palestinian organizational and social life, noting where participation in the PLO and in guerrilla parties' programs, economic efforts, and cultural activities fostered particular types of connections among families, friends, and neighbors and indeed throughout "formal" political life. It pursues each of these goals with the explicit end of providing essential background to readers as it draws upon a large body of exceptional existing work that has been done on Palestinian history and contemporary society in Lebanon.[8]

Palestinian politics in pre-1982 Lebanon can be divided into three broad periods. The first lasted from the Nakba in 1948 to 1969.[9] This period includes the founding of the Arab Nationalist Movement (ANM) in 1952 in Beirut; Palestinian political organizations' illicit operation under the Lebanese *Deuxième Bureau* (Military Intelligence Directorate); and the growth of Palestinian refugee communities in 16 UNRWA-administered camps as well as in non-camp settlements and in urban neighborhoods. Politically, it represents a time of continued influence of historically village-based governance structures, centered on the figure of the traditional *mukhtar*. It also saw Palestinian guerrilla groups' initiation of attacks against Israel from Lebanese territory, the founding of the PLO, and the conclusion of the 1969 Cairo Agreement, which ceded control of Palestinian camps in Lebanon to the PLO.

The second period spans 1969 to the early months of 1975. It includes the formal entry of the resistance parties into the refugee camps, the aftermath of the 1970 Black September events in Jordan, clashes between Palestinian resistance organizations and the Lebanese Army in 1973, and the lead-up to the first phase of the Lebanese Civil War. It was characterized by a massive expansion of the PLO's apparatus in Lebanon, a presence that many observers likened to the construction of a state within a state. The third period extends from the beginning of the Lebanese Civil War in the early months of 1975 to August of 1982, when the PLO and guerrilla organizations evacuated Beirut as part of a negotiated agreement. This last phase of organizational development witnessed several important trends, including the consolidation of internal Palestinian opposition to the PLO and growing tension between the PLO and the Syrian government.

Palestinian Refugees under the *Deuxième Bureau*, 1948–1969

At the time of the Nakba in 1948, between 100,000 and 130,000 Palestinian refugees crossed into Lebanon from what had been Mandate Palestine (Y. Sayigh 1997, 39).[10] During this period, as one scholar notes, "there was no single Palestinian authority, no united Arab leadership, no policy either of mass resistance or mass evacuation. Especially in the countryside, there were no other sources of organization than the villages' own defense committees" (R. Sayigh 1979, 64–65). Refugees largely settled in or near Lebanese cities where they had friends or family; members of village communities often collectively fled violence in Palestine, traveling to Lebanon together and then reestablishing what had been locally based governing committees.

Initial conditions in the refugee camps that sprung up in Lebanese cities were difficult; both those who had lived in the camps during this time and those who had grown up in more middle- or upper-class Palestinian homes often referenced these conditions when they discussed the importance of the PLO and their own motivations for political activism. The five-year-old Lebanese state, organized under the confessional power-sharing provisions of the 1943 National Pact, dispatched police to pacify large groups of refugees and to corral them into different camps (R. Sayigh 1979, 106–107).[11] Some refugees in Sur and the Bekaa Valley occupied shelters that Armenian refugees had abandoned, while others gathered in old French military barracks. Those in other locations initially stayed in shared tents provided by the International Committee of the Red Cross (ICRC). At the end of 1949, the United Nations established UNRWA as a means to channel international aid to Palestinian refugees across Lebanon, Syria, Jordan, and Gaza.

UNRWA became active in the spring of 1950, providing education, health services, and in some cases new housing for 726,000 registered refugees (UNRWA n.d.; Salah 2008, 10). Organizations such as the ICRC and the American Friends Service Committee (AFSC) also played a key role in aid management and service provision (Y. Sayigh 1997, 4; Feldman 2007).

The Lebanese government subjected Palestinian refugees to harsh restrictions on housing, employment, and political organizing. Palestinians could not build permanent homes, work in over seventy professions (particularly in prestigious vocations such as medicine, law, and engineering), or form political parties (R. Sayigh 1979, 1994, 1995; Suleiman 1999; Khalili 2007a). The state justified denying Palestinians civil and social rights on two grounds: to prevent permanent settlement (*tawtin*) and the ostensible threat it would pose to Lebanon's confessional demographics, and to maintain the Lebanese government's political stance that Palestinian refugees should return to their homes in Palestine.[12] However, particularly in the early years, Lebanese administrations also feared the influence of leftist and often cross-national parties associated with Arab Nationalism, communism, and Nasserism. Cold War tensions pitted the pro–Eisenhower Doctrine Chamoun administration against domestic Lebanese currents that leaned toward the United Arab Republic and Arab Nationalist trends, resulting in a civil war and US military intervention in 1958.

Within this context, the Lebanese *Deuxième Bureau*, one of the state's many intelligence and security forces, monitored Palestinian activities closely, frequently interrogating individuals suspected of political involvement and their families (R. Sayigh 1979, 151; al-Hout 2004, 24–25). This relationship with state authorities both fomented Palestinian resentment toward Lebanese authorities and forced politically active Palestinians to learn underground organizing skills. The state's repressive tactics also tended to isolate poorer Palestinians who lived in the camps, who lacked the connections or finances to protect themselves (R. Sayigh 1979, 132–33). Families who had previously owned and farmed their land were left landless and competing for jobs with thousands of other poor Palestinians and Lebanese. While middle- and upper-class Palestinians were, in many cases, able to retain their social status—drawing on both family wealth and socioeconomic ties to the Lebanese elite—they were still subjected to discrimination.[13]

Many Palestinians who were politically active during the 1970s and 1980s grew up during this period and relayed being deeply affected by the conditions in which they lived and the repression they experienced. They vividly recalled the zinc roofing and shared toilets of the pre-1969 camps. Middle-class Palestinian refugees often looked on the camp populations with pity. For example, in her autobiography, Leila Khaled (1973), a long-term leftist militant whose family fled Palestine and took refuge in Sur, recalls that children from the nearby camps lived in deep poverty, lacking shoes or proper clothing (her family had a stable income and could afford a small apartment outside the camp). Several of my interlocutors whose older siblings had been politically active vividly recalled their parents' concern for the family's safety because of the *Deuxième Bureau*'s constant surveillance. While they resented the political repression, people also noted that being raised by constantly worried parents both affected their social freedom and sometimes made them hesitant to tell their parents when they *did* mobilize.

Despite varying restrictions on Palestinian refugees in host Arab states, key Palestinian political organizations appeared in the predominantly middle-to-upper-class arenas of Arab university campuses during this period. Three core strands developed: A leftist, secular, pan-Arab vein in Beirut; a more socially conservative, explicitly Palestinian nationalist strand among affiliates of the General Union of Palestinian Students (GUPS) and Palestinian members of the Muslim Brotherhood; and, a bit later, a third line cultivated by Palestinian officers in the Syrian army that blended leftist, Baʿthist ideology with social conservatism. At the American University of Beirut (AUB), a group of radical students led by George Habash (a Greek Orthodox Palestinian), Wadi Haddad (also a Greek Orthodox Palestinian), and Hani al-Hindi (a Syrian), founded the socialist, pan-Arab, secular Arab Nationalist Movement (ANM) in 1951.[14] The organization's clandestine membership gradually grew among Lebanese and within the Palestinian refugee community; it was frequently the first of many political affiliations that my older interlocutors mentioned.[15] Habash, Haddad, and their followers later split from the ANM, forming the revolutionary Leninist-Marxist Popular Front for the Liberation of Palestine (PFLP) in 1967.

This initial split foreshadowed several more within the leftist elements of militant Palestinian politics. For example, the Palestinian Popular Struggle Front (PPSF) split from the PFLP in 1967, the Arab Liberation Front (ALF) in 1968, and the Popular Democratic Front for the Liberation of Palestine, later known simply as the Democratic Front for the Liberation of Palestine ((P)DFLP, led by former ANM and PFLP leading member Nayef Hawatmeh), in 1969.[16] In the late 1950s, then Kuwait-based activists Yasir Arafat (Abu Ammar), Salah Khalaf (Abu Iyad), and Khalil al-Wazir (Abu Jihad) founded Fatah, a broad-based nationalist organization dedicated to using armed struggle to liberate Palestine.[17] Other Palestinian organizations also emerged in the late 1950s, including the Palestine Liberation Front (PLF)—the forerunner of the PFLP-General Command (founded in 1968)—which Palestinian Syrian army officers Ahmad Jibril, Ali al-Bushnaq, and Abd al-Latif Shururu created.[18] During its 1964 meeting in Cairo, the Arab League established the Palestine Liberation Organization (PLO), an umbrella organization dedicated, in its words, to freeing the territory of Mandate Palestine and establishing right of return for all refugees; Ahmad al-Shuqayri became the PLO's first chairman.

While support for the growing number of Palestinian resistance organizations varied across communities in the region, the ANM and the Palestine Liberation Front-Path of Return, the latter of which was a leftist-Nasserist group founded in Beirut, gained the two largest followings among Palestinian refugees in Lebanon during the late 1960s (Y. Sayigh 1997, chap. 6). At the international level, Fatah emerged as the leading Palestinian militant organization by 1967; its main rival within the PLO for years to come would be the PFLP (R. Sayigh 1979, 144–45).[19] However, the March 1968 Battle of Karameh between Fatah and the Israel Defense Forces in Jordan monumentally improved Fatah's reputation among Palestinians and augmented the group's ability to recruit in Lebanon. At this juncture, Fatah began moving significant military resources into the Arkoub region of South Lebanon, opening training sites and launching attacks into the Galilee.[20] This series of actions foregrounded the tense relationship between the Palestinian refugee community and the Lebanese state.

At this time, the PLO was organized around the Palestinian National Council (PNC), its legislature, and an eighteen-member Executive Committee. It also included a conventional military arm, called the Palestine Liberation Army (PLA), which eventually established battalions in Syria, Jordan, and Egypt. While highly competitive, the various emergent militant organizations cooperated extensively on military matters, funneling weapons to each other and sharing training camp space in the late 1960s (Y. Sayigh 1997, chap. 6). As they progressively joined the PLO, members of guerrilla parties quickly assumed control of the initially independent organizational apparatus.

Lebanese support varied for the growing Palestinian political project in Lebanon. Large portions of the population of South Lebanon, along with urban leftists and a majority of Lebanese Muslims, supported the Palestinian *fida'iyyin* (guerrillas/resistance fighters)[21] in the region (R. Sayigh 1979, 156; Traboulsi 2007, 152-153). Particularly because many communities in South Lebanon were socially marginalized and lacked state services, "supporting the Palestinian Revolution became a means of protesting against a corrupt and negligent regime" (R. Sayigh 1979, 157). However, tension between the fida'iyyin and the Lebanese army increased, not least because repeated Palestinian cross-border military operations into Israel elicited that state's reprisals on Lebanese territory. Israel's occupation of the West Bank, East Jerusalem, and Gaza during the 1967 war elevated the importance of South Lebanon, a location from which to stage these assaults. In April 1969, the Lebanese military sealed the village of Bint Jbeil to capture fida'iyyin returning from an operation in Israel. The guerrillas' subsequent surrender and imprisonment in Sur set off a wave of urban protests that mobilized the Palestinian camp community as well as thousands of Lebanese sympathizers. Throughout the summer, attacks on the *Deuxième Bureau*, the Lebanese police, and the Lebanese military increased, even though camp populations were unarmed. By the end of the year, Palestinians had forced the Lebanese to abandon control of the refugee camps and had replaced *Deuxième Bureau* offices with party and PLO headquarters. In November 1969, representatives from the PLO and the Lebanese army finalized the Cairo Agreement, which gave the PLO and its constituent parties permission to base their armed struggle on Lebanese territory and formally transferred refugee camp governance into Palestinian hands.

"We Could Finally Breathe": 1969–1975

The Cairo Agreement prompted a restructuring of political life in the refugee camps and allowed Palestinians to openly organize. It afforded the PLO the opportunity to establish camp Popular Committees, which included representatives from each guerrilla party as well as the general unions. My interlocutors who had lived in the camps during this time frequently used language such as "we could finally breathe" to describe the freeing nature of the transition. Palestinian militant groups used this autonomy to launch repeated armed incursions into northern Israel. These operations targeted both IDF installations and civilian communities; multiple operations resulted in Israeli civilians' being taken hostage or killed. Palestinian guerrilla incursions and Katyusha rocket attacks on settlements in the Galilee led the IDF to target South Lebanese villages to eliminate militant bases and to force the local Lebanese population to halt its support of the Palestinians. These attacks displaced tens of thousands of predominantly Christian and Shi'a Lebanese, many of whom settled in the slum districts surrounding Beirut where several of the Palestinian camps were also located.[22]

During the Black September events of 1970 in Jordan, deep disagreements between the PLO (particularly its leftist elements such as the PLFP) and the Hashemite Kingdom sparked open warfare between Palestinians and the Jordanian government. Jordan outlawed Palestinian parties and guerrilla groups from operating within its borders; in summer 1971, the PLO relocated its command structure and its fighters to Lebanon.[23] The PLO and the guerrilla organizations transferred both their massive military apparatus and a significant social and economic sector that became the largest employer in Lebanon; Jaber Suleiman (1997) estimates that approximately 65 percent of Palestinians in Lebanon were employed by the PLO's social and economic apparatus. Funded by Arab states, the Soviet Union, and a 5 percent income tax on Palestinians working in Gulf countries such as Kuwait and the United Arab Emirates, the PLO acted in many ways like a deterritorialized state apparatus. Areas of West Beirut and South Lebanon became near-autonomous regions within the Lebanese state.[24] Reflecting the organizations' broad influence, people referred to the Arkoub region as "Fatahland" (Traboulsi 2007, 152) and the West Beirut neighborhood that housed the PLO's administrative buildings as the "Fakhani Republic." The PLO became Lebanon's largest employer, running industrial operations through organizations such as Samed, medical institutions through the Palestinian Red Crescent Society (PRCS), and popular organizations such as the General Union of Palestinian Women (GUPW) (Suleiman 1997). The GUPW alone counted 21,000 members (Rubenberg 1983b, 73).

People like Yunis, a middle-class, left-leaning, half-Lebanese/half-Palestinian who grew up in Beirut's eastern suburbs during this period, frequently emphasized that mobilization at this time was not simply about military aims. When he described to me his pathway into the GUPS, he started by stressing conditions in the camp and then connected his activism to efforts to instill a sense of shared history and collective dignity among Palestinians and between Lebanese and Palestinians, given the new atmosphere:

> YUNIS: People were deprived [*mahrumin*] in Tel al-Zaʿtar, the toilets were all shared, they were living in a very bad situation. There was darkness [*zalam*], they lived under zinco [zinc] roofs, people were poor. In 1970, 1971, I was working with the Students' Union in East Beirut, I was in the union with Lebanese and Palestinians who wanted freedom.
>
> ME: What was the union's role?
>
> YUNIS: Teach ideas about Palestine, share with the Lebanese. We were cultured [*muthaqafin*], we had the brève, the BAC, the BAC II [high school certifications], we wanted to teach people about Palestine, about freedom, about their roots. The idea was to pass information from generation to generation. The military stuff happened later.[25]

Here, Yunis emphasizes building ties among Palestinians, between Palestinians and Lebanese, and across strong class divides. Often, Palestinian militants later called upon these ties during the Israeli occupation and the 1985–1988 War of the Camps.

The PLO and guerrilla parties also quickly became deeply entwined in domestic Lebanese politics. Interviewees from multiple parties referred to this involvement as a mistake, referring to Lebanese politics as "a sickness" or an "infection," both terms conveying that Palestinians felt their own sociopolitical projects had been infected or sullied by Lebanese politics (Parkinson 2016, 978). Palestinian groups dealt extensively with Lebanese political parties, particularly members of the leftist, secular, pan-Arab Lebanese National Movement (LNM) led by Kamal Jumblatt, which included the predominantly Druze Progressive Socialist Party (PSP), the Syrian Socialist National Party (SSNP), the Independent Nasserite Movement (Murabitoun), the Lebanese Communist Party (LCP), and smaller leftist parties such as Saida's Popular Nasserite Organization (PNO). Coordination among the PFLP, DFLP, and Lebanese leftists was particularly strong; Fatah tended to operate more toward the political center, even maintaining relationships with many of the right-wing Christian parties such as the Kata'ib (also known as the Phalange) and Camille Chamoun's National Liberal Party (NLP) (Abu Iyad and Rouleau 1981).[26] Palestinian parties, particularly Fatah's Force 17, also helped to train members of Amal, a party that recruited heavily from the marginalized Lebanese Shi'i population that lived in the south, the Bekaa Valley, and the slum districts surrounding Beirut.

Yet the Lebanese army's repeated skirmishing with Palestinian guerrilla forces, its relative weakness in South Lebanon, and the government's refusal to allow a military response to Israeli attacks, including the April 1973 assassination of three PLO leaders in Beirut, put it at odds with Palestinian forces (Khalidi 1985, 24). In May 1973, with the support of the Kata'ib and the NLP, the Lebanese military attacked Shatila and Burj al-Barajneh camps using tank-supported ground and air assaults. Palestinians and leftist Lebanese staged multicity protests, roadblocks, and attacks on police barracks that prompted the declaration of a state of emergency in Lebanon. Subsequent negotiations culminated in the Melkart Protocol on May 17, 1973, which further outlined guidelines that governed Palestinian military activity in Lebanon, including the cessation of attacks on Israel (Y. Sayigh 1997, 316–17; Picard 2002, 87).

In 1974, the PLO had to contend with a strong wave of internal dissent following its adoption of the 10 Point Program at the 12th session of the Palestinian National Congress. Seen as a possible harbinger of the PLO's willingness to accept a two-state solution with Israel, the PFLP, DFLP, ALF, PPSF, al-Sa'iqa, Fatah-Revolutionary Council, and the PFLP-GC formed the Rejectionist Front. Several factions left the PLO. The PFLP—the first organization to formally protest—resigned from the PLO's Executive Committee but remained in the organization (Cobban 1985, 62). Others also remained as opposition groups but refused to attend Central Council meetings (Cobban 1985, 151). The Rejectionist Front remained as the primary collective opposition body until it dissolved in 1978. By then, the Palestinian experience of the Lebanese Civil War moderated many of the dissenting organizations' unfavorable stances on establishing a "Palestinian National Authority" (Cobban 1985, 150).

Individual factions continued to use Lebanese territory to launch attacks on Israel. For instance, the DFLP was responsible for the May 1974 killing of twenty-four people, the majority of them schoolchildren who had been taken hostage, during an attack in the northern Israeli town of Ma'alot.[27] The PFLP-GC had carried out a similar attack on the northern Israeli town of Kiryat Shmona, in April 1974. Operations such as these were frequently aimed at coercing the Israeli government to release Palestinian prisoners, or, in the late 1970s, to sabotage Egyptian–Israeli peace talks. In response, Israel retaliated against Palestinian forces and against civilian communities in South Lebanon more generally, seeking to engender resentment toward the Palestinians; between "June 1968 and June 1974, the Lebanese army counted more than 30,000 violations of their national territory, including Israeli 'policing' operations, control measures taken with impunity using patrols and fixed observation points, blows at the civilian population in the camps or at resistance leaders in the cities, and attacks aimed at Lebanon itself" (Picard 2002, 83).[28]

The Lebanese Civil War, 1975–1982

In the late winter and early spring of 1975, simmering tensions escalated into violence between the leftist LNM/Palestinian alliance and the right-wing Lebanese Front—an alliance including the Kata'ib (affiliated with the political party of the same name and the Gemayel family), Tigers (affiliated with Chamoun's National Liberal Party), Marada (also known as the Zgharta Liberation Army, affiliated with the Frangieh family), Guardians of the Cedars, and al-Tanzim. A dispute between predominantly Sunni fisherman and the government-supported, Christian-dominated Proteine Company, a seafood consortium that was encroaching on Saida's traditional fishing trade, resulted in the fatal wounding of Maarouf Saad, then the city's mayor and founder of the PNO, during a February protest. Following Saad's funeral in March, leftist Lebanese and Palestinian demonstrators clashed with the LAF (el-Khazen 2000, 268–73). Many of my interlocutors thought of this event as the start of the Lebanese Civil War, particularly given the way that the clashes mobilized intersecting modes of identification that ranged from economic and class-based (elite-run corporate entity versus traditional fisherman), political (rightist versus leftist), and sectarian (predominantly Maronite and Greek Orthodox versus Sunni and anti-sectarian). To my interlocutors, this event embodied the diverse underpinnings of what became innumerable ongoing conflicts in a context of a broader state breakdown.

These events served as precursors to the April 13, 1975, bus attack in the East Beirut neighborhood of Ain al-Rummaneh, which is more broadly understood and memorialized as the beginning of the Lebanese Civil War (Haugbolle 2012). During this episode, Kata'ib militiamen attacked a bus full of Palestinian members of the ALF who were returning to Tel al-Zaʿtar after a rally in Shatila, killing twenty-six. While buses carrying members of Palestinian and Lebanese militant groups regularly traversed the city, Kata'ib members were on high alert following a shooting only hours earlier, when Palestinian gunmen from another faction fired into a church where a member of the Gemayel family, which founded Kata'ib, was attending services, killing several bodyguards (el-Khazen 2000, 285–88).[29] The event prompted LNM organizations and Palestinian militants to mobilize both diplomatically and militarily against the LF and its allies. This chain of events eventually triggered the Lebanese government's collapse in May as well as militia fighting and sectarian massacres throughout the remainder of 1975.[30]

Right-wing Lebanese militia attacks on Palestinian civilians and camp communities during this period served as later reference points for Palestinian activists and militants during the 1980s. In January 1976, Maronite militias renewed their attacks on the East Beirut refugee camps Tel al-Zaʿtar[31] and Jisr al-Pasha as well as on proximate Shiʿa neighborhoods such as Nabʿa. These areas were centers of leftist labor and political organizing as well as being strategically located near major industrial zones on the main highway between Beirut and the Christian heartland in the Metn.[32] Right-wing Lebanese militias, in some case led by elites with economic interests in local industries, laid siege to the Tel al-Zaʿtar and Jisr al-Basha with heavy artillery. In the same month, right-wing militias overran Dbayeh Palestinian refugee camp north of Beirut before expelling its residents. On January 18, the right-wing militias expelled and massacred hundreds of Palestinians, Syrians, Shiʿas, and Kurds from the left-leaning Maslakh-Karantina slum district in East Beirut, another geographic hub for cross-national organizing.

In response, Palestinian fighters attacked the seaside Christian town of Damour on January 20, 1976. At Damour, Palestinian fighters affiliated with the PLA, Fatah, and al-Saʿiqa committed numerous atrocities to avenge these East Beirut killings, including the rape, expulsion, and murder of hundreds of Lebanese Christian civilians (Hanf 1994, 211–12; Y. Sayigh 1997, 374–76). When ordered to retake Damour, the Lebanese army in the southern city of Marjayoun split down sectarian and ideological lines, producing the Muslim-led Lebanese Arab Army (LAA) commanded by Colonel Ahmad al-Khatib and the Christian-led Free Lebanon Army (FLA) led by Major Saad Haddad.[33] The PLO and LNM Joint Forces moved into the Christian heartland of the Metn, further straining the capacities of right-wing Maronite militia forces.

Tel al-Zaʿtar as a Historical Touchstone

For many of my interlocutors, the 1976 Tel al-Zaʿtar siege became emblematic of the Palestinian struggle in Lebanon as well as a harbinger of future attacks on the refugee camps. As Hala, a former PFLP militant and former member of the Tel al-Zaʿtar branch of the GUPW told me, "Before, Tel al-Zaʿtar didn't know war . . . before the 70s, there was security, we never thought war would happen."[34] The siege came to represent how she, and many others, understood war. Individuals' experiences of malnutrition, snipers, constant shelling, and medical shortages—which left the camp without antibiotics, anesthesia, or plasma supplies and led to widespread gangrene—were coupled with the reality of being unable to leave the camp for fear of torture, rape, or murder upon exit. Interviewees repeatedly emphasized memories of severe dehydration, asking me to pinch my arm to watch how my well-hydrated skin bounced back into place, imploring me to imagine how during the siege people became so dehydrated that their skin would stick in place. These visceral, embodied memories of the physical hardships of siege, survivors of Tel al-Zaʿtar explained, informed their future mobilization as well as the risks they were willing to take during the 1980s. The shared experience of siege had important downstream effects on people's notions of political and social affiliations, including a willingness to override factional affiliation in order to protect communities. Zahra, for example, told me: "[The siege of] Tel al-Zaʿtar canceled all affiliations. I am not from the village, I'm from Tel al-Zaʿtar. If there is happiness, if there is pain, if there is a problem, all of us from Tel al-Zaʿtar, we are coming."[35] I asked her if this was perhaps due to people's shared political affiliations in the camp: did everyone who "stuck together" belong to the same militant party before the siege? She immediately responded: "no, no, because of the siege."[36]

In January 1976, right-wing, predominantly Christian militias established a military cordon around Tel al-Zaʿtar and Jisr al-Basha. At this time, civilians living in the camp received what would be the last deliveries of fresh food, including produce and meat. In the camps, local militiamen, guerrillas, and PLA soldiers battled the Lebanese Front and elements of the Lebanese military. Throughout the following months, the Lebanese Front increasingly sought to use the camp as a bargaining chip against the PLO and LNM. The Joint Forces' (PLO and LNM's) military successes in the spring of 1976 resulted in direct reprisals against Tel al-Zaʿtar. On April 9, the Syrian government, fearing that further fighting would result in an untenable regional security situation, moved armor and infantry into Lebanon (Y. Sayigh 1997, 385; Traboulsi 2007, 197). Tel al-Zaʿtar received its last supply shipment of preserved food, hygienic supplies, and medicines on April 24 (Y. Sayigh 1997, 396). On June 20, the Tigers—led by Dany

Chamoun, son of Lebanese Interior Minister Camille Chamoun—escalated the confrontation; according to Sayigh, during the assault, "up to 5,000 shells landed on the camps, damaging up to 70 per cent of their housing" (Y. Sayigh 1997, 396). Jisr al-Basha fell on June 24.

Concerned by the prospect of the PLO and LNM seizing control of Lebanon, and foreshadowing its later operations against the PLO in the 1980s, the Syrian regime switched its support away from the left-wing, Palestinian–Lebanese Joint Forces and allied with the right-wing Lebanese Front. The Syrian military, including PLA units, consequently began providing artillery fire against Tel al-Zaʿtar while militarily sustaining the Front against the Joint Forces in battles across central and northern Lebanon. Intensifying attacks severed Palestinian forces' supply chain via the Beirut River, meaning that goods and replacement fighters ceased reaching the camp; near-starvation conditions followed. A July ceasefire negotiated between Syrian president Hafiz al-Assad and PLO chairman Yasir Arafat collapsed in early August; the Kataʾib occupied Nabʿa, expelling approximately 200,000 Shiʿa Lebanese from Beirut's eastern neighborhoods (Traboulsi 2007, 201). Tel al-Zaʿtar eventually succumbed on August 12, 1976; between 9,000 and 12,000 civilians fled. The Lebanese Front's militias executed between 1,000 and 2,000 people as they evacuated the camp; my female interviewees who had endured the siege emphasized that the militiamen also sexually assaulted women as they attempted to escape.[37] Approximately 4,000 people died over the course of the siege (Berggren et al. 1996; Y. Sayigh 1997, 401; Fisk 2002, 85–86; Picard 2002, 110; Faris 2007; Khalili 2007a, 51).[38] Members of the Lebanese Front immediately bulldozed the entire community.[39]

Cross-Border Operations and the Israeli Invasion of 1978

Cross-border armed operations into Israel, planned by different guerrilla factions, began in the 1960s and continued during the late 1970s into the 1980s. A March 1978 civilian bus hijacking near Tel Aviv, led by Sabra-born Fatah cadre Dalal al-Mughrabi and carried out with thirteen members of her unit, killed 37 people. My female interlocutors frequently referenced al-Mughrabi's skill as a commando, specifically, as an inspiration in their own careers. They considered the operation a success, though it also prompted an immediate, massive Israeli reprisal (Cobban 1985, 96).[40] Three days after the hijacking, on March 14, the IDF launched Operation Litani, which, according to Israeli journalists Ze'ev Schiff and Ehud Ya'ari (1984, 24), "[aimed to] destroy the PLO bases that were the continuing source of harassment to settlements in the Galilee and of terrorist raids farther inland; and to extend the territory under the control of Lebanese Major Saad Haddad [one of the founders of the Army of Free Lebanon in 1976] and the local militia he had recruited among the Christian population of the area—Israel's surrogate and client force in South Lebanon."

A 25,000-strong IDF force occupied South Lebanon, with the exception of Sur (Cobban 1985, 94); the Lebanese government protested to the UN Security Council. Approximately half of the region's population—around 285,000 people—fled the area and some 2,000 died. As a Syrian officer told the journalist Robert Fisk, the Syrian military prevented many people from fleeing because the Israelis would otherwise "claim that they had found another land without people" (Fisk 2002, 130). The Security Council responded by passing Resolutions 425 and 426, which established the UN Interim Force in Lebanon (UNIFIL) and called for the immediate withdrawal of Israeli forces. Haddad's militia, supported by the IDF, greatly restricted UNIFIL's access to the area; the decision to base the peacekeeping force at the coastal town of Naqoura restricted its capacities and gave the FLA a chokehold over the mission's attempts to patrol the interior. The FLA also continuously abused Shi'a civilians in its zone of control (Fisk 2002, 137–55).[41]

Skirmishes between the Israel–FLA alliance on one hand and Palestinians and Lebanese leftists on the other took an increasing toll on South Lebanon; they also helped Palestinian militants to build guerrilla skill sets and to learn the terrain. Yet, these clashes also had a devastating effect on the region, given that "in one period of under six months in 1979, there were 175 Israeli land, sea, and air attacks on the area. Villages were hit repeatedly, their residents made refugees time and again, and it became difficult to see what they or the P.L.O. were achieving from this war of attrition in which civilians paid the main price" (Khalidi 1985, 28). Palestinian militant organizations continued to cross into northern Israel to conduct operations and to shell the northern settlements from their base at Beaufort Castle,[42] undeterred even by the IDF's July 1980 bombing of the PLO headquarters in Beirut. These attacks created considerable Lebanese resentment against Palestinian forces operating in the region, even if many communities simultaneously sympathized with the Palestinians' larger aims.

In the early 1980s, Lebanese support declined with continued Israeli attacks and Palestinian militants' abusive treatment of Lebanese civilians. Rashid Khalidi muses: "If the relationship between a successful guerilla army and the society it operates within is accurately described by Mao Zedong's metaphor of 'fish swimming in the water,' the P.L.O. was flopping helplessly on dry land in Lebanon on the eve of the 1982 war" (Khalidi 1985, 17). He further emphasizes: "It was of particular importance that immediately before the war, this alienation had begun to affect communities and groups traditionally well disposed to the Palestinians and which benefited politically from the P.L.O.'s presence" (Khalidi 1985, 17–18).

The Social Infrastructure of a State in Waiting

The PLO and various guerrilla organizations spent the 1970s constructing a massive military, social, civic, and economic footprint in Lebanon. In the following sections I provide a brief description of some of these capacities, thus sketching, in part, the social infrastructure that undergirded militant organizations in the lead-up to 1982. Specifically, given the frequency with which my interlocutors mentioned them, I describe military training, healthcare, and scouting and recreation programs. Some data on healthcare and scouting and recreational institutions are available in a 1981 report by Team International Engineering and Management Consultants (TIEMC) that was submitted to the Economic Commission for Western Asia. However, they are primarily self-reported and only represent projects that fell under the factions' social wings. For example, Fatah's scouting programs did not fall under its social wing; in fact, the PLO's supervision of scouting activities was located in the Department of Mass Organizations rather than under Social Affairs (Rubenberg 1983a). Likewise, in the section regarding the PFLP's Medical Committee, the report says only: "The Committee supervises health and medical care provided to martyrs' children and families and the Palestinian people in the camps" (TIEMC 1981, 31). Although the PFLP had a well-known and respected history as a medical provider in many camps (notably Tel al-Zaʿtar, where it opened the first clinic in the camp in the 1970s), no further geographic, financial, or workforce details are provided.[43] It must also be noted that brick-and-mortar facilities are only a rough starting point from which to analyze the nature and degree of the PLO and the guerrilla organizations' social embeddedness. Only by examining the content of social network ties generated by these establishments and the ways in which people perceived the influence can we understand a fuller picture of militant social presence.

Not all forms of social engagement were equally prioritized across the factions. This may be due to the variant nature of ties; medical institutions, for example, can be used to employ many people and to provide services; they also are not age-specific. By contrast, nurseries and kindergartens employ fewer people, and the nature of service provision is to a family (centering on mothers and young children); interactions at childcare institutions have, however, been demonstrated to generate new social network ties for parents via interactions during drop-off/pickup and class activities (Small 2010). Ideology may well have influenced this variation; reports from the era indicate that leftist organizations tended to run more social, cultural, and recreational facilities than, for example, Baʿthist and Syrian-supported groups. The leftist organizations' general tendency to combine recreational facilities and activities may indicate a broader commitment to grassroots social change and political education.

Military Capacity and Training

Engagements such as those in East Beirut and Damour involved a diverse array of Palestinian armed forces. The Palestinian military apparatus in the 1970s and in the early 1980s comprised three main levels, all of which played varying roles in the conflicts of the time. Local, camp-based militias were formed to manage community-based defense; members were not necessarily party cadres. They received less training and were not as well armed as guerrilla cadres or the PLO's official military force, the PLA. Militia members did not commonly attend specialized training programs in other camps. The PLA and the guerrilla organizations, by contrast, fielded uniformed fighters and support staff who received varying levels of formal indoctrination, training, and supplies.

The PLA and guerrilla factions were deeply embedded in Palestinian communities. Recruiters often worked close to home, enrolled people they knew, and sent them for basic drilling nearby before transferring promising new cadres for specialized instruction elsewhere. PLA soldiers frequently trained alongside the Egyptian, Syrian, or Jordanian national armed services. They were, as a result, familiar with conventional military organization, discipline, and tactics. The PLA initially comprised three brigades—the Ain Jalut Brigade (originally stationed in Egypt), the Qadisiyya Brigade (originally located in Iraq and moved to Jordan and Syria in 1967), and the Hittin Brigade (originally based in Syria) (Hamid 1975, 105; Rubenberg 1983a, 12).[44] Elements of all three forces participated extensively in the Lebanese Civil War, some under Syrian command. In early 1982, a fourth brigade, the Badr Forces, deployed in Beirut and in the hills above Damour. When Israel invaded in June 1982, between six and ten thousand PLA soldiers were stationed in Lebanon, some of whom had combat experience from the events of Black September, from the 1973 war (during which Palestinian contingents fought in Egypt and Syria), or from the Lebanese Civil War (Rubenberg 1983a, 12).

The guerrilla organizations' armed elements varied widely in size, training, and capacity. In 1968, Fatah had some 2,000 guerrillas; in 1970, the PFLP, PLF/PLA, and al-Saʿiqa each comprised approximately 1,000–1,500 guerrillas (Y. Sayigh 1997, chap. 12). These numbers rose notably in the decade leading up to the 1982 invasion, in part due to heavy recruitment and conscription within the refugee camps in Lebanon. Of the seven guerrilla organizations that filled seats on the 1981 PLO Executive Committee, Fatah had approximately 14,000 guerrillas organized into five brigades—Yarmouk, Karameh, Qastal, Ajnadayn, and Force 17, the latter of which was Arafat's personal bodyguard—and 26 battalions (Rubenberg 1983a, 11; Schiff and Ya'ari 1984, 130; Y. Sayigh 1997, chaps. 19–21). Fatah historian Mahmoud al-Natour (2014a, 1:600) claims the faction could field 3,000–5,000 fighters in South Lebanon alone, in addition to 50–60 Soviet T-34 tanks and 50–60 cannon. Many fighters had previous battle experience; the approximately 4,000-man-strong Yarmouk Brigade included a large number of former Jordanian Army soldiers and had been active since 1971. Based in Syria but deployed in South Lebanon in 1982, the Yarmouk Forces consisted of "three infantry battalions, an artillery battalion and other combat support units, and a full complement of support units (medical, communications, engineering, supply, transport, and workshop)" (Y. Sayigh 1997, 295–96). These preexisting ties came into play during the 1983 Fatah rebellion, when many soldiers in the Yarmouk Forces sided with dissidents led by the former battalion commander Colonel Saied al-Muragha (Abu Musa).

Other guerrilla organizations fielded smaller combat forces in comparison. Al-Sa'iqa only had the ability to put 3,000 guerrillas into combat. The 6,000-soldier-strong DFLP organized thirteen battalions, "eight infantry, two gun artillery, one rocket artillery, one air defense, [and] one security" into regional brigade commands, which would have theoretically allowed military commanders tactical independence (Rubenberg 1983a, 11; Y. Sayigh 1997, 451). The PFLP's 6,000-strong guerrilla combat forces comprised ten battalions, while the 500-person-strong PFLP-GC fielded six; in both cases, the faction's central leadership had direct control of combat forces rather than creating independent brigade commands (Rubenberg 1983a, 11; Y. Sayigh 1997, 451). However, manpower varied widely across battalions, which could consist of anywhere from 60 to 150 men. Sayigh (1997, 451) emphasizes that "on this basis, even the miniscule ALF could claim three battalions, as well as artillery, mortar, and anti-tank sections."

Several interviewees cited their participation in military training and operations as a deep source of pride. They also noted how it affected their relationships with their families, friends, and communities. Others saw mass participation in armed resistance as a harbinger of social change, especially when it came to gender. When I asked Zahra, whose story is detailed in the introduction to this book, about gender relations during initial recruitment, she told me: "there were equal numbers of men and women in Fatah." Her statement, however, does not pan out in official records or research, which indicate higher male participation in fighting roles (Peteet 1991). Rather, it likely indicates her personal sentiment that the resistance elevated women and placed them on a more equal footing with men. Mahmud, a guerrilla from South Lebanon, also referenced shifts in gender roles that military training facilitated, recalling both his shock the first time a woman shared the barracks with him in Shatila and his ability to view her as "one of the guys" after she told a raunchy joke (which would have been highly taboo and to some extent still was at the time of the interview).

Healthcare

In 1982, Palestinian healthcare infrastructure in Lebanon was geographically widespread, financially accessible, and well-regarded by both Palestinians and Lebanese. These organizations created overlap between people's everyday relationships, their professional ties, and military organizations, though they also often reified factional divisions. Concentrated in Beirut, Saida, and Sur, the PRCS hospitals were among the PLO's social anchors in Lebanon; they provided patient services, educational campaigns, and employment to the Palestinian community. In 1980, for example, the PRCS managed nine hospitals and twelve clinics, treating 425,682 Palestinian and Lebanese patients (Rubenberg 1983a; Khalidi 1985, 32).[45] The PRCS funded programs to train nurses, technicians, and paramedics and ran preventive health and mother-child health programs (Rubenberg 1983a, 22–24; TIEMC 1981, 9–10). Guerrilla factions administered over thirty additional medical and dental clinics (Rubenberg 1983a; TIEMC 1981).

Healthcare organizations provided key spaces and institutions through which the PLO established ties to Palestinian and Lebanese communities through employment and service provision.[46] Julie Peteet (1991, 104) notes, for example, that leftist institutions' preventive medicine projects drew their employees from the camps. PLO-subsidized healthcare services were both financially and geographically accessible. Employees of the PLO and their families received medical care for free, highlighting the strong exchange of employment and services that membership incurred. However, all Palestinians and Lebanese could access PRCS services; patients paid approximately US$1 for a clinic visit, US$5 for inpatient hospital care per day, and, on average, US$60 for surgery (US$2.94, US$14.69, and US$176.27 in 2021, respectively) (Rubenberg 1983a, 21).

During and following the invasion, protecting and maintaining medical establishments—which were often targeted by the IDF and right-wing Lebanese militias—were military and social priorities (Ang 1989; Cutting 1989; Giannou 1990). After the invasion, hospitals' and clinics' needs drove logistics and smuggling considerations while continuing to provide employment for skilled Palestinian workers. Building or rebuilding a hospital or clinic became a way to combine old organizational logics with new civil society-derived practices. Starting in the mid-1980s, institutionally independent medical facilities paid for by foundations but managed by militant parties began operating.

Scouting and Sports

Scouting organizations paved the way for many young Palestinians to later enter military divisions of the guerrilla organizations. While all the scouting organizations included at least elementary military training, my interviewees distinguished the scouts (sing.: *kashaf*, plur.: *kashafa*) from the male Lion Cubs (sing.: *shibil*, plur.: *ashbal*) and the female Flowers (sing.: *zahra*, plur.: *zaharat*); the Lion Cubs and the Flowers were expressly militarily oriented (TIEMC 1981; author interviews). Yet few people explicitly mentioned ideology or indoctrination when they spoke of their experiences of the scouts; those who grew up in the 1960s tended instead to contextualize scouting organizations as places where young Palestinians could be proud of their heritage and feel as if they were part of a broad social and political project. For example, when I interviewed Amjad, a member of the PFLP who had grown up in Tel al-Zaʿtar in the 1960s, he emphasized the historical role of the scouts, especially during the *Deuxième Bureau* era. He noted that unlike the *ashbal*—whom he remembered as boys marching off to the forests with sticks (not guns, at that point) for military training—the *kashafa* were "just in schools." Yet Amjad still underscored the *kashafa* organization's particular influence on its members, explaining that "to the outside, they were scouts," but on the "inside" they were "something for Palestine." Sports clubs, he explained, encapsulated the same inside–outside dichotomy: on the "inside"—under the table, so to speak—they were "something for Palestine." Especially in the context of the 1960s, Amjad's memory of the scouts and sports teams emphasizes how people carved out small spaces of collective resistance, even in contexts of surveillance and state repression, and also how people's pathways into later high-risk activism incorporated many different, and differently risky, starting points.

Scouting and sporting organizations did more than simply build physical skills; as in other settings, recreational facilities generated lasting social and political ties among their members. Sporting clubs have long been a source of political and military organization building, licit and otherwise. Scholars have noted the importance of fun in political activity (Royko 1988; A. Cohen and Taylor 2001; Volkov 2002; Verkaaik 2004), suggesting that participation in party-sponsored recreational activities may have been an important aspect of continued membership and cohesion, rather than simply a path to recruitment. In Soviet Russia, the United States, and the United Kingdom, participation in sporting clubs has for decades also been linked to involvement in riots and violent enterprises (Royko 1988; Buford 1993; Volkov 2002). In Lebanon, politically affiliated football clubs have a long history of facilitating friendships and reinforcing political boundaries among Palestinians; several of my interlocutors had played in the leagues since shortly after the ANM's founding and were still friends with football buddies who had changed factions. For example, Abu Husayn informed me on several occasions that he had met members of other Fatah battalions and other guerrilla organizations because he played on the football team. Abu Riyad, who played in the same football league, noted, almost offhandedly, that these programs had obviously broadened his contacts within the sprawling institutions of the Palestinian resistance. Even the ALF and the PLF—both leftist factions that showed comparatively little comparative interest in social efforts such as childhood education—were deeply involved in the world of cultural and sporting clubs (TIEMC 1981).

Understanding the relational environment in Palestinian refugee communities at the beginning of the 1980s is a critical foundation from which to understand processes of organizational adaptation and emergence over the following decade. By 1982, Palestinian guerrilla organizations and the PLO itself had deeply embedded in refugee communities and developed complex ties with Lebanese political parties. They benefited from the backing of regional and global state patrons. Military, social, cultural, and economic projects mobilized hundreds of thousands of ordinary people. These projects also provided a scaffolding upon which a complex social infrastructure developed. Palestinian organizations also became deeply entwined in domestic Lebanese politics, causing broad resentment and attracting incendiary political rhetoric. The early stages of the Lebanese Civil War, shaped by Syrian and Israeli interventions, introduced new generations of Palestinian refugee populations to the lived realities of armed conflict and created new frames for collective identification and mobilization. Of particular import for the processes described in this book are the various ways in which people who were engaged with militancy interacted across subdivisions, factions, and the Lebanese–Palestinian divide.

As the vignette regarding Ain al-Hilweh at the beginning of the chapter suggests, the actors at the center of this study—militant organizations—demonstrate dynamism and malleability in their organizational structures over time, a theme that the remainder of this book deepens. In other words, while the factions being studied retain their names over time, their organizational structures and behaviors change as they experience and respond to violence and repression. Attention to organizational metadata—for example, in Ain al-Hilweh, to distinct performances of militarized hypermasculinity in one camp—can help to reveal historical ruptures and provide evidence of comparative differences in adaptive processes. The following chapter lays out initial distinctions in regionalized repertoires of violence that shaped these adaptive trajectories; those chapters that follow trace the processes of adaptation and emergence that produced new organizational forms.

3

SOCIAL NETWORKS AND WARTIME VIOLENCE

Comparing Repertoires during the 1982 Israeli Invasion

On June 6, 1982, Israel invaded Lebanon. Prompted by the fringe group Fatah-Revolutionary Council's June 3 attempted assassination of the Israeli ambassador to the United Kingdom, the Israel Defense Forces bombed Palestine Liberation Organization offices in Beirut. In retaliation, the PLO launched missiles from South Lebanon toward civilian settlements in northern Israel. Heavily influenced by Prime Minister Menachim Begin, Defense Minister Ariel Sharon, and IDF Chief of Staff Raphael Eitan, the Israeli cabinet launched a long-planned invasion to destroy the PLO's armed forces (Schiff and Ya'ari 1984, chaps. 1–6; Cobban 1985, 120; Y. Sayigh 1997, 505–21). Intensive aerial and artillery attacks began on June 4. The land and sea invasion began on Sunday, two days later.

This chapter highlights core aspects of wartime repertoires of violence from the invasion's first days to September 16–18, 1982, when the Sabra and Shatila massacre took place. My goal is neither to provide a complete history of the engagements nor to analyze the belligerents' decision making, which are available in other works.[1] Rather, this chapter has three primary goals. First, I describe five distinct components of the Israeli and Lebanese parties' repertoires of violence in the summer of 1982 as relayed to me by my interlocutors and as drawn from archival sources and memoirs. This discussion provides a foundation for the following chapters' analyses of resulting social network adaptation and emergence. While aerial bombardment, street-to-street combat, incarceration, "mopping-up" campaigns, and mass killing could, for example, all fall under the umbrella of "indiscriminate," each tactic resonated within social networks in specific ways that later played out via hyperlocal processes of organizational evolution.

Second, I use this thick description of violent repertoires during the summer and fall of 1982 to problematize two oft-used conceptual dichotomies in (counter)insurgency research: that between "indiscriminate" and "selective" violence (Kalyvas 1999, 2006; Downes 2007, 2008; Lyall 2009; Kocher et al. 2011; Souleimanov and Siroky 2016) and that between "direct" and "indirect" strategies, the latter of which involves the use of "brutal" or "barbaric" tactics that "seek to destroy an adversary's will to fight" such as murdering noncombatants and mass internment (Arreguín-Toft 2001, 101–105, and 2005; Hazelton 2021, 18).[2] Despite the causal significance assigned to these categories in (counter)insurgency studies, I suggest three reasons that both the terms themselves and the ways they are employed lack the precision necessary to predict subsequent militant and civilian behavior (e.g., further attacks, new mobilization). First, each label subsumes very different forms of violence. Counterinsurgency campaigns almost always deploy multiple tactics concurrently, rather than à la carte; that is, "indiscriminate" tactics such as aerial bombardment accompany forms of face-to-face, "selective" violence such as assassination and nonlethal techniques such as disinformation. The concurrent usage of tactics from both categories blurs the incentives associated with each, muddying proposed causal pathways to (counter)insurgent success or failure.[3] Second, scholarship focuses on perpetrators' intentions rather than targeted populations' experiences. That is, belligerents' intentions do not translate into militant and civilian perceptions. People targeted by counterinsurgent violence will often experience ostensibly "selective" tactics (such as incarceration) as indiscriminate and will respond according to their interpretations, regardless of perpetrators' aims. Third, there exist substantial challenges to reliable application of the terms; one reasonable person may code certain tactics, such as blanket incarceration of adult men from a certain village, as indiscriminate whereas another would code them as selective.

While other scholars have argued that extant measures of counterinsurgent success are problematically based on artificially truncated parameters (e.g., a short timeline for follow-up attacks; see Souleimanov and Siroky 2016), my contention is that the very categorization of violent tactics into categories of "selective," "indiscriminate," "direct," and "indirect," with the goal of predicting political outcomes neglects the fact that variation in choice of tactic does not consistently map onto organizational or social impact. That is, because these oft-used scholarly categories obscure the micro-level, complex network interactions between repertoires of violence and militant organizations, they are insufficiently precise to analyze the unexpected military decisions and surprising social processes that these tactical repertoires produce. I instead argue that organizational networks and the social infrastructures that underlie them mediate both the material effects of and context-specific meaning-making processes that follow from counterinsurgent violence, affecting outcomes such as militant mobilization, decision-making, and organizational capacity. The implication is that extant scholarly findings mask significant political processes and ignore important modes of organized resistance, thus overstating the chances for and degree of counterinsurgent "success."

To achieve this goal, this chapter carefully details the tactical components that constituted Israeli and Lebanese repertoires of violence, linking them to network effects (e.g., the meanings associated with a death versus a disappearance) and examining how the meanings associated with them shaped understandings and narratives of violence and repression, which came to infuse social ties. This approach to understanding the contextual and symbolic weight of intrastate war and occupation violence underscores the unexpected ways that tactics interact with each other over time, disrupt social systems, and generate new behaviors and meaning-making among local actors, rather than assuming that these tactics' deployment plays out as belligerents planned.

Third, and finally, this chapter provides an empirical outline of the regional and within-region comparisons that undergird this book's analytical framework. It was one of my interlocutors, Kamal, who made the transformative and entirely practical suggestion that I simply ask my interviewees: "Why is the South different?" Posed at the right moment in an interview about factional history, the question had an almost cinematic flashback effect; people immediately started talking about the 1970s and 1980s. A former Lebanese member of Fatah's al-Asifa Forces,[4] Kamal immediately started talking about how he used to descend with his unit from South Lebanon into Israeli-controlled territory in the mid-1970s. He directly linked these operations to the 1978 Israeli invasion of South Lebanon and the growing power of Israeli-allied Lebanese militias such as the FLA. Kamal spent approximately twenty minutes of our three-hour interview describing the effects of the IDF's tactics during the 1982 invasion, including mass incarceration and the deployment of white phosphorous on Lebanese towns. Yet he also spent equal time discussing the War of the Camps in Beirut, which he described as "the hardest time, the hardest politics, the hardest personally" because Palestinian factions were fighting each other and also because Syria was arresting members of pro-Arafat parties. This period, he explained via a direct comparison, "harmed the Palestinians more than the Israelis in 1982. . . . Mazzeh, Tadmor, Qism Falastin, Sadnaya, there were people dying in prison."[5] Interactions such as this one helped me to understand people's lived experiences of the invasion and occupation beyond the violence covered in journalistic and most historical accounts. They thus allow for a deep comparison of how Palestinians in (and within) South Lebanon experienced the invasion versus how those in Beirut experienced the Siege of Beirut, the various "mopping-up" campaigns, and the Sabra and Shatila massacre. This part of the chapter also foregrounds the work of qualitatively comparing network micro-processes (Parkinson 2021) and assembling cases (Soss 2018) of organizational emergence in the following chapters both by noting subtle differences in repertoires of violence across space and by showing how they differentially affected militant networks and broader communities.

The Invasion in South Lebanon

The Israeli government initially anticipated clearing a limited border zone to prevent future PLO missile attacks and guerrilla infiltrations from the border to the Zahrani River south of Saida and Lake Qaraoun in the eastern Bekaa Valley. On the morning of the invasion, journalists were still being informed that the IDF's goal was "to push the PLO and its artillery out of range of the frontier and the northern Galilee area of Israel" (Fisk 2002, 201). Instead, Israeli troops moved into Lebanon via the coastal road, the Arkoub region, and naval landing points just north of Saida. The IDF progressed north up Lebanon's coastal highway, defeating the PLA units, Lebanese and Palestinian guerrilla forces, and camp-based militias. Once troops were on the ground, high-ranking government officials directed the IDF to continue north to Beirut (Schiff and Ya'ari 1984, chaps. 7–11). Many Palestinian guerrillas and militiamen stationed in South Lebanon, including several commanders, fled during the onslaught, which disrupted the chain of command and military discipline. Two of the clearest shared narratives that emerged from my interviews and ethnographic engagements were ones of complete material destruction and the gendered partitioning of social networks as a result of mass incarceration.

Aerial Bombardment and Community Destruction

Intensive Israeli aerial bombardment dislocated Palestinian as well as Lebanese communities and rendered people dispossessed. Entire populations from South Lebanon relocated over the course of the summer of 1982, disrupting community- and kinship-based networks that provided people with emotional, social, and financial support.[6] Tens of thousands of Palestinians fled north or into the mountains to villages such as Abra or Wadi Zeini, while others continued on to Beirut.[7] The American Friends Service Committee (AFSC), a US-based Quaker organization that organized humanitarian operations in Lebanon at the time, estimates that the IDF's destruction of the southern refugee camps left approximately 200,000 Palestinians homeless.[8]

Many people shared their escape stories from South Lebanon as a means of illustrating their collective confusion, panic, and concurrent search for information related to the invasion. For example, Abu Wissam, who grew up in al-Buss camp in Sur, described a scene from the initial days of the Israeli campaign:

> It was the night of my cousin's wedding, but they [the IDF] started shelling. We decided to flee to Ain al-Hilweh, but our car was damaged. So, we took the wedding car![9] We reached Jal al-Bahr [about 3 km up the road from al-Buss] and we saw cars getting hit. The whole road was getting bombed, everything was destroyed. We saw people dead in the cars, entire families, all burned. We turned off the main road and headed through the orchards; we were driving through the orchards east of Jal al-Bahr with the lights off and drove right up to an Israeli tank! In front of me was an Israeli tank! It was the first time in my life I saw Jews. But they didn't know what was going on—I didn't either! I didn't even know it was an invasion! I got scared and pushed the gas pedal harder![10]

In this particular case, Abu Wissam found dark humor (driving a flower- and tulle-covered wedding car while fleeing an invasion) and self-deprecation (noting that his reaction to the Israeli tank was to slam on the gas pedal), despite an objectively grave, terrifying situation. His experience underscores the oft-surprising coexistence of absurdity and horror in the civilian experience of war; he was obviously scared, but he was not, for example, cowed into immediate submission despite what he saw on the road. Recognizing such tensions in these moments helps to deepen understanding of people's lived experiences of the invasion and occupation, especially by underscoring their emotional complexity.

The destruction of homes, the interruption of lives, and the displacement of hundreds of thousands of Palestinians and Lebanese created clear collective perceptions around Israeli intentionality; people understood aerial bombardment as being disproportionate, expressly targeted at civilians, and aimed at obliterating Palestinian communities rather than the purported goal of stopping rocket attacks. Unlike what would happen in Beirut, the southern camps of Rashidiyeh, Burj al-Shamali, al-Buss, and Ain al-Hilweh were almost entirely physically destroyed during the invasion and its aftermath. Ground-based artillery and aerial bombardment by a modern military had devastating human and infrastructural consequences, magnified by the IDF's subsequent bulldozing of large portions of the southern camps with the goals of eliminating them as potential staging areas for guerrillas and disincentivizing the return of civilians. An AFSC report cites a June 23, 1982, UNRWA estimate detailing "damage to camp housing as follows: Rashidiyeh 70% destroyed; Bourj el Shemali 35% destroyed; el Buss 50% destroyed; Ein al Hilweh totally destroyed; Mieh slightly damaged"

(Advisory Committee on Human Rights in Lebanon 1983, 18). Drawing on UNRWA figures, the historian Hilana Abdullah (2008, 53) estimates that 70 percent of homes in Burj al-Shamali were destroyed.[11] Several PRCS facilities—often Palestinians' only source of healthcare—had to close.

While Palestinians in Beirut would later experience the city's besiegement and the Sabra and Shatila massacre, they did not witness the same extent of infrastructural destruction and demolition. People from the southern refugee camps often described discrete, galvanizing moments of collective shock, horror, grief, and failure both during and following the 1982 Israeli invasion. These moments formed bases for collective identification among Palestinian civilians as well as reference points for future repurposing, remapping, and mobilization. Yet, in their accounts, my interlocutors emphasized it was not simply a specific tactic—for instance, aerial bombardment—that influenced their interpretations of events. Rather, it was a combination of the tactics used, the perceived manner of targeting (intended or accidental, homes, hospitals, or militant positions), the social consequences, and the subsequent assignment of responsibility that all resonated. For example, Kamal, the former member of Fatah quoted above, shared precise, analytical recollections of military operations—such as leftist guerrillas successfully downing an Israeli helicopter, or a group of eight Israeli soldiers capturing two PFLP-GC guerrillas who were stationed between Arnoun and Nabatiyeh. He explained that the IDF and Mossad took prisoners such as these men to Israel to interrogate them regarding past operations. He understood both of these events as representing normal practices of war. He then relayed vivid, emotion-laden recollections of Israeli jets dropping white phosphorous—a self-igniting compound that both burns through tissue unless it is deprived of oxygen and severely irritates the eyes and lungs—onto both military and civilian targets.[12] This tactic still shocked and upset him decades later. Abu Riyad, a Fatah officer from al-Buss who fought during the invasion, described each jet-delivered bomb as "clearing the space of a football [soccer] field," which I interpreted to mean a disproportionate use of force given the significant amount of territory affected (i.e., potentially several dozen homes in his geographically tiny camp).[13] Yahya and Khalid, both PFLP-GC fighters from Burj al-Shamali, told me that the Israelis encircled the semi-urban camp with twenty-three tanks while conducting air raids, which would have disincentivized escape and contributed to the notion that the IDF was trapping people in the camp as they bombed it. The resulting destruction was so extensive, they recalled: "You wouldn't know where your house was; a family of 36 all died in the shelling."[14] Their emphasis on relaying precise numbers—twenty-three tanks and thirty-six members of a family (which is significant for both the number of dead and the implication that multiple, spatially distinct households were destroyed)—as well as the graphic visual of being unable to locate one's own home in the rubble underscore feelings of proximity to the battlefield and their shared experience of devastating loss to the point of social disorientation.

These collective experiences of violence initially spurred strong feelings of linked fate across distinct political affiliations, village backgrounds, religious denominations, and other forms of identification, especially as seemingly overwhelming numbers of people perished or simply vanished from their immediate social networks. Even decades later, multiple people from different political groups in Burj al-Shamali often explicitly anchored their experiences to collective events—for example, by asking if I had visited a memorial in the camp that commemorates ninety-four civilians who died when the IDF dropped a bomb on the Nadi al-Houli, a clubhouse maintained by a Palestinian village association, on June 7, 1982 (the second day of the invasion).[15] By asking this question, they sought to highlight a moment that people believed shaped the camp community's shared trajectory in the following years; for example, several people linked the Nadi al-Houli massacre and its explicitly civilian casualties to the community's later decision not to engage in direct hostilities with the Syrian-backed Amal militia during the War of the Camps (see chapter 7). In the fall of 1982, narratives of vulnerability, PLO failure and abandonment, and Israeli aggression toward civilians crystallized as months-long delays in UNRWA's tent construction for homeless Palestinians in Saida and Sur left people sleeping in the open as the winter approached. The situation was so dire that US officials—usually strong Israeli allies—publicly criticized the Israeli government for "doing the minimum for the refugees despite the coming winter."[16]

The Role of Camp-Level Militia Forces

Foreshadowing the realities of command-and-control and challenges to formal hierarchies in the following years, Palestinian guerrillas and camp-based militias operated with very little oversight after the first day or so of the invasion. Local camp-based Palestinian militias long outlasted the technically better-trained guerrilla forces and PLA battalions (Schiff and Ya'ari 1984, chap. 8), seeding a future bias among many militants toward local coordination and reliance. Several high-ranking officers deserted or were killed; contact with PLO headquarters in Beirut was extremely limited (Schiff and Ya'ari 1984, 136; Cobban 1985, 121; Khalidi 1985, 61, 74; Fisk 2002, 219).[17] Rashid Khalidi (1985, 61) notes that "regional and large unit commands frequently failed to respond to the emerging situation, particularly in the south in the first three or four days of the war." Israeli journalists who covered the invasion emphasize that "the real war in South Lebanon was not fought by the Fatah's semi-regular forces but by the homeguards in the refugee camps. It was a static, tenacious battle fought in built-up areas cut through by narrow alleyways that barely accommodated a vehicle but afforded the Palestinian irregulars excellent conditions to fight back and defy the Israelis to the end" (Schiff and Ya'ari 1984, 137).

Using a combination of small-unit tactics and home-field advantage—that is, a deep knowledge of the labyrinthine alleyways of the refugee camps and the bunker systems that had been built into their foundations—irregular Palestinian forces delayed the IDF's advance for days. Yet the resilience of specifically local, irregular, defensive forces fighting within the camps marked them as unexpected challenges for the Israeli forces, even in comparison to more traditional targets. Israeli journalists Ze'ev Schiff and Ehud Ya'ari (1984, 138) explain that "the conquest of Nabatiye, for example, where the semiregular forces had six T-34 tanks and were supposed to be prepared for a long holding action, took all of three hours without costing the Israelis a single casualty. But the fighting in the refugee camps around Tyre went on for days, and the defenders of the Ein Hilweh camp adjoining Sidon, held out for an entire week." Rashidiyeh held out for four days; Burj al-Shamali continued fighting for three and a half (Schiff and Ya'ari 1984, 139). Burj al-Shamali's militia forces managed to destroy a number of IDF tanks and wound several Israeli officers (Abdullah 2008, 50). Palestinian fighters in Ain al-Hilweh held the IDF off for over a week, delaying the overall Israeli advance by two full days (Schiff and Ya'ari 1984, 142; Yermiya 1984; Khalidi 1985).

Ain al-Hilweh and the Invasion

The battle for Ain al-Hilweh meant that the camp had a unique experience of warfare even when compared to the other southern camps. It was longer, more intimate, and involved a broader array of IDF tactics and weaponry that included incendiary armaments. The camp's defenders' refusal to submit prompted Israeli forces to take a particularly aggressive stance toward it during the occupation.[18] Throughout this book, I argue that these nuanced differences in counterinsurgent tactical repertoires such as the ones described here influenced variation in Palestinian organizational emergence.

Led by a combination of militiamen, Muslim religious authorities, and scouts, Ain al-Hilweh's defenders battled Israeli troops starting Thursday, June 10 (Schiff and Ya'ari 1984, 144–47; Khalidi 1985, 51; Rougier 2007, 44–45).[19] As they retreated, small, isolated groups of fighters wove between the camp's buildings, targeting the Israeli armored personnel carriers and tanks with light arms as they attempted to penetrate the camp. As a result, the IDF sacrificed any territorial gains made during the day when they pulled troops out of the firestorm for safety each night. After the initial push to clear the camp's arterial north road failed, the IDF repeatedly bombed the camp. By Friday, June 11, several days into the invasion, the IDF was attempting to negotiate the remaining militiamen's exit via camp elders; the militiamen and camp youth refused to leave, saying that they would win or be martyred (Zeidan 2017, 284). Israeli forces resorted to bombing the camp with conventional ordnance and incendiary weapons such as napalm (Schiff and Ya'ari 1984, 148; Y. Sayigh 1997, 525; Khalili 2007a, 52).[20] Nevertheless, Ain al-Hilweh held out for several more days.

In both Saida and Sur, these urban battles provided important learning experiences for surviving militia members in terms of tactics, understanding of Israeli forces, and the inadvisability of relying upon higher command for direction. The collective planning, coordination, and toolkits they developed became some of the constitutive elements of emergent guerrilla practices during the ongoing occupation. Neighborhood-based defenses and extensive systems of earthworks, shelters, and arms caches enabled camp residents with small arms to repel the Israeli forces longer than trained forces did. Later, during the War of the Camps, fighters from Burj al-Shamali would transfer a similar, but updated, defensive model to Shatila and Burj al-Barajneh, an example of knowledge transfer that relied on preexisting networks.[21] The PLO's and factional regulars' largely weak response to the invasion also seeded narratives of abandonment that were only amplified in local guerrilla networks between 1982 and 1985, creating a cleavage between on-the-ground forces and exiled elites.

Gendered Incarceration

In the summer of 1982, thousands of politically and militarily active Palestinian and Lebanese men from South Lebanon—as well as thousands of male civilians and hundreds of women—were arrested and detained in Israeli internment facilities. According to the AFSC, "[i]n November 1982 Israel announced that a total of 9,064 persons had been taken prisoner during its invasion of Lebanon. About two thirds of those arrested were Palestinians and the remainder were Lebanese and foreign nationals."[22] In her work on the Ansar prison camp outside Nabitiyeh, an open-air military prison where the IDF detained thousands of inmates in tents, Laleh Khalili (2008, 101) estimates the total number of individual inmates imprisoned at Ansar between June 1982 and May 1985 at 12,000 to 15,000 people.

While aerial bombardment is often cited as the quintessential "indiscriminate" tactic, different forms of incarceration have been treated in a more varied manner by counterinsurgency scholars. To understand how mass arrests and internment affected Palestinian organizational and social networks, it is helpful to consider the roles that each interned person may have filled, as well as the effects of their removal from those roles. Each arrest took a family member—a father, brother, uncle, or son—from their social networks; economically, it separated breadwinners from families while, from a societal perspective, it removed civic leaders, teachers, doctors, and other central social actors from communities. Underscoring the broad, socially disorienting scope of the arrests, rather than reflecting detailed knowledge of actual numbers, former guerrillas from al-Buss and Burj al-Shamali refugee camps separately estimated that approximately 1,500 to 2,000 men from each of their camps were sent to Ansar. To put this number in perspective, the registered population of al-Buss at this time was 5,133 people; in Burj al-Shamali, it was 10,644.[23] In short, people in al-Buss felt that about 40 percent of the camp's population had been incarcerated. Fatah, the largest Palestinian faction, had 3,000 to 3,500 fighters stationed in South Lebanon before the invasion. Many of them were killed or fled before the arrests (al-Natour 2014a).

Men in Black Masks

The Israeli forces' use of mass arrests, interrogations, and internment also revealed the role of secret Palestinian and Lebanese collaborators with the Israelis, shifting how people perceived trust and threat within their own social networks. This is another aspect of the invasion and occupation that distinguished South Lebanon from Beirut, where collaboration was much less central to the repertoire of violence. While collaborators superficially facilitated mass detainment and provided a veneer of selectivity for Israeli forces, few Palestinians saw their role as anything but personally instrumentalist.[24] For example, after the invasion, the IDF evacuated Saida, moving civilians and soldiers en masse to the beachfront. A PRCS doctor, Chris Giannou, who was present on the beach at Saida, paints a vivid picture of the denunciation process that followed:

> The males were paraded one by one in front of three parked jeeps. In each one was a man with a hood over his head and an Israeli soldier. As they walked by, certain people would be singled out and taken away with an X or something in Hebrew written on their backs. Eventually 5,000 to 6,000 people were arrested on simple denunciations by a hooded man.
>
> We ended up being taken to a convent school close by. There we found ourselves first in a small courtyard and then in a large schoolyard where about 500 to 600 prisoners were being kept. There were new groups of prisoners being brought in and taken out all the time, but the constant population was 500 to 600 . . .
>
> . . . we knew some of the people were not fighters. Nobody in this schoolyard had been taken with arms in their hands. Now, in the other

courtyard, where I'd examined the wounded prisoners and they were lashed to the trees, they were just about all wearing military uniforms. I would assume that they were caught armed. (Chris Giannou, quoted in Cobban 1982, 81–82)

Mahmoud Zeidan, who was a child living in Ain al-Hilweh at the time, recounts similar memories, reflecting how Palestinian youth experienced the process:

> The Israelis would stamp people's ID cards, they would tear it from the side of the photo and stamp it with a Hebrew stamp. Everyday new people arrive at the sea, and they would go through the same procedure [of walking in line in front of the informants who would indicate who should be taken in for interrogation]. The Israelis would tell people to go to the sea. Every day, I would go and watch the procedure. In reality, I felt like I was a young man, and that's why I went to the sea. Maybe my appearance did not suggest that, which is why the Israelis wouldn't make me walk in front of the collaborators. The Israelis would ask people 15 years old and over to go to the sea, and they arrested many of our friends with whom we used to play, including Suhail Abu al-Kul who was 14 years old at the time, despite his small and short body. He later died in the Ansar prison in one of the uprisings of the prisoners. (Zeidan 2017, 280–81)

Without exception, militants I interviewed who fought during the invasion explicitly highlighted their awareness of Palestinian as well as Lebanese collaborators in black hoods who pointed out their personal rivals on the beaches of Saida and Sur.[25] No one to whom I spoke believed that local collaborators' "identification" of militants was anything but their personal revenge toward the individual in question.

Palestinians and Lebanese perceived on-the-spot interrogations and arrests as arbitrary—an example being Zeidan's memory of his small, short-statured, fourteen-year-old friend being sent to Ansar—and designed to generally intimidate the population, rather than to effectively identify individuals engaged in military activity. This particular aspect of the Israeli forces' tactical repertoire appears to have provided Palestinians a clear, shared narrative frame and a perception of imminent threat that required response. Many people whom I interviewed described, often with an air of residual incredulousness, how Israeli soldiers had simply approached them as they sifted through the rubble of their homes to ask, "Do you work for any organization [implying a political faction]?" as if someone would boldly reply "Why, yes, I'm a colonel in the PFLP! Why does it matter?" Most people assumed they would be detained no matter what they answered, which lowered any potential deterrent capability and opened new pathways for small, nonviolent acts of resistance that, as scholars such as James Scott would predict, later became routinized, particularly among civilians (Scott 1987; 1990) (see chapter 5). For instance, Abu Haytham, who had never been militarily active, eventually became so fed up with this repeated questioning that he actually answered a young IDF infantryman with a wide-eyed, innocent "Yes!" in order to enjoy the soldier's shocked look before patronizingly explaining that he was a teacher, and thus a member of an educational organization.[26] Arrests, interrogation, and incarceration do not seem to have disincentivized later high-risk activism and militancy. Demonstrating the sheer absurdity of the situation, Mahmud, who *was* a member of Fatah and a former militia member (though not an active combatant) at the time he was arrested, simply informed his Israeli interrogator in Ansar "no," when asked if he was a member of a faction; he was unceremoniously released a few weeks later.

Despite the sweeping nature of arrest campaigns, at least some Israeli operations targeted specific Palestinian positions, units, or individuals. Several of my interviewees described this experience firsthand; Abu Riyad, Yahya, and Khalid were all captured as part of their units and immediately sent to prisons in Israel. Their subsequent experiences illustrate two possible trajectories that high-level prisoners took; Abu Riyad (who had little knowledge of clandestine operations) was transferred to Ansar after a few months, whereas Yahya and Khalid remained in Israel until the IDF released them during a prisoner exchange years later. The AFSC emphasizes both that the Red Cross did not have access to these facilities and that the majority of interrogations occurred outside Ansar.[27] Yet, given the broader context of mass incarceration and heavy policing of Palestinian and Lebanese men, the fact that someone like Abu Riyad often served similar terms to civilians with no militant history emphasizes a lack of predictability in incentives and also alludes to one source of widespread feelings that the Israeli repertoire of violence was focused predominantly on collective punishment.

At the level of individual families and units, incarceration both removed people—mostly men and boys—from networks and produced overwhelming uncertainty among those who remained outside. The archipelago of Israeli- and Lebanese-militia-run prison camps, military detention facilities, interrogation centers, informal jails, and other internment sites, combined with varying patterns of sweeps and targeted arrests, meant that many Palestinian families simply did not know what had happened to their kin. Some arrests were short-term or involved multiple transfers, increasing the likelihood that neither prisoners nor their families knew where they were, where they would be, or for how long. Besides Ansar, smaller internment facilities in settings such as government buildings and schools held thousands of men and women prisoners across South

Lebanon on a more temporary basis. The IDF frequently held detainees in Saida at secondary internment facilities such as the Safa Orange Factory, the government hospital, St. Joseph's convent, or government administrative buildings, to determine whether they would be sent to Ansar, Israel, or released.[28] This scenario could last years; at least a hundred families later learned from the Israeli authorities that their relatives had died in prison.[29]

These three aspects of the larger repertoire of invasion and occupation violence—aerial bombardment, close quarters battles in Ain al-Hilweh and the Israeli forces' subsequent repression of the camp's population, and mass incarceration—shaped both militant and civilian trajectories in the following years. While each of these tactics might reasonably be classified "indiscriminate," analyzing them independently and in concert demonstrates their distinct network effects and narrative influence. They spurred network remapping that relationally distanced active guerrillas from formal chains of command, produced gendered roles within underground guerrilla cells, motivated civilian women's collective as well as community-based advocacy, and spurred the development of cross-generational counterintelligence networks. These processes are the focus of chapters 3, 4, and 6.

The Siege of Beirut and Its Aftermath

By June 8, 1982, West Beirut was crowded with refugees from South Lebanon, many of whom flooded into neighborhoods that were subsequently bombed (Fisk 2002, 216). After moving up the coastal highway in an initial push, the IDF encircled Beirut over the next five days, isolating Lebanese, Palestinian, and Syrian forces, decimating Syrian anti-aircraft facilities in the Bekaa and cutting transit routes between Beirut, the Bekaa Valley, and Damascus. Between June 14 and June 26, the IDF fought to control the mountainous heights that encircle the city (Khalidi 1985, 48). Between June 26 and August 12, the IDF besieged the capital, cutting off roads, water, and electricity while shelling West Beirut.

The political dynamics and effects of siege and blockade often receive comparatively little scholarly attention, in comparison to those associated with conventional or insurgent warfare. With notable exceptions, such as Sarajevo in the early 1990s, sieges may receive minimal on-the-ground journalistic coverage, given the sheer difficulty and risk associated with reporting from them (Borri 2013). While millions of people might be affected, they can be harmed or killed in less visible or enumerable ways than in battle (whether through starvation, dehydration, or building collapse). However, from Changchun to Grozny to Aleppo, sieges have featured in dozens of twentieth- and twenty-first-century wars and have killed or wounded hundreds of thousands of combatants and civilians while affecting millions more.[30] Siege is generally treated as an indiscriminate or indirect tactic. Yet, as the limited number of scholars who seriously examine sieges, blockades, and similar tactics almost universally note, there is a particular set of organizational, psychological, economic, and social dynamics that accompanies them (Andreas 2008; Finkel 2017).

The experience of siege shaped later organizational and social evolution among Palestinians in Beirut. Rashid Khalidi describes the Siege of Beirut as "intensive air, naval, and artillery bombardments and agressive [sic] psychological warfare directed both against the defenders of the city and its civilian population, and included calculated pressure on the morale of the besieged via the cutting off of food, water, and electricity" (Khalidi 1985, 49). In contrast, the Israeli Kahan Commission report notes in its background section that the capital was "occasionally shelled and bombed by the I.D.F.'s Air Force and artillery" (Kahan Commission 1983). Intense resentment of the Israeli military grew as the IDF bombed residential areas and deployed anti-personnel weapons such as cluster bombs and white phosphorous in civilian neighborhoods (Fisk 2002, 278). The siege also created feelings of solidarity among civilians across national lines—an unsurprising finding, given classic sociological theories of conflict dynamics (Simmel 1964).

The PLO had unevenly prepared for an onslaught of this magnitude. Its military organization was deeply flawed and inconsistent, incapable of matching the Israeli onslaught (Khalidi 1985, 60–61). However, the PLO had shifted reserve forces to Beirut; stocked supplies such as arms, ammunition, medicines, and fuel; and provided military training for Palestinian civilians (Khalidi 1985, 59), including in and near the camps. Sabra, Shatila, and Burj al-Barajneh withstood constant shelling, though not of the destructive magnitude seen in the south. The IDF targeted the PLO's massive weapons dump in the Camille Chamoun sports stadium next to Sabra and Shatila as well as Palestinian anti-aircraft guns that had been placed in West Beirut, which were concentrated more heavily in Fakhani, Sabra, Shatila, and Burj al-Barajneh (Fisk 2002, 205, 210).

Beirut-based militants did not have the discipline, training, manpower, or firepower to indefinitely hold off the Israelis, to interact professionally with civilians, or to manage public opinion in West Beirut. Of the night of June 21, for instance, journalist Robert Fisk (2002, 259) writes: "Fatah guerrillas could be seen parking their truck-mounted recoilless rifles beside hotels and apartment blocks, inviting destruction on the civilian population. Several Palestinian officers did their best to organise relief services, guiding ambulances through the streets from the American University Hospital. Others behaved less heroically, threatening civilians with their rifles and harassing the few Western correspondents who ventured onto the streets." Despite these realities, it also became evident that the Israeli forces would have to accept massive casualties if they faced Beirut's full defenses—the Joint Forces of the PLO and the LNM, local Lebanese militias, and camp-based defense committees—in open battle in order to take the city (Cobban 1985, 122).

Ensuing negotiations lasted for most of the summer and were punctuated by failed ceasefires that took a further toll on Beirut's population. The Israeli government would not speak directly to Palestinian representatives, and Lebanese President Elias Sarkis would not meet with PLO Chairman Arafat; instead, Lebanese Prime Minister Shafiq al-Wazzan served as the communication channel between Arafat and Sarkis. Sarkis, in turn, dealt with US Ambassador Philip Habib, who held consultations with the Israeli government. When they reached a ceasefire agreement two months later, the Multi-National Forces (MNF), a peacekeeping force composed of soldiers from France, the United States, Italy, and the United Kingdom, moved in to monitor the ceasefire, the Palestinian and Syrian forces' evacuation of Beirut, and an IDF withdrawal from the city.[31] The PLO's international bureaucracy and guerrilla fighters from multiple parties (14,398 personnel and soldiers total, including at least 11,000 fighters and 1,500 political staff) evacuated Lebanon at the end of August.[32] The MNF deployed in Beirut and its southern suburbs. The PLO relocated its headquarters to Tunis while fighters dispersed to Tunisia, Yemen, Syria, and other Arab countries.

After the PLO's 1982 evacuation of Beirut, Palestinians lacked direct communication with the PLO and the various guerrilla groups' exiled command apparatuses. Instead they focused on reestablishing relationships with each other on the ground. Remembering the massive air and ground assaults of June and July of 1982, Zahra, the now-retired military trainer, simply said: "We couldn't do anything."[33] In the space of a few months, my interviewees recalled initial feelings of communal strength and optimism giving way to helplessness and vulnerability.

From "Mopping Up" to Massacre

Even before the PLO's departure from West Beirut, the IDF and right-wing, predominantly Christian Lebanese militias had begun arrest and disarmament campaigns in the camps. Schiff and Ya'ari note: "The first attempt to 'straighten out' the situation in Beirut took place on August 23, 1982 in the Burj al-Barajneh refugee camp, which was surrounded on three sides by IDF units. On [the leader of the right-wing Kata'ib militia Bashir Gemayel's] orders a battalion of the regular Lebanese army entered the camp, began making mass arrests, and searched for arms caches" (Schiff and Ya'ari 1984, 251–52). Following the withdrawal of the PLO leadership, guerrilla fighters, and their families at the end of August,

Lebanese government forces led by Kataʾib asserted control over West Beirut. Underscoring a broader, complementary narrative centered on the fighters' defeat, the micro-level disarmament of the camps, and the resultant vulnerability of Palestinians left behind, the author of one history of Shatila camp writes that they departed "wearing civilian clothes and holding their individual weapons" (Kallam 2008, 43).

In the eyes of Palestinian residents of West Beirut, the immediate aftermath of the evacuation began a period of acute community insecurity. In September 1982, the Lebanese army initiated a "security plan" throughout West Beirut and Dahiyeh, a demographically mixed area of the southern suburbs adjacent to Burj al-Barajneh camp. Palestinians who were living in these communities remembered feeling helpless and overwhelmed during the invasion and its immediate aftermath, especially in light of the symbolism of the LAF entering neighborhoods it previously refrained from entering due to the 1969 Cairo Agreement, which ceded control, security, and management of the camps to the PLO (al-Hajali 2007, 66–67).[34] Photographs in historical collections depict Lebanese soldiers removing arms caches from basements and bunkers in Palestinian-populated neighborhoods in Fakhani, Tariq al-Jdideh, and Burj al-Barajneh (al-Din 1985, 100–103). The PLO and guerrilla factions had transferred many of their weapons stores out of the camps and to their Lebanese allies before the evacuation. Small numbers of fighters, including a group who had survived the Tel al-Zaʿtar siege, kept their personal weapons for self-defense, arguing that they had no way of knowing what would come to pass. However, there was also considerable community-level pressure to hide or dispose of individual small arms, since they could be used by Israeli and Lebanese forces as a pretext for violence against districts inhabited predominantly by civilians (al-Hout 2004, 40–42). With fighters gone and the Cairo Agreement abrogated, Palestinians who remained in the camps felt exposed and under constant threat.

The Sabra and Shatila Massacre

On September 14, less than a month after the PLO's formal withdrawal and the MNF's stationing in West and South Beirut, a bomb planted by a Maronite Syrian Socialist National Party member ripped through Kataʾib headquarters in Ashrafieh, killing Lebanese President-elect Bashir Gemayel (Hanf 1994, 268).[35] Operating on the Israeli government's preexisting claim that Palestinian fighters remained in the city, the IDF immediately occupied West Beirut. It established positions on major access routes to the Shatila district, the area comprising the Palestinian camp itself as well as the adjacent, demographically mixed neighborhoods of West Shatila, al-Daouk, Sabra, Hay Farhat, Hay al-Miqdad, Hay

Arsal, and Horsh Tabet (al-Hout 2004, 43–44).³⁶ On September 15, militiamen affiliated with the Lebanese Kata'ib, the South Lebanon Army, and other right-wing Christian militias surrounded and scouted the neighborhoods surrounding Shatila. Swee Chai Ang (1989, 55), a PRCS volunteer from England who worked as a surgeon in Gaza Hospital in Sabra and was present for the subsequent massacre, notes: "People who tried to leave the camp returned and said that all roads leading out of the camps were blocked by Israeli tanks. . . . At 5 p.m. we were told that Israeli commandos were on the main roads of the camps." Maps published by witnesses indicate Israeli military positions on the Kuwaiti Embassy corner and along major streets on the camp's periphery (Kallam 2008, 48). Two groups from Shatila, one of male community elders and the other made up of women and children, attempted to reach and peacefully negotiate with IDF commanders in the area, yet Lebanese militiamen abducted, raped, or killed members of both parties (al-Hout 2004, chap. 2). On September 16 and continuing through the morning of September 18, Lebanese militiamen entered the district and killed or disappeared between 2,000 and 3,500 predominantly Palestinian civilians, many of whom were also subjected to beatings, torture, and sexual violence. Significant numbers of Lebanese and other nationalities were also victimized (Schiff and Ya'ari 1984, chap. 13; Ang 1989, chap. 6; Y. Sayigh 1997, 539; Fisk 2002, chap. 11; al-Hout 2004, 296). Throughout the massacre, IDF troops prevented people from leaving, illuminated the area with flares (Traboulsi 2007, 218), and, especially in the early stages, shelled the district. This last act forced residents into underground shelters whose locations Lebanese militias had deliberately surveyed; they became one of the first places where the militias found and subsequently killed civilians (al-Hout 2004, chaps. 2–3).³⁷

The deployment of siege tactics and the use of "mopping-up" campaigns that culminated in mass killing and atrocity during the Sabra and Shatila massacre created constitutive bonds of shared vulnerability that motivated later cross-city organizing in Beirut. The PLO's original video footage of the massacre's aftermath reveals aspects of the tableau visible to any resident of Mar Elias, Tariq al-Jdideh, or Burj al-Barajneh who ventured down the road to see what had happened: Red Crescent workers wearing branded vests and face masks while spraying lye over bodies lying in the streets; volunteers digging mass graves and laying dozens of bodies in them; screaming women searching for children and elderly parents. The camera gives some idea of what it might have been like to wander through the area's tight alleyways as a Palestinian or Lebanese from elsewhere in South Beirut; it selectively zooms in on the corpses of women and children, often half-buried under haphazardly bulldozed rubble. It repeatedly focuses in on everyday household objects such as children's toys in a clear effort to further dramatize the militias' targeting of children. In terms of the perspective taken, the PLO cameraperson is insistent on conveying the idea that civilians—specifically, women, children, and the elderly—were killed brutally and intimately in their own homes and businesses. In October 1982, Palestinians' fears were further compounded when government forces loyal to newly elected President Amin Gemayel (Bashir Gemayel's brother) arrested and imprisoned hundreds of Palestinian men at the Lebanese Ministry of Defense in Yarze. These arrests involved broad round-ups; a photo chosen to represent this period in a well-known history of the Lebanese Civil War shows at least 15 Palestinian men sitting or being loaded on an open-bed truck by two armed men in fatigues and helmets while a driver stands in the cab (al-Din 1985, 102–104).[38]

While siege, mass killing, and "clean-up" campaigns each easily fit into the category of "indiscriminate tactics," the close examination of their micro-level network effects and narrative influence in the following chapters demonstrates how they shaped Palestinians' experiences and perceptions in distinct ways, in comparison to South Lebanon. The confinement of numerous men at home initially cut communication channels, but Palestinians soon reestablished them via a woman-led courier-system similar to that in the south. However, rather than being cross-regional, these processes occurred at the city level. Moreover, the specific targeting of civilians by Lebanese militia forces during the Sabra and Shatila massacre created bonds across political persuasions as well as the militant-civilian divide. The narratives it seeded became key relations that undergirded the development of camp defensive fronts later in the decade. These processes are the focus of chapter 6.

By all accounts, the PLO and the guerrilla factions had been defeated by September 1982. Few Palestinian fighters remained in Lebanon; among the limited number who did, an even lower number retained their personal weapons for self-defense. Many extant studies of counterinsurgency would predict that in this context, indiscriminate targeting of civilian communities (Lyall 2009) and brutal, indirect tactics (Arreguín-Toft 2001, 2005; Hazelton 2021) would successfully suppress Palestinian militancy and "drain the sea" of civilian support. The following chapters demonstrate that they did neither. In fact, the repertoires of violence and repression that both Israeli and Lebanese actors deployed created new collective grievances among Palestinians and Lebanese while laying the network foundations for new, adaptive modes of organized resistance.

Approximately 19,085 Lebanese and Palestinians were killed and 30,302 were wounded between June 4 and August 31, 1982, a period inclusive of the Israeli invasion, the Siege of Beirut, and the PLO's withdrawal (Rubenberg 1986, 281). However, these numbers do not capture how the lived experience of the invasion and occupation immediately affected and continued to shape social networks. Regional differences arose between Beirut and South Lebanon based on the repertoires of violence people faced and their agentive decisions regarding how to manage it. The massacre at Sabra and Shatila instilled in many people that civilian communities had to be robustly defended. Claims that the IDF and Lebanese militias wanted to selectively root out "terrorists" in Shatila had little believability in the wake of mass civilian death. Likewise, arguments that collaboration and mass incarceration in South Lebanon only targeted fighters held no credibility when the IDF, its Lebanese allies, and Palestinian collaborators continuously harassed, exploited, and violently targeted people who had no involvement with armed activities.

Repertoires of violence that felt indiscriminate and brutal conclusively taught Palestinians that they would be targeted independently of their individual or collective decisions. However, it would be wrong to argue that a distinction between selective versus indiscriminate violence or direct versus indirect violence determined Palestinian organizational outcomes. Rather, distinct, regionalized repertoires of violence shaped both the material content of and collective meanings embedded in Palestinian social networks, thereby affecting processes of organizational and social change at the local level.

The rest of this book closely examines those experiences of violence and repression and their effects, revealing how intersecting social networks mediate both organizational and social responses to violence. It suggests that current understandings of counterinsurgent success often erase the human cost of military tactics by relying heavily on body counts as a measure of their effects. Building a deep understanding of how communities experience and collectively process violence allows scholars, policymakers, journalists, and other observers to better comprehend the spectrum of violent and nonviolent organizing that emerges to challenge states' and other belligerents' power during intrastate wars. This is especially true when considering how repertoires of violence affect people differentially in terms of gender, age, social class, and geography—dynamics that the more general language of "indiscriminate" and "indirect" obscure.

The following chapters build from the ontological and empirical foundation this chapter has provided by pursuing the regional and within-region comparisons of violence, network adaptation, and emergence. Each chapter cases instances of organizational emergence both by tracing subtle differences in repertoires of violence across space and by showing how they differentially affected militant networks and broader communities. In doing so, each chapter continues to problematize the concepts of indiscriminate and indirect violence and to insist on a more complex understanding of the human experiences of violence and participation in intrastate war, all while looking at the unexpected consequences for both armed organizations and civilians.

4

BEYOND THE LINES

Gendered Mobilization and Organizational Resilience in Militant Groups

Intisar stormed through the front door, noticed the electricity was off, and marched out to the balcony looking for us. Her workday had been frustrating and she needed to vent. Several demoralizing interactions with higher-ranking male colleagues had amplified the everyday annoyances of her office job. These apparently began with dismissiveness and culminated in some sort of extremely gendered or lewd comment directed at her. As she hit the climax of her story, she thundered: "They wouldn't even be here if it wasn't for us."

"What do you mean?" I asked.

Sawsan, her sister, gave it a little thought. "In the past," she began, as Intisar sat down and accepted an arguileh, *"women worked like men; they were wounded, they lost limbs, they're still injured. Now everything is like there was nothing. Our sisters fought, but now girls see that it was for nothing, and they're back to acting like girls."*

"Can you tell me more?" I prodded.

The sisters nodded and took turns explaining the history to me, each jumping in with additions or explanations. It was forbidden to be Fatah in the 1990s in Beirut [because of the Syrian occupation], but it was different in the South [where Fatah could still have offices and public activities]. In Beirut, men in Fatah couldn't move around and couldn't safely meet—they reminded me that their father had been alive then and had to be careful.

Women, they explained, "kept the party alive," specifically through a publication and money-smuggling apparatus. A ranking woman in each neighborhood organized the smuggling operation. Women would "go to the beach" or "go visit

family" in the South and come back packing issues of al-Quds magazine—Fatah's main publication in Lebanon—under billowing clothing or carefully secreted away in her luggage. Intisar, Sawsan, and their sister Hind took turns listing the strategies; women would seal the magazine in plastic in the bottom of a pot and cover it with food; wrap it in stacked loaves of thin, round bread; or (they told me giggling) they'd stuff it down their cleavage. These women would distribute the magazines to others, usually those in professions that were either mobile or where women could congregate.

Certain professions and spaces were ideal for facilitating the distribution of al-Quds and for meeting with other members of Fatah. The sisters enthusiastically explained how women could "naturally" congregate in salons, which consequently became hubs of underground political activity. Hind put on a ditzy, high-pitched, bourgeois Lebanese accent to demonstrate what a woman would say if she were asked what she was doing: "Oh, I'm going to the hairdresser, I want to do my hair!" Her affect implied that the women were deliberately playing on gender stereotypes to manipulate the police officers, intelligence agents, or militiamen they might encounter. Medical workers' ability to make house calls, access hospitals, and work in mixed-gender spaces meant that they were ideal distributors. Similarly, cooks and tailors were central to the operation; they delivered to offices and visited people's homes. It was impossible for the Syrians to target all these workers for systematic checks; the system mapped onto the relationships that constituted everyday life. The sisters added that female officers would also distribute monthly salaries and welfare payments to families; each regional representative held the list of families in her neighborhood and would strap enough cash for each of them to her body. So, the sisters concluded, women had all the meetings, paid all the salaries, and relayed news to the men, or women traveled under the pretext of meeting other women and spoke to the men.

Sawsan had an afterthought, and leaned forward, lowering her voice. "You know, there were times where someone would marry someone who didn't know their affiliation. You know Shadia, from the camp? Shadia got married, and she was secretly Fatah. Her husband didn't know. One day, she said she was going to the hair salon and he said he was going to drink coffee with a friend. They both showed up to the same meeting and were totally shocked. Afterward, they could work together." Intisar jumped in to underscore that this overlap of affiliation with marriage made them a powerful, central couple in the faction.[1]

This chapter returns to the period that Munadileh, the woman whose story opened this book, described as when "the world became black." Drawing from interviews and participant observation I conducted following my conversation with Intisar and Sawsan, I trace how a clandestine information, intelligence, finance, and supply apparatus emerged to support small-scale Palestinian guerrilla operations in the aftermath of the 1982 Israeli invasion. Gendered counterinsurgent repertoires of violence mobilized women and youth as male cadres were deported, imprisoned, confined at home, or forced underground. By remapping ties within militant organizations but across subdivisions, women mobilized into emergent roles as intelligence agents, couriers, document forgers, bankers, and weapons smugglers. Leveraging the plasticity of mixed-gender, trust-based quotidian networks—especially kinship and marriage ties—provided safe, alternate pathways onto which militants remapped communications, supply, and financial flows when counterinsurgency campaigns rendered formal organizational pathways inaccessible. Palestinians reconfigured relations that spanned geographic, substantive, and political subdivisions across the PLO, various guerrilla organizations, and the Lebanese–Palestinian national divide. These processes facilitated the emergence of male combat units, reconceived as small, mobile cliques that operated relatively independently from the formal chain of command.

Prewar networks mattered for how these processes took shape, but did not lock outcomes in place. Specifically, the initial compartmentalization of PLO and guerrilla organizations' social, military, and political offices, as well as many guerrilla organizations' social embeddedness in camp-based and middle-class communities, facilitated gendered patterns of organizational remapping. Before 1982, both men and women cadres received military training, but women were more likely to work in the social or political apparatuses than in front-line combat roles. During the occupation, the IDF broadly targeted men as well as boys for arrest and interrogation, though it also incarcerated high-ranking women and the wives of elite men. The lasting focus on men and boys as active militants throughout the occupation created space for trained and socialized militant women to move into more central roles as information and financial brokers in the military apparatus, including within high-risk intelligence and commando positions that put them in direct contact with enemy forces. Strong, trust-based quotidian relationships linked militant organizations' subdivisions when counterinsurgent tactics and exile severed formal chains of command.

These remapped militant networks produced semiofficial auxiliary information channels and alternative military hierarchies through which organizational supply, maintenance, and learning flowed. They consequently emerged as new organizational subdivisions whenever mixed-gender guerrilla apparatuses adopted new routines and practices. Over time, these networks bypassed established organizational hierarchies, informally linking an increasing number of organizational subdivisions. Palestinian factions in South Lebanon stopped operating cohesively and instead crystalized into small, mobile, localized, and personalized combat cells.

The following section briefly sketches the prewar compartmentalization of labor within the PLO and guerrilla factions. The chapter then outlines the emergence of clandestine apparatuses in relation to localized, gendered patterns of violence, in particular the way that mass incarceration isolated men from organizational structures. Focusing on the brokerage roles that women assumed, it demonstrates how logistics, finance, and intelligence networks underwrote ongoing political and military activities. It links this clandestine apparatus to the reconstitution of combat units populated primarily by men, and addresses the ways that mass incarceration did or did not affect male militants' networks through a close telling of one former prisoner's story. Finally, the chapter analyzes the role of underground party publications in organizational maintenance and change via a deep reading of one such newspaper, *Sawt al-Mukhayyam*.

Women as Intra-Organizational Brokers

Before the 1982 invasion, quotidian social connections played a central role in cadres' mobilization into the various factions (R. Sayigh 1979, chap. 4, and 1998; Peteet 1991, chap. 4); when asked how they were recruited, Fatah members tended to note family connections, while PFLP and DFLP members more often cited friendship.[2] However, once cadres were recruited, quotidian ties were not systematically used for "formal business"; recruits' assignment into different subdivisions depended on many factors, including interest, skill, intelligence, perceived social appropriateness, connections, and need. Though some women participated in combat units, they were largely placed in administrative offices, social services (e.g., kindergartens, literacy programs, health services), or in support units such as information divisions, though patterns varied across factions (Peteet 1991, chap. 5; Kawar 1996, 70–73).

Factors such as education, training, migration, recruitment patterns, and marriage meant that individuals' personal networks frequently spanned geographic, political, subunit, and gender divisions, both within individual factions and across them. For example, attending an UNRWA vocational or teacher program could introduce both men and women to new Palestinian friends from across Lebanon. These quotidian ties also frequently spanned the Lebanese–Palestinian national divide as Palestinian factions cotrained and codeployed with Lebanese parties such as the Progressive Socialist Party (PSP), the Lebanese Communist Party (LCP), Amal, and the Lebanese National Movement (LNM).[3] For example, one woman I interviewed had worked in a joint PLO-LNM media office in the early 1980s and had befriended her politically active Lebanese coworkers. Post-invasion, these past connections provided the social infrastructure onto which militants remapped and reconsolidated military units' communications, finance, supply, intelligence, and other operations. The following addresses these processes in detail, focusing on how variations in wartime repertoires of violence drove regional differences in organizational adaptation.

Repurposing Kinship and Marriage Ties

The first organized, post-evacuation of Beirut smuggling activity began in South Lebanon in direct response to material conditions in the camps. The "first movers" who took on clandestine roles tended to be women with preexisting ties to militant organizations, whether officially through party membership, the scouts, a social service job with the PLO, or activism through the GUPW, or informally by association through a spouse, fiancé, or family member. These women had often become heads of household when the IDF rounded up Palestinian men who survived the summer military campaigns. While there were shortages of food and building materials in the areas surrounding the camp, goods were still available in occupied Saida, and institutions such as banks were open. Under these circumstances, women started volunteering to "visit" PLO-affiliated family members in the Bekaa Valley and Trablous, areas in which the Palestinian resistance still had a presence.

Women mobilized into new, task-based roles because of strong, trust-based ties that bridged organizational subdivisions and everyday networks. Their initial trips out of Saida served two purposes that reflect the general challenges of conflict-affected spaces. First, as in many war zones, "there was no communication, and people wanted news."[4] Second, again reflective of many civil wars, families were destitute and hungry; they needed cash. Khadija, a courier from Ain al-Hilweh interviewed by Dana Abourahme, emphasizes how the humanitarian crisis in the camp influenced her decision to assume the role she did: "My secret political work was a response to our reality. We woke up from a nightmare, and everything was different in 1982. I felt like any small deed, like delivering a salary to a family in need, was an accomplishment" (Abourahme 2010). Dalal explained how quotidian ties influenced who ventured east: "If the woman had a son in the resistance, she would volunteer and go alone to get money."[5] When I asked if it was just mother-and-son dyads that engaged in these transfers, she elaborated: "Maybe her father, maybe her husband, maybe from her neighbors."[6] Women would visit a trusted, personal connection, would pick up cash or organize a bank transfer, and would then return through the Shouf and occupied South Lebanon.

These trips assumed a third, explicitly military purpose as well. Munadileh, a trained cadre who had brothers and an uncle in other leftist organizations, noted: "For women, there was a social role and a military role," thus distinguishing the idea of "everyday" resistance through mutual social support from participation in underground guerrilla activities.[7] Military roles, by her definition, included gathering intelligence on the IDF, making food, sewing uniforms, and liaising with guerrilla units operating in the Shouf and around the southern camps. Women like Munadileh were particularly valuable in this context. As someone with medical training, she provided essential care; as someone who had formally joined the organization, she was also well-known and trusted by the guerrillas. Participating in public prewar social activities, such as dance teams or the scouts, may have also meant that some women were recognizable members of factions, even if they had never before participated in military operations.

The nascent underground organization was marked by constant loss and uncertainty, compelling militants to develop new secrecy protocols and more complicated routines over time, a nonlinear process of adaptation and feedback that varied in response to local environments. Some interviewees frankly described moments of panic or indecision, often in self-deprecating ways, emphasizing that it took time to learn new tactics, to grow accustomed to the changing context, and to negotiate the tension between the threats to their families and political work. These moments demonstrate that adaptation was neither path-dependent nor preplanned; rather, network change followed complex, often highly contingent processes shaped not just by preexisting networks, but also by people's in-the-moment understanding of the context. For instance, Umm Karim, whose husband was an official in the PLO, had been left with a bag of money for Palestinian fighters. Yet she describes how "the invasion was in the house, here [*al-ijtiyah kan bil bayt, hun*]" and that, especially since that she had several young children, she decided to flee. As the family left ahead of the IDF's incursion into Ain al-Hilweh, Umm Karim's fear that she would be discovered led her to throw the bag of money into a valley; she describes the bag unexpectedly splitting wide open in the air and the money floating away on the wind, meaning it could not be retrieved.[8] Women operating in clandestine operational roles were also well aware of the risks.[9] They could easily get caught in the ever-shifting web of Israeli and Lebanese militia checkpoints. As time went on, deaths were rarely confirmed or formally recognized by Palestinian organizations; individuals simply disappeared, leaving uncertainty and speculation as to what could have happened to them. As Dalal recalled, "they never came back . . . many of them are martyrs."[10]

Remapping Combat Units in South Lebanon

Cadres consciously remapped critical organizational structures—in particular, communication channels that carried information, intelligence, and orders—in reaction to an environment controlled by occupation forces, collaborationist militias, and informants. Reconnecting isolated members of local subunits to larger organizational structures provided both the information and the financial resources necessary to reestablishing militant operations. As fighters began to emerge from hiding or to be released from prison, these dynamics reconsolidated militant networks in South Lebanon into small, operationally autonomous cliques. That is, while they retained many of their previous military capabilities, they existed in a state of quasi-independence from official command-and-control structures.

Their form also evolved over time in response to counterinsurgent repertoires of violence. In other words, occupation violence shaped militant networks by cutting ties between local militants and organizational hierarchies and between local units via the fragmentation of space and the use of collaborators. Early mistakes, such as an initial lack of compartmentalization, left the entire network vulnerable. For example, in late 1982, the IDF captured one high-level guerrilla who operated around Ain al-Hilweh. Following his interrogation, the IDF arrested twenty-two other guerrillas and sent them to an Israeli prison. In this case, an entire network map disappeared, rattling those who escaped arrest.[11] However, moments like these were also crucial for organizational learning and updating.

Palestinian militant organizations consequently adopted a tight cell structure similar to those employed by insurgents in Algeria or Vietnam; small cliques such as these protect guerrilla organizations by limiting the number of people with operational information and restricting what individual militants know about the rest of the organization's activities and membership. Men and boys who remained free tended to move in small groups, based predominantly in the nearby Shouf Mountains (where people had contacts in the PSP) or in the rocky hills of South Lebanon (where they had contacts with Amal and the LCP), so as to avoid detection by informants. Kamal, a Lebanese member of Fatah, described these cliques as tiny, mobile units consisting of only two to three men who communicated with superior officers through female couriers who could move more safely than men.[12] Yusif and Dalal, both of whom worked within the cell structure over several years, confirmed this arrangement, noting some flexibility on the numbers of men in each group. This adaptation meant that the capture of a cell member would only endanger the two to three other members of his cell, rather than dozens. Still identifying as parts of the different factions, cells technically operated under the direction of country-level command structures, which remained active in both eastern and northern Lebanon. There were at least some attempts at a coordinated insurgent strategy; for example, military commanders who remained in the Bekaa, alongside the LNM and various Islamic groups, formed a coalition to plan armed resistance operations against the Israeli forces and their Lebanese allies in the South (Nofal 2006, 27).

These two operational structures—one based on remapped, ground-level, and informal militant networks and the other a formal coalition of established groups that recognized prewar roles and hierarchies—communicated and coordinated through the emergent, woman-dominated logistics and information network. Together, they formed a loose web of guerrilla cliques that was still defined by prewar affiliation.

Militants experimented and improvised in the ways that they repurposed and subsequently remapped ties, blending their prior training with new experiences. Their logic of organization evolved in response to Israeli and Lebanese militia tactics. When asked how the guerrillas avoided detection, Yusif reminded me that working out the appropriate routines, practices, and organizational structures involved trial, error, and conscious learning. Referencing the previously mentioned capture of nearly two dozen people, he recalled: "that was early on. They went to prison in Israel. After that, if you were a leader, you could only run three groups; that was the limit. There were three to five persons in each group, but they only knew their leader. We were searching for security."[13] Members of the emerging underground remained mobile, went into hiding, or assumed cover identities. They consciously adapted past guerrilla training or, especially in the case of leftist parties that emerged in Lebanon, experience in past underground student movements (Khaled 1973, 63–64), a reference to how previous experiences of violence and repression shaped militants' skill sets.[14]

The diversity and depth of organizations' links to different community-level actors produced organizational flexibility, particularly among deeply embedded actors such as the PFLP, DFLP, and Fatah.[15] However, it also made Palestinian militants profoundly dependent on their limited connections within highly compartmentalized organizations. They channeled information through relationships rooted in preinvasion affiliations to avoid getting caught, but they also drew upon prior training and toolkits. Both Yusif and Kamal described how the guerrillas used co-members' local networks to locate friends with whom they could stay; to reach safe houses owned by Lebanese members of Palestinian groups; or to secure rooftops (which were less likely to be searched even if the house was). Yusif explained that undercover Palestinian activists in Saida would often sleep in the houses of people incarcerated in Ansar because no one looked for clandestine fighters in abandoned homes. Hussam, another former clandestine fighter, remembered using a friend's shop in Old Saida (the neighborhood feared by the IDF and its allies) as a safe house; the friend would lock him inside when the business closed at 7 p.m. each night.[16]

Old political alliances gained new resonance in this setting as both Palestinians and Lebanese reestablished communication with each other via personal connections rather than through formally established, top-down alliances. On the regional level, Palestinians in South Lebanon connected with their allies in the PSP, then fighting its own war against the Lebanese Forces and Kata'ib in the Shouf. Many Palestinian guerrillas leveraged past relationships with PSP members during this time period; the PSP could locate weapons in old Fatah stashes in houses, caves, or buried in fields, for example. Fighters from both groups cooperated to transfer recovered weapons in ambulances to smaller units, establishing a crucial supply chain for the Palestinian guerrilla cells. Palestinian organizations in the Bekaa, in turn, transferred weapons to the PSP for its own operations in the Shouf (Nofal 2006, 28). Other Lebanese or Lebanese–Palestinian political organizations in Saida, such as the PNO, the LCP, and the *Jama'a Islamiyya* (an Islamic movement), also provided material aid to clandestine Palestinian organizations with which they had prior relationships (Y. Sayigh 1997, 581).[17] The resilience that these organizational-level ties provided and their flexible uses allowed guerrilla cells to experiment with different approaches to organizing clandestine operations and to increase attacks on the IDF, resulting in an upsurge in Israeli attacks on Ain al-Hilweh.[18]

The Organizational Consequences of Mass Imprisonment

These network adaptations occurred in response to mass arrest and internment campaigns that targeted men and boys between the ages of fifteen and sixty. Counterinsurgent forces use mass arrests for the ostensible deterrent and information-gathering payoffs, as well as for punishment and control. From a blunt social network perspective, incarceration removes individual actors from networks. However, at the mass scale, internment on the collective level can sever ties and create cleavages between the incarcerated and those "outside"—it breaks chains of command, disrupts information networks, and removes actors from operational availability, for instance. At the social level, incarceration often removes key economic and protective actors from households, increasing their vulnerability; at its extreme, mass detention can also be used as a tactic of ethnic cleansing (Downes 2008).

Prison and detention camp populations fluctuated over time, meaning that some people returned to and then reexited networks over time. By April 8, 1983, after initially detaining approximately 10,000 prisoners, the IDF reported that it was still holding 3,300 Palestinians, 940 Lebanese, and 380 Syrians, along with over 100 prisoners of other nationalities.[19] However, guerrilla attacks increased in the spring of 1983, prompting the IDF to launch a new program of mass arrests. The AFSC's Advisory Committee on Human Rights in Lebanon report notes that these numbers only represent those held in indefinite detention; "[i]t does not include those arrested in the course of security sweeps but released within a day or two after questioning—a much larger number." The report estimates that the IDF interred approximately 400 "new" detainees by May 25, 1983, but that the IDF also arrested approximately 700 Lebanese during the last week of the same month and the first week of June (Advisory Committee on Human Rights in Lebanon 1983, 24). By 1983, the Israelis were releasing small numbers of men (e.g., 100 in early September, 1983), while others were beginning to come out of hiding.[20]

The Politics of Prison Life: Abu Riyad's Story

Abu Riyad, an officer from al-Buss, had been involved with the factions since his childhood; he played in a football league with other politically active youth, joined a militant group, went through guerrilla training, and was assigned a job in the organization's military wing. He didn't tell me much about the early days of the invasion, except that he remembered civilians dying in their cars trying to escape up the highway to the Awali River north of Saida; many had been hit by Israeli ordnance, an act he referred to as "state terrorism [*irhab al-dawleh*]." The IDF captured him shortly thereafter and sent him to a military prison in Israel. Four months later, the IDF transferred him back to South Lebanon, where he spent the following two years in Ansar prison camp.

Ansar was its own political and social world. The IDF divided the prison into two sections—Ansar I and Ansar II—and further divided detainees into fifteen "pens" that interviewees referred to as *muʿaskarat* (sing. *muʿaskar*, meaning "camp(s)," though with a military connotation). Each *muʿaskar* was surrounded by barbed wire fences and held between 250 and 300 prisoners in ten to twelve tents that could sleep twenty-five people each (Khalili 2008, 103).[21] Abu Riyad and I took turns sketching a map of the *muʿaskar* where he played a supervisory role in my notebook, drawing the location of ten tents and a shared kitchen before marking circles for the six guard towers around the perimeter. With a hint of what seemed like residual satisfaction, he then put the pad of his index finger on a spot by a guard tower on the long side of the fence, instructing me to fill in a circle where inmates eventually managed to dig an escape tunnel.

Ansar strictly controlled inmates' interactions by limiting them to their *muʿaskar* and deploying multilayered surveillance (Khalili 2008, 103). Yet it also worked by mixing inmates from different political backgrounds, separating people from their subunits and any family members who had also been incarcerated. Abu Riyad explained that there were men from "all of the factions" in each of the tents, as well as militants from the Lebanese parties. Conversation among co-members of various factions was consequently difficult; communication between inmates was highly regulated and political discussions nearly impossible (R. Sayigh 1985; Khalili 2008). Exchanges thus had to be both limited and strategic; guards patrolling outside the tents could hear almost any noise through their canvas walls. Ziyad, a former guerrilla and Ansar I inmate from Ain al-Hilweh, told me in a separate interview that the Israeli forces inflicted physical punishments for violating the communication rules; he himself had his hands bound in front of him and was hit on several occasions for violating them.[22] It was thus hard for militants to develop new connections and difficult to inject any nonessential content into existing connections.

When Ansar inmates did "talk politics," they discussed immediate concerns within the prison camp. Abu Riyad explained that detainees in his pen eventually organized several public acts of resistance, which were predominantly linked to humanitarian conditions in the camp and tied to religious or political holidays.[23] On Lebanese Independence Day, for example, the prisoners drew flags on pieces of paper and raised them in unison at 8 p.m. Abu Riyad lightheartedly noted that he and his fellow prisoners even formed a scout team, making a drum out of an empty gas canister to pound on during protests. During one Eid al-Adha, when inmates launched the "Eid Uprising," the Israeli guards fatally shot seven prisoners. Eventually, the prisoners managed to dig a tunnel that ended past the barbed wire fences; seventy-three inmates escaped. In response to the "Great Escape," the Israeli forces transferred some 2,000 prisoners to a new prison camp in Wadi Jahannam that contained four *muʿaskarat* (Khalili 2008, 107).

Despite the profound effects of mass incarceration, internment appears to have had few long-term organizational effects in terms of seeding network connections or inspiring group restructuring. This finding sets Ansar, specifically, apart from settings such as Soviet gulags or US military prisons in Iraq—both of which fostered the growth of illicit networks and brokerage between members of various organizations (Handelman 1997; Volkov 2002; Chulov 2014; Warrick 2016). Abu Riyad recalled, with what I perceived as a bit of frustration, that everyone from Ansar went back to their own region and their faction after release. When he was eventually freed in 1984, he fled to North Lebanon, later returning to the south via boat. By the end of 1984, he was arrested again for guerrilla activities in Qasmiyeh, a Palestinian gathering just north of Sur; he was sent to a prison facility in Saida until the Israeli forces withdrew to the border zone in 1985. His wife, in the meantime, served as a money smuggler between Beirut and Saida.

This dissimilarity across conflicts very likely relates to the way that Ansar's set-up interacted with Palestinian social networks. Former detainees distinguished the consequences of time spent in smaller, usually local interrogation facilities from longer stints in Ansar or in high-security prisons in Israel. Individual stories of interrogation at smaller facilities, shared through everyday relationships and often published in underground newspapers, helped to promulgate a collective narrative of Israeli brutality. Rahaf, for example, detailed her interrogation in a facility in Saida (likely at St. Joseph's Convent, from her description), where she was held in a stress position in solitary confinement for days and forced to urinate in a bucket while male guards watched her. This expressly gendered technique was designed to shame her and encourage her isolation from her family. Rahaf refused drinking water to avoid having to urinate, a choice she explicitly framed as a form of resistance. Demonstrating how family connections could be leveraged against activists in prison, the soldiers guarding Rahaf's brother, who was simultaneously incarcerated and able to hear her scream, told him that they were planning to rape her if he did not provide information.[24] The leftist underground newspaper *Sawt al-Mukhayyam* regularly published articles that summarized these tactics, as well as those used in Israeli raids, emphasizing the use of beatings and psychological torture. The cumulative effect of word-of-mouth and written-word descriptions of raids, arrests, and interrogations was to create a shared understanding of the Israeli forces' repertoire of violence as well as to reinforce already-accessible frames among a broad population that supported resistance activities.

Though Abu Riyad did not discuss it in our interview, the IDF also deployed informants and collaborators within Ansar. This tactic disincentivized detainees from forming strong new ties and seems to have reinforced both intrafactional relationships and the salience of other social boundaries. Mixing members of different factions and cities in the tents meant that people did not necessarily know one another; the general belief was that all factions and all social circles were infiltrated and that anyone could be an informant. While the inmates' leadership spanned formal political groups, several former prisoners to whom I spoke indicated that other detainees uniformly saw members of the Israeli-appointed inmates' leadership as collaborators. Mahmud once illustrated this point graphically, asking me: "Sarah, do you know about those fuckers in the black hoods on the beach, the ones who told the Israelis who were *fida'iyyin*?" When I answered affirmatively, he told me: "Those guys were traitors, and they became the leadership in Ansar. This one guy, he held his Kalashnikov over his head and said '*kis ummhu* ["his mother's cunt"] Abu Ammar [Yasir Arafat]' in front of everyone on the beach! He is still in the leadership!"[25] Mahmud's revelation regarding the leadership in Ansar offers one explanation as to why shared experiences of imprisonment may not have led to the later reconsolidation of new activist networks, as well as emphasizing additional, emerging cleavages between elite officers and foot soldiers in South Lebanon. These prisoners often faced mortal threat upon their release, which may explain Abu Riyad's choice to escape to North Lebanon for a time. In some cases, inmates even asked not to be released. For example, an AFSC report notes the presence of "an unknown but significant number of detainees at Ansar who have been cleared for release by Israel but who have asked to remain at the detention center in protective custody, in accordance with provisions of the Fourth Geneva Convention. They [had] been warned by relatives that they would be in danger of reprisals or vengeance killings in South Lebanon if they were freed. Also, a few released Palestinians have asked to be reinterned after receiving threats upon their return home" (Advisory Committee on Human Rights in Lebanon 1983, 27–28).

This note reveals several important lessons about the way that suspicion, selective violence, rumors, and social network isolation operated in this environment. First, the setting forced detainees' family members to consider their own safety as they prepared for a relative's impending release and the potential to reconnect with them. Was the detainee an informant? Would other families assume that they were? Would a rival use the situation to spread false rumors of collaboration to gain an unrelated advantage (e.g., ensuring that a competing shop lacked customers)? If family members were to house a suspected or rumored collaborator, they would inevitably be tainted by association: they could suffer social exclusion or become targets themselves. These considerations occurred in an environment where individuals' extrafamilial relationships often mitigated the effects of surveillance, poverty, powerlessness, and homelessness; surviving as a former member of the prison leadership often involved top-down protection or patronage. A second lesson is that Palestinians' asking to be rearrested and returned to a prison camp indicates that the prison itself was set up to perpetuate fragmentation and atomization by seeding negative perceptions of inmates, thus hamstringing their social reintegration and fomenting isolation. Actively sowing suspicion and distrust within the prison camps was key to the IDF's strategy of maintaining militant group and social fragmentation.

In many ways, Abu Riyad's story reflects common patterns that surfaced in my interviews. Upon release from Ansar, people who had been members of the PLO or guerrilla factions usually reported returning to their old organizations rather than choosing to coordinate in new ways with their co-detainees. The IDF's close control of prisoner relations meant that militants simply rejoined old, trusted factional cohorts upon their release rather than building on relatively shaky new ties. In its approach to control, the prison camp counterintuitively fostered expressly factional survival. In part because of its seeming arbitrariness—former detainees assessed that their chances of arrest or death were equal, whether they participated in resistance activities or not—and in part because of the broad, general resentment that the occupation and mass incarceration generated, detention did not work as a deterrent from returning to violent or nonviolent resistance activities. Most of the former Ansar prisoners I interviewed returned to militant work after their release, often taking on more high-risk positions or activities because of the desire to be mobile and to avoid recapture.

However, there were also variations in people's choices. For example, Mahmud, who married soon after his release, never returned to organized armed activity after his release from Ansar. However, he did get into a physical fight with an Israeli officer who tried to steal his new car. His calculus was that he was as likely to wind up in Ansar simply for being a Palestinian who did nothing as he was for being a Palestinian who punched an Israeli soldier, so he chose to act. Despite their experiences, Rahaf and her brother both immediately returned to underground activities upon their release; both took on higher-risk, clandestine roles following their imprisonment, in part because they suspected they would be rearrested if they took on roles closer to home when ensconced in their own community.

The Emergence of Intelligence and Logistics Apparatuses

Emerging clandestine intelligence, logistics, and combat networks in 1982–1985 South Lebanon reflected a fundamental change in how the PLO and the guerrilla organizations operated in relation to their formal chains of command. Starting as early as 1983, organizational elites in Lebanon and in exile worked to adapt remapped, gendered grassroots operations to more systematized political and military ends. Top-down organizational demand for these informal roles and practices resulted in their rapid institutionalization and routinization. While these moves may have generally represented efforts to ensure organizational survival, they also represented leaders' reassertion of control over cadres they had left behind in 1982. Some on-the-ground cadres welcomed the reestablishment of formal command, but others saw elite efforts as attempts to co-opt effective military structures for personal gain.

Elites in the PLO and the guerrilla organizations adopted the emergent grassroots network as the official conduit for underground cadres' salaries, which they routed from Tunis through the Arab Bank in Saida. An initially uncomplicated money transfer process anchored by women who carried cash from the

Bekaa into South Lebanon evolved into an international financial apparatus. Yusif, one of the Fatah officers responsible for distributing guerrillas' salaries, underscored how the strategy of using women in the supply chain quickly scaled up to the national level once the PLO started funneling salaries into Saida:

> "[*Me: How did people get paid?*] The money would go to Saida, to the bank from Tunis. Two, three, four people who were leaders would go to the bank. They then distributed it down to two or three guys each who maybe each controlled around one hundred guys.
>
> We used women to move the money.... It was like a grape, meaning everything is tied to everything, what is the group called? [*Me: A bunch?*] It was an *anqud*—a bunch of grapes... like a cluster bomb! [*Laughter*] ... No one can talk to the people below you. It protects people.... We were searching for security. [*Me: How was it structured?*] Like this." [At this point Yusif drew a diagram in my notebook with a central stem and branches jutting off. I asked where the women would be in the diagram, and he indicated the branches linking the grape/male nodes to each other via the stems/female ties].[26]

Yusif noted that the funding that arrived in the Arab Bank was subsequently divided between guerrilla organizations, each of which had its own segmented courier network: PFLP for PFLP, Fatah for Fatah, DFLP for DFLP. This reorganized underground network contained three- to five-person cells.[27] Women working as couriers moved information between each level of the evolving hierarchy, thereby institutionalizing relations between freshly delineated roles.

As this emergent organizational network—one with defined positions, hierarchies, and routines—interacted with the broader conflict environment, it also prompted diversification of the noncombat apparatus. As the IDF, Lebanese militias, and the Syrian military responded to increased guerrilla activity by building more checkpoints and hunting women couriers and intelligence operatives, Palestinian militants further expanded their toolkits, adapting old skill sets and acquiring new ones. For example, underground cadres established an information office to forge documentation. Dalal's university professor, an older man, recruited her into this division. Her military training in the scouts, her education and reputation for intelligence, and her party membership meant that higher-ranking officers likely saw her as capable and trustworthy; the intersection of her university-based relationship with a professor and his role as a high-ranking officer provided a specific mobilization vector. Given both her skill set *and* her position in webs of overlapping organizational and quotidian networks, Dalal was more valuable to the underground as a document forger than she would have been as a fighter.

Clandestine activists in Saida also remapped family, friendship, and cross-national relationships to develop chains of safe houses, allowing them to move members of the Palestinian resistance deep into the cities rather than relying on ad hoc arrangements as early-stage clandestine operatives did. Houses owned by Lebanese members of Palestinian groups, homes belonging to imprisoned family and friends, and rooftops all remained prime hiding spaces; the difference lay in the degree of routinization and connectedness.[28] The sheer amount of work involved in establishing and managing the minute details associated with the safe house system helped maintain people's ties to formal political organizations. For example, Kamal returned from exile in the Gulf via Trablous, moving to South Lebanon through the Bekaa and the Shouf by leapfrogging between safe houses maintained by PLO sympathizers. His Lebanese Christian heritage and kinship ties in South Lebanon afforded him added mobility and protection in areas patrolled by right-wing militias, making him a valuable asset to the organization. Yet his movement through this clandestine geography concurrently, if episodically, invoked his hosts' organizational ties, thus reinforcing remapped relations even under conditions marked by surveillance, fragmentation, and extreme repression.

Still, the environment was also marked by pervasive and persistent suspicion. Rumors and distrust continued to affect relations between the factions throughout the period to the extent that they were reported in clandestine newspapers:

> One official in a Palestinian organization is spreading a rumor that another Palestinian front is spying on him and sending their men to follow him because they want to assassinate him. This official is paranoid. He thinks anyone walking behind him is following him and he doesn't take his bulletproof vest off.[29]

This note, in a section of a newspaper devoted to rumors and gossip, appears to mock the official, indicating that he is both performing a particular status (of someone who might be assassinated) and disparaging the other Palestinian organization by "spreading a rumor." However, the simple mention of this behavior belies the way in which narratives of spying, collaboration, and plotting shaped relationships between guerrilla factions during this time, changing the content of relationships between organizations and reinforcing distance between them.

Socialization and Indoctrination as Organizational Maintenance

For Palestinians in South Lebanon, organizational resilience meant reestablishing communication among militants, supporting families, and reconstituting combat units. Rather than attempting to maximize military and political outcomes in a purely "rational" sense, members negotiated issues as they were confronted with them, patching holes rather than fixing them and attempting to balance diverging individual- and community-level concerns, approaches that have previously been identified as common and predictable behaviors for organizations under stress (Cyert and March 1992).

Research that focuses on rebels' ability to mount military missions or engage in negotiations often ignores these critical behind-the-scenes behaviors, despite their effects on organizational strength and resilience. For instance, research that focuses only on the frequency or count of lethal rebel attacks may ignore rebel training, strategy, socialization, community engagement, and overall military effectiveness. The problem with this tack is that it confounds short-term, easily observable activity with long-term capability and goals. It also assumes that lethal violence is the organizational goal, rather than survival. Focusing only on rebels' ability to carry out violent acts ignores the organizational upkeep and solidarity-building that often occur behind the scenes in reaction to different combat environments. The following section explains how the publication and sharing of a clandestine leftist newspaper, *Sawt al-Mukhayyam*, served essential organizational maintenance and survival purposes via mechanisms of socialization and narrative creation.

Publications as Socialization

Distributing money, one of the core functions of the Palestinian underground, could conceivably be construed either as a humanitarian act or as instrumentalist resource distribution. However, circulating political publications during civil war is less ambiguous; one cannot eat or drink a magazine, nor can one use it to bribe soldiers. Why would militants risk their lives to print and distribute newspapers? Reading political publications and debating their content socialized militants and created shared political narratives among Palestinians living in South Lebanon.

Publications such as *Sawt al-Mukhayyam* ("The Voice of the Camp"), a bimonthly clandestine newspaper that local militants published in Saida in the mid-1980s, established that members of militant organizations concerned themselves with far more than launching attacks, paying soldiers, and civilians' material welfare.[30] *Sawt al-Mukhayyam*'s editors published articles that targeted social norms, pushed political agendas, and shared news of military successes and failures. Over coffee at a seaside restaurant, one of the former editors laughed, in retrospect, over the massive risks they took to do so. He vividly recalled printing the twice-monthly issues under cover of darkness on a sympathetic Lebanese political party's Xerox machine in Saida before handing them off to the smuggling network that delivered them. The editorial board also wound up paying increasingly hefty bribes to the company repairman the editors had to call when the machine repeatedly broke due to overuse.[31]

Publications add content to informational networks, helping people to establish shared narratives and understandings of the realities in which they live. In Lebanon, papers such as *Sawt al-Mukhayyam* reinforced and deepened a cleavage between Palestinians living under occupation in a war zone, on one hand, and the PLO and guerrilla organizations' leadership-in-exile on the other. In spite of a clear leftist bent, *Sawt al-Mukhayyam* bolstered weak ties across factions and between the guerrillas and civilian communities. The effect was a specific form of socialization that privileged both the shared experience of occupation and the collective experience of being Palestinian in South Lebanon. The ties that it established were not necessarily premised on absolute ascription to the ideologies or perspectives contained in the publication, but rather on continued interaction with it and participation in the conversation (Wedeen 1999).[32] *Sawt al-Mukhayyam* painted a picture of a community of people struggling for survival in the context of mass violence while painting a picture of a withdrawn, corrupt, entrenched elite. For example, its August 1984 issue leverages two accusations of elite corruption in a first-page article:

> A "big" Palestinian leader received a check of 30 million dollars from an oil exporting Arab country. Though he was supposed to transfer it to the PLO National Fund, the check didn't reach its destination, causing the fund to suffer.
>
> A Palestinian official who is working in humanitarian services bought a villa in Amman worth 100,000 JD [Jordanian dinars]. She spent 30,000 JD for the decor and furniture. It is worth noting that the sum of all the paychecks she received since she started working for the PLO is nowhere close to that.[33]

Claims such as these do not simply report news; by focusing on both elites and money, they also inject an explicitly moral discourse into the conversation between clandestine militants and civilian populations (Parkinson 2016). By focusing on money and corruption, underground writers articulated boundaries of acceptable behavior, marked cleavages between elites and people on the ground, and created shared understandings of the world of Palestinian politics.

Publications also establish norms and offer evidence of organizational priorities. Another article in the same issue of *Sawt al-Mukhayyam* sketches women's involvement in the Vietnamese Revolution, highlighting the varied roles that women played and the way they benefited the organization. The piece serves at least two, interrelated purposes of recruitment and normative change:

> In 1945 when the armed revolt against French colonialism began, women took a big leap forward. Women's groups were taking the place of the Revolutionary Committees in some areas. They were also part of the operations in the mountains and helped protect bases. In many cases, women had better results than men. In addition to jobs like logistics for the army and supplying food, there were women's militia groups responsible for protecting the roads, building barricades, executing traitors, and attacking enemy bases. The women's groups made up 36% of all militia groups. In Bayan city alone, there were 1 million women participating in civil tasks. They were able to penetrate deeper into enemy lines. They used better techniques to recruit soldiers and they collected information on the ones who refused. In 1953 they were able to recruit 17 army soldiers and convinced them to change sides.[34]

Publishing articles with this genre of content created a discursive infrastructure for further debate over women's current and potential roles in ongoing Palestinian political and military activities. By lauding Vietnamese women's participation in the revolution; by explicitly celebrating their logistics work as well as their organizing and combat roles; and by underlining their successes relative to men, this kind of article effectively resituates the Palestinian women who were taking on similar roles in remapped networks as surpassing the contributions of men and acting as agents of broader, positive social change. It also situated the Palestinian struggle in Lebanon as a comparable revolutionary struggle, even as the exiled PLO and guerrilla leaderships' priorities began to shift to other venues.

Publishing and smuggling newspapers required significant logistical effort and helped to reinforce ties between clandestine agents. Bassam, the editor, described elaborate systems for transferring organizational publications from secret printing sites into besieged camps and to underground members of organizations. Militant organizations' local and regional leaders were clearly concerned not only with prolonging military activity, but also with cadres' repeated performance of organizational affiliation and expressly local loyalty.

Militant organizations' leaderships wanted to ensure that even otherwise inactive individuals and families made explicit political statements of loyalty throughout civil war and occupation by receiving salaries and literature via clandestine networks. In effect, these exchanges of money and information preserved Palestinian militant organizations through iterated acts of individual risk acceptance on behalf of a group. Giannou, the Greek-Canadian surgeon who worked in South Lebanon before the invasion, highlights the dual nature of the organizational salary in his own memoir: "Belonging to a [sic] organization and receiving a monthly salary was (and still is) much more of a political statement than belonging to a political party in a Western parliamentary democracy. The allegiance could cost you your life."[35] Munadileh agreed that accepting a salary symbolized at the very least a tacit statement of support.[36] Moreover, these actions situated the militant organizations and their members as the central financial and information brokers within the Palestinian civilian community.

In South Lebanon, gendered repertoires of counterinsurgent violence that were centered on the mass incarceration of men and boys eventually led to the emergence of cell-based combat units and clandestine logistics, communication, and intelligence apparatuses. The specific context of Ansar prison camp and other sites of internment largely disincentivized the development of new political ties among Palestinian men, reinforcing factional loyalties. As subdivisions of larger rebel organizations, emergent clandestine supply networks resolved two critical challenges that Palestinian militant organizations faced: providing material support to their associates and allowing for organizational maintenance when formal pathways were inaccessible. By serving as the social and informational interface—specifically, by transmitting feedback between the conflict environment and core organizational structures—clandestine networks came to serve as primary sites of organizational learning.

On the individual level, these processes reveal how cadres' roles in broader organizational apparatuses both flowed from and reshaped their everyday relationships, driving broader social change. In Lebanon, the prewar PLO and many guerrilla factions consolidated cadres into their organizational structures along gendered lines. Previous membership in the PLO and in guerrilla organizations' social institutions combined with militants' kinship and friendship ties to create potential for mobilization. This social infrastructure of overlapping quotidian and organizational ties created categories of participants with prior activist histories who were "structurally available," two key determinants of high-risk, clandestine action (McAdam 1986, 65, 69–71; della Porta 1988). As a result, women who inhabited specific positions as brokers—either "officially" through the *zaharat,* party membership, or the Women's Union, or "unofficially" through a spouse, fiancé, or sibling—mobilized within an organizational context and via remapped, trust-based strong ties. Quotidian social ties acted as bridges between organizational subdivisions, forming the basis of the clandestine network.

Ongoing mobilization under conditions of occupation is not particularly surprising. However, the processes elaborated here establish that repertoires of violence, militants' understanding of them, and configuration of ties all matter for organizational outcomes. That is, emergent organizational forms such as small, factionalized cliques of combatants or clandestine apparatuses were not the "natural" outcome of preexisting social relations. Rather, people's mobilization into specific roles depended on their location in overlapping social networks—often those constituted by social organizations and kinship groups (della Porta 1988)—as well as those networks' experiences and interpretations of the violence and repression that they faced.

The noncombat roles described in this chapter—document forger, intelligence agent, money smuggler, courier, journalist—were essential to militant operations, organizational adaptation, and community survival. These roles require training, socialization, trust, intelligence, and emotional fortitude. Nearly all of my interlocutors emphasized that they had to develop specialized skills, plan for countless contingencies, cultivate relationships, leverage varied experiences to do their jobs, and repeatedly bear the risks of front-line or behind-the-lines action. This labor was crucial to negotiating the core challenges that asymmetric warfare presents and required that cadres and affiliates alike pursue it with secrecy and nuance, given their understanding of the threats posed to themselves, their organizations, and their communities. They did not mobilize due to the presence of a critical public mass. Rather, they moved into clandestine roles as part of larger processes of remapping social ties in response to violence.

These findings contrast portrayals of militant women as serving either in second-tier, low-status "support" roles (posed as a foil to "high-status" combat roles) or in inherently "feminine" roles in some studies of militancy (R. M. Wood and Thomas 2017; Thomas and Wood 2017). The lack of public recognition for women who served in the clandestine apparatus did not mean that their *roles* were understood as being "low status" by either organizational leaderships or the Palestinian community writ large. Indeed, in the context of occupation and militia warfare, public status rewards would have meant their certain deaths. As coming chapters will demonstrate, and in line with other accounts of women in asymmetric conflict (MacFarland 1994, 72–73; Sheldon 1994, 42), the factions *invested* in many women who were part of the clandestine logistics and intelligence apparatus. In a one-to-one comparison, they very likely proved more valuable to the organization than the average male fighter. The backstage roles women assumed were, and were collectively valued as, integral to political—not simply military—operations.

5

CROSSING COLLABORATORS
Emotion, Informing, and Civilian Mobilization in Occupied South Lebanon

As we leave the camp, [Abu Houli and I] walk through a checkpoint. The guards on duty cheerfully greet us; their weapons lean against the wall and one is trying to chase a neighbor's stray chicken out of the hut. As we walk down towards the main road, I carefully ask Abu Houli about the Palestinian National Guard [a collaborator militia] in Saida, and whether there was "a similar problem" in Sur. Right off the bat, he says, "oh, one of those guys [whom you just interviewed] was a collaborator; he was a kid [when he did it]. The guy was with [a Palestinian faction] and his father was an officer in the PFLP. He brought him to a car that had a bomb in it and the father was martyred in the explosion." I am entirely shocked by Abu Houli's nonchalance regarding a former Israeli spy in his social circles.[1]

The Israeli forces' and Lebanese militias' tactics in South Lebanon between 1982 and 1985—which included aerial bombardment, mass incarceration, raids, curfews, infiltration, disappearances, arson, and evictions—reshaped camp-level social networks in Saida and Sur. These repertoires of violence severed relationships and aggressively introduced collaborators into noncombatants' social relations. Deploying collaborators and cutting ties between male youth and adults on one hand and young children, women, and the elderly on the other spurred the remapping of ties between women and across generational cohorts. These processes led to the emergence of collective, women-led advocacy efforts and community-based counterintelligence apparatuses. Narratives of shared fear, resentment, and vulnerability; resistance toolkits; and, eventually, practices of unmasking and anticollaborator violence constituted these networks.

These findings complement previous work on civilian agency, information networks, and support for militants (Petersen 2001; E. J. Wood 2003; Tse-tung 2007; Arjona 2016; Kaplan 2017; Lewis 2017, 2020; Bulutgil 2019). However, they also strongly imply that civilians' roles in irregular wars expand far beyond attitudinal, material, informational, or even symbolic support of or resistance to armed actors. Moving beyond the body-count approach to wartime violence, this chapter explicitly examines how highly visible aspects of violent repertoires—e.g., mass incarceration—interacted with less easily observable tactics—e.g., the infiltration of social networks with collaborators—to catalyze adaptation in civilian social networks. It argues that, contrary to the long-standing finding in studies of mobilization that activists must *overcome* fear to mobilize or that those with high thresholds for mobilization must feel "safety in numbers" to act in high-risk environments (Granovetter 1978; Kuran 1991; Pearlman 2013), pervasive fear, resentment, and suspicion embedded networks with new, collective understandings of the threat people faced and engendered new motivations for them to act.

Not all resistance is public or visible (Scott 1987, 1990, 2010). In South Lebanon, the repression of Palestinian communities and the emotions it engendered did not act exclusively as a deterrent or an inspiration; in interviews, people consistently reported being afraid and continuing to act even as they confronted militias in their homes and spotted informers next to them at protests. In this environment, fear influenced the narratives that people developed; the way they organized; the skill sets they acquired; and the tactics they subsequently deployed. In other words, intense fear, resentment, and suspicion shifted how people negotiated risk (Mercer 2010) rather than universally depressing political activity. I demonstrate that the people in the resulting emergent roles achieved important social ends and contributed to broader political goals while operating independently from and without explicit cooperation with formal organizational hierarchies.

This chapter first examines how the repertoires of violence deployed activated Palestinian civilian networks in South Lebanon. It then delves into the gendered and generational effects of the IDF's and right-wing Lebanese militias' tactics at the hyperlocal level, focusing on how mass incarceration and infiltration spurred network processes that initiated home-based resistance, mass protest, and organized counterintelligence efforts. Then, it expressly compares how the organization of Palestinian collaborators in Saida, versus Sur, shaped the remapping of Palestinian civilian networks in distinct ways, resulting in highly public anticollaborator identification and violence in Ain al-Hilweh, versus more nuanced modes of response in Rashidiyeh.[2] The chapter concludes with a discussion of how these processes can deepen and inform understandings of civilian agency and behavior in war.

The Gendered Effects of Counterinsurgency Campaigns

In the summer and fall of 1982, the Israeli forces' on-the-ground counterinsurgency practices physically and experientially divided Palestinian communities along both gender and generational lines. Together with the sheer level of physical destruction and the flight it often entailed, the mass removal of men and boys from social networks via incarceration, hiding, disappearance, and death had instantaneous social, economic, psychological, and political effects. Dalal, a member of Fatah then based in Ain al-Hilweh, emphasized that "[i]mmediately, everything was different."[3] Fatimah, a community worker in Saida, underscored the confusion and terror that ensued as she recalled Israeli soldiers taking prisoners to the Rabat School and women asking where the men were; she emphasized that the IDF took away any man they found.[4] Umm Karim, the wife of a PLO official, recalled "... we didn't see men. There wasn't a single man. We didn't know where they were [ma shufnish rijal... ma fi walla zalama... ma arifna waynun]."[5] Tala, a Burj al-Shamali resident with family in Fatah, the PFLP, and the PFLP-GC, emphasized that she stayed in the camp's ruins when the IDF imprisoned her husband and brothers-in-law, leaving her the only adult to manage the family.[6] Dalal emphasized the June 1982 invasion's gendered effects on her immediate family: "First thing, they [the IDF] took my brother, he was 16, and my father, and my grandfather."[7] Halimah, another employee at Fatimah's community-based organization, recalled that her brother's arrest occurred in the middle of Ramadan when everyone was fasting; he remained in Ansar for four months.[8]

These broad detainment sweeps felt random to Palestinians; to observers, they clearly included many more men—for example, teenage brothers and grandparents—than the subset of male combatants that was ostensibly the raids' target. The demographic shift was so palpable that European journalists who visited Ain al-Hilweh in July 1982 expressly noted the absence of men and boys.[9] Men in South Lebanon essentially disappeared from the Palestinian camps, a process that created strong feelings of insecurity among women, children, and the elderly. Incarceration also amplified economic precarity in Palestinian communities; the AFSC notes that by September 1983, a year into the occupation, female heads-of-household had increasingly turned to prostitution to support their families.[10]

Militia Violence and Increasing Uncertainty

The IDF sought to leverage gendered insecurity to exert control by seeding mass distrust, instability, and fear in civilian communities. This environment was also conducive to what Laia Balcells (2011; 2017, 6) defines as direct violence—that is, violence "perpetrated by individuals with small weapons (e.g., machetes, handguns, rifles) . . . produced by armed groups in collaboration with local civilians"—by right-wing Lebanese militias against Palestinian civilians. By October 1982, there were clear signs that militias such as the predominantly Christian Kata'ib and the Lebanese Forces were carrying out targeted killings of Palestinians around Ain al-Hilweh.[11] These militias also explicitly aimed to disrupt Lebanese–Palestinian relationships, often among leftists, by violently disincentivizing coworking and co-organizing. Chantal, a Lebanese woman and then-employee of a makeshift kindergarten located in a hospital's ruins, recalled walking to work one day in the fall of 1982 when her companion stopped to light a cigarette, offering her one as well. Pausing to tie her son's shoe, Chantal looked up just as a car bomb exploded in front of the building. Emphasizing their luck, her precarity, and the overarching unpredictability of deadly violence during that time, she noted (a bit jokingly, given the health warning label printed on her current pack): "I smoked a cigarette, I escaped a massacre [*shribit sijarra, harbit majzara*]."[12]

These attacks occurred in places where there was significant prewar mobilization. Right-wing militia violence stemmed from perceptions of threat, from desires for revenge, and also from bids for control, as theories of civilian targeting would predict (Balcells 2017, 5). By February 1983, international humanitarian groups were receiving firsthand reports that the LF and Kata'ib were evicting Palestinians in and around Saida. In this environment, many Palestinians saw the IDF as being responsible for allowing and, in some cases, actively encouraging these evictions to take place.[13] Mahmoud Zeidan (2017, 299), who was a child in Ain al-Hilweh at the time, recalls:

> We started hearing that the Kata'ib militias were in the Saida area, and its eastern side, and that their numbers were growing. And about the assaults of Saad Haddad's militias [the South Lebanon Army], who started kidnapping people from their houses, or through establishing flying checkpoints.[14] A few days later we heard that the Kata'ib were about to attack our camp, and that day many people fled their homes that were on the public road and came to our neighborhoods to stay in our houses. We did not close our eyes that entire night, or even the following nights. The fear would generate conversations that wouldn't stop until dawn. Fear accompanies silence, which is why we were never silent.

Yusif, who alternately fought with Fatah, the PFLP, and the DFLP, sketched a number of network processes, painting a picture that reveals efforts to eliminate key actors while generally feeding an atmosphere of suspicion and distrust.

He noted (in English): "The Lebanese Forces [in Saida] killed a lot of people, they used to kidnap people and would later throw [them] dead on the road." *[Whom did they kill, and why? Was it mostly political people, because it seems like it was more random?]* "It was a way to show they could do it."[15] According to the AFSC representative on the ground, "[i]n February 1983, the outgoing head of the ICRC's [the International Committee of the Red Cross] Sidon [Saida] delegation, Thomas Ruegg, said that murders, disappearances and other violent actions against Palestinians living outside the camps had created a climate of panic among Palestinians who feared a repetition of the Sabra and Shatila massacres" (Advisory Committee on Human Rights in Lebanon 1983, 20). This particular reference usefully demonstrates how certain violent events resonated far beyond the days on which they occurred, even as they were being reinterpreted in the context of more local experiences.

The situation in Saida eventually became so dire that the IDF itself attempted to clamp down on Lebanese militia violence against Palestinians. The international media also began reporting on the violence, alongside articles about high-level diplomatic engagements and the status of the US Marines in Beirut. For example, an Associated Press wire dated April 8, 1983, reports the discovery of three Palestinians' bodies, two of which had been repeatedly shot and one that had suffered ax wounds. The wire emphasizes that the victims were found "two months after Israeli occupation forces ordered more security for Palestinian areas in the city to stop a terror campaign in which 12 Palestinians were killed," and states that Israel "blamed the earlier killings on the right-wing Christian militiamen of the Phalange [Kata'ib] party" (Associated Press 1983). Another Associated Press report eight days later underscores that the IDF was actively arresting Lebanese civilians who threatened Palestinian families with murder and describes a series of incidents where men dressed in military green had repeatedly threatened displaced families who had taken shelter in religious sanctuaries. A fifteen-year-old Palestinian girl, Maha, who spoke to the reporter, relayed that after the families staying alongside hers in a church refused the men entry: "'They broke open the door and came inside. There were six of them, some in uniform and some in jeans and shirts. They hit the men in the stomach and forced seven of them into the hall. They made them lie face down, and the uniformed men kicked them on the head and necks. Blood poured out of their mouths." Maha then added that one of the uniformed men informed them "'Today, it's a cup of coffee. Tomorrow, it's a cup of blood'" (Faramarzi 1983).

Despite the IDF's recognition that these dynamics fed instability, it and its Lebanese allies continued to employ extrajudicial violence, some of which clandestine militants reported in secret newspapers, feeding collective perceptions of threat and unpredictability. For example, an August 1984 report on the funeral of Muhammad Mabruka from Ain al-Hilweh describes just such an event: "[Mabruka] was arrested by the occupation and was taken to an Israeli intelligence center in Taʻamir [a Lebanese neighborhood that borders Ain al-Hilweh]. A military vehicle dumped the body in Saida three days after his arrest. The martyr was shot several times in the head and chest. His body showed he had been tortured."[16] Given his injuries and the way his body was released, Palestinians saw this chain of events and others like them as engineered to engender terror (a term used repeatedly in underground newspapers). Mabruka's death prompted camp-wide protests that followed a related strike against the occupation forces' treatment of civilians.

While my interviewees clearly distinguished between violent acts carried out by Israeli forces, by their local Palestinian collaborators, and by right-wing Lebanese militias, they also interpreted this violence as being facilitated by and a direct result of the broader occupation. This cognitive move shaped how collective discourses developed among civilians and enabled the remapping of everyday ties into advocacy networks based on a simple narrative of shared experience and blame.

Narrative Networks and Internationalizing Advocacy

The IDF's approach to counterinsurgency and the Lebanese militias' targeting of Palestinian noncombatants activated both cross-generational and gender-based civilian networks. Specifically, while occupation tactics shattered predominantly male combat networks across South Lebanon and physically segregated male youth and adults from children, women, and the elderly, they appear to have also facilitated the formation of new ties between noncombatants across factions. Dalal told me that at this juncture, "the role of women began" as the women, youth, children, and elderly who were left behind collectively struggled to build shelters, tend to the wounded, and secure stable sources of food and water.[17] The clustering of Palestinian women, youth, children, and the elderly in and around the camps and their shared experiences of violence and repression facilitated new modes of communication and cooperation among these groups, in addition to novel ways of collectively narrating the lived experiences of occupation. Palestinian women became visible agents of public, expressly political protest against the IDF occupation, its Lebanese militia allies, and frequently UNRWA.[18] In doing so, they effectively replaced the PLO and guerrilla organizations as the local social and political advocates for Palestinian civilians, segmenting political advocacy and military work in new ways.

Gendered Counterinsurgency and Civilian Narrative Networks

Shared narratives grounded by the gendered nature of occupation violence, the insecurity said violence propagated, and the perception that the IDF intentionally targeted civilians and civilian infrastructure all provided a discursive framework that facilitated the remapping of expressly civilian networks across political affiliations. Even in the contemporary era, interviewees from the southern camps repeatedly foregrounded our conversations by describing the loss, destruction, and violation of homes. Some people recounted, in detail, being unable to locate their home in the destruction and wandering through the ruins. Others described the experience of physically digging through the rubble of their homes with their bare hands to the point where they bled, all while searching for items such as children's clothing. Still others fixated on the loss of a special possession—for example, a new appliance such as a refrigerator that the family had saved for and then lost. News reports from the fall of 1982 reflect similar discursive patterns; one resident of Ain al-Hilweh told a United Press International reporter of the Israeli army: "I was hoping they'd be merciful . . . they destroyed our houses" (Nadler 1982).

The specific meanings that people associated with the physical devastation of and intrusions into their houses—the destruction of *homes* in both the material and the social senses (as fathers, husbands, uncles, sons, and brothers were in Ansar and as families were separated)—served as an accessible, emotion- and meaning-laden, collective frame for new political demands on actors such as the IDF and UNRWA.[19] Home raids became associated with random acts of violence, especially as the IDF used them in response to increasing guerrilla attacks through 1983 and 1984 (see chapter 3).

The continuing use of home raids continuously fed into a cross-cutting narrative focused on the violation of intimate, family space and of explicitly, brutal violence against residents of the camp that was fundamentally distinct from aerial bombardment. Mahmoud Zeidan (2017, 298–99) describes how this perception of violence shifted everyday domestic practices such as sleeping arrangements when Palestinians heard that Lebanese militias were coming to the camp or surrounding neighborhoods:

> We would sleep on the roof with our neighbors, who stayed with us for a long time. Our bedrooms and living room were on the ground floor. The living room contained two sofas that would turn into beds, where my brother and a guest would sleep, whether a relative, a neighbor, or a friend, and we had a large library in the living room, and three win-

dows: one looking toward the house, one overlooking our neighbor Abu Salah's yard, and another overlooking my aunt's yard. We used to keep those windows open, but that day we had to close them and we never reopened them. We stopped sleeping on the ground floor, fearing a sudden attack and being found by the murderers.

My sister and I were terrified of being slaughtered. That night I felt terrified more than any other time. The situation involves slaughter! I thought to myself. I was not afraid of shelling/bombing, because in bombings a human dies suddenly and without feeling pain, but death through slaughter takes time. And that's a different affair, one which causes more pain. We started recalling the slaughter scenes of sheep or chicken in regular or Eid al-Adha days. The slaughtered animal [*zabiha*] would twitch with its blood splattering. Our bodies would shiver at the scene.

These raids continued throughout the occupation and were repeatedly described by the underground newspaper *Sawt al-Mukhayyam* through 1984:

> The night of August 10, the Zionist occupation forces in the South raided the northeast area of Ain al-Hilweh, searching homes and emptying them of their contents under the guise of looking for weapons and explosives. Once the forces did not find what they were looking for, they gathered the residents in a neighborhood close by and interrogated them about the vandals among them, beating and cursing them. Before leaving the neighborhood, the Zionist elements shot above the heads of the detained to terrorize them and drove six camp residents in front of them [the forces] under the pretext of interrogating them. Armed forces also attacked a young man in Ta'amir and left him soaking in his blood in the street after they assumed he was dead.[20]

The underground newspaper's publication of articles that emphasized the tactics used in these raids, their operational fruitlessness, and their public brutality—especially the fact that houses were emptied or ransacked, that the soldiers did not find anything, and that they beat and cursed noncombatants—both reflect and help to reinforce the experience of these raids as a collective, unwarranted abuse suffered by the community as a whole. Even if an individual was not herself targeted, she could empathize with those whose homes and family had been.

The consistency and ongoing nature of this repertoire of violence prompted the repurposing and remapping of cross-cutting ties between women in and around Ain al-Hilweh. Civilians began to publicly and collectively invoke narratives based around gender, human rights, and humanitarian accountability. This collective action fostered the creation of new social ties via shared participation, narratives, and demands, eventually constituting a reconstituted network identity in its own right.[21] As in many contemporary movements in the region (Allam 2018, chap. 2), Palestinian women strategically capitalized upon, rather than avoiding, Western media stereotypes of women in the Middle East so as to bring attention to their very real vulnerability. For example, they began to cite the absence of men as the reason why the IDF and UNRWA were responsible for civilian communities' support and protection. Evoking the narratives of groups like Madres de Plaza de Mayo (Asociación Madres de Plaza de Mayo n.d.), their advocacy *as women* invoked broad, accessible, and heavily feminized themes that drew in a broad range of participants and was tailor made for international media. Residents of Ain al-Hilweh eventually began protesting conditions in the camp; attacks by the SLA, LF, and Kata'ib; and mass imprisonment.[22]

Local Advocacy, International Ties

Women in Ain al-Hilweh sought to make the ostensibly "collateral" damage of war visible and to demand accountability from both the IDF and the United Nations via organized sit-ins, demonstrations, protests, tent burnings, and road blockages.[23] Some of these actions became routinized events; for example, an article in *al-Safir* dated October 4, 1982, describes Palestinian women's daily protests at the Israeli army's general command center. Fatimah, the civil society worker, explicitly remembered marching in a demonstration to the Serail (a main government building) demanding to speak with the authorities in order to argue that the seven-year-olds in Ansar were not combatants. Other actions were one-offs. Another employee of the same community organization, Zahrah, recounted a story of women marching up to the Kata'ib office in Saida to complain about the militiamen—whom she describes as worse than the IDF—standing around the kindergarten with guns and kidnapping people from the camp. Though the officers there informed the women that the situation was "*hasabtu*"— essentially, their collective responsibility as Palestinians, given past violence committed by Palestinian guerrillas—Zahrah retorted that everyone was responsible for themselves and that she knew nothing about the fighters.[24] While the group won no concessions, for Palestinian women to directly confront Kata'ib to demand accountability was a significant shared risk and a political act in and of itself. Given these public, collective actions' growing visibility, informants working with the Israeli forces soon began infiltrating them. Later in her interview, Fatimah recalls what seems to be a different demonstration, when she and friends were there to demand their rights. She emphasizes the presence of collaborators and infiltrators, one of whom had a gun and another who started harassing her friend with the butt of a Kalashnikov rifle in front of children.[25]

As women developed new skill sets and reinforced connections to each other, they expanded the protest movement to the international stage by mounting information campaigns that established fresh ties to diplomatic as well as to humanitarian actors. A write-up from July 11, 1983, demonstrates these increasingly sophisticated tactics; by then, the women of Ain al-Hilweh and Saida were attempting to cut off major urban thoroughfares while sending press releases about the conditions in Ansar to human rights organizations, Arab governments, and the United Nations.[26] Employees of one community organization in Ain al-Hilweh deliberately cultivated its center as a space to share news and have conversations, inviting everyone they knew from the camp. They then began bringing journalists and humanitarians to interact with the residents of Ain al-Hilweh, in effect generating new ties between camp-based activists and international actors. Halimah, who was involved in this effort, underscores that this was how they at the organization, specifically, came to know foreigners.[27] Nonviolent public protests, the symbolic burning of what people saw as inadequate UNRWA-provided tents, and sharing information with human rights and political organizations thus became central common practices among Palestinian women in Saida.

These networks also explicitly channeled collective emotions such as fear, rage, and grief to call for accountability and protection; for example, on September 17, 1984, thousands of people demonstrated in memory of the Sabra and Shatila massacre.[28] *Sawt al-Mukhayyam* covered the event in detail, carefully outlining specific tactical and discursive repertoires:

> Ain al-Hilweh camp witnessed the largest march in the south since the Zionist invasion. It had more than ten thousand people holding Palestinian flags and black banners while speakers played national songs and announcements, calling for resistance against the occupation and their collaborators.
>
> Starting the morning of September 16, the camp had a general strike, all entrances and roads leading to the camp were blocked with burning tires and rocks. Palestinian flags were hung up on the entrance alongside black banners saying "We won't forget, won't allow another massacre."
>
> At 10 [a.m.], thousands gathered in Armed Struggle Square and began the protest, which lasted hours, going around the camp. They chanted against occupation and fascism. Flyers were distributed calling for revenge against the criminals, and promising martyrs their justice.[29]

The newspaper reveals clear evidence of the emergence of a broad-based Palestinian protest movement grounded by a clear set of skills, practices, and common narratives deployed in response to the occupation and militia violence: marching with Palestinian flags and black banners; broadcasting national songs; organizing strikes; burning tires; throwing rocks; chanting; and distributing literature. These are all signs of a network of protestors linked by shared, constitutive understandings of identity and experience. This nonviolent activism took place in an overarching environment of intense violence and movement fragmentation yet still demonstrated extensive local coordination and solidarity. Its members' efforts later complemented—intentionally or not—resurgent militant violence, particularly in its emphasis on identifying and resisting collaborators.

Collaboration and Community-Based Counterintelligence

In this context, the Israeli forces' and the Lebanese militias' expanding use of collaborators and constant attempts to recruit members of Palestinian communities seeded the environment with deep suspicion. The IDF's and Israeli intelligence agencies' approaches to managing Palestinian collaborators in Saida and Sur had long-term effects on Palestinian community relations and militant organizational structures, owing to the way that they shaped social networks. They shifted social interactions; people who lived in the southern camps during this time consistently emphasized intense fear, following up with comments emphasizing that the fear still didn't stop them from acting. In both archival footage and my own interviews, people describe staying in their homes more, not trusting acquaintances, and watching their neighbors carefully for signs of collaboration. In network terms, these practices indicate social fragmentation and fostered the closure rather than the expansion of social networks.

Coping with collaborators within community-based, civilian networks became a key aim in the camps. Yet ground-level responses to Palestinians who worked with Israeli forces were not regionally uniform. Rather, evidence shows that city- and camp-level variations in the Israelis' management of collaborators—and specifically how each set of regionalized tactical repertoires influenced community-level social network relations—directly shaped the evolution of organized counterintelligence capacities. Specifically, I demonstrate that while people in both Saida and Sur targeted collaborators with violence, whether or not a large number of collaborators were organized as a militia and were anonymous put distinct network mechanisms into action. Anonymity and collaborator groups' institutionalization spurred the emergence of civilian anticollaborator networks in Saida; I have found no evidence of the same level of institutionalization or coordination in Sur. The following sections examine this comparison in depth.

Understanding the Network Effects of Collaboration

Palestinians who collaborated with Israeli forces did so for a number of reasons. In addition to seeking power or personal revenge, many people were socially isolated, vulnerable, or even blackmailed. Though people hated and resented collaborators, some also sought help from them; Mahmoud Zeidan (2017, 299) explains the dynamic as being one where:

> Fear was suffocating our lives, and the infiltration of [our community by] collaborators and their control over our community suffocated our lives even further. Some people would ask them to help get their sons out of prison, or to verify they are ok at Ansar prison, or would ask them for assistance, or to help them with various affairs such as receiving materials for construction, or a travel permit. And that is how their role in our daily lives and securing our basic needs became increasingly institutionalized.

In the context of military occupation, physical destruction, economic uncertainty, mass incarceration, and extreme poverty, broad segments of the population often had extremely limited choices if they wanted to survive—or if they believed a relative's survival seemed contingent upon their cooperation. However, as scholars of civil war violence such as Stathis Kalyvas (2003, 2006) and Laia Balcells (2017) would predict, others were simply opportunistic, given the environment of the occupation; they used collaboration to seek status, power, or economic rewards.

Across the camps in Saida and Sur, my interlocutors emphasized that resisting collaboration frequently demanded choices that severed potentially useful relationships. In an environment characterized by mistrust and social atomization, high-risk, public performances of noncooperation could, however, convey key signals to a broad segment of the population when direct, reliable communication was difficult, thus reinforcing a resister's position and trustworthy reputation. Yusif, for example, recalled a Lebanese neighbor's attempt to recruit him. A member of Kata'ib, the neighbor took to performing an intimidating role by "wearing dark glasses; he looked like *mukhabarat* [indicating government intelligence, whether civilian or military]." One day in fall 1982, the neighbor saw Yusif in public, gripped his elbow, and told Yusif to "walk with him in Saida and point out *fida'iyyin*"; in other words, he tried to use his ostensible position in overarching power structures and his social proximity to pressure Yusif to denounce other Palestinians, a move that would have irreversibly shifted Yusif's own position within Palestinian social networks. Yusif told me that he escorted the neighbor to the entrance of Old Saida, where many pro-resistance fighters hid, because "they [Israelis and Lebanese militiamen] were all afraid of Old Saida." In his telling of the story, Yusif then attacked the man in the street and darted into the neighborhood, where he could be protected.[30] He remained in Old Saida for some time after the incident. Yusif's experience underscores both the cost he paid for refusal (mobility restrictions, as well as the protection and material rewards he might have received from collaborating) and his choice to publicly pay it in order to send a message to his attacker as well as to those with sympathies similar to his own. The fact that people also witnessed these public acts increased trust in Yusif across segments of the community, priming him for future clandestine roles.

The incentives to inform and the prices people paid to avoid collaboration typified the complex and painful choices the Israeli occupation forced many Palestinians and Lebanese to make. My interlocutors emphasized that violence was often driven by hyperlocal and often intimate factors, which in many ways meant that its effects reverberated through personal as well as professional relationships. Emphasizing how the IDF explicitly leveraged collaborators' social embeddedness to eliminate hard-to-reach "problematic" actors, Abu Houli, the former commando from Burj al-Shamali, relayed the story of a Popular Front for the Liberation of Palestine (PFLP) officer whom the Israelis assassinated with the help of the man's son, who was himself an officer in a different leftist faction. The two men's immediate family, most of whom were politically active, either strongly suspected or knew about the son's role in the assassination at the time. Using the man's son had three effects: (1) it demonstrated the very real threat of the IDF infiltrating even familial relationships, emphasizing the Israeli forces' ability to reach into people's homes and pick off their enemies; (2) it isolated the son from his kin, making him further dependent on the IDF for protection; and (3) it heightened tensions both between the PFLP and the son's faction and within the son's faction. Abu Houli's choice to reveal this detail underscored an underrecognized aspect of this particular tactic: that while the IDF only targeted the PFLP officer and clearly chose him because of his role in a militant group, killing him by enlisting his son as a co-assassin produced a very different understanding of the act than if the IDF had deployed a Special Forces team. The act represented the son's violation of intimate kinship relations as well as the IDF's ability to shift loyalties and shatter even the most intimate of networks; it was extraordinarily personal and reverberated through kinship and political networks in a distinct way as a result.[31]

The Israeli forces also attempted to recruit or develop informants across social domains, including within UNRWA and other local Palestinian governing bodies. This move weakened trust-based relationships among Palestinians, the UN body tasked with their education and healthcare, and the few potentially representative bodies that existed. Foreign aid workers repeatedly recorded instances when the IDF attempted to recruit UNRWA workers as collaborators in Saida. For example, according to AFSC documents, the IDF attempted to influence the UN's Siblin Vocational Training Center to hire a principal of its choosing and then pressured the principal who was chosen to allow it access to students.[32] While a local committee called the Palestinian Social and Humanitarian Committee superficially appeared to work on behalf of Palestinians, e.g., by demanding that the IDF increase patrols in order to cut the right-wing Lebanese militias' attacks on Palestinian civilians, a handwritten note on an AFSC translation of an *al-Safir* article that mentions the group comments that "[t]his committee—in its make up and its ties with the Israelis—is taking on definite Village League qualities."[33] Created in the late 1970s, the Village Leagues were Palestinian governance bodies in the Occupied Territories headed by tribal elders who worked with the Israeli military. Likely due to the sensitivity of the topic and the way that it implicated contemporary Palestinian organizations, my interlocutors did not mention the apparent collaboration of at least some members of UNRWA in Saida.

Cross-Generational Counterintelligence Networks in Ain al-Hilweh

In Ain al-Hilweh, initial collaborator anonymity profoundly heightened distrust in social networks, resulting in the remapping of preexisting social relationships into generationally as well as gender-defined, task-oriented cliques. The IDF formalized and routinized ties among members of its collaborator network in the camp, creating a uniformed militia dubbed the "Palestinian National Guard" (PNG), which policed the camp and denounced political activists. The top-down creation of this organization suggests the IDF believed that providing collaborators with power, socialization, camaraderie, and support would help the occupation forces to maintain control. It also enabled them to leverage the PNG as a tactical force both within the confines of the camp and in neighboring Saida. The PNG forces do not appear to have been particularly professionalized or indoctrinated; in line with theories of armed group socialization, residents of the camp reported frequent and expressly gendered civilian abuse (E. J. Wood 2006b, 2009; D. K. Cohen 2016; Hoover Green 2018). Hala, who was a civilian and student in the early years of the occupation, recalled having to traverse a checkpoint at the entry to the camp manned by spies who would regularly stop and harass girls, describing the experience as "every day, you pay the toll [*kil yawm, tidfaa ajaar tariq*]."³⁴ For Hala and other girls, encounters such as these represented a particular difficulty of navigating the militarized city and added a dimension to how they understood the threats the PNG posed.

In some cases, the IDF simply chose what Mahmoud Zeidan (2017, 299) refers to as "the thugs [*zuʿaran*], drug addicts, and those with a bad reputation to be its eyes."³⁵ Yet, it also recruited or coerced members of civil society, UNRWA, and local leaders to collaborate in far less public ways. Not knowing anonymous PNG and civilian collaborators' locations in social networks forced people to be extra careful in how and with whom they shared information, in addition to whom they critiqued, complained about, or otherwise confronted (given the potential for revenge). This shift in how people understood their relationships with friends, neighbors, and even kin spurred the emergence of a decentralized, grassroots, explicitly anticollaborator network that divided roles across age groups. While older members of the community educated children about the risks collaborators posed, youth and young men targeted collaborators with unmasking and, along with the rest of their families, pushed back with everyday resistance techniques. Publicly unmasking collaborators allowed underground guerrillas (see chapter 4) to move in and target collaborators with lethal violence.

The PNG's actions in the community generated broad fear alongside intense resentment, prompting small, nonviolent acts of resistance and defiance that involved entire families. Perhaps the most typically mentioned sensory representation of this time period among my interlocutors from Saida is the loud, aggressive, unexpected knock at the door. In interviews, several people mentioned refusing to open the door, booby trapping exits, wedging chairs against doors, and teaching children to pretend not to be home if someone knocked. These actions stood in contrast to the discursive euphemism some used to embody collaboration: "opening the door to Israel." The Israeli forces also delegated after-dark patrols in the camp to the PNG, likely because of the potential risk or, as Umm Karim put it, because the IDF soldiers were scared.³⁶ These nighttime forays amplified the acoustics of repression. Umm Karim and her daughter Hala recollected the PNG's nightly patrols as being marked by the sound of glass bottles shattering because the PNG guys were "posing/fronting a lot [*ytzaharu ktir*]"³⁷ and drinking alcohol on duty.³⁸ These nighttime patrols and arrests, in particular, terrified families and often inspired small confrontations. One woman recounted someone in her household yelling "outside, dog!" at the men who arrived for one of the family's sons. Though the family gave up the son, this move was understood as an act of control and dignity.³⁹

Both the Lebanese media and my interlocutors linked the PNG's creation with an uptick in assassinations, kidnappings, disappearances, and attacks on Palestinian political figures. The strong belief was that the group's organization and membership amplified possibilities for violence and abuse.[40] Almost everyone from Saida whom I asked about this time period remembered people they knew personally being assassinated, kidnapped, or disappeared. For example, Fadi, a former member of the DFLP, recalled the disappearances of both a member of the LCP's Central Committee and a member of an elite family affiliated with *al-Jamaʿa al-Islamiyya*. Fadi also associated previous personal vendettas with collaboration; he explicitly underscored the idea that "there was a lot of violence because of revenge."[41] In this regard, the environment in South Lebanon facilitated the enactment of personal feuds for superficially political reasons; in other words, Palestinian and Lebanese militants used the macro-cleavages of conflict to facilitate personal ends, an outcome predicted by classic civil war scholarship (Kalyvas 2006).

People in Ain al-Hilweh repeatedly relayed that the PNG's members targeted people without cause and violated the rules of war. "They would take anyone, even children. . . . we felt it could be anyone who could be taken" notes Fatimah.[42] For instance, Halimah and Fatimah, who worked together in a civil society organization, recall a colleague named Umm Nizar being taken from the office by Palestinian men wearing civilian clothing while Israeli soldiers waited in a jeep outside. In the POHA interview, they debate the extent to which people knew the men as collaborators. Their ongoing conversation about a colleague's arrest in the office emphasizes how even people who worked closely together might not have shared the same connections or access to information regarding who was an actual collaborator:

> FATIMAH: People knew who they were.
> HALIMAH: I didn't know, they were wearing civilian clothes!
> FATIMAH: I knew them, those . . . it was known that they were working as collaborators, that they were collaborating with Israel.

Fatimah goes on to emphasize that the men demanded that Umm Nizar accompany them to the Serail as the woman's colleagues cried and pleaded with them, demanded that they take everyone, and invoked norms by arguing that the men couldn't take people from a school and that the targeted woman wasn't with a faction.[43]

The degree of fear, resentment, and uncertainty the PNG fostered in Saida created urgent, collective incentives for civilian communities to unmask, isolate, and neutralize informants. In the absence of robust military counterintelligence, the actions of identifying, locating, frustrating, marking, and revealing collaborators in their midst fell to children, youth, women, and elderly civilians. To do so, Palestinian activists mobilized along generational lines, with the various age groups assuming distinct roles.

Resisting collaborators involved repurposing and remapping close relations by laying new channels of knowledge transmission and socialization onto them. Parents, community workers, and teachers actively developed age-appropriate means of teaching young children how to cope with the presence of collaborators. These efforts relied on the plasticity of everyday ties such as those between teachers and students and between parents and children to remap new networks of anticollaborator and anti-occupation practices and norms. Fatimah explains that children were a particular concern because they repeat what they hear adults say. She outlines how teachers instructed children who attended school at her organization not to tell secrets, how to behave in the community, not to be afraid, how to stay strong and be proud. One method teachers used to instill these values was storytelling, which often featured a Palestinian resistance fighter as the main character but cast the child as a hero helping the revolution. Fatimah shares one storyline (paraphrased):

> I'm telling them the story of a resistance fighter [*fida'yi*]. There's a guerrilla who is going to do an operation, he comes to the door, says I'm Palestinian like you [*zayii, zayik*], and he hides. Israel comes to the door, the kid says there is no one here, mama is not home, and he goes away.[44]

Zeidan, too, references the deliberate socialization of children, but by masked, resistance-affiliated youth and fighters who started coming at night, pretended to arrest the children, and then let them go. Yet rather than impressing upon kids that one group was bad and one was good, Zeidan (2017, 300) writes that it taught them "we didn't know who was with us or against us." Quite simply, children often feared anyone who wore a mask, a concept he calls "foreign" to the community, because of the ways that masked people sought to control people's lives.

Cross-generational, remapped quotidian connections facilitated the spread of new norms and practices—even those as simple as "don't open the door" or "trust no one" in a community where doors had previously been kept open—that supported community-based security and counterintelligence. Stories such as these taught even very young children not to open doors to strangers—with the understanding that the guerrilla was Palestinian, "like" the child, and not a stranger—and not to tell people if there was a weapon in the house, and above all not to talk and not to answer people's questions.

For a child, society was simply laid out as including two networks—good actors and bad actors—with the understanding that the children might not be able to discern the difference. Learning exchanges taught children how to be *appropriately* suspicious, given the networks in which they were embedded, and considering their cognitive capabilities. Yet at the same time, community workers insisted that children had to simultaneously be comforted and supported, particularly because children were terrified of the shelling and because many had fathers in jail. The underlying implication of this approach is that children who had psychological and social support were better equipped to deal with coercive situations. While these changes in everyday networks would not manifest in a material analysis of network structure—children had connections to the same people as before the war—the very content of their relationships with people such as teachers changed due to the active repurposing of those relationships for protective and resistance ends.

By contrast, acts of retribution, whether a threat, beating, or homicide, remained predominantly the purview of older individuals with factional affiliations and salaries, though not necessarily former combatants. By the summer of 1983, small, reconsolidated cliques of underground militants were clashing with members of the PNG in Ain al-Hilweh, bombing shops that provided goods and services to the IDF, and assassinating collaborators.[45] A cyclical pattern of attacks developed between the PNG and these underground cadres.[46] Evidence indicates that children and youth who were prior members of groups such as scouting organizations and culture clubs played a central role in identifying and these targets. Newspaper reports from the era indicate that resurgent youth wings of Palestinian political organizations began posting flyers bearing the images of suspected Israeli collaborators around the camps.[47] Anticollaborator violence escalated throughout 1983 and 1984, eventually attracting the attention of international reporters. For example, in November 1984, an Associated Press wire report covered the apparent assassination of two Palestinian collaborators in Ain al-Hilweh by what it describes as a previously unknown, underground group calling itself "The People's Court, Forces of the Palestinian Martyrs." The wire relays that the group circulated a printed statement in the camp shortly following the attacks that read: "This is a warning. Every other collaborator with the enemy should leave the camp or he will executed, too" (Associated Press 1984).

The reconsolidated anticollaborator network relied on specific, shared norms—skills that were specific to certain age cohorts and level of closeness to the factions—and the faith that completing one's tasks would set the stage for the next steps in the process. Anticollaborator efforts did not rely on direct communication or top-down orders between all segments of these networks. Rather, they seem to have operated largely based on the assumption that one task-driven clique would take care of its job and then leave the next step to others; everyone operated on a need-to-know basis. Children didn't let anyone but people "like them" into the house and were appropriately suspicious of anyone wearing a mask. Women blocked doors and hurled insults at home invaders. Youth and women publicly identified collaborators and then stepped back for militants to assassinate them. Few people were directly in touch with active guerrillas, protecting both them and civilians; the one hint people had was whether a family member or neighbor stopped sleeping at home or attending evening activities (Zeidan 2017, 299–300). Even high-ranking officers did not know the identities of civilians in the anticollaborator network. For example, Bassam, the editor of *Sawt al-Mukhayyam*, remembered an old woman—he never knew her name or where she lived—who used to "conveniently" drop papers or groceries whenever a collaborator walked past her in the street, thus revealing the agent to anyone nearby who knew the proper signal.[48] All he knew was to look for her signal.

Negotiating with the Devil You Know in Sur

In the Sur camps, IDF soldiers maintained a more on-the-ground presence rather than delegating control to an institutionalized collaborator militia and informants. In contrast to Ain al-Hilweh, where PNG members were institutionalized, uniformed, and often anonymous, a comparative lack of collaborators' anonymity in Rashidiyeh, Burj al-Shamali, and al-Buss led to different forms of anticollaborator organizing and action. In Rashidiyeh, for example, the IDF manned a base within the camp and patrolled its roads; collaborators were largely known, not uniformed, and were not operationally independent. Moreover, according to one AFSC report, the extent of efforts to recruit collaborators was not as far-ranging:

> UNRWA is not overtly involved in the collaboration [handwritten note inserted: "with Israel"] as it is in Sidon, but is handicapped in its job by the persons described. The situation is more stable in Tyre as far as camp structures go, but the IDF wield a freer hand as international pressure is less and the camps are more integrated and smaller than Ein el Hilweh (Sidon). In addition, there is not the concentration of intelligentsia in the Tyre [Sur] camps as we see in Sidon [Saida] and therefore the collaboration does not have the complexities of the more subvert [sic] approach of the doctors and teachers of Ein el Hilweh [Ain al-Hilweh].[49]

This report indicates a fundamentally different set of social conditions in Rashidiyeh in comparison to Ain al-Hilweh. Specifically, it compares the IDF's more direct interactions with the inhabitants of Rashidiyeh to those it pursued in Ain al-Hilweh, notes that UNRWA has not been compromised to the same degree, and links the situation in the camp to the comparative lack of international pressure.

These two models elicited distinct responses from civilian populations, in part because they produced very different collective experiences of surveillance. The IDF relied on a more personalistic structure in Sur than the PNG's paramilitary-like organization. Unlike in Ain al-Hilweh, the IDP minimally regulated the local strongmen who collaborated with them. In Rashidiyeh, for example, the primary IDF contact, Abu [Jaradh], is described as being poorly disciplined (approaching an AFSC worker "with alcohol clearly on his breath"), notorious for attacking UNRWA officials and other humanitarian workers, and adept at extorting money from the camp's residents.[50] After Abu [Jaradh] threatened an AFSC representative with a pistol in the camp, the humanitarian worker wrote in internal correspondence that:

> The tactics the IDF use to keep the people under their control show the lack of real concern for the welfare of the Palestinians. The [IDF] officer was pleased when I told him I had been scared of his "agent"—as I am in the face of any angry, drunk and armed person. The disreputable thugs and extorsionists [sic] like Abu [Jaradh] whom the IDF have chosen as quislings indicate the intent of the IDF to use division and dissention among the Palestinians to strengthen their hold on the camps.[51]

These conditions, among others, spurred distinct processes of network remapping and reconsolidation in Sur. That is, while people both in Sur and in Saida clearly feared collaborators, their specific experiences and subsequent network responses diverged. Knowing the network positions inhabited by collaborator strongmen and their associates in Rashidiyeh often had the unexpected effect of keeping those persons alive and social relations more stable. General awareness of collaborators' roles across social domains—collaborator, shop owner, cousin of an important factional officer—meant that people in Sur could interact with them accordingly whether at home, at a neighbor's house, or at a store without the ambiguity that people in Saida faced. In Sur, people also staged lethal, public attacks on both Israeli forces and collaborators; given the different geography and demography of the city, Palestinian efforts also overlapped more frequently with those of leftist and Islamist Lebanese militant organizations such as Hizbullah, Amal, and the Syrian Socialist National Party. Efforts in Sur thus sought to remove collaborators from Palestinian social networks through social isolation, intimidation, flight, and, in some cases, death.

In certain ways, these efforts did mirror the violence that emerged in Ain al-Hilweh. For instance, in al-Buss, a camp in the heart of Sur, civilians described a situation that felt unpredictable and out-of-control. Abu Haytham, then a teacher in the camp, recalled seeing both Israeli and Palestinian bodies in the streets following Palestinian guerrilla operations. When I asked how the occupation affected his school, he explained that "teaching started again, but there was always fighting. I sometimes went home very late because we couldn't leave the school due to fighting. It would go into the night, sometimes, and it was too dangerous to go out."[52]

However, there were also more nuanced means through which Sur-based activists worked to disembed or simply counterbalance informants, making them less effective sources while leaving them alive. In Rashidiyeh, semipublic knowledge of the main collaborators' identities seems to have meant that militants carefully targeted the collaborators themselves along with people in their immediate networks. As one report noted: "Two handgrenades have been thrown in Abu [Jaradh's] direction, one injuring his wife and one debilitating a fellow collaborator."[53] Here, the goal was to neutralize the source and threaten his immediate support network. These grenade attacks may well have been attempted assassinations. However, several former militants made it clear to me that simply knowing who collaborators were, and isolating them either with or without their knowledge, could have a steadying effect on social relations. People knew to behave with caution around those individuals or to avoid them—whether it was the son who betrayed his father or the local strongman—so that doing very little, or even nothing, became viable tactical options. Harassing or subtly isolating an informant without actively removing them from service to the IDF, as well as targeting family members who knew of their position, facilitated community solidarity, demonstrated organizational resolve, acted as a warning to potential future informants, and prevented recognized collaborators' replacement with unknown parties.

In many ways, Israeli occupation and counterinsurgency tactics worked against both its own and its allies' attempts to control Palestinian populations. Mass incarceration, the physical destruction of homes and communities, and collaboration all activated community-level, civilian networks in South Lebanon. However, local repertoires of violence produced divergent organizational outcomes in Saida versus in Sur. While not initially visible to outsiders, the way that collaborators' presence affected social networks and disrupted home life activated cross-generational civilian networks that became collectively focused on identifying and deterring collaborators. There were subtle differences between how communities in Saida and Sur handled these tasks; these distinctions stemmed from whether civilians knew the identities of key collaborators (as in Sur) or whether they were anonymous members of the Palestinian National Guard (as in Saida). Recent research similarly demonstrates that tactics of state repression designed to fragment local coordination and stymie organizing, such as the Israeli government's extensive use of checkpoints in the West Bank, simply reshape resistance networks and often prompt further violence (Gade 2020).

The Palestinian experience in South Lebanon instead indicates that forms of community-based defense can both emerge from grassroots relational processes and operate independently from, if in a complementary fashion to, formal militant organizations. These networks operate in a distinct manner from community-centric neutrality enforcement and dispute resolution committees (Kaplan 2013; 2017) and have different aims from communities that resist rebel rule (Arjona 2015). Rather, Palestinian community defense networks in South Lebanon actively sought to combat three immediate threats to civilian welfare: Israeli forces' and Lebanese militia infiltration, shelter and livelihoods, and mass incarceration. They did not rely exclusively or even predominantly on trust-based networks. But, while socially fragmented and suspicious of each other, civilians still mobilized for high-risk action. They did so based on a broad, collective frame characterized by intense, shared sentiments of fear, grief, resentment, solidarity, and vulnerability—a surprising assessment, given past findings that fear drives risk aversion and depresses political activity.[54] In doing so, civilians influenced a larger trajectory of conflict by denying the IDF and its Lebanese allies intelligence, by compelling belligerents to expend resources in attempting to control them, and by internationalizing advocacy campaigns, bringing outside attention to the plight of Palestinians in South Lebanon.

6

THE FACE OF THE CAMPS
Leadership and Loyalty in Combat Units

Yasir Arafat's image is an omnipresent sight in Palestinian communities in Lebanon. His visage invariably looks down from PLO office walls. Fatah cadres in the camps spend hours designing and hand-making frames for poster-sized prints of his face using spare kaffiyehs and Palestinian flags. Elite officers often display high-quality, glass-protected portraits in their workspaces. Stencils of the "Old Man's" face flutter on yellow flags above party offices and adorn the uneven surfaces of walls in camp alleyways. In their homes, retired militants proudly hang pictures of themselves shaking Arafat's hand at a rally, receiving a plaque, or touring military installations at his side. My interlocutor's one-year-old baby, when asked who the man in the photo was, readily identified Arafat as "Abu Wa Wa," *wa wa* being the Arabic version of the English "boo-boo." Not yet old enough to understand death, the child simply associated Arafat with being hurt or wounded.

Few Palestinian leaders approach this particular status of visual icon. Others who inhabit office walls and whose pictures feature on banners at camp entrances—the PFLP's Leila Khaled, Hamas's Shaykh Yassin, the PFLP's George Habash, Fatah's Dalal al-Mughrabi, and Fatah's Abu Jihad (Khalil al-Wazir), for example—are still not as ubiquitous as Arafat. As a consequence, it can initially be surprising, given the competition, to see small, modestly displayed, often original photos of a different bearded man around Fatah offices in Lebanon. His face—often enlarged from grainy, creased, decades-old prints—appears on banners at many party and PLO events. In recent years, dozens of photographs of the same bearded man were scanned and uploaded to a Facebook page titled "The Martyr, the Leader Ali Abu Tawq" [*al-shahid al-qaʾid Ali Abu Tawq*].[1]

In many ways, Ali Abu Tawq, the man in these photos, could be the poster child for a successful career in the Palestinian National Movement. According to the Facebook page, Abu Tawq was born on July 7, 1950, to a family from Haifa then living in Homs, Syria. He joined Fatah at the age of 16 or 17 and spent his early career active in student unions and Palestinian militias in Jordan. In 1971, he fought in the battles of Black September. By 1972, he had relocated to Lebanon. Elected to the General Union of Palestinian Students, he set about constructing relationships with Lebanese student organizations. Abu Tawq fought in early engagements of the Lebanese Civil War and participated in operations against the IDF invasion in 1978. During the 1982 invasion, he served around Nabatiyeh with Fatah's Jarmaq Battalion as an operations and logistics officer in the PLA. Drawing on specialized training he received in China, Abu Tawq helped construct the famous system of subterranean earthworks under Beaufort Castle, a strategic asset that towers above the Israeli border southeast of Nabatiyeh (see Y. Sayigh 1997, 881). Following the PLO and guerrilla organizations' defeat in 1982, Abu Tawq transformed into a full-fledged guerrilla fighter. He served in clandestine armed cells in South Lebanon before moving to Trablous to help defend the camps there against a mutiny by Fatah dissidents led by Colonel Saied al-Muragha.[2] By 1983, Abu Tawq was a key figure in the secret supply network that supported underground guerrilla cells in Beirut and South Lebanon.

In short, Ali Abu Tawq had a long, distinguished political and military career that introduced him to a broad array of Palestinian and Lebanese activists and militants. He had experience in both combat and logistics as well as conventional and guerrilla warfare. Yet Abu Tawq is best known for commanding Shatila's and Burj al-Barajneh's defenses during the War of the Camps from 1985 until his assassination in 1987.

Abu Tawq is a paradox when it comes to theories of military socialization and discipline. He joined voluntarily, completed multiple modes of formal indoctrination, participated in intensive military training, and consistently demonstrated respect for military discipline, all traits associated with military obedience and loyalty (Hoover Green 2017, 2018). In line with theories of military socialization and norm construction (Manekin 2017, 609–11, and 2020), Abu Tawq's everyday social affiliations reinforced his commitment to Fatah and the PLO. Yet during the War of the Camps, when the Lebanese militia Amal, backed by the Syrian government and elements of the Lebanese military, besieged Palestinian refugee camps with the goal of expelling pro-Arafat guerrillas, Abu Tawq repeatedly bent the rules, violated the spirit of the orders he was given, engaged in insubordinate behavior, and refused exiled leaders' direct commands. This profile put Abu Tawq in direct opposition to Yasir Arafat himself. However, during a three-hour, coffee-fueled midnight debate about the state of the current Palestinian leadership, a regional-level Fatah officer told me that Abu Tawq is recognized and respected because "No one could say 'no' to Abu Ammar [Yasir Arafat]. But Ali Abu Tawq said 'no.'"[3]

Rather than being shunned within Fatah for his public, documented, and at times game-changing insubordination toward Arafat, Abu Tawq has emerged as a hero, an idol, and a symbol for many Palestinians throughout Lebanon, including non-Fatah members. Instead of people suppressing or banning tributes to the man who unapologetically disobeyed Arafat, Abu Tawq's face seems to be featured in more official events every year. Why is the man who defied Arafat revered and not reviled?

Abu Tawq was not the only militant in Beirut to disobey orders during the War of the Camps. In fact, disobedience was relatively commonplace across factions in the largest Beirut camps, Burj al-Barajneh and Shatila. According to firsthand interview accounts, memoirs, and secondary literature, militants from nearly every faction repeatedly defied discrete top-down operational orders—e.g., orders to fire on Lebanese militia positions—from exiled leaders. Despite alliance structures that pitted Fatah members against affiliates of the Palestinian National Salvation Front (PNSF)—a coalition of anti-Arafatist parties formed in 1985 that included the PFLP, PFLP-GC, PPSF, Fatah al-Intifada, al-Sa'iqa, and a wing of the PLF—militants often cooperated on matters of camp defense and community survival. Unlike in Saida, militants institutionalized cross-factional defensive fronts in both camps, which facilitated community protection in spite of the clear, competing rationalist power considerations that many scholars argue drive militant behavior (Christia 2013; P. Krause 2017).

This chapter traces the remapping of independent factional combat apparatuses and the emergence of camp-level shared defensive fronts in Beirut in response to citywide repertoires of violence between 1982 and 1988. Patterns of violence against Beirut-based Palestinians from 1982 to 1985, specifically those surrounding the Sabra and Shatila massacre and the "mopping-up" campaigns in fall 1982, activated neighborhood-level ties. Militants then repurposed kinship and marriage ties to share money and information between various geographic locations, a move that facilitated the remapping of combatant networks into locally based cells that predominantly women couriers linked across neighborhoods. The PLO's subsequent co-optation and strengthening of these underground operations (e.g., by adding flows of money and official orders) situated Abu Tawq, who assumed an official role in this hybrid apparatus, as a broker between community-level, cross-factional networks and formal command hierarchies. In effect, he became a robust actor—that is, someone who acts as a broker between two networks based in distinct constitutive domains (Padgett and Ansell 1993), affording him considerable power among Palestinian militants in Lebanon.

The War of the Camps (1985–1988) challenged exiled Palestinian elites' attempts to assert command and control via the Beirut underground. Yet this difficulty was not due to poor military training or to lack of political education. Rather, I argue that the context of the deployment—specifically, operating among civilian communities during a siege—interacted with militants' local identities and also with their past guerrilla socialization to produce disobedience.[4] That is, siege violence activated ground-level networks of people linked by previous socialization practices that broadly emphasized civic engagement, Palestinian nationalism, and community defense. This interaction prompted similar practices of disobedience across factions as a result of shifting logics of appropriateness, a process that has been observed in other settings (Manekin 2017, 610–11). Specifically, when the Syrian-allied Lebanese militia Amal targeted Shatila and Burj al-Barajneh from 1985 to 1988, Palestinian guerrillas were primed to understand violence in terms of threats to the entire Palestinian community, rather than in factionalized terms. Despite the tension between military socialization and reality, guerrillas applied and reinterpreted aspects of their training to understand the situation they were in, leaning on socialization and past networks rather than top-down orders via the formal chain of command.

Militants in Beirut faced tensions between their organizational affiliations, command hierarchies, and financial networks on the one hand, and their community identifications, guerrilla training, and conflict environments on the other. Under the guidance of officers such as Abu Tawq and the PFLP's Abu Mujahid, militants repurposed various types of quotidian ties—such as those between neighbors and former classmates—and coordinated military operations across cross-factional, allied fronts in Shatila and Burj al-Barajneh. These locally evolved, remapped organizational forms drove priorities that came into direct competition with formal, transnational military hierarchies. Abu Tawq, as well as other local commanders, experienced role strain (Hundman and Parkinson 2019, 651–53) when given orders that contravened their feelings of obligation and loyalty to local troops and communities. Their decisions to disobey produced collective insubordination that in turn reinforced these emergent hybrid organizational forms. The result was an adaptive process through which local cadres managed conflict within larger organizational systems. As Palestinian militant groups' exiled leaderships issued orders from Tunis and Damascus, their commands clashed not only with local fighters' feelings of moral obligation to their communities, but also with the tactical decision-making of newly emergent organizations.

Militant Adaptation in Beirut, 1982–1985

After the 1982 evacuation of Beirut, Palestinians lacked direct communication with the PLO leadership and with guerrilla groups' exiled command apparatuses. Members consequently focused on reestablishing relationships with each other on the ground. News of the Sabra and Shatila massacre (see chapter 3) activated community-level networks. Though the guerrilla factions' formal communications chains were mostly silent, neighbors, friends, and families quickly spread word of "something horrible" happening at Sabra and Shatila. The information that flowed through them contained few details, some inaccuracies, and many ambiguities, all of which only heightened the perception of immediate collective threat. Aisha, for example, remembered that people rushed to Burj al-Barajneh saying that a massacre was happening, and that Israel was killing people; the role of Kata'ib and SLA militiamen was initially lost in the version relayed to her. Emphasizing the camp population's related feelings of exposure and vulnerability, Aisha described an armed panopticon that led Palestinians in her neighborhood to believe that they were next: "There were [Israeli] tanks on the perimeter of the camp, in the neighborhood close to the camp, and in its surroundings."[5]

For Palestinian refugees remaining in Beirut, the massacre at Sabra and Shatila echoed the 1976 massacres at Tel al-Za'tar, Jisr al-Pasha, and Maslakh-Karantina in East Beirut. People living in the camps, in particular, understood the Sabra and Shatila massacre as proof that they had to collectively organize to protect themselves in the absence of the recently departed fighters.[6] By early 1983, small groups consisting mostly of men began to meet covertly in private homes to discuss community defense.[7]

Nader's Story

The personal narrative Nader conveyed to me captures many of the initiatives that underground militants explored and the ways they worked to adapt prior organizational structures to new realities. By 1982, Nader, like many of his colleagues, had a long history of activism and extensive social ties at his disposal. In 1970, when he was eleven years old, he was already a member of the local chapter of the military scouts, where he received basic combat training. When the April 13, 1975, bus massacre happened near his East Beirut neighborhood, he quit school and joined the local militia along with his brothers, an uncle, and a grandfather. Nader fought in Maslakh in January 1976 and during the same year's sieges of Tel al-Za'tar and Jisr al-Pasha. He eventually joined Force 17, the special forces brigade that comprised Yasir Arafat's bodyguards. Post-September 1982, his military history and the fact that he was a known member of Fatah severely limited Nader's movement and ability to communicate with his colleagues.

Nader described a process whereby members of the fledgling underground network added content to preexisting quotidian relationships or established new ties in the interest of local organizing. In 1983, despite the restrictions placed upon Palestinian men, Nader and a small group of local militants and activists started holding secret meetings in their houses. He explained that after the massacre at Sabra and Shatila, "We wanted to start again, so we made very small, secret groups." They recruited subtly—in his word, "indirectly." When he or another militant ran into someone on the street, they would chat with them for a while and look for signs that they wanted to be politically active. Nader or another vetted militant would then invite the person to a meeting to discuss things. Whenever they met, they'd have coffee, music, and food, to make it seem "normal" if an enemy was nearby. Nader and his friends also had an advantage because, as he explained, the Israelis thought that the neighborhood where he lived was Christian and thus "didn't know about it."[8]

Leveraging Connectedness

In 1983 and 1984, amid ongoing civil war violence, members of these clandestine cells began forming small, secret militias in West Beirut. Unlike in South Lebanon, many members had not previously been involved in combat actions; they mobilized because they felt that Palestinian communities were threatened and required organized protection. While these militants eventually came to work at least partially in tandem with the exiled leadership in Tunis, they were focused first on creating information chains and defensive capabilities rather than assuming the trappings of political affiliation.

These militia members leveraged two sets of ties to achieve this end. First, members of the underground worked to connect small, localized cells such as Nader's by remapping personal ties with comparatively mobile female kin and co-cadres, appointing women as couriers, cash smugglers, and intelligence officers. With women serving as city-level brokers between clandestine cells, these groups quickly consolidated a reliable organizational infrastructure on which to base riskier and more broad-reaching activities. Second, using the broader social and geographic reach that the mixed-affiliation, local, cell-based structure afforded, Beirut-based Palestinian militants contacted former colleagues among Lebanese fighters who had served in the LNM, the PSP, or Amal, repurposing and remapping what had previously been high-level alliances to more local ends.

With Lebanese allies and a reliable, redundant communication network based on personal ties to women cadres, local Palestinian militants were able to then connect with higher-ups in Trablous and overseas. They began moving weapons and PLO cash into West Beirut. In particular, the PLO and Fatah co-opted small militant cells such as Nader's to reinfiltrate fighters such as Ali Abu Tawq into Beirut.[9] The cell structure in Beirut was much looser than in South Lebanon; local commanders would be responsible for distributing salaries to between fifty-five and sixty-five people, a system that became vulnerable to corruption and abuse as local leaders added "ghost cadres" to the payrolls.[10] The PLO also opened a "bridge" between Tunis and Beirut that led through Cyprus. Paying US$50,000 a launch, the PLO started to send fighters through Beirut's fifth port and through the northern port of Jounieh (Picard 2002, 133), both controlled by Lebanese Christian militias. Capitalizing on increased money flows as well as personal relationships with Lebanese militia members, operatives bribed the Christian militias and Amal to allow fighters into West Beirut and the refugee camps.[11] One former high-level PLO intelligence officer who sneaked into Lebanon via Cyprus during this time relayed that he, like others of his rank, passed through Jounieh using forged documents directly provided by the Lebanese Forces and Kata'ib, a process facilitated by bribery.[12]

Lebanese groups such as the PSP, the Murabitoun, and Amal were mobilizing against the Lebanese government and the Multinational Forces (MNF). In August 1983, leftists from these militias regained control of southwestern Beirut from the government (Hanf 1994, 284). Palestinians and the leftist Lebanese militias closely supported each other in these efforts. For instance, Palestinian fighters aided the PSP in its war against the Lebanese Forces and Kata'ib in the Shouf (Hanf 1994, 288). I interviewed one former guerrilla who fought under direct PSP command at this time and who simultaneously used this position to smuggle Palestinian fida'iyyin into Beirut. Another interviewee lost a close relative who fought with the PSP when the American navy shelled the Shouf. Resistance to the regime came to a head on February 6, 1984, when this coalition expelled both the government and right-wing Christian militias from West Beirut and took control of the streets.

The 1984 collapse of the Lebanese government and the withdrawal of the MNF afforded Palestinian militants in Beirut new opportunities to organize. Specifically, it allowed the trickle of returnees to increase, adding personnel to emergent organizations and increasing the weapons and money flowing through local ties. According to Yezid Sayigh, "A number of veteran officers took advantage of the change of government to return illicitly. They set up 'safe houses', communications networks, and weapons stores in Beirut and Trablous and revived sections of the local organization" (Y. Sayigh 1997, 580–81). While Sayigh refers to the local cells as "dormant," it is clear that the cadres who remained in Beirut after 1982 constructed much of the organizational and financial infrastructure that allowed higher-ups to reinfiltrate Beirut. Indeed, the evidence presented here indicates that the organizational maintenance and learning functions that they performed constitute important resistance work in their own right.

Small cells like Nader's shaped returnees' experiences of participation by alerting reinfiltrating officers to the heavy presence of both dissident Palestinian organizations and Syrian intelligence, as well as by keeping members in close communication with each other throughout the return process (see also Y. Sayigh 1997, 581). In doing so, they deployed new skills and routines associated with organizational membership, including but not limited to physical evasion tactics and clandestine, cross-regional communication. Processes such as these, along with the partial reestablishment of formal military hierarchies, resurrected systems of formal factional affiliation; in contrast to Saida, Beirut-based militants whom I interviewed invariably referred to returning officers as their military superiors.

However, some returnees seem to have adopted the urban underground's organizational norms and practices, especially the reliance on cross-cutting quotidian social networks and generally flattened military hierarchies. For example, Abu Hassan, a Fatah military cadre who worked in the financial arm of the PLO's underground apparatus in Beirut, told me that he once entered his office to find Abu Tawq and two fighters sleeping on a mat of cigarette cartons in the antechamber rather than the internal sleeping quarters. Abu Hassan asked Abu Tawq, technically the superior officer, why he had not slept inside on his cot. Abu Tawq responded that the interior office was "private space" and that he preferred sharing with his men. Abu Hassan, along with several other Fatah cadres present when he told the story, used the incident to highlight Abu Tawq's respect for the people under his command; the vignette was intended to show that Abu Tawq was literally "with his men" at all times while Arafat was comfortable in Tunis.[13] Scaled up to the city level, the result was a type of hybrid local military organization with distinct modes of interfactional communication, intelligence-sharing, and structures of obligation that undergirded factional structures.

Unified Command in the War of the Camps, 1985–1988

These processes of repurposing and remapping fed back through the local environment, triggering substantial blowback. Many Lebanese feared a return of the PLO to Lebanon, given its potential to provoke Israel and escalate violence associated with the Israeli occupation and Lebanese resistance to it in South Lebanon. The consequences also reverberated geopolitically; the Syrian government was engaged in a protracted power struggle with Arafat over the direction of the Palestinian National Movement.[14] It and its allies actively battled a resurgent PLO apparatus in Lebanon, culminating in the 1985–1988 War of the Camps. During this period, Amal, the Syrian-allied Lebanese militia, and the Sixth Brigade of the LAF bombarded the camps with tank fire, rockets, and mortars. Syrian intelligence and its local allies surveilled, imprisoned, and tortured suspected pro-Arafat Palestinians. Amal blockaded the Shatila and Burj al-Barajneh camps from May to June 1985, for four days in January 1986, for twenty days the following April, and for thirty-five days in July–August the same year. In early September that year, Amal began a six-month complete blockade of Rashidiyeh that it extended to Burj al-Barajneh in October and to Shatila in November. During the sieges, no food, medicine, medical supplies (e.g., gauze, plasma, surgical tools), or fuel were allowed into the camps. When Amal did periodically lift the siege, the militia continued to strictly enforce bans on moving goods such as fuel, batteries, building materials, and weaponry into the camps and frequently attacked relief convoys as they attempted to access the camps during ceasefires. People in the camps eventually exhausted their food supplies and resorted to eating mules, grass, rats, dogs, and cats. The explicitly collective character of these violent repertoires recalled the 1975–1976 attacks on Tel al-Zaʿtar and Maslakh-Karantina as well as the 1982 campaigns against Palestinian camps in Beirut, a fact noted almost immediately even by external observers (Aruri 1985, 4).[15]

Learning from the Massacre: Factional Alliances and Civil Defense

The reaction to the 1985 attacks on Burj al-Barajneh and Shatila evolved directly from collective understandings of the Sabra and Shatila massacre. Sami, a longtime resident of Shatila and a former member of the camp's engineering committee, told me "we learned from the massacre" (referencing Sabra and Shatila).[16] Activists planned ahead and often worked outside formal chains of command; people in both Shatila and Burj al-Barajneh had extensive procedures for military and civil defense in place by the mid-1980s.

Officers' overlooking or outright ignoring of formal factional alliances and the Arafat-Assad rivalry provide evidence of a new, localized organizational form's emergence. Naseer Aruri notes that "in the battle for the camps . . . both Amal and Damascus seemed to have miscalculated. Unlike the Tripoli battles of 1983, the pro-Syrian Palestinian forces refused to join the campaign against ʿArafat. On the contrary, they suspended their political difference with him and defended the Palestinian camps side by side with his forces" (Aruri 1985, 7). Abu Tariq, the former leader of an ostensibly Syrian-allied, anti-Arafat faction under the umbrella of the PNSF, confirmed that technically illicit discussions regarding cross-group organizing within Shatila started as early as February 1985. In his memory, officers in the camp formed a joint social committee that included both PNSF and PLO members; these efforts created a new set of mid-level, cross-cutting ties characterized by shared communication and norms within the larger organizational field. Illustrating the diversity of membership from his perspective, Abu Tariq emphasized that Amneh Jibril, the head of the GUPW and a member of Fatah, was a leading participant, and that the political committee spanned organizational divisions.[17] Other sources concur. For example, Dr. Chris Giannou, a Greek-Canadian surgeon who worked in the Shatila PRCS hospital during the War of the Camps, writes, "I noticed that the contending faction leaders in Shatila . . . had established a *modus vivendi* among themselves. As a rule, PNSF leaders did not meet with Arafat top leaders, but second-echelon officers, often childhood classmates and friends, did. Some served as intermediaries between the organizations, as during the Four-Day Battle, to set up the work teams and co-ordinate the many services—water, electricity, distribution of building materials, or food, building of fortifications—necessary to organized life in the camp and resistance to Amal" (Giannou 1990, 43).

The civil defense and political committees that activists created via remapping were as essential to the camp community's survival as the military front. The engineering committee, for example, which included members of Fatah, the DFLP, and the PFLP, managed infrastructural projects such as building repairs in Sabra, al-Daouk, and Shatila; Burj al-Barajneh's own committee did similar work. These committees were also instrumental in building "underground cities" of tunnels and shelters that protected the civilian population during bombardments and allowed fighters to move beyond the camps' boundaries to conduct raids.[18] During the sieges, the committees operated generators on previously stockpiled or stolen fuel—both being products of planning by the city-wide underground. Moreover, the camps maintained functional PRCS hospitals with minimal space and equipment throughout the sieges; the PLO's original footage from the period plainly shows groups of men ferrying fighters away from the front on stretchers to the central hospital facility.

In direct, ongoing contradiction to each organization's formal alliances, PLO and PNSF organizations cooperated on civil defense matters throughout the War of the Camps. According to Giannou (1990, 45), "In spite of fierce political rivalry, responsible and broad-minded leaders, Ali Abu Toq and some of the PNSF officers overlooked the entry of food, supplies, and even smuggled weapons and ammunition into the camp by other rival organizations. They knew that in time of war, with Shatila under total blockade, everything within the camp would be considered common property and distributed among all. Pragmatic co-operation, and even co-ordination, in times of need tempered the antagonistic public pronouncements and insults traded among groups." Other firsthand accounts of the siege reinforce this description of the militants' collective, practical, and cross-factional approach to survival. Pauline Cutting (1989, 64), an English surgeon who volunteered for the PRCS in Burj al-Barajneh during the Camps War, reports similar behavior: "In Burj al-Barajneh, [the political organizations] generally managed to submerge their differences and unite against the common enemy outside."

Organizational leaders also went out of their way to demonstrate to their leaderships that they deeply disagreed with Amal's strategy of collective punishment and that it was influencing their microlevel organizational decision-making. Abu Tariq, for instance, noted that activists in Shatila would try to send letters to the outside, and particularly to the press, in attempts to draw attention to the growing humanitarian disaster in the camp. These letters represented their obligation to and activism on behalf of civilian communities and local organizations, rather than to factional bodies. He eventually learned that his organization's national-level leadership, headquartered in Mar Elias camp, would change his reports before forwarding them to Damascus; his commanding officers repeatedly downplayed the carnage in order to protect their allies in Amal and to avoid offending Syria. Seemingly motivated by moral outrage and frustration, Abu Tariq paid 500 Lebanese pounds for a satellite telephone, smuggled it into his office, hid the antenna in a chimney, and started calling the local and international press himself.[19] On air, he would identify himself as a leader of a PNSF organization and tell anyone who would listen: "I hate Amal!" This was extremely high risk; according to Abu Tariq, Amal would get on the radio to him and yell, "We hear your voice! We know it's you!" His response was, in his words, either "Go to hell!" or, in mockery of Amal's threats, "I'm just talking to my wife!"[20] While Abu Tariq's choices were highly individual, he was also acting as a representative of the local members of his organization. Not only did he defy the elite leadership, he also drew a distinct line between himself and local members of his faction (who did not stop him) on the one hand, and their national leadership on the other.

Organizational Hybridity

The blending of emergent organizational forms with recently reasserted military hierarchies produced strategic as well as tactical innovation. For example, Beirut-based militants adopted defensive tactics from the southern camps as southern militants migrated to Beirut. These knowledge flows produced and reinforced new understandings of community defense in the face of patterns of enemy violence.[21] Prior to the War of the Camps, and with the input of Shatila's representatives, seven guerrillas from Burj al-Shamali camp had developed a military strategy for Shatila. Based partially on lessons from combat in the south during the Israeli invasion, the strategy preserved factionally based chains of command at the camp level while leveraging emergent, cross-factional organizations such as intelligence and supply networks. In network terms, the addition of new nodes (the fighters from Burj al-Shamali) to Beirut networks produced what was known as the *"mihwar"* (intersection/axis) system: a defensive strategy premised on remapped cross-factional forces based on nonhierarchal, community-level ties. This system required each organization to help defend a particular slice of the camp's perimeter associated with a major intersection or landmark. Fighters would use tunnels leading from the camp into their assigned *mihwar* to unexpectedly appear behind enemy lines near the camp.[22] Burj al-Barajneh employed an identical arrangement.

Strategic practices, remapped combat units, and patterns of incumbent violence coevolved and created a mutually reinforcing dynamic that deepened throughout the War of the Camps. By the Four Day Battle in Shatila in 1986, "Each political organization had an allotted area of the battle-front periphery as its military responsibility.... everyone scrambled to his respective position as each organization, pro- or anti-Arafat or neutral, posted a platoon or two of men at every critical point" (Giannou 1990, 33). Burj al-Barajneh operated in the same way; as I stood on a rooftop at the edge of the camp in 2012, former fighters and supply officers identified landmarks where each organization had assembled its section of the defenses, including entrances to each group's committee-constructed tunnels. However, they always emphasized that, as in Shatila, the organizations operated under a shared command. These Shatila- and Burj al-Barajneh-specific cultures came into relief when replacement officers assumed new posts in the camp; Giannou notes the "narrow factionalism" of a Fatah officer who arrived in Shatila, emphasizing that it was "just as alien to the spirit of Shatila as was the brainwashed extremism of the dissident factions brought in from Damascus" (Giannou 1990, 212).

New cross-organizational supply and reinforcement ties mapped onto previously established community-based relations between members of dissident organizations such as the PFLP-GC and affiliates of its erstwhile enemy, Fatah. For example, a friend's mother—the wife of a former PFLP-GC officer in Shatila—smuggled grenades for Shatila's shared defenses in his swaddling.[23] As the spouse of an officer in a Syrian-allied organization, she had safe passage when other women did not. The woman's instrumental use of her infant child to smuggle military goods, and her choice to endanger both herself and baby by transporting live ammunition, demonstrate deep emotional and moral obligations to the broader Palestinian community that constituted these emergent defensive fronts. Other fighters violated military orders to preserve supplies for their own members and often ignored commands to turn their weapons on members of other organizations within the camp. Pro-Syrian Palestinian militants responded to Amal's violent repertoire by challenging their alliance; PNSF organizations also repeatedly fired upon their ostensible pro-Syrian, Lebanese ally despite orders from their leadership (Y. Sayigh 1997, 583).

For members of the PNSF organizations, military cooperation with the PLO had serious ramifications. George Habash, Secretary General of the PFLP, fled Syria at the end of May 1985 to avoid retribution by the Syrian government; the PFLP had participated in the PNSF's shelling of Amal from positions in the mountains above Beirut (Y. Sayigh 1997, 583–84). Syria "ordered the PNSF and DFLP to cease artillery fire, blocked their reinforcements and combat resupply, demanded full personnel lists and detailed inventories of weapons and ammunition, and suspended publication of the PFLP, DFLP, and PFLP-GC weeklies" (Y. Sayigh 1997, 583). The dissident organization Fatah al-Intifada shot at least one of its members in Shatila for fighting alongside the PLO; he survived and subsequently left the organization.[24] Syria's actions were both punitive and aimed at regaining control; the Syrian regime's order to suspend several Palestinian allies' weekly publications betrayed a fear that powerful, community-based sentiments on the ground would spill into the organizations' propaganda. Syria also attempted to preempt further insubordinate behavior among the Fatah dissidents by ordering "33 combat officers and senior cadres (including the head of the regional command) to return to Syria" (Y. Sayigh 1997, 599).

The Role of Mixed-Descent Militants

The creation of the opposition PNSF and Amal's attacks on the camps introduced a new political dynamic during the camp sieges. Quotidian relationships between PLO-allied militant organizations, the PSP, and the recently-formed Hizbullah on the one hand and PNSF supporters and Amal on the other became especially significant throughout the sieges. These alliances challenge arguments that favor the primacy of ethnic and sectarian affiliations in civil war and within "deeply divided" societies (Horowitz 2000; Toft 2005; Cederman and Girardin 2007; Cederman et al. 2010; Chang and Peisakhin 2019), instead highlighting the ways that personal relationships and shared frames of reference undergird networks of loyalty, obligation, and protection.

Remapped cross-ethnic and cross-organizational ties benefited both militant organizations and civilians, yet did so in a predominantly unofficial way via quotidian relations. More than simply providing insurance, these relationships provided literal free passes to the network of barriers and local prisons that Amal used to constrain and threaten Palestinians' movement. Fatah- and DFLP-affiliated women with quotidian ties to members of PNSF factions or Amal became especially valuable to the clandestine apparatus. Aisha and her cousin Ibtisam, also a Fatah cadre, explained that when Amal periodically lifted the blockade, they would pick up weapons from male officers and then smuggle them through the remaining checkpoints into the camp.[25] Their uncle by marriage, who was both Lebanese and a practicing Shi'a, was an officer in Amal to whom they could appeal if they were caught.[26] Abu Husayn, a Fatah cadre, former member of the underground, and former PLA officer who identifies as Shi'a, deliberately selected his wife to smuggle arms through a network of tunnels and sewers under the camps. Between his two brothers in leftist factions and his contacts from the Shi'i community, they assessed that if she were to be caught, his contacts in the PNSF could protect her.[27] Murid, a member of the DFLP, was introduced to a Syrian intelligence agent who staffed one of the southernmost checkpoints outside Beirut by his sister and brother in-law, both members of PNSF-affiliated organizations. He was subsequently able to move largely unchallenged between combat theaters for several years, using only that crossing.

Politically affiliated women with combat experience were redeployed to critical, high-risk underground positions. Many were caught and imprisoned. For example, Zahra, who was working in a kindergarten during the War of the Camps, started smuggling salaries into the camp by using her teaching position to cover her movements. However, her Fatah affiliation was semipublic knowledge in the camps; in 1986, she was denounced by members of a PNSF organization and imprisoned by Syrian intelligence. Upon her release, Syrian-allied groups set up a checkpoint under her apartment in West Beirut, forcing her to sleep outside her family home and to curtail her activities. Zahra began working in a humanitarian aid division of the GUPW, providing food and clothing to civilians rather than returning to clandestine work. Aisha, the smuggler from Beirut, underscored how Amal's and the Syrians' constant updating influenced clandestine militants' organizational routines and strategy:

> The Syrians learned that we were smuggling things in our clothes and started making us pull our shirts tight when we crossed the checkpoints. Like this [Aisha pulls her shirt tightly over her stomach and chest]. So what did we do? [Aisha leans closer to me and takes a drag of her Marlboro Red, looking for me to solve the puzzle. I wait.] We strapped guns and money to our thighs! [Aisha slaps her inner thigh, laughing heartily]. Not even the Syrians would search there![28]

Aisha later noted that the difference between women's and men's roles in the defense of the camps often inverted expectations about risk acceptance. She emphasized that due to the stationary fronts, smuggling and logistics roles fundamentally became front-line positions: "Women died going to get food and water . . . women came face to face with Amal and the Syrians. They were searched, threatened, beaten . . . they were raped and killed while the men hid and shot at [Amal]."[29] The pathways that women smugglers used to enter the camps consequently earned the moniker "Corridors of Death" (Nofal 2006, 40, 49). Aisha emphasized the contrast in men's and women's risk acceptance, noting that she had to move through the camp—exposed and under fire—to deliver food, ammunition, and sandbags to the front while male fighters hunkered in fortified positions.[30]

Militants refined and routinized clandestine operations during the War of the Camps, reinforcing new, hybrid organizational forms. Beyond simply moving information, finances, and supplies, clandestine networks allowed organizational politics to assume an increasingly dual character as militants used quotidian ties to bypass formal alliances. Militant organizations increasingly sought to create redundancies by engineering quotidian brokers into their structures. Marriages, specifically, formed new bases for militant organization and provided marked career advantages for both female and male Palestinian rebels.

Emergence and Disobedience

In the context of the War of the Camps, PLO as well as PNSF cadres—in addition to many members of Lebanese militias—regularly disobeyed commands. Evidence strongly indicates an important role for alternative membership in and loyalty to community-based networks that undergirded armed community defense fronts. Interviewees from Shatila and Burj al-Barajneh emphasized that the repertoires of violence associated with the sieges made political divisions at the local level (i.e., prewar organizational ties) irrelevant, even though almost all of them had been politically active at the time. The siege's devastating effects on civilian communities provided both shared motivation and fodder to critique people seen as "playing politics" at the expense of people in the camps. A telex sent by foreign aid workers in Burj al-Barajneh in January 1987 underscores the collective humanitarian catastrophe of the camp sieges:

> The camp has now been under attack with a complete siege more than 12 weeks and we, along with the 25,000 residents of the camp[,] are being subjected to conditions of deprivation and misery. Drinking water is the most basic human need. Most houses do not have running water and it has to be collected daily from taps in the street at great risk for the personal safety. Several women have been shot and killed by snip-

ers while collecting water for their families. Foodstocks have been completely depleted.[31]

We are still under siege and now the people are beginning to starve. We have seen children hunting in garbage heaps for scraps of food. Today one woman was shot while trying to collect grass on the outskirts of the camp. . . . Some women and children are taking the risk of leaving the camp and many small children have been taken prisoner.[32]

In this setting, people strongly believed that there was no space for organizational politics. Local loyalties and obligations reigned instead; in this atmosphere, "organizational" politics became synonymous with "elite" politics, which people viewed as the cause of the siege in the first place.

Rhetoric and orders that emphasized official ideological differences seemed not only absurd, but even dishonorable and immoral when the community was literally starving under the blockade and bombardment. Zahra, emphasized how shared routines, tasks, and sentiments came to constitute emergent defensive fronts in response: "There was no Fatah, Popular Front, General Command. Everyone worked in the siege. They cooked. They made sandwiches. They helped in the hospital. Everyone was together."[33] Abu Tariq simply said: "The camp had to look for survival and protection. . . . there was no time to think about organizations." Ibrahim, who fought in Burj al-Barajneh when he was only fifteen years old, emphasized that even though he is now a loyal member of Fatah, during the siege he "did not think much about Fatah." Instead, he explained, his first thought when Amal attacked was that "they were coming for my house and my camp, Burj al-Barajneh camp."[34]

These rhetorical distinctions worked to discursively constitute defensive fronts that de-emphasized organizational affiliation. Even when many militants were arrested by the Syrian allies of the PNSF factions and Amal, they highlighted their shared humanity; Abu Hassan, for example, told me of his arrest by Syrian forces, insisting: "In our cells—the cells in Murr Tower—we were facing guys from Amal, guys who had helped Palestinians. They were saying 'Allah, Muhammad, Qur'an, Yassir Arafat, Palestine.' They were reading Qur'an and we were reading Qur'an. Their general told us 'we refused to fight you.'" Abu Hassan's emphasis on the Qur'an not only works to render the predominantly Sunni Palestinians and Shi'a members of Amal alike; it also emphasizes his association of morality with Lebanese milititamen who disobeyed commands to fight with people in the camps.[35]

This distinction between elite leaderships and local commands reflected emergent, camp-level solidarity patterns that crisscrossed organizational affiliations. Abu Tariq emphasized local actors' agency in the camps, noting that his larger group was allied with Syria, "but we [members in Shatila] were also not toys in Syrian hands."³⁶ His political perspective demarcated local members of Fatah, to whom he was personally tied and against whom he held no grudge, from Fatah's leadership, people whom he saw as traitors for negotiating with the Israeli government: "I was against the arresting of Fatah people, it's not right. Arrest the leadership, not the Fatah people in the streets."³⁷ Yet Abu Tariq alluded to an even deeper political schism between the international leadership and his situation on the ground: "When the Camps War started, maybe the leadership knew. We weren't informed as *local* leaders [author's emphasis]."³⁸

While political officers like Abu Tariq superficially performed their stated political roles—in part owing to the presence of Syrian spies in the camp—they constantly violated political boundaries. This choice was often simply a matter of survival. For example, when Abu Mujahid, the local PFLP leader as well as the head of the camp's Popular Committee, needed to repair water mains, he deliberately worked through a politically neutral intermediary in order to secure supplies and funding from the PLO:

> Since Abu Moujahed was a leading official of a [sic] organization of the National Salvation Front, he could not negotiate the funds for payment directly with Ali Abu Toq, who as the head of Fatah controlled the PLO budget. Syrian spies in the camp watched to see who received 'Arafat money.' I assumed the task of negotiating the payment between my two friends. As the responsible official of the Palestine Red Crescent Society, a civilian institution of the PLO, I knew no such constraints. (Giannou 1990, 68–69)

Technically, the PNSF officers should have done anything possible to prevent the PLO and its members from persevering in the face of Amal's attacks. Quotidian ties thus served to broker between those who could not publicly violate role expectations.

Yet disobedience went beyond securing the material necessities of survival and acquired a new meaning as a result of local understandings of Amal's tactical repertoires. Remapped relational ties based on shared camp affiliation undergirded this cooperation. At the grassroots level, helping neighbors became a moral obligation for those who stood against Amal's blockade, sniping, and shelling. This dynamic fed fighters' motivation to flout orders from above. Abu Adnan, a Fatah officer who survived the War of the Camps in Burj al-Barajneh, noted explicitly (and despite his later expulsion from the camp by a pro-Syrian organization) that everyone distributed their supplies regardless of the recipient's organizational affiliation.³⁹ I asked Aisha how camp life changed during the sieges and how people from different organizations acted toward each other. Her immediate response was that everyone shared any supplies that they had: "If you had some coffee or *labneh*, and someone else had another thing, you'd divide it all." She also remembered that people in the camp actively shunned and shamed those who did not share, noting that to have an egg and not split it with the family next door was *haram*. Her use of the term for something that is religiously forbidden was especially indicative of the moral implications of selfishness in a particular conflict environment.[40]

The Puzzle of Ali Abu Tawq

Ali Abu Tawq embodies the overarching tension between elite leadership and local emergent organizations; examining both his actions and the way people remember them offers insights into the role that community-level networks played in shaping militant action in Beirut during this era. When Yasir Arafat ordered him to violate a ceasefire with Amal in 1986, Abu Tawq refused; he had been quietly communicating with local Amal leaders via personal connections he had generated in the 1982–1985 Beirut underground. Arafat promptly cut Abu Tawq's payroll allowance, punishing his subordinates and seeking to sever the financial and loyalty bond among them (Y. Sayigh 1997, 592).[41] I asked several former militants who served under him what they made of Abu Tawq's choice; rather than criticizing a renegade officer who defied Arafat and who cost them their salaries, they universally defended the choice as honorable, ethical, and appropriate.

Many Beirut militants drew clear lines between the "games" that exiled leaders played on one hand and local commanders' moral stands for their communities on the other. Given these tensions, coupled with fighters' perceived moral commitments to camp communities, it is not difficult to see why Palestinians in Beirut might hold the leaders who defied orders to protect them in high regard. Yet, Abu Tawq still seems to eclipse his contemporaries. Narratives surrounding his memory paint him as the leader of Palestinians, emphasizing his humility, tactical genius (particular with reference to guerrilla skills such as tunnel building), and the resulting social embeddedness among both Palestinians and Lebanese. This theme occurred across interviews; Abu Tawq frequently emerged as a symbolic foil to former as well as contemporary members of the elite leadership, especially when they were seen as engaging in "political theater" or "political games."

Sami and Abu Houli, the latter being one of the fighters from Burj al-Shamali who smuggled materials into the Beirut camps, told me that, unlike Arafat, Abu Tawq "was living the reality." This statement was not only a testament to the perceived competence with which he made decisions for his people, but also to his moral right to do so.[42] Abu Tawq came "from the same school as Abu Ammar," said Ibrahim, the former fighter from Burj al-Barajneh, who wanted to demonstrate the high regard in which people viewed the man. Ibrahim's response to my subsequent question about Abu Tawq's insubordination—"No one could say 'no' to Abu Ammar. But Ali Abu Tawq said 'no'"—strongly implied that Abu Tawq had not only moral standing, but also popular support.[43]

Despite the combat setting in which it occurred, Abu Tawq's ultimate assassination stunned residents of the Beirut camps. On the orders of Fatah al-Intifada's military commander, four Fatah dissidents assassinated Abu Tawq in Shatila on January 27, 1987, detonating a buried 82mm shell in Shatila's defensive earthworks. He died along with his deputy, who was announcing the birth of his son to members of the cross-factional defensive front (Giannou 1990, 136–39). The move—specifically, targeting the shared trenches—seemed to go against all the organizational and community norms that people had worked to establish. In a move that seems designed to "de-Palestinize" his assailants and distance them from the camp community, the Facebook page dedicated to Abu Tawq's life attributes the assassination to "isolationist forces" and "Arab fascists," rather than to Fatah al-Intifada specifically by name.

The devastating effects of the Sabra and Shatila massacre and the confinement of many Palestinian men to their homes led to the emergence of camp-based, often cross-factional militant cells based on neighbors' shared perceptions of immediate threat. People repurposed everyday kinship and marriage ties, deploying female couriers to facilitate communication between cells and, eventually, salary payments. The PLO co-opted this apparatus, but never managed to completely control it.

The War of the Camps (1985–1988) challenged exiled Palestinian elites' command and control of military and political apparatuses. The specific use of siege tactics reinforced militants' identification both with camp communities and with previous socialization practices, subsequently producing disobedience. Feedback into neighborhood-based relationships facilitated the remapping of combat apparatuses onto quotidian ties, resulting in the emergence of united defensive fronts in Shatila and Burj al-Barajneh. A woman-dominated network of smugglers who were often connected to members of Amal or PNSF factions via kinship and marriage ties worked to resupply the camp with ammunition, bribe money, food, and medicine. Hybridized siege fronts facilitated tactical innovation and new forms of political contention via acts of disobedience and insubordination. Participants largely understood the conflict as a political one driven by geopolitics and elite rivalries between the PLO and Syria, rather than as a sectarian conflict between Shiʻa Lebanese on one hand and Sunni and Christian Palestinians on the other. This understanding undergirded network connections between Palestinians and Lebanese Shiʻa that militants remapped to facilitate organizational survival.

Local organizations' repeated successes in challenging elite leaderships and bringing horrific humanitarian conditions to light led to the erosion of international support for the Amal-Syrian axis, particularly from Libya and Iran. Palestinian organizations that had previously maintained strained relations with Syria changed their positions, as well; by the end of the War of the Camps, "the DFLP and PCP [Palestinian Communist Party] had already resumed the political dialogue with Fatah, while the PFLP, PPSF, and PLF tacitly followed Fatah's political lead in the camps, prompting a disgruntled Birri [the leader of Amal] to observe that he could no longer distinguish the PNSF from Fatah" (Y. Sayigh 1997, 595). However, Amal, the Syrians, and their Palestinian allies also expelled known surviving Fatah officers at the end of the War of the Camps. Fatah members who remained in Beirut went underground; those who left Beirut filtered into the southern camps, into a distinct political system where they were forced to negotiate new roles for themselves and protection for their families.

These events have had lasting consequences. In contemporary Beirut, one frequently sees subtle traces of these past organizational configurations and alliances. Walking through the Sabra market with Abu Houli, the former commando from Burj al-Shamali, he sometimes introduced me to members of the PFLP and PPSF who stopped to exchange high-fives with him and ask about his children; he often told me that they know each other "from the siege." Friends of mine tell me that they consider themselves to be from Shatila, not because they were born in that camp but because they were there for the entire six-month siege. Sometimes, the organizational resonance is less nuanced. For example, medical aid teams based in the camps almost immediately mobilized during the 2006 July War when the IDF bombed Dahiyeh and other nearby neighborhoods. Unified fronts among the camps' inhabitants also emerged in times of danger; for instance, a cross-factional collective closed the camp during Hizbullah's May 2008 invasion of West Beirut.[44] Organizationally, one of the lasting effects of the sieges has been a generalized disdain for elite leaderships, though this dynamic has certainly been reinforced over time by broad feelings that the Ramallah-based leadership has abandoned Palestinian refugees in Lebanon. However, given the history, the meanings embedded by lasting public and private displays of Ali Abu Tawq's face are hard to misread.

Viewing these dynamics via the lens of remapping and emergence emphasizes both the material effects of violence and the ways that violent repertoires—particularly siege dynamics—interacted with factional apparatuses and everyday relationships to produce specific understandings of threat and obligation. The use of siege tactics, in particular, amplified elite distance from the battlefield, bringing distinctions between long-standing socialization on one hand and realpolitik on the other into stark relief for those on the ground. That cleavage caused a shift in conflict dynamics, whereby the militants in the camps fought for themselves often independently of orders. In name, each of the factions "survived" and, for the most part, still exist today. However, the inherent changes to their structures, motivations, goals, and practices force us to problematize the concept of "survival" and to think more seriously about how emergence localizes conflict dynamics and drives divergent patterns of organizational adaptation.

7

"EVERY FACTION FOR ITSELF"
Personalized Militias and Fragmented Battle Lines

"Crazy bastard!!" *A foot-high stack of accordion folders shudders and tilts precariously as Abu Hadi slams his tiny Nokia mobile onto the massive wood laminate desk. A UNRWA employee in South Lebanon, Abu Hadi is about four hours into what is usually a twelve-hour day. Staying with his family, I have quickly learned that he is lucky if people don't call late at night to ask for information or, often, to ask some sort of favor.*

This call, at a more respectable hour, falls into a third category. A man is upset that his child is doing poorly in school and has called to complain about the teacher. Abu Hadi has had to intervene with the family previously; the child has serious behavioral problems that the parents have consistently failed to address. The father has called to inform Abu Hadi that if his son does not receive better treatment from the teacher, he will show up at the school with his gun and shut it down until Abu Hadi does something to change the situation.

The end of his cigarette glows orange as Abu Hadi takes a deep, annoyed drag. "Want to get some ful?" he asks.[1] It's still breakfast time, but we ate with his family before leaving home. I realize that whatever he is about to do, Abu Hadi wants to leave the office to do it; in South Lebanon, it seems like someone is always hovering by a door or "coincidentally" arriving with coffee. I agree and we hop across town to one of his favorite cafés and sit outdoors: fewer people there, and more street noise to mask our conversation. Snapping a lighter toward a fresh, unlit cigarette with one hand, Abu Hadi picks up a second, personal mobile and dials someone in his address book. I startle as he adopts a bubbly, upbeat, familiar tone.

"Issam, habibi, how are you?[2] How is your health? How is the family? I hear from her teacher that your daughter is progressing quite well in class. . . . Yes, praise God. Me? Oh habibi, I am so stressed, this job is killing me. . . . Why? Oh, don't worry about it, it's just the nature of the . . . well, of course you know how people are . . . oh, you know, it's no one in particular, it's just guys like this bastard who just called me about his son, threatening to come down to the school with a gun . . . yes, him. Yes, the kid is quite out of control, but haram you know how the parents are . . . no, no of course that doesn't excuse his behavior . . . no, Issam, don't worry, seriously, you know there are many people like this . . . Issam . . . you know I can't support that . . . well of course, I can't stop you, but really, you know how I feel about this kind of thing . . . habibi, I really don't think you should . . . you have to go? Okay Issam, I will see you soon, God willing . . . okay, bye."

I can tell that my eyebrows have involuntarily shot skyward, and revise them into an expression that I hope combines an unspoken question with a bit of shock at what I think I have just witnessed. Abu Hadi drags on the cigarette, balancing it on an impish grin, and explains: "You know, my old friend Issam, we were together during the war. His loves his daughter very much, of course, and he gets upset when people threaten to disrupt the school; it's very hard on a child."

I am somewhat at a loss, and only manage to say that I probably don't want to know what he has just done. Abu Hadi laughs: "You saw me; I didn't do anything. Issam is a bit angry about the situation, though. He has a slight temper; he was threatening to go get his brothers and to go straight to the guy's house to explain what will happen if he takes his gun to the school tomorrow. I'm hoping this doesn't happen." I can't help matching his sarcasm: "I'm sure," I reply.

Abu Hadi winks conspiratorially at me as I realize, with some concern, that elsewhere in town, Issam is probably already out the door. Ten minutes later, as we are starting in on the ful, Abu Hadi's mobile blasts scratchy music. He walks down the block—he doesn't seem to want me to hear this part—and has a quick conversation. After he hangs up, he reseats himself in his plastic chair and digs contentedly into the platter. "You know, I don't think we will have a situation at the school after all."[3]

People across postwar communities in fragile states share Abu Hadi's challenges and, sometimes, his problem-solving techniques. In many cases, social networks that consolidated during war or under conditions of harsh repression provide the relationships necessary to launch vigilante and other reactive violence (Smith 2015, 2019; Bateson 2017, 2021; J. Krause 2019). A former fighter and member of the PLO's administrative apparatus, Abu Hadi was one of many who had quit his faction and moved into humanitarian and social work in the mid-1980s. He was known for battling corruption and trying to end patronage hiring in his organization, making him unpopular with certain segments of the Palestinian refugee population in Lebanon.

Yet, paradoxically, Abu Hadi's effectiveness as an unaffiliated social service administrator was largely based on the social networks that he had built up during the 1980s, rather than on formal bureaucratic channels. Why didn't he work through the formal bureaucracy, and, if necessary, with local police to defuse the situation described above? First, the school was located in a refugee camp; Abu Hadi could call either *al-kifah al-mussalah* (literally: "armed struggle," a PLO-affiliated organization that acts as a police service) or members of an armed faction. But he also understood the potential for escalation if the vigilante then called his own backup; there would almost certainly be a clash between armed Palestinian factions (though that still existed with a more private encounter such as the one he initiated). Second, he didn't want to risk a public incident; given the setting, the media would almost certainly appear, identify the man waving a gun in front of a children's school as Palestinian, and spin various editorials about violence in the Palestinian refugee community. But most important, Abu Hadi didn't trust the formal bureaucracy to get anything done, much less quickly, simply, or quietly; not only was his school staffed with members of factions who had their own interests, but he also knew that several of his employees actively spied on him. His old military buddies were a sure bet when it came to diffusing a complex, threatening situation.

Being able to do things safely and effectively in South Lebanon is often a byproduct of relationships generated long ago. This chapter argues that from 1985 through 1988, past experiences of infiltration and collaboration interacted with hyperlocal patterns of violence, producing camp-level processes of organizational adaptation and emergence. In Saida, violence reinforced emerging insular, personalistic militia structures in and around Ain al-Hilweh. The reinfiltration of elite PLO officers into Saida after the IDF's withdrawal further galvanized localized, primary-group-level ties among local combatants and reinforced vertical stratification between different factions' chains of command. Fighting a guerrilla war against Amal in Magdousheh, a village in the hills above Ain al-Hilweh, mobilized people across factions. However, in contrast to Beirut, both the mode of combat (front-based, rural guerrilla war that privileged small, mobile units) and Yasir Arafat's centralized command style only reinforced factional chains of command, to the exclusion of overarching, community-wide loyalties.

Meanwhile, the prospect of and subsequent reality of camp sieges in Sur combined with people's knowledge of the grave situation in the Beirut camps. As in Beirut, the threat from the Lebanese militia Amal activated community-level, cross-factional ties. However, in contrast to Beirut, collective framing primarily referenced the invasion and occupation rather than the Sabra and Shatila massacre. Citing the catastrophe of 1982, events such as the Nadi al-Houli massacre and the camp's location adjacent to a Lebanese Shiʻi neighborhood, residents of Burj al-Shamali collectively declared neutrality during the War of the Camps.[4] In other words, the community was able to demand loyalty from active fighters by activating broad, community-based ties associated with the proximate memory of 1982. However, residents of Burj al-Shamali also formed a local clandestine supply apparatus to aid those trapped in Rashidiyeh, which fought Amal. Faced with a siege, Rashidiyeh's residents fought as a unified front, relying on underground logistics apparatuses fielded by Palestinians in Saida and the rest of Sur. In contrast to civilian communities that draw on strong networks to refuse rebels support (J. Krause 2018; Kaplan 2017), Burj al-Shamali's inhabitants instead in effect split the difference by supporting other communities while strategically preserving their own territory. Tiny al-Buss camp was never besieged, but experienced encirclement by checkpoints, arson, kidnappings, and other attacks. Because it did not collectively fight, the camp was able to staff a local strategic communication center that directed smuggling into Rashidiyeh.

This chapter examines concurrent processes of organizational adaptation and emergence, focusing first on Saida and then on Sur. It traces the emergence of factionalized, personalized militias in Ain al-Hilweh and details the consequences of elite officers' return and attempted co-optation of these localized units. It then turns to Sur, discussing how similar processes of activation in response to repertoires of violence interacted with camp histories, producing different outcomes. The third part of the chapter returns to the gendered processes of remapping that staffed clandestine supply networks, emphasizing how these dynamics interacted with the fragmented environment of South Lebanon to produce elite-ranking women cadres who operated cross-regionally, engaging in some of the most high-risk militant work of the period.

Emergence in Saida during the War of the Camps, 1985–1988

Guerrilla groups in Saida and Sur displayed vastly different pathways of remapping and emergence during the War of the Camps. I argue that this divergence was largely the product of the interaction of hyperlocal experiences of violence with evolving social networks. That is not to say that local experiences were completely different. Mamdouh Nofal, a DFLP commander, observes that Amal tortured many prisoners, a practice that people noted across both cities (Nofal 2006,

39). Actions such as these influenced network activation and shaped overarching understandings of the conflict with Amal; former militants repeatedly cited these tactics and others such as arson as having influenced their decision either to continue engaging in militancy or to mobilize for the first time. Even so, other aspects of both localized and overarching conflicts affected organizational structures to the point where they evolved into different forms across space.

Atomization and Infighting in Saida

On February 16, 1985, the IDF withdrew from Saida, though it continued to intermittently bomb Ain al-Hilweh over the following years.[5] The withdrawal, Yezid Sayigh notes, spurred "a dramatic rise in guerrilla attacks [on the IDF], which reached 160 in February and 200 in March" as well as resulting in the murder of sixty alleged collaborators as "the Israeli-armed 'national guard' collapsed," leaving members of the organization without the protective umbrella of the IDF (Y. Sayigh 1997, 581).[6] However, right-wing militias such as the Lebanese Forces continued their attacks on the camp.

Emergent, localized, personalized organizations coalesced in the face of PLO reinfiltration into Lebanon. After the IDF withdrew from Saida, the city became a primary port of entry for returning PLO officers, particularly those in Fatah. These officers were supposed to reestablish command over the small, semi-independent guerrilla cells that had been receiving salaries but operating autonomously for nearly three years. However, many fighters who had been present throughout the occupation resented those whom they labeled "the foreigners," who locals felt lacked local experience and connections.

Palestinians in South Lebanon reported that the shared, emotional experiences of occupation violence—mass imprisonment, protesting at IDF installations, fearing infiltration, rooting out collaborators, being on the run and hiding out—linked them together in ways that were impenetrable for those who had been living in villas in Tunis or Damascus and safely sending their children to school every day. By 1985, the underground newspaper *Sawt al-Mukhayyam* had published a steady series of articles critical of the factions' leaderships—even those with which it ideologically sympathized. For example, its columnists wrote that "[DFLP leader Nayef] Hawatmeh has committed many subversive crimes against that masses and against the revolution," referred to the "treasonous policies of Arafat," and argued that "we should start embracing the motto of taking down the traitorous leadership and opening the doors wide to the theoretical, political, and organizational discussions."[7] The January 1985 issue—the final one accessible in the archives—featured articles that took stock of twenty years of armed revolution. It roundly criticized both the way the Palestinian National Movement had used military operations and its relationship with ordinary people:

> Military operations have been used politically thus far: publicity, retaliation, intimidation and then the establishment of smaller political parties. In the face of all that, we must confirm that armed resistance is the primary method for liberation. We must purify it from all of the distortions that it has been through. To connect it directly to the public, and to act upon it, not just say it.
>
> The relationship with the public was unrevolutionary. It was arrogant, bureaucratic, tribal, and self-righteous. This mentality created many mistakes and it became the norm. Palestinian action became against the public. It put organizations in the place of the people and put a regime on top of them, that considered people useless save for elections and rallies. Correcting this relationship requires radically criticizing, and connecting the people to the cause through commitment and awareness, not through corruption and money.[8]

To be clear, this is not to argue that there was universal agreement with or acceptance of these stances. Rather, I am demonstrating the existence of grassroots narratives that highlighted divides between the Palestinian "people"/"public" in Lebanon and elite political and military leaders. While one might argue that the paper's stance represents a clear factional bias—it uses leftist terminology such as "comrades" and emphasizes the corruption of the "bourgeoisie"—it also explicitly and deliberately distinguishes itself from factional papers such as *Palestine* (published by the PFLP) and *Tariq al-Watan* (published by the DFLP).[9]

Many active guerrillas in South Lebanon resented returnee "outsiders" because of their materially privileged lives in exile, their lack of military expertise in the theater of South Lebanon, their proximity to disliked elites, and their exclusion from the small cliques that kept their members alive under the Israeli occupation of Saida. In short, they deemed the returnee officers untrustworthy, a key predictor of disciplinary breakdown within units (McLauchlin 2020). Emotion-laden, remapped ties constituted by personal experiences of violence, coordination, and participation under the occupation made new forms of political contestation possible. For example, in a quiet conversation over coffee that occurred only after I had known both men for years, Abu Houli and Nader shared that fighters in Saida conspired to kill returning elite officers, whose actions were perceived as disrespectful toward the locals who had protected the camps and survived Ansar. Meso-level officers who were supposed to transfer high-level officers from the docks to their command stations assassinated them instead; the idea was both to remove troublesome actors and to maintain local command earned under the occupation.[10] This wave of murders seeded even deeper suspicion among the sub-units of Fatah, producing smaller, more insular Fatah-affiliated cliques that operated more like private militias (Andoni 1988).[11]

These mutinies were not as simple as research on military discipline would predict. They did not occur simply because of poor physical conditions or officers' unsatisfactory leadership skills (Rose 1982; Gal 1985). Rather, Abu Houli and Nader explained that these dynamics were linked to what is commonly referred to as primary group cohesion (Shibutani 1978; Grossman 2014), that is, close bonds between unit mates. Though cohesion is generally associated with control and discipline, in this case it facilitated unified resentment and coordinated violence. Nader drew on the commonly used examples of home and family to explain: "It was like someone coming into your living room and saying to your wife, your children: 'I'll pay you to be with me instead of him.'"[12] Nader's use of the family metaphor implies that while the returning officers sought to reassert a long-standing, recognized, formal military hierarchy, their attempts were read as presumptuous and inappropriately instrumentalist by militants who privileged the intimacy, loyalty, and trust embedded in their on-the-ground relationships and gained through collective experience.

Ongoing violence and top-down incentives entrenched these emergent organizational forms in Saida. When recalling this era, my interlocutors detailed an evolving organizational dynamic characterized by small, entrepreneurial, and explicitly personalized militias. Yet this intimacy was not all perceived as normatively good; several former militants emphasized that the network dynamics that led to these groups' emergence also laid the foundations for violence and corruption. Referencing the idea of dirty money, Yusif likened the targeting of returning, cash-flush foreigners to organized crime, telling me that "there was a big mafia involved in this"—"this" being plans to kill returning leaders and claim the money.[13] A former member of various Marxist parties, George, explained that the meso-level commanders concealed what was occurring from exiled leaders so they could be promoted rather than punished. For example, he told me that after the death of Abu Alaa, a Palestinian political leader, the customary martyr poster said that he had been killed by Mossad, the Israeli intelligence agency. In reality, George informed me, Abu Alaa was killed by a local leader who wanted his position.[14] He knew this because his friend worked with the leader who killed Abu Alaa. Because the local leader's family included high-level guerrillas, he added, the killer was protected. His point, which he emphasized, was that "the revolution was corrupted.... I saw corruption, clashes between Palestinian groups, plots against people.... it's just a mafia."[15]

Affiliation as Protection

In contrast to the processes of branching out and consolidation that characterize early stages of successful rebellion (Lewis 2020), individual and organizational survival in this environment relied on cliquish behavior focused on personalistic segments of larger factions. The broader implication is that to survive in environments characterized by infiltration and collaboration, many ongoing insurgencies must begin to prioritize operational security in the form of network closure (Burt 2005), rather than widespread, open recruitment. Ironically, these modes of surveillance may drive adaptive processes that lead to more organizational splintering and, as a result, violence (Gade 2020).

Severing chains of command by killing returning officers bolstered rising local leaders' attempts to assert their status and control over local branches of the guerrilla factions by situating those locals as brokers between the militant units under their control and external actors, including exiled factional leaderships, regional governments, Lebanese parties, and even religious institutions. According to Abu Ali, a former member of a PNSF member organization, those leaders created new relations with external actors by seeking to establish independent funding streams for the local sub-units of larger guerrilla factions. This move cemented their semi-autonomy from their exiled leaderships while placing them in competition for patrons. This practice channeled top-down financial flows into local cliques, bypassing transnational organizational hierarchies. Localized factions began to recruit specifically to aid a group's reputation, soliciting renowned fighters or well-respected men. Abu Ali put it quite simply: "They [the organizations] all wanted to be on top."[16] This competition branched into various domains; by 1987, for example, locally emergent Islamic factions were holding Sabra and Shatila massacre commemoration ceremonies and opening cultural centers in the camps.[17]

Publicly joining a faction became a financial, physical, and social survival strategy, representing a fundamental shift in what constituted "membership" in a militant organization. Rather than joining for revolutionary reasons, Yusif recalled that "everyone was in an organization to protect himself."[18] He added that people who had family members in the militant groups felt more "freedom" because they had patrons; leaders would put their entire families on an organization's salary list so that they would have a bloc within the organization.[19] It also provided access to information that could protect people from plots, rumors, or revenge. Unsurprisingly, the factions leveraged this risk in recruitment; officers would ask unaffiliated people rhetorical questions such as "What if something happens to you? What if you are arrested? What will happen to your family?"[20] Nonparticipation thus became increasingly costly compared to the relative risks of joining a group, a dynamic that emerges across intrastate conflicts (Kalyvas and Kocher 2007).

Local leaders sought to leverage these ties to ensure loyalty and obedience to themselves first, shifting basic logics of command and control within the guerrilla factions and centering them on midlevel commanders. Mobilization via personalistic ties to leaders replaced older recruiting practices that required members to sign up through a representative in a recruitment office that would then assign them to a unit.[21] An endogenous dynamic emerged; because some people joined, others felt compelled to affiliate themselves, as well. Belonging to an organization, receiving a salary, and benefiting from its military and social protection kept a fighter ensconced in a web of locally based loyalties that would "have his or her back."

Factionalism and Community at the Magdousheh Front

The international PLO-PNSF cleavage further reinforced segmentation among Palestinian factions; the prior necessity of operating in small, mobile cells, together with the difficulty of communicating in Ansar and the factionally-specific salary payments, had previously disincentivized coordination. Rising tensions between PLO and PNSF-affiliated forces, which could now operate more freely in Saida, were so bad that officials were forced to issue statements denying clashes among Palestinian organizations.[22] These events further fortified the organizational boundaries and patronage ties that divided Palestinian militant factions in Saida. Without the need to cooperate against the IDF, or the shared responsibility to protect Palestinian civilian communities (in contrast to the situation in Beirut and Rashidiyeh), divisions between the Fatah and Fatah-allied organizations such as the DFLP and the PNSF organizations came to the fore.

While meso-level officers in Beirut were quietly discussing joint political and engineering committees (see chapter 6), the PNSF and PLO factions in Saida remained divided. On January 1, 1986, the PNSF announced the formation of its own security force within the Saida camps—a force that would necessarily compete with the PLO's *al-kifah al-mussalah*.[23] The PNSF also began meeting with Fatah's traditional Lebanese partner in Saida, the PNO, situating itself as the PLO's rival for local alliances.[24] By February, *al-Safir* was publishing reports that PNSF-affiliated militants were applying their own justice system in Ain al-Hilweh, including one that described six armed cadres publicly executing two men in front of some 10,000 of the camp's residents for the crime of raping and killing a fourteen-year-old boy.[25] Meanwhile, the DFLP embarked on a social-cultural agenda by holding conferences, opening art galleries, and throwing festivals to commemorate the anniversary of its establishment. While it is likely that *al-Safir*—the leftist, Arab Nationalist, generally pro-Syrian newspaper that ran these stories—was somewhat more sympathetic toward the PNSF factions and typically sought to amplify their power, the important takeaway is that organizations tried to distinguish themselves by engaging in heavily localized, faction-to-faction status competition.[26]

The War of the Camps in Beirut and Sur made the situation in Saida increasingly tense. Amal units moved into the villages east and southeast of Saida and began to intermittently shell Ain al-Hilweh, though they never completely blockaded the camp. On October 5, 1986, the PNSF signed a ceasefire agreement with Amal (called the "Damascus Agreement") (Nofal 2006, 43). Yet despite these elite-level political deals, Mamdouh Nofal, then the DFLP commander in the area, writes that he met with both Fatah and PSP representatives to coordinate an operation to expel Amal from Saida's eastern suburbs and overlooking villages. PLO forces and their allies subsequently opened a front against Amal in Magdousheh (a village in the hills southeast of Saida) to force Amal to lift its sieges of Burj al-Barajneh, Shatila, and, by then, also Rashidiyeh (Y. Sayigh 1997, 593).[27] Walid Jumblatt, the PSP's leader, pledged to provide Fatah and the DFLP weapons and ammunition for a major operation against Amal; Arafat's representative agreed to obtain funding from Tunis (Nofal 2006, 53–55).

Engaging in guerrilla combat across hillsides and villages reinforced local, emergent organizational forms. Rather than fighting side-by-side in trenches and bunkers around a shared community (e.g., a camp), combatants dug in to hillsides and darted through village alleyways. Organizational divisions at the various fronts were stark; unlike the carefully organized defenses of Shatila and Burj al-Barajneh, each group operated autonomously under its leader in its own sector. Certain organizations shared sectors, but did not cooperate militarily or share supplies; if something went wrong, my interlocutors noted, the local factions would all blame each other.[28] Problems were so endemic that militants in Burj al-Shamali, who technically reported to a central command room in Ain al-Hilweh, recalled managing operations predominantly within their own camp to avoid Ain al-Hilweh's countless rivalries and flying accusations. Munadileh, the Marxist cadre and former nurse from Ain al-Hilweh, fought in the campaign and emphasized that during battle it was "every party for itself."[29]

Some mid- and high-ranking officers, in particular Nofal of the DFLP, attempted to manage these battlefield rivalries because they detracted from the organizations' military effectiveness.[30] However, the segmented, personalistic nature of the guerrilla groups in Saida meant that officers did not employ informal quotidian communication channels to coordinate across groups. At the time, Nofal actively wondered whether the centralized communication system that linked on-the-ground commanders to PLO offices in Tunisia was expressly designed to curb local leaders' independence and to control locally emergent groups (Nofal 2006, 241). Secondary sources also note that the highest levels of the PLO encouraged divisions between factions and even within Fatah:

> The ability to maintain direct voice and fax contact with individual combat officers in Lebanon, for example, encouraged petty rivalry and jealous competition for resources, as each sought the chairman's [Yasir Arafat's] ear. It also impeded the emergence of an integrated field command: when a joint operations room was formed with the other guerrilla groups in Ain al-Hilweh in November 1986, six Fatah battalion commanders and senior officials insisted on being present in addition to Arafat's personal representative 'Isam al-Lawh, while the local Force 17 commander, who was not invited, petulantly refused to join the offensive on Maghdusha as a means of registering his protest. (Y. Sayigh 1997, 604)

Arafat's micromanaging of the Magdousheh campaign, specifically of the Fatah commanders, reinforced the personalized militia form that had emerged in Saida. Evidence strongly indicates that owing to the local structure of militant organizations, meso-level officers in Saida had organizational incentives to jockey for Arafat's attention and money.

Even if the factions acted independently of each other, they did mobilize for similar reasons. Palestinians in Ain al-Hilweh interpreted Amal's decision to shell the camp as a collective attack on the community, prompting local PNSF affiliate factions to join the Magdousheh battles. Syrian-allied groups such as the PFLP and the PPSF eventually entered combat with the PLO-allied factions against Damascus's orders, as did Fatah-Revolutionary Council, a radical dissident organization. Other dissident organizations such as the PFLP-GC and Fatah al-Intifada fought to defend Ain al-Hilweh, but did not participate in the attacks on Magdousheh.[31] While moral commitments to Ain al-Hilweh and other Palestinian camp communities drove these local Palestinian units to open the Magdousheh front, the cross-cutting command institutions that linked members of the organizations in other cities did not materialize. When I asked Yusif about the dissident factions' disobedience at Magdousheh, he immediately responded:

> Look, I want to tell you something. People in Fatah did this so many times, they kept fighting when they were supposed to stop. But the people in PFLP, in Fatah al-Intifada, the guys on the Syrian side, they

were supposed to stay out of it and they fought. For them, Amal was sniping at the camp from Magdousheh. People were dying in the streets. They said "these are my parents, my brothers and sisters," and they made the decision to fight. They were sons of the camp first.[32]

Yet in the end, these sentiments seem to have amplified organizational segmentation in Saida. In contrast to foreign humanitarian workers in Beirut, who repeatedly emphasized behind-closed-doors coordination between ostensibly rival organizations, Barbara, the AFSC liaison in Saida, repeatedly encountered political impediments to aid delivery. While attempting to coordinate health aid, she reported: "We have had tremendous difficulties in this so-called coordination, with political struggles emerging as the root cause of some of those problems. I will not describe this in detail here, but suffice it to say that inter-Palestinian politics affects all aspects of life."[33] Fighting against orders or refusing to stop fighting exacerbated the distance between local militias and their exiled leadership. Fighters' insubordination further remade the relationship between expressly personalistic subfactions and international leaderships. Unable to give up their footholds in Saida, particularly as PLO members were expelled from Beirut in 1988 and 1989, organizational elites were forced to accept this status quo.

The War of the Camps in Sur

Patterns of remapping varied across the three camps in Sur, with distinct effects on conflict dynamics. While Amal sometimes deployed a blanket tactical approach to Palestinian communities in Sur, for instance when it launched a broad harassment and arrest campaign in al-Buss, Burj al-Shamali, and Rashidiyeh in December 1985, each camp had a distinct experience of the 1985–88 period. According to aid workers with the AFSC, Amal began sporadically shelling Rashidiyeh and sniping at civilians in its surroundings in summer of 1986. In the fall of 1986, in response to these escalations and events in Saida and Beirut, Palestinian militants attacked an Amal outpost, killing four militiamen.[34] At this point, Rashidiyeh's experience diverged from the two other Sur camps as Amal besieged it. And, unlike Beirut, clandestine operations acquired geographic footprints within the southern camps that were not under siege, representing a routinization of clandestine activities and the emergence of a robust organizational apparatus across Palestinian communities in South Lebanon.

Amal laid siege to Rashidiyeh, a camp of approximately 15,000 people, in the fall of 1986; a shared defensive front repulsed Amal's attempts to overrun the camp.[35] However, 590 people were injured and approximately 200 houses destroyed

(Nofal 2006, 44). Burj al-Shamali, by contrast, was the only camp to openly declare military neutrality during the War of the Camps. Abdullah (2008, 56) explains:

> As far as Burj al-Shamali camp is concerned, it did not enter the War of the Camps militarily for a number of reasons, the most important of which were: agreement between the actors and the political forces in the camp and their neighbors [referring to the surrounding Shi'i Lebanese neighborhood] not to enter into this war, in order to preserve the current relationship between the camp and the neighbors. The [modest] military capacities of Palestinian armed factions at the time also played a role in this.

Abdullah emphasizes that the camp's geographic location—an urban neighborhood in a predominantly Shi'i area of Sur—made it incredibly difficult to defend; Burj al-Shamali residents relayed that, at the time, they knew what was happening in Burj al-Barajneh (surrounded by a demographically mixed neighborhood with a large Shi'i population from which Amal recruited) and did not want to risk the same outcome.[36] However, in addition to supporting other camps, Burj al-Shamali's inhabitants also developed an advocacy organization called the Committee for the Defense of Palestinian Prisoners, which issued statements in support of Palestinian prisoners of Amal and criticized the Lebanese militia for arrest campaigns targeting the camp.[37] This collective effort built directly on more individualized prisoner advocacy efforts linked to mass incarceration under the Israeli occupation. Similar to the situation in Beirut, and in spite of the PLO-PNSF rivalry, individual-level practices similar to those employed in Beirut evolved in Sur when Amal besieged Rashidiyeh in 1986. For example, many Palestinians relied on personal contacts in Shi'a communities to protect them, though these practices do not seem to have been as institutionalized as they were in Beirut. For instances, Abu Zaki, a humanitarian worker from Rashidiyeh, explained that when Amal kidnapped him, he had no organizational apparatus to intervene on his behalf. He was released only when the Palestinian Shi'a parents of a child he had helped intervened by invoking kinship ties with Amal's regional head of security, who was also both Shi'a and Palestinian.[38] The large family's members belonged to both Palestinian and Lebanese political organizations, providing leverage for an under-the-table concession.

The Emergence of Cross-Regional Clandestine Networks

Within South Lebanon, a cross-regional clandestine relief apparatus emerged as a product of a perceived shared threat and the by-then well institutionalized, factionalized underground supply system. Burj al-Shamali's residents, for instance, collectively mobilized to support Rashidiyeh's besieged population with supplies such as food and cash (for bribes). To explain their reasoning, Tala, the wife of a PFLP-GC officer, told me: "The camp [Rashidiyeh] was besieged.... there were operations in every camp. We had to stick together."[39] In other words, though Burj al-Shamali itself was not besieged, its residents still felt that they were being targeted as Palestinians—whether through the starvation of their friends and family in Rashidiyeh or via less-dramatic repertoires involving arrests and arson.

Women, including many who had previously been uninvolved in military operations, related taking on clandestine roles that approximated those of women in the Beirut camps at this juncture, but with a larger geographic range. Tala pointed out that, despite overarching political divisions, women in her politically divided family smuggled money and food from Saida to Sur by using repurposed kinship networks that criss-crossed multiple militant organizations as cover for their travel and political contacts. Nadia, who worked for a social aid group in Ain al-Hilweh, would travel to Beirut to obtain funds before physically smuggling cash into Rashidiyeh and reporting back to her supervisors on local conditions in the camp. Her behavior was not unique; members of her organization living in Burj al-Shamali sent unaffiliated family and friends to Saida to pick up money from Nadia, which they subsequently returned to the Burj al-Shamali office to be transferred onward to Rashidiyeh.[40]

During the siege, people in Burj al-Shamali and al-Buss also organized secret nautical supply routes into the camp; unlike in Beirut, these groups consisted of small clusters of men who would fill coats with food, wait for nightfall, and launch small fishing dinghies and "military boats" (inflatable skiffs), to access the camp via the sea.[41] This strategy explicitly leveraged participants' well-honed boating skills and professional networks from the fishing industry in South Lebanon. Tala; her husband, Salah; and her brothers-in-law described how increasing attacks on Rashidiyeh and al-Buss, and thus the need for relief missions, inspired the creation of "[military] operations rooms" in the southern camps as well as underground emergency rooms to treat those injured during smuggling assignments, indicating similar counter-siege institutionalization as in Beirut.[42]

Women's Work as High-Risk Work

Within these zones, women's roles often shifted more frequently than men's as the organizations sought to adapt the regional logistics and intelligence apparatuses to the exigencies of the environment and the combat units' needs. Syrian and Lebanese armed groups also updated their own tactics and toolkits. For instance, Nofal emphasizes that Syrian army and intelligence forces began explicitly targeting women, given the crucial role they played. At one point, he explains, the Syrians caught one of his couriers and referred to her by name, indicating both that Syrian intelligence had at least partially penetrated the DFLP and that they were hunting individual women because of the roles they played. Nofal also describes a situation where the Syrians imprisoned two female DFLP cadres to explicitly try to force the DFLP to withdraw from Magdousheh, given the factions' reliance on women (Nofal 2006, 365).

Organizationally, as in Beirut, the General Union of Palestinian Women played an increasingly central role in coordinating wartime smuggling activities.[43] It was the hub through which women in the underground connected to families in the camps and, in some cases, also to the military leadership. Yusif noted that by 1985 or 1986 "there was a woman's office that managed all women's activities" including both smuggling and other logistics work. As the Lebanese and Syrians caught on to this system, the PLO began using organizations such as the General Union of Palestinian Students as well as humanitarian associations—frequently staffed by women who had served as smugglers—to funnel money into Lebanon.[44]

Repression led to the further professionalization of women who took on these roles via training and socialization, driving adaptation and the development of new overarching organizational capabilities. The GUPW took on a brokerage role that linked formal hierarchies and "on-paper" subdivisions to the emergent and informal logistic, financial, intelligence, medical, and supply apparatus. By time of the Battle of Magdousheh in 1986, the GUPW in Ain al-Hilweh had assumed management of previously more decentralized clandestine operations and was helping to coordinate support and medical services for fighters. By 1987, it had organized and was graduating entire classes of women educated in first aid.[45] Locating these roles under the GUPW, rather than under the command of individual factions, meant that women from across different factions worked together in status-equivalent roles under the same authority, in effect occupying hybrid positions in which they worked for the GUPW and individual political groups simultaneously. For example, the GUPW hosted a seminar on International Women's Day in March 1987 that explicitly incorporated both pro-PLO and PNSF-affiliated women while also reaching out to women in Lebanese factions to form a joint women's leadership in the region.[46] Munadileh noted that serving in these functions "brought women together. There were people from all of the organizations together. It [the GUPW] shared the revolutionary work with the men."[47] In Ain al-Hilweh, this unity contrasted the fragmentation and stricter political divisions that men in combat units faced.

Engineering Brokerage through Marriage

Nawal's experience illustrates the progressive feedback between a woman's political activity and her everyday relationships, in addition to the career trajectory of one of the most elite clandestine agents in the system. Currently an official in GUPW and a Fatah cadre, Nawal was encouraged by her family to join the *zaharat* in the late 1970s to "become strong." Her father worked in a central office in PLO headquarters; her brother had joined the *ashbal* as a child and became a cadre during the war. At the beginning of the War of the Camps, teenage Nawal and three of her friends from the *zaharat* started sneaking supplies such as food and cigarettes into Shatila, telling the Amal militiamen that they were simply visiting children. Nawal and her friends had no contact with or direction from higher authorities at this time.[48]

Hisham, a regional officer in Fatah and a former underground guerrilla in Beirut, explained that after he noticed the girls' ad hoc humanitarian operation, he took a liking to Nawal and eventually asked her to marry him.[49] Hisham brokered between Nawal and regional officers in Saida, leading to Nawal's advancement within both Fatah and the GUPW. Nawal recalled:

> During the second siege, I got married; I was [a teenager]. My husband wanted someone smart, someone who knows politics. He took me to his colleagues in the organization, and I began working in the Women's Union. I learned how it worked, I met the officer for the area. I shared in activities. [Me: *Like?*] Opening a kindergarten . . . cultural activities . . . bringing women to the Union.[50]

Hisham subsequently arranged for Nawal's military, ideological, and emergency first aid training through Fatah. As a trusted, well-trained cadre, Nawal began traveling as an emissary between Saida and Beirut offices, bridging various regional and functional divisions using remapped kinship ties (through her brother), marriage ties (through Hisham), and friendship ties (through old connections in Beirut).

The interaction between her quotidian relationships and organizational role resulted in Nawal's increasing centrality in both Fatah and the GUPW. Fatah promoted her as a military cadre in 1986, when she fought against Amal in the battle of Magdousheh :[51]

> The War of Magdousheh happened in 1986. I brought food to the soldiers. [Me: *Did you share in the battle?*] I was a soldier! I was with the guys! [Me: *How was the relationship between the guys and the women?*] It was like we were siblings. [Me: *How many women participated?*] There

were 20 women above who brought supplies like food and clothing to a couple hundred men below [in the battle]. All the girls were with their husbands. But if anything happened, we were soldiers! I was in battles!⁵²

Nawal's combat experience demonstrates how marriage ties could guide women into elite roles, creating new modes of militant organization such as the co-ed guerrilla front at Magdousheh. Their quotidian network relationships formed institutional bridges that granted many women access to new divisions of militant organizations.

Many husbands also advanced because of their wives' activism. Hisham was more likely to be selected for central roles because of Nawal's reputation, skill set, and influence in the GUPW. Other women also described how their marriages both served organizational ends and advanced partners' careers. Munadileh and her husband, Ashraf, whom she married in the mid-1980s, were selected as another elite spousal team to fight at Magdousheh; her previous experience in combat during the 1982 invasion and her marriage to a fellow cadre made her husband a more attractive candidate for front-line roles. These dynamic processes of organizational and social feedback thus established new pathways to accruing influence within the guerrilla party system while also creating new understandings of individual "eliteness" within the factions and broader society.⁵³

Remaking Gender Relations?

Other offices within the factions' military, political, and social apparatus were not always as welcoming toward women, nor were all male cadres supportive of women moving into high-responsibility roles (or even their entry into the workforce). In a climate where women were participating alongside men and accepting extreme levels of risk, many women continuously confronted sexism as well as unwanted advances from their own colleagues.

Yet, it also appears that women also increasingly complained to their chain of command when they encountered these behaviors, demonstrating how women's changing roles in emergent organizations positioned them to demand accountability. Given the roles that women played, sexist and predatory behavior became unacceptable in new ways. In one case, Nofal received a complaint from a nurse who was being harassed by her supervisor, Abu Fahad, a doctor in the clinic. In addition to accusing Abu Fahad of corruption, she informed Nofal: ". . . and most importantly, this brother believes that every girl working in the revolution or anyplace outside her house is a whore." The woman specifically requested that Nofal reassign her to "private work . . . transferring arms to the interior" as a means to escape the doctor's unwanted advances. She also proposed obtaining a foreign passport for operations, noting her UNRWA education and history as someone who had "rebelled against her family since she was small" as evidence of her competence for the job. The woman finished her request by informing Nofal "I joined the revolution for my honor and my people's honor, and I will not accept to be insulted by Abu Fahad or anyone else." Nofal writes that he mentioned "the nurse's request and her reasons" to Abdulkarim [another official in the DFLP]; Abdulkarim then informed Nofal that "her problems with Abu Fahad were expected" and suggested transferring the woman to another clinic while they investigated whether her foreign passport plan was feasible (Nofal 2006, 296).

Nofal's description of this interaction, which occurred during the Magdousheh engagement, reveals much about gender dynamics within the DFLP at the time. While he does not seem to find Abu Fahad's behavior entirely surprising, it does seem that both Nofal and Abdulkarim recognized the man's behavior as a distinct problem in view of how the local DFLP organization had evolved in terms of staffing and philosophy. Though it was a Marxist organization, there were still members of the DFLP who felt women should not work outside the home. The unnamed cadre was not the first woman in a leftist group to undergo this stark realization; in her autobiography, Leila Khaled (1973) explicitly writes that she experienced sexism in meetings she attended in Sur in the early 1970s. However, by the mid-1980s, at least some women seem to have decided to formally report harassment to a military chain of command; in this case, the woman's superior officers took seriously her report, her request for transfer, and her proposal for future clandestine missions.

During the War of the Camps, direct threats to these communities produced a spectrum of local responses; Burj al-Shamali's neutrality flowed from the historical experience of collective targeting and the practical assessment that that the camp could not sustain a siege given its geography or resources. This unified dynamic played a key role in residents' choice to support resisters in Rashidiyeh, where the camp community mobilized a shared military front. In Saida, past and contemporary repertoires of violence—dominated by denunciation, betrayal, and assassination—encouraged individuals and families to affiliate with local, personalized militias to ensure their protection. The guerrilla wars in Magdousheh between Palestinian organizations and the Lebanese militia Amal further reinforced this system; local leaders fought for power and failed to build a cohesive military front. Critically, insubordination during this time allowed local commands to challenge elite authority, thus enhancing their relative status and remapping local branches of larger factions into personalistic militias. Perhaps unsurprisingly, several key leaders in Saida subsequently created their own named organizations, trading their within-faction autonomy for independence.

These were neither linear nor path-dependent processes. As Palestinian groups in South Lebanon faced counterinsurgent and ethnic cleansing strategies, locally specific organizational forms emerged in response to exogenous "push" factors (e.g., evictions by Lebanese militias) and endogenous "pull" factors (e.g., widespread suspicion of returning prisoners and resentment toward reinfiltrating officers). Contingent factors also played a role. Yasir Arafat, chairman of the PLO and leader of Fatah, employed a number of leadership strategies across the camps and met with different responses from meso-level officers. His micro-management of Fatah fighters during the guerrilla war in Magdousheh entrenched fragmented cells in Saida, leaving groups open to manipulation and infighting.

Soon after the War of the Camps, Fatah and Fatah-Revolutionary Council fought a gruesome war over Ain al-Hilweh. In Beirut, Amal, the Syrians, and their Palestinian allies expelled known surviving Fatah officers. Fatah members who remained in Beirut went underground; those who left Beirut filtered into the southern camps, a distinct political system in which they were forced to negotiate new roles for themselves as well as protection for their families.[54] For violating orders at Magdousheh, Syria punished PFLP leaders from Saida, PPSF officers, and the DFLP politburo in Damascus (the politburo for its inability to control the DFLP contingent in Saida) (Y. Sayigh 1997, 593–94). The PFLP subsequently resumed relations with Fatah and the PPSF withdrew from the PNSF.

Organizational dynamics throughout the 1980s shaped possibilities for the 1990s. For example, one study conducted in Ain al-Hilweh in 1991 found that 70 percent of residents felt "unfree" in the camp and that "[t]he proliferation of armed factions in the camp has often led in the past to bloody clashes many of which have been instigated by trivial issues." The study strongly hints at political fragmentation and alienation from the mainstream factions, with only 11.5 percent of residents reporting allegiance to the PLO, 2 percent reporting loyalty to pro-Syrian Palestinian factions, 3.4 percent to Palestinian nationalist groups, 16.4 percent to "local Islamic groups which appeared only in the 1980s," and 58.9 percent of the random sample reporting no allegiance to any group (Khashan 1992, 15). However, researchers also learned that over 90 percent of the camp's residents identified Syrian intelligence as the biggest threat to their personal safety (Khashan 1992, 7–8), despite the fact that the Syrian occupation ended north of Saida, thus emphasizing the multilayered political context in which people lived.

Abu Taha, a member of the DFLP's Central Committee, pointed out the longer-term, shared consequences of the War of the Camps: "In the war, entire areas of South Lebanon were destroyed, and people couldn't leave to work during the sieges. Afterwards, people haven't been as well educated, there is no money for scholarships, the universities are expensive, and healthcare—especially access to operations—is a major issue."[55] Abu Taha's comment represents a common view of the regional consequences of the 1980s wars; issues related to destruction, immobility, and economic opportunities during wars have filtered through social networks and compounded across generations. I turn more deliberately to some of these issues in the conclusion.

Conclusion

ECHOES OF ORGANIZATIONS

On November 12, 2015, a massive suicide bomb planted by Islamic State in Iraq and Syria (ISIS) ripped through a neighborhood adjacent to Burj al-Barajneh camp. Immediately after the explosion, I watched from the United States as friends in the camp took to social media calling for blood donations, including by sharing specific requests for A negative and B negative type blood from local hospitals. Someone started the hashtag "With South Dahiyeh" and attached it to these posts. Friends from the camp told me, via Facebook Messenger and WhatsApp, that the camp mosque was also announcing the blood drive on its speakers.

Years before, my interlocutors had explained that during the War of the Camps, everyone—including even very young children—was taught what their blood type was, in case they or anyone else were ever in need of a transfusion during the siege. This simple, potentially lifesaving piece of knowledge is something that many of my own North American and European friends don't know about themselves. The practice of teaching it originated during the War of the Camps, when Palestinians were cut off from external supplies and the hospitals in Burj al-Barajneh and Shatila were frequently in desperate need of blood donations.

Much of what I was able to observe as a researcher in Lebanon fell into the category of what I term holdover practices: constitutive knowledge, skills, practices, and routines developed under dire conditions that have been worked into the everyday banalities of more peaceful times. For example, one employee of a civil society organization once commented to me that her group was able to address gender-based violence by employing women who had worked in the underground during the Israeli occupation and the War of the Camps. She explained that having smuggled money to families left those women with trust-based ties as well as intimate awareness of family dynamics that allowed them to reach out in ways that others could not. I witnessed countless moments when people invoked the past—when women like Intisar were sexually harassed; when people like Abu Hadi had to solve a problem related to an aggressive, armed, potentially violent parent; or when they reached for old connections and points of reference. I listened as people occasionally spoke wistfully about the days of the War of the Camps, when, at least to them, people were together. These holdover practices hinted at the lasting influence of organizational and community-level adaptations to past violence and repression.

This book argues that militant groups' adaptive trajectories flow from interactions between formal organizational hierarchies, repertoires of wartime violence, and the social infrastructure of quotidian network relationships that undergird, intersect with, and sometimes challenge official chains of command. It emphasizes that the plasticity of social ties facilitates militants' repurposing and remapping of their relationships, enabling organizational adaptation. Moreover, it demonstrates that militant adaptability is not simply a function of inherent group attributes or capacities. Rather, people individually and collectively interpret repertoires of wartime violence as actors embedded in multiple social networks and respond to the everyday challenges that occupation and civil conflict pose in a relational context. I have used the setting of 1980s Lebanon—during conflicts that have become stereotypes of "complexity" (Leenders 2012, 1; Ghosn and Parkinson 2019, 494)—to illustrate how discrete elements of belligerents' tactical repertoires restructure social networks, driving organizational adaptation and emergence, processes that in turn shape the military and social dimensions of ongoing conflict and its aftermath.

This theoretical and empirical perspective takes complexity and dynamism seriously, especially in terms of feedback between formal organizational and quotidian social worlds. That is, it provides an alternative to linear understandings of causality, event-based models of conflict, and rationalist assumptions of militant decision-making in favor of analytically emphasizing the messy realities of war via a relational, multiple-network perspective that systematically captures the interactions that collectively bring about organizational as well as and social change. Such a perspective spotlights a far greater realm of possible trajectories for both organizations and communities in conflict than what research and policy currently postulate.

The dynamics this book explores provide a nuanced, grounded, and holistic account of the organizational and social processes that constitute intrastate conflict. This type of approach is particularly significant in a time when internationalized intrastate conflicts such as those in 1980s Lebanon are becoming more prevalent (Dupuy et al. 2017). One need only look at Ukraine, Libya, the Central African Republic, Syria, Iraq, the Philippines, or even Mexico's cartel wars to conclude that the analytical simplicity of an event-based "rebels versus the state" model of intrastate warfare frequently cannot capture the political, geographic, economic, or social processes that characterize contemporary conflicts. Understanding these armed struggles necessitates theoretical and empirical approaches that embrace complexity. In the following pages, I explore some of the implications of this approach for ongoing and future research trajectories. Specifically, I focus on lessons for researchers interested in militant organizations' behavior in war, gender and conflict, and understandings of the social legacies of war and violence.

Rethinking Intrastate Warfare

This book offers several broad lessons for those interested in civil or intrastate war, political violence, insurgency, and asymmetrical warfare. First, rather than focusing on abstract and subjective concepts of militant "success" or "failure" or on more simple measures of "survival" or "death," this volume complicates scholarly and policy-oriented understandings of organizational behavior and outcomes in armed conflict. Specifically, it introduces a new category of analysis—emergent organizations—and points to their significance in conflict processes. In so doing, it shows that formal organizational design and institutional structure cannot independently predict or ensure "success" in terms of a group's resilience or survival, nor can it reliably predict the use of violent versus nonviolent tactics. Rather, the structure of organizational networks, the degree of militants' social embeddedness, and local environment all matter for how organizations adapt and behave. This perspective complements and moves beyond scholarship that analyzes militant groups' behaviors solely through formal, macro-structural traits such as cohesion/fragmentation or centralization/decentralization (Humphreys and Weinstein 2006; Weinstein 2007; Johnston 2008; Gutiérrez-Sanín and Giustozzi 2010; Sinno 2010; Serena 2014). While certain types of formal stratification or fragmentation may have high potential for change, outcomes fundamentally depend on how militants adapt in the moment, which is a product of how violence shapes the networks in which they are embedded and their own interpretations of it.

In emphasizing militants' perceptions and understandings of their environments via the lens of multiple-network embeddedness, this book demonstrates how the intersection of organizational and everyday networks both creates and forecloses possibilities for militant groups. Specifically, the social infrastructure that undergirds and intersects with militant structures shapes both the ways that people understand repertoires of violence and repression as well as how they respond to them. This finding has particular salience for recent conclusions that the relationship between rebel governance and military capacity is highly contingent and conditional (Stewart 2020, 27–29). For example, it explains why an ostensibly ideal initial combination of resource endowments or connections with civilian communities may produce an expected set of "positive" outcomes, such as a set of robust governing institutions and the absence of factional violence, in one locale but not in another. Militants may benefit, as Palestinian organizations did, from the ties that governing institutions generate and deepen because they lay the groundwork for future repurposing and remapping across organizational divisions that in turn produce, for example, dispute resolution mechanisms and social service provision. Yet deep connections to civilian communities may also elicit tensions between on-the-ground militants and distant elite leaderships, producing friction and the potential for disobedience, as they did in both Beirut and South Lebanon.

Relational Plasticity, Social Infrastructure, and Organizational Change

Analytically leveraging the concept of relational plasticity—the innate malleability of social relationships that allows militants to reshape their social relationships to organizational ends and vice versa—embraces the fact that actors are inherently socially embedded, conflicted by shifting modes of organizational and quotidian belonging, and infinitely creative in how they leverage social ties. Centering relational plasticity emphasizes interpretive potential in social networks, rather than assuming that specific types of connections—e.g., family ties (Pedahzur and Perliger 2006)—naturally or consistently do certain types of political work. The plasticity of ties is particularly important to understanding how social infrastructure and organizational hierarchies interact to influence militant behavior and broader community dynamics. For example, rather than leveraging marriage ties as Palestinian factions did in Magdousheh, many militant organizations actively seek to break down or simply reformat, rather than exploit militants' existing, everyday relationships. Jeff Goodwin (1997), for example, points out that the Huk leadership saw romantic ties as impediments to military discipline and solidarity and therefore forbade them, a move that could conceivably limit adaptive options for the group. In some contemporary national resistance projects, such as the Kurdistan Freedom Movement, members abstain from sexual relations "as pushback to patriarchal conditions," which in turn constitutes part of a larger political project that challenges and reconceptualizes existing romantic norms and gender identities ("Open Letter to the Public" 2021). Other groups seek to engineer relations in particular ways, according to their ideological leanings (Asal et al. 2013; Thomas and Bond 2015). For example, leftist organizations such as the Eritrean People's Liberation Front (EPLF) trained and deployed men and women together, meaning that women in the EPLF were not situated as brokers between organizational subdivisions. Indeed, clandestine networks in the EPLF did not flow through marriage ties (which were frequently engineered within units); rather, non-cadre women *bartenders* liaised with militant men who acted as smugglers and couriers (Wilson 1991, 82–84; Bernal 2001; Pool 2001). In a different vein, Afghan militant groups approached embeddedness with local *qawm* or tribal structures in very different ways. For example, Hezb-i-Islami (led by Gulbuddin Hekmatyar) espoused the practice of *hijrat*, or evacuating land inhabited by infidels. Hezb-i-Islami fighters—who consisted predominantly of nontribal Pashtuns (Roy 1986, 133)—consequently cleared the land that they controlled of local tribes and villages, depending fully on training, a disciplined Leninist military structure, and external support to command the battlefield. One obvious question to ask is whether designing and institutionalizing organizational structures based on a strict Marxist-Leninist or religious ideology, including the explicit breakdown or rearranging of quotidian ties, could render a group relationally hypo-plastic, in other words, unable to remap relations in order to adapt. The relationship between plasticity, embeddedness, adaptability, and social change merits further investigation.

In a different vein, it seems improbable that organizations with high proportions of foreign fighters—such as Jabhat al-Nusra in Syria, or the Arab Mujahidin in Chechnya—lean heavily on local quotidian ties. When do these types of organizations seek to develop such relationships over time by, for example, marrying into local populations, as many foreign Islamic State fighters did (Moaveni 2015, 2019)? What outcomes are associated with the development of those quotidian ties? Pauline Moore (2019), for instance, finds that while insurgent groups that recruit foreign fighters are more likely to abuse civilians than those who don't, foreign fighters who are locally socially embedded are associated with comparatively lower levels of harm. Further examination of these dynamics would provide crucial insight into a growing number of protracted armed conflicts that feature organizationally complex and strategically sophisticated militant groups that recruit internationally and at times also operate alongside private military organizations. Moreover, it could also provide insight into broader processes of social change linked to community-level adoption of organizational norms and practices.

The concept of relational plasticity in analyses of organizational decision-making and behavior applies beyond the realm of militant organizations. For instance, viewing organizational adaptation through the lens of repurposing, re-mapping, and emergence provides insight into issues such as political party development and democratic accountability. Overlap between organizational and quotidian networks is an inherent aspect of political life. Members of American pharmacist networks that intersect with particular religious organizations refuse to dispense prescriptions, Chinese government officials provide public goods to certain localities in light of their inclusion in local moral solidarity networks (Tsai 2007), and Israeli bureaucrats facilitate settlement activity because of their location in religious-nationalist activist networks (Haklai 2007). Depending on context, certain social network identifications will be more salient *or have the potential to become more salient as political conditions change*. Rather than analyzing actors in isolation from the multiple social networks in which they are embedded, scholars should incorporate relational context into a broader range of research. Studying the ways in which particular configurations of overlap produce unexpected political and social outcomes is a productive line of future inquiry.

Insiders on the Outside

This book repeatedly demonstrates that significant cleavages arose between on-the-ground cadres and exiled leaderships during the period studied. In South Lebanon and in Beirut, schisms between those who gave top-down orders from exile and those who fought and lived through the occupation and civil war deepened significantly over the course of the 1980s. Disobedience, violence, and local narratives entrenched a local-versus-exile dynamic that repeatedly disrupted chains of command. These cleavages have continued to influence Palestinian factional politics in Lebanon, especially via moral narratives surrounding authenticity and power (Parkinson 2016).

Despite media attention to similar "insider-outsider" dynamics in conflicts such as the Syrian Civil War (Abouzeid 2013) and empirical similarities to organizations such as the African National Congress (Ellis 2013, 151–204), royalist Afghan *muhajidin* groups, and Palestinian Hamas, limited research expressly examines the politics of exiled leaderships, their relationships with militants and communities on the ground, and conflict outcomes. In one example, Wendy Pearlman's (2011) research on cohesion and fragmentation in the Palestinian National Movement recognizes this insider/outsider distinction with regards to the divide between the PLO/Fatah leadership in Tunis and on-the-ground organizers in the West Bank; other research has examined the emergence and politics of Fatah's "New Guard" in the West Bank (see, e.g., Harb 2009). Exile dynamics affect command and control as well as local militant cultures and patterns of mobilization. These factors, in turn, have substantial potential to affect processes of negotiations, demobilization, and on-the-ground peacebuilding, especially if on-the-ground militants do not see their internationally recognized leadership as representative, trustworthy, empathetic, or accountable. The commonality of these inside-outside dynamics, and the informal power associated with meso-level commanders, imply serious disconnects between those who represent rebel groups on the international stage versus those fundamentally responsible for implementing ceasefires and peace agreements at the local level. Indeed, research has shown that meso-level commanders, rather than members of elite leadership, hold unique power to remobilize local soldiers under their command (Daly 2014; 2016). This study had gone even further by revealing how the localized nature of violence and organizational evolution in intrastate wars may create entirely different organizational forms and institutions across space and time, meaning that programs and policies that work in one region may fail in another. More research must be done to acknowledge the challenges and opportunities that these variations provide.

Ethnicity, Insurgency, and Network Analysis

Even as the ground–elite distinction played out across Palestinian factions, other potential cleavages—including those of an ethnic and sectarian nature—did not operate the way that prominent civil war literature would predict (Horowitz 2000; Toft 2005; Cederman and Girardin 2007; Cederman et al. 2010). Rather, strong, trust-based quotidian relationships that formed, for example, via military training, joint labor organizing, marriage, or co-membership on a football team acted as bridges between Palestinians and Lebanese, Muslims and Christians, and Sunnis and Shi'as. These bridging relationships proved central to sustaining community-level mobilization, organizations' armed operations, and clandestine information and logistics efforts. The salience that militants assigned to various modes of identification, whether based on class, ideology, gender, or neighborhood, varied based on how repertoires of violence activated and resonated within people's multiplex networks.

The argument and evidence put forth in this volume concur with previous research indicating that group-level analysis is simply too coarse a measure to explain outcomes such as conflict onset and variations in mobilization. For example, in his research on the Syrian conflict's trajectory, Kevin Mazur (2019, 996) finds that "the social units possessing the relevant network properties are often not entire ethnic groups. Rather, clans, extended families, and towns are more likely to contain such networks and thus, act in solidarity."[1] Mazur points to how network "frontiers"—that is, boundaries between dominant and marginalized groups—and dense, local social networks shape mobilization. He demonstrates that in Syria, pro-regime, clientelistic brokers' control over tight-knit local solidarity networks disintegrated in the face of regime violence and "acts of misrule"; dense, local, trust-based ties subsequently provided grounds for mobilization based on shared grievance (Mazur 2019, 482–483, 487–488). While Mazur emphasizes how clientelistic ties provide ethnically exclusive regimes control over dense local networks in times of stability via brokerage across network frontiers, his deeper theoretical point pertains to the importance of brokers and dense, community-level relations in shaping conflict dynamics. While ethnic and patron-client relationships may be strongly influential in some contexts and time frames, we should not assume the uniform primacy or salience of any one mode of collective identification or organizing across either space or time.[2]

This book emphasizes people's systematic creativity in actively remapping social network ties in the face of a variety of repertoires of violence. It demonstrates that strong quotidian relationships in one domain—whether familial, neighborhood-based, team-based, or congregational—frequently connect populations that appear to be "divided" in another domain—whether between majority and minority ethnic groups or militant parties. These network bridges facilitate myriad adaptations. The localized repertoires of violence that belligerents use to target organizations and communities activate various modes of identification (e.g., those based on gender), inspire new collective narratives (e.g., of vulnerability and international responsibility), prompt network repurposing and remapping (e.g., based on neighborhood ties), and produce emergent modes of organizing resistance (e.g., a protest movement). This is why deliberate attempts to fragment one type of social network via a repertoire including, for instance, mass incarceration, collaboration, or checkpoint building (Gade 2020) will almost always initiate unexpected responses; those deploying it do not consider the complexity of social ties.

It's worth noting that my interlocutors actively distinguished between Palestinian and Lebanese parties, their members (as a collective), and individual cadres and affiliates. For them, specifically local party organization and cultures shaped outcomes—whether among Lebanese militias, units within the IDF, or camp-level branches of different Palestinian factions. They refused to treat party membership, group-level sectarian categorization, and personal religious belief as coterminus. Put differently: no one in this study reported making decisions simply because others were "Sunni" or "Palestinian." From a practical standpoint, this granular view of individuals' social affiliations makes sense. Assumptions of group-ness weren't viable decision-making heuristics during the wars of the 1980s, in terms of patterns of collaboration, shifting party alliances, and the reality of intermarriage, friendship, and labor solidarity in everyday social networks (especially in the demographically mixed neighborhoods of Beirut's "Belt of Misery"). Lebanese trained with and served in Palestinian organizations (and vice versa); Christian Palestinians and Lebanese were victims of right-wing, Lebanese Christian militia violence despite their religious beliefs; members of rival Palestinian ideological currents put them aside to protect friends and family. This behavior isn't surprising. It squares with extensive scholarship that challenges "sect-all-the-way-down" framings of Middle East politics (Cammett and Issar 2010; Clark and Salloukh 2013; Cammett 2014; Salloukh et al. 2015) and emphasizes the need to understand conflict through the lens of local histories (Makdisi 2000; Wedeen 2008, chap. 4; Philbrick Yadav 2014) and cross-cutting ideological currents (Schulhofer-Wohl 2020, chaps. 3 and 4).

Attention to these micro- and meso-level network relationships clearly offers important insights for understanding intrastate wars in terms of mobilization, the roles individuals come to play, and organizations' ability to sustain operations. The significance of these ties suggests that reducing conflicts in the Middle East to "these fights between the Sunni and Shi'a side of the region," as US policymakers continue to do (Sen. Chris Murphy, quoted in Petti 2021), does a severe disservice to understanding conflict and its on-the-ground consequences. More research should focus on how regimes strategically "sectarianize" and "ethnicize" conflicts (Fielding-Smith 2015; Majed 2016; Gordon and Parkinson 2018; Mazur 2021) and the role that both elites and foreign actors play in reifying ethnic, sectarian, national, and other identity categories, often for domestic political goals (Lawrence 2010, 2013; Torbati 2019).

Gender and Conflict

This book also holds lessons for incorporating gender-based analysis and feminist approaches more centrally into conflict studies. The experience of Palestinian militants in Lebanon reaffirms previous findings that militants' and civilians' experiences of war are deeply gendered (Tétreault 1994; Enloe 2000; Alison 2003, 2004; Viterna 2006, 2013; Sjoberg and Gentry 2007; E. J. Wood 2008; Coulter 2009; Eriksson Baaz and Stern 2009, 2013; Sjoberg 2013; Gowrinathan 2017, 2021; Eggert 2018; Kinsella 2019). It also underscores the reality that, given the militant roles that women play and the effects that conflict has on their lives, it is absurd to study intrastate war or its aftermath without addressing gender, a point that feminist scholars have repeatedly made (Lake 2014; Tripp 2015; Berry 2017, 2018; Lake and Berry 2017).

This book builds upon this prior work by demonstrating that many of the gendered hierarchies, motivations, and roles that outsiders project on to rebel work do not pan out on the ground. That is, the idea that intelligence, financial, social service, and logistics-centric labor—often assumed to be "women's roles"—are naturally less prestigious, less risky, or less important to armed conflict (Thomas and Wood 2017; R. M. Wood and Thomas 2017) does not align with militants' own assessments of the organizational distribution and value of labor. These tendencies may be compounded by what Timothy Wickham-Crowley, among others, has called the "high newsworthiness" of gun-toting female fighters (Wickham-Crowley 1992, 21). Collectively, these portrayals of women in war contribute to both a systematic underestimation of support, logistics, and intelligence units' importance and a biased representation of female rebels. In keeping with feminist research that emphasizes the need to move beyond stereotypes of militant women as "mothers, monsters, [or] whores" (Sjoberg and Gentry 2007), this book emphasizes how gender intertwines with and shapes mobilization, organizational hierarchies, and noncombatant activism. It eschews external categories in favor of serious engagement with militants' own complex experiences and recollections, thus helping to recalibrate scholarly and policy understandings of the gendered nature of intrastate warfare.

Women *do* frequently take on backstage roles during civil war and anti-occupation movements. In Cuba, women served as couriers, underground publishers, money smugglers, and officers in the clandestine Action and Sabotage brigades; many came to the movement via family or neighbors (Klouzal 2008, 59, 62–63, 87, 89). The Association of Indonesian Women funneled women activists into the nationalist movement during the Indonesian campaign against the Japanese occupation; there, they carried out intelligence operations, provided logistic and medical services, and organized social services in addition to participating in active combat (MacFarland 1994, 197). Women have been centrally involved in clandestine operations in, for example, Irish, Algerian, and Eritrean civil wars well as serving as ground troops (Wilson 1991; Amrane-Minne 1992, 2004; Klouzal 2008). Evidence indicates that the same pattern may hold for recent conflicts in Libya, Syria, and Iraq (BBC 2011; Holmes 2012; *Economist* 2013; Moaveni 2015, 2019; Bond et al. 2019).

However, the argument presented in this book is that women often play these roles because of the *structural* positions that they inhabit rather than because of innate social characteristics. Indeed, in other contexts of intrastate war, revolution, and anti-occupation or liberation movements, other actors conduct this brokerage-based labor owing to their relational context, trustworthiness, and skill sets. During the siege of Sarajevo, members of Serb and Muslim families who had intermarried acted as smugglers (Andreas 2008, 65). So did local employees of foreign humanitarian organizations; they had access to the coveted "blue cards" that allowed for safe passage (Andreas 2008, chap. 2). In Zimbabwe, children who attended boarding schools served as informational brokers between urban areas and more rural communities, updating their mothers about the anti-colonial struggle during holidays at home. Those mothers subsequently participated in underground operations by providing food, compiling intelligence, transferring money, and serving in—and leading—village committees (MacFarland 1994, 72–73; Klouzal 2008). This variation speaks not only to organizations' social resources, but also to interactions between social infrastructure and repertoires of violence, with context-specific brokers emerging as a result. The role of these informal structures is broadly overlooked by the extant literature, in part because they are rarely covered by journalists, identified as power centers by mediators or NGOs, or chronicled by militant organizations themselves.

Violence beyond the Headlines

While usually portrayed as politically defining, most intrastate conflicts aren't decided by rapid-fire battlefield engagements, nor does combat alone dictate organizational trajectories. Rather, insurgency and other forms of intrastate conflict may be best described as grueling military, political, and social tests of organizational endurance and innovation. They usually last for several years, if not decades (Fearon 2004; Hegre 2004; Cunningham 2006; Balcells and Kalyvas 2014). This book's emphasis on the various forms of labor—from intelligence to logistics, sabotage, publishing, social services, protest, advocacy, and combat—demonstrates how both violent and nonviolent labor complement and shape each other's impact on organizational and broader political outcomes. While most work on rebel groups has focused disproportionately on young male combatants, the evidence presented in this book portrays a more nuanced picture of the labor of armed resistance. Here it is also important to underscore the fact that people who are front-line combatants one month may be teachers the next; as in other political organizations and vocations, many militants move across subdivisions as they progress through the ranks, making their professional trajectories an important point of analysis in rebellion.

To focus only upon violence that can be seen, heard, and quantified is a mistake (Parkinson 2015). Scholars such as Timothy Pachirat (2011) have argued that hidden or less-commented-upon violence carries significant analytical heft in terms of understanding broader politics and political systems. Shifting analytical focus off spectacular, performative violence produces an account of war that recognizes the local and global sociopolitical significance of patterns of violence and repression that may be hard to measure but that have long-standing effects. These include forced disappearance and incarceration, in addition to starvation and withholding of medical treatment. Collaboration, infiltration, denunciation, and intimate betrayals—as well as deep loyalties—are features, not bugs, of any civil war or occupation, as both research and artistic renditions such as the Palestinian film *Omar* (Abu-Assad 2013) and the Canadian film *Incendies* (Villeneuve 2010) recognize. And yet they are frequently omitted from scholarly and policy-based representations of conflict.

This reality is attached to a macabre arithmetic in the contemporary Middle East, where multiyear (and sometimes multidecade) internationalized intrastate conflicts in Syria, Iraq, Afghanistan, Turkey, Yemen, Libya, and Sudan accounted for approximately 90 percent of an estimated 102,000 global battle deaths in 2016 (Dupuy et al. 2017, 3). Casualty numbers are, however, a matter of contention in any conflict (Andreas and Greenhill 2010). In 2014, the United Nations stopped updating its overall death count for Syria, acknowledging that it no longer had the ability to reliably update and verify the numbers (Ohlheiser 2014); in 2016, casualty estimates for the duration of the Syrian Civil war ranged from the mid-100,000s (caveated for being low) and the high 400,000s (Taylor 2016). Yet the oft-hidden aspects of civil war and occupation violence are extraordinarily salient for political outcomes in the contemporary Middle East. Siege has been a feature of wars in Syria, Yemen, and Iraq, as it was in Chechnya and the former Yugoslavia. Despite a long media focus on Aleppo, Syria's second city, over a dozen Syrian cities and huge neighborhoods of Damascus, including Yarmouk and Eastern Ghouta, have experienced protracted sieges since the war began in 2011.

The erasure of conflict and its constitutive labor may also occur via other mechanisms, such as siege, which may grind on so long that it loses media and public attention (Andreas 2008; Borri 2013). Indeed, multiple studies demonstrate that these "fatigue effects" and other journalistic biases (Davenport 2009) affect analyses of conflicts from First Intifada in Palestine to the US invasion of Iraq (Gerner and Schrodt 1998; Pérez-Peña 2008). Moreover, casualty counts only speak to those killed as a direct consequence of armed conflict, not due to disease or disappearance (for example), which are both notoriously hard to measure. Focusing exclusively on battlefield deaths ignores those who perish while incarcerated in prisons such as Saydnaya in Syria, where an estimated 17,723 people died between March 2011 and August 2016 (Wainwright 2016). The Syrian Network for Human Rights estimates that belligerents in Syria—primarily the state itself—had disappeared over 100,000 people (Syrian Network for Human Rights 2020, 2); 3,364 medical personnel, professionals who are protected under international law, were arrested or disappeared (Syrian Network for Human Rights 2021, 5). In Yemen, battlefield casualty numbers do not account for nearly 4,000 people who have died from cholera or the estimated 2,510,806 people who have been infected (Electronic Disease Early Warning System 2018; World Health Organization 2020). Nor does an emphasis on battlefield casualties encompass the immediate social repercussions of the fact that "the main causes of avoidable deaths in Yemen are communicable diseases, maternal, perinatal and nutritional conditions (together accounting for 50% of mortality)" (World Health Organization 2017).

Scholars of civil wars, including those in Mozambique, the United States, and Afghanistan, have also noted regional differences in incumbent violence and militant behavior (Roy 1986; Rubin 2002; Lubkemann 2008; Geiger 2010). How militants interpret patterns of violence and resolve challenges that stem from the nonlethal and indirect aspects of wartime repertoires—ways to transfer information, identify collaborators, feed communities, educate children, and replenish their ranks—make all the difference in the forms that they take. In other words, while certain aspects of violent repertoires may never make it into the global headlines or into scholarly data sets, they have a profound effect on how organizations as well as communities understand war and participate in organizational politics related to it. They shape people's participation in militant organizations, grassroots social movements, and wartime contentious politics.

These realities speak to one of this book's core underlying themes: that while wartime casualties matter, deadly battlefield violence is only one piece of the puzzle when it comes to how people experience wartime violence, how they interpret those experiences, and how their understandings interact with broader politics. Indeed, combat medicine has drastically reduced the incidence of battlefield death, making nonlethal battlefield injuries more prevalent (Fazal 2014, 96); compared to past eras, more people are living to participate another day after experiencing various forms of violent contention. To capture this reality, this book has sought to center the common, often less spectacular, and slower-paced (when compared to conventional warfare) modes of violence—incarceration, collaboration, harassment, starvation, besiegement—that shape millions of peoples' experiences of war and their resulting participation in organizational politics. The processes described in this book do not flow from individualized reactions to death. Rather, they are the results of militants', survivors', and bystanders' complex, relational, strategic, emotion-laden, and above all *human* decision-making. Bystandership and survivorship, in of themselves, have profound effects on individual participation, organizational adaptation, and social change in war.

Violence is not simply death; militants are not merely men with guns. Embracing complexity in the study of intrastate conflict highlights how militant social embeddedness, capacities for organizational improvisation, and contingency make prediction of civil war outcomes both difficult and problematic. This book demonstrates that two of the strongest militaries in the Middle East could not eliminate either Palestinian military or political organizing in Lebanon, despite those organizations' repeated battlefield defeats. Furthermore, it suggests that their efforts to do so inspired fresh mobilization, reanimated survivors, taught militants new skills, and helped to produce organizationally diverse modes of both violent and nonviolent resistance. Simplified accounts of organizational decision-making and behavior mask the processes that shape these outcomes, presenting a sanitized, if parsimonious, account of intrastate conflict dynamics. The approach outlined in this book de-emphasizes casualty counting and battlefield scorecards in favor of analyzing how individual experiences of armed conflict influence organizational trajectories. The larger point here is not that either of these measures is irrelevant. It is that scholars of intrastate conflict—together with policymakers interested in the same—should work toward a more holistic understanding of the lived experiences and complex dynamics of asymmetric conflict if they are interested in finding durable pathways out of it.

Appendix A
METHODOLOGICAL APPROACH AND ETHICAL CONSIDERATIONS

This book is based upon years of engagement with Lebanon and with Palestinian refugee communities. My time there included the summers of 2007 and 2008; a year from October 2009 to 2010; May–June 2011, May–June 2012, and January and May–June 2014; and two weeks in 2018. Over the course of these trips, I visited eight of the twelve UNRWA-recognized refugee camps, spent time in multiple Palestinian gatherings (small settlements that are not recognized as camps but that receive some UNRWA services), and lived in Lebanese-Palestinian neighborhoods in Beirut and Saida as well as in a refugee camp in South Beirut.

From 2009 to 2010, I lived in three predominantly Lebanese neighborhoods in West Beirut (Raouche, Caracas, and Sanayeh) where Palestinian associational and political officials also lived and where my Palestinian friends were comfortable visiting me.[1] When I returned in 2011 and 2012, I lived with Palestinian friends in Tariq al-Jdideh, a Lebanese-Palestinian neighborhood in South Beirut near the Beirut Arab University, just north of Sabra. Starting part time in 2012, continuing full time in 2014, and returning in 2018, I lived with one of my interlocutors and her family in Burj al-Barajneh, a refugee camp adjoining the Beirut suburb of Haret Hreik. I also spent several weeks staying with my interlocutors in and around Saida. I visited family homes and political offices regularly, shared meals, helped children with homework, participated in household chores, attended weddings, and exchanged gossip, jokes, and news. Living in the camp allowed for participation in some of the most informative and frankest conversations about my research, as I was around when friends dropped by, when news flashed across the TV screen, when storylines came to a dramatic climax on soap operas, or when people stayed up late relaxing after a long day.

Aware of existing resentment toward researchers in some of the refugee camps, as well as of the extractive dynamics that characterize many research plans, I endeavored to productively contribute to the communities where I worked. During the summer of 2008 and from October 2009 through October 2010, I volunteered with three civil society organizations, each of which was loosely associated with a different Palestinian political current. In the summer of 2008, I taught English for a well-known social association focused on educational and social support for women and girls in the camps. From fall 2009 to summer 2010, I worked for a small civil society organization that focused on training Palestinian journalists, which was run by a member/former member of various leftist parties. Over spring and summer of 2010, I spent increasing time at this educational association's office, helping my supervisor with translations, grant applications, and research projects. Like other associational employees, I participated in human rights workshops in Beirut and South Lebanon, led a workshop of my own regarding the role of the international media in the camps, and spent hours discussing the educational situation for Palestinian refugees with parents, political officers, and United Nations officials. My work came to the attention of the camp's Popular Committee's leader, who asked if I might be willing to tutor primary-school students in a locally managed, United Nations Children's Fund–supported community center, an offer that I accepted. Throughout my time in Lebanon, I tutored children; helped youth navigate their foreign university, scholarship, and job applications; and clarified questions about immigration lottery procedures.

As a US citizen, I could not feasibly work with some civil society groups—specifically, groups linked to certain Islamist and Salafi factions, as well as those linked to the PFLP. This was because of legal restrictions stemming from these organizations' association with factions the US government has declared foreign terrorist organizations (FTOs).[2] My volunteering was consequently limited to organizations historically linked to specific secular-nationalist and specific leftist parties. This constraint meant that my everyday interactions with secular-nationalist and leftist parties were much more extensive than my experiences with Islamist parties, though I made every effort to consult materials that represented the latter's ideological standpoints.

Given the social and legal precarity that shapes Palestinian refugee communities in Lebanon, I wanted to be as open as possible with my interlocutors so that people could make decisions not only about whether to engage with me, but also to what extent. Volunteering for months before I began more intensive ethnographic work allowed people a chance to get to know me, ask me questions, and form opinions about my character. In my consent procedures, I extensively discussed my funding sources, including the distinctions between the fellowships I was awarded through the National Science Foundation (which supported several years of my graduate education), and through organizations such as the Social Science Research Council on one hand and fellowships that I did not have that are administered through the US Department of Defense and the US Department of Education (e.g., Fulbright) on the other. For example, many interlocutors were especially wary of Fulbright grant holders; they associated them with espionage. However, many of the people with whom I was working were also well-versed in the idea of organizations such as foundations supporting students; many Palestinian students earn grants to study abroad, in view of the limited access to higher education for them in Lebanon. I also extensively discussed participant observation and my interviewing approach. Many people were enthusiastic, pushing me to "live the reality"; others repeatedly asked if I wanted to record or film them "like a journalist." Assuring them that I would request neither audio nor video recording was often the reason that someone agreed to speak with me. Some people also declined to be interviewed, including several cadres to whom I was close and whose personal histories I knew; even if I know those stories, they have been omitted from this volume.

The project received ethical approval under Institutional Review Board protocols H10075 and H07177 at the University of Chicago and protocol 1312S46161 at the University of Minnesota. All research occurred under conditions of confidentiality, and all names provided herein are pseudonyms. Where essential to preserving confidentiality, identifying details have been masked or omitted. Research was conducted predominantly in Arabic, with some interviews in English.

Organizational Ethnography

My growing familiarity with the camp's political parties and social associations allowed me to observe the relationships that undergirded organizational politics in sharp relief and in multiple contexts, whether in parties' offices, in schools, or in private homes. To understand what kinds of roles, relationships, and social network ties exist within Palestinian political factions, I conducted participant observation in Palestinian communities, including ten months of organizational ethnography among members of Fatah's Women's Office.[3] I observed meetings (at the camp, regional, and national level, open-invite as well as invite-only), visited party offices, collected and studied the party's publications, watched its television channels, socialized in members' and affiliates' homes, attended events such as poetry readings and demonstrations, and gathered materials such as party-produced yearly planners. I also studied sites of political discourse such as an email listserv for publicizing party events and public Facebook pages. Pursuing long-term, intensive research with Fatah members afforded me an opportunity to study the interface between members' formal organizational networks and their quotidian ties, which include kinship, marriage, and friendship. Research with "public" organizations led to sustained participant observation in more "private" spaces. At least partially owing to my status as a young, unmarried, female researcher, I was increasingly invited into family homes and to social gatherings.[4] Developing and maintaining long-term ties within Fatah afforded me the opportunity not only to observe contemporary organizational practices and hierarchies, but also to introduce comparative questions about the past to my interlocutors.[5] Conversations about veterans' healthcare and salaries, for example, presented the opportunity to ask about party funding and how it had operated in the 1980s.

Over the years, I developed close relationships with seven families linked to Fatah. By "close" I mean that I communicated regularly with more than one family member (e.g., via text or WhatsApp), visited family members frequently at home or work, regularly ate meals at and slept over in family homes, helped with household chores, and attended party events with family members. I came to know members of multiple generations. For example, in one family, I repeatedly interacted with twenty-nine members whose birth dates fell between the late 1940s and the present—a widow born in the late 1940s, her children born between the mid-1960s and the mid-1980s, her children's spouses and their mothers, and her grandchildren (born between the 1980s and the present).[6] Half of the children born between the 1960s and 1980s currently serve or have served in a formal office in Fatah; several others would identify as being "with" Fatah. Another family with whom I was similarly close invited me to stay with them in their house in one of the camps; treated largely like a visiting cousin, I held myself to many of the same standards as other young women in the same family (e.g., observing a curfew when staying in the camp and contributing to housework). This approach allowed me to follow and participate in discursive networks that spanned multiple organizational and quotidian domains, operated across genders, and bridged generations.

Participant-Driven Ethnohistory

As described in chapter 1, I came into the Fatah fold in late April 2010 after a friend casually asked me to copyedit her weekly report of the office's activities. I then participated in the office's woman-centric projects and events surrounding Nakba Day, sharing in conversations related to the design of a poster and pamphlet that featured notable Palestinian female fighters and politicians.[7] Discussing this poster's design and attending the subsequent exhibit at the Nakba Day events facilitated many of my introductions to women who had worked in the clandestine support network described in chapter 6.

Two weeks later, the Mavi Marmara incident occurred; I participated in the subsequent demonstration in Beirut with members of the Women's Office.[8] Women who were present repeatedly cited my presence at this event when they later introduced me to other members. Around the same time, a longtime US White House Press Corps member, Helen Thomas, resigned after being criticized for making controversial remarks about Israel; I shared in a meeting where the Women's Office members drafted a formal statement of support not of Thomas's comment (though they did not oppose it), but, in their words, of a fellow woman's right to freedom of political expression. This in-depth conversation about women, politics, and journalism prompted one Women's Office member to unearth a binder of media clippings from the early 1980s, which she had assembled as an employee in a joint PLO-LNM media office and preserved throughout the following decades. The officer gave me the binder, telling me that she didn't want the "dusty thing" taking up space in her house anymore and that she hoped it could help in my work.[9] She did this immediately following the meeting about the Helen Thomas statement, in front of other members of the office. Since the officer was known as a figure of authority and someone who was not easy to please, her decision to do me a clear favor served as an informal approval of the project, paving the way for my more in-depth, prolonged engagement with the Women's Office.

Members of the Women's Office often facilitated my relationships with other camp-level and regional offices within Fatah. I began visiting some offices several times a week and developed working relationships with several local officers, which deepened over the course of that year. I began spending extended periods of time with Fatah members: stopping by their offices a few days a week, tagging along on house visits, attending festivals and commemorations, sitting in on scout meetings. I spent many evenings with Fatah members, former members, and those close to them, smoking *arguileh*, watching soap operas, slicing potatoes or coring squash before dinner. In addition to observing members' behavior, I participated in a number of formal events by doing anything from engaging in political discussions during rallies to singing and dancing *dabke* (a traditional line dance) at scout meetings. My presence at these types of events also allowed me to collect and analyze what Schatz (2009, 6) terms "human artifacts" such as custom-printed kaffiyehs that parties gave to members on formal occasions, t-shirts from scouting clubs, jewelry that youth activists wore, key chains that members of the Woman's Office traded, and commemorative plaques that officers exchanged. My engagement further intensified during my return trips when I continued to regularly visit party offices—by 2012, across three camps—began living with current and former cadres, and was allowed to observe a camp-level women's Central Committee meeting. In 2012, largely thanks to these long-term connections and my own shifting positionality as someone who was increasingly known by members of Fatah and around South Beirut, the Fatah representative for Beirut granted me permission to conduct formal historical interviews with military leaders. With official sanction, I could ask officers directly about their strategies and tactical decisions during the 1980s and their aftermath, which enabled me to assemble critical evidence related to meso-level changes in organizational practices and routines over time.

Though my ethnographic engagement with Women's Office members gave me special access to Fatah, I built strong working relationships with members from other political factions and currents as well. I socialized with members of other factions and recognized over time that people tracked how close I was to members of each one. Before I left my volunteer position at the association that trained journalists, I spent hours every week talking politics with my supervisor, a long-time leftist who had retired from his organization, and his friends, who belonged to multiple left-wing factions.[10] There were days when I would go from mid-morning coffee with a former member of the PFLP, to a Fatah-affiliated family's house for lunch, and to the apartment of a former member of the DFLP for dinner. As noted in chapter 1, I also spent extended periods of time with UNRWA employees in offices, schools, and clinics, discussing everything from healthcare policy to garbage disposal to factional interference in school activities.

An ethnographic approach also allowed me to progressively build working relationships (Fujii 2017) and trust with my interlocutors, gaining access to insider perspectives, experiences, and meaning-making practices while situating them in local and historical context, rather than taking external categories of participation or behavior for granted (Burawoy 1998, 2003; Bayard de Volo and Schatz 2004; Pachirat 2009, 143–44; Wedeen 2009, 2010; Yanow 2012). Gathering knowledge of changing funding, communications, and supply structures over time made it possible to ask about and consequently map changing social network flows. Ethnographic immersion also granted me the perspective necessary to asking the right people informed questions about factional histories; for example, I learned that despite their ranks, many national officers knew little of critical clandestine operations during the 1980s (see chapter 1). Trust and analytic insight gained through this kind of long-term engagement are crucial to accessing and situating restricted information that is unlikely to be gathered in a one-shot interaction and that is not captured in documents or other accessible historical material.

Interview and Life History Approach

My access to research participants depended heavily on the reputation that I developed through my ethnographic work, volunteering, and "off-hours" socializing in various Palestinian social and political circles. For example, one day, a group of former military cadres from Shatila drew me a detailed map of the camp's 1985 defensive front and described the specific network of fighters from Burj al-Shamali who designed it; they had originally stopped into a party office to see if their new ID cards had been completed. They recognized me from several previous interactions and started to ask about my research as they waited. Almost all my interviewees, including this group, participated in the project after knowing me for several weeks, if not months, in a more casual, passing context; many initiated conversations on the topic of more sensitive events themselves, in the context of a more general interview or conversation. Several interviewees put me in contact with friends, relatives, or colleagues who had also participated in political activities over the years; I approached these individuals to schedule interviews only after ensuring that my initial contact had already explained who I was, where I was from, the nature of my project, and the types of questions that I would ask to the potential interviewee. Only after the potential interviewee had granted permission for me to establish contact did I suggest an interview.

While I interviewed each participant for at least an hour, I spoke to the majority of them on at least two occasions and was able to interview many people for up to twelve hours across multiple sessions. This count excludes interactions with the families with whom I stayed for days or weeks at a time, the informal interviews that I conducted, and the conversations in which I participated on an almost daily basis as part of my participant observation in militant organizations' offices, social associations, UNRWA installations, and private homes.

Central to this effort, I conducted twenty-four extended life history interviews with members of emergent—and largely underground—organizations that are described and analyzed in this book. During life history interviews, I recorded each interviewee's demographic information (e.g., age), family attributes, their home village in Palestine, their birthplace and other places of residence, their current and former affiliations and organizational roles, whether they were imprisoned or deported, and, critically, their position in relational flows (specifically their handling of information, finance, and material goods such as weapons and publications). I cataloged much of the same information for their family members; one of the early questions that I asked was "can you tell me about your family?" Later in the interview, I often learned that family members had been wounded, beaten, imprisoned, or even killed; many had also emigrated for safety. At other times, my interviewee had already invited family members to join our conversation. Additionally, I queried interviewees about general trends, behaviors, and decision-making processes within their respective organizations or social organizations.

I strove to conduct interviews in a way that afforded my interviewees maximum agency. While my questions focused on organizational dynamics, I was still cognizant of the potential that engaging with them could surface upsetting memories. I always started interviews with open-ended, broad questions. I did not ask for details about people's involvement in specific violent events, avoided requesting details of my interlocutors' own victimization, and checked in with my interviewees throughout our conversations by asking how they were doing, if they wanted to take a break, or if they wanted to move to a different topic. However, I also did not stop people from discussing issues related to their participation in resistance or their victim/survivor status, which some people did choose to share. During difficult moments, we often took smoke breaks or stopped to share coffee or a meal before continuing. I always emphasized that I could return if they wanted to continue a conversation another time, or that we could simply end our exchanges on a certain topic at that moment. Several interviewees asked to revisit conversations when I encountered them months or even years later.

Though I had the most expansive access to members of Fatah, I was able to approach historical interviews in a fashion that more evenly represented both the PLO loyalist organizations and former Palestinian National Salvation Front (PNSF)[11] members. Organizations' members often articulated that I needed "get the real story," and seemed almost universally pleased to discuss the 1980s. Though I spoke to members of over a dozen different Palestinian militant organizations, ranging in ideology from communists to Salafis, I was never able to formally interview long-term, current members of Fatah al-Intifada or al-Saʿiqa. These groups, along with others whose members I was able to interview such as the PFLP-GC and a wing of the Palestine Liberation Front (PLF), are the most strongly aligned with Syria. I had hoped to approach members of these organizations when I returned to Lebanon in 2011 and 2012. However, these trips, as well as later ones, occurred in the midst of the Syrian revolution. The heightened presence of Syrian intelligence agents and a shifting political environment made establishing new contacts ethically questionable for me because of the contentious nature of the Syrian government's past and current activities in Lebanon. In some cases, I knew secondhand that people had relatives suffering in besieged communities in Syria and felt it would consequently be insensitive to propose an interview about the War of the Camps.

Talking about the Past

Researchers, as Elisabeth Jean Wood (2003, 33) explains, face at least three challenges to evidentiary quality when conducting historical interviews: "the accuracy and intensity of the respondent's initial memories, the subsequent shaping of those memories through social and cultural processes, and the respondents' objectives in the ethnographic setting of the interview itself." With the first, factors such as temporal distance from events may make people likely to forget details or to misreport how events transpired. However, time may also afford people the opportunity to process, evaluate, reconstruct, and analyze. Both social scientists such as Wood (2003, 33–34) and psychologists such as Mark Freeman (2010, chaps. 2, 4–6) emphasize that intense memories can also become clearer and more vibrant over time, and therefore are often more likely to be subject to recall. Indeed, many of my interlocutors had trouble identifying the exact sequencing of certain events or, for example, the months in which events occurred. In other moments, though, their memories of specific occurrences or practices—e.g., the rumors that swirled in the aftermath of the Sabra and Shatila massacre; the changing ways soldiers frisked women at checkpoints; the way a high-ranking officer slept on the floor with his men—were frequently sharp, focused, detailed, visceral, and vivid. These contrasts helped me to assess which events might have been relatively more important in my interlocutors' personal trajectories and enabled me to search for commonalities in important themes across interviews and field notes.[12]

People also interpret their memories through the lens of contemporary contexts, politics, and relationships (Zerubavel 1996; Auyero 1999; E. J. Wood 2003, 34–35) and often relay them in the context of intersubjective encounters with a researcher. In my research, what initially seemed like romanticized memories surfaced, often seemingly paradoxically, about deeply trying times.[13] Methodological techniques exist to help researchers to generate and leverage insights to be gained from encounters with incomplete or "rose-tinted" memories. For instance, Jocelyn Viterna (2006, 13) notes that she "structured [her] questionnaire around past events rather than past attitudes because memories of events are more reliable." I emulated this technique in my life history and other in-depth interviews, especially as I sought evidence of actions taken resulting from collective interpretations of violence. Additionally, I structured my questions according to levels of detail. If, for example, I was assembling data to reconstruct an interviewee's social network over time, I would ask them about their family and close friends early in the interview, then return to family as we discussed their different roles over time (e.g., "Could you tell me what your sisters were doing when you were smuggling cigarettes?"). This technique flagged my interest in family and friends early in the interview, priming respondents to mention others' roles as they discussed their own. However, I also became interested in the role that comparatively "rosy" memories of difficult periods played in contemporary organizational politics, treating those discourses as contemporary organizational data, specifically evidence of intraorganizational cultures, in their own right (Parkinson 2016).

Javier Auyero notes that memories of particular salience in the present day—in one interlocutor's case, her memories of all the gifts the Peronist Party had given her—might be clearer and more accessible to them because of contemporary contextual factors (Auyero 1999, 332). In my own work, the changing present-day salience of events in the 1980s—initially heavily focused on issues related to factional funding and access to social services such as healthcare—provided a pathway to discussing the more "concrete" issues of roles and relations within 1980s guerrilla organizations. Many party cadres also saw the 1970s and 1980s as a golden age for the factions (Parkinson 2016). However, the project also gained new resonance during the Arab Uprisings, as people were excited to talk about their own past activism in light of contemporary movements in places such as Egypt, Syria, and Yemen.

Political Change and Issue Sensitivity

Following 2011, the Syrian Civil War's escalation dramatically shifted the political context in which I was conducting research. Hundreds of thousands of Syrian refugees as well as Palestinian refugees from Syria came to live in the Palestinian camps where I conducted much of my work, often renting apartments from my interlocutors and socializing with them. A wave of foreign journalists and researchers followed, as well as Syrian and Lebanese intelligence services, quickly contributing to people's existing feelings of research fatigue, surveillance, and exploitation (Nayel 2013; al-Hardan 2017; Sukarieh and Tannock 2019).

I grew increasingly concerned that attempting new formal interviews and reaching out to participants I had never met before would endanger both my interlocutors and myself, in view of the Syrian government's past role in training and supporting both Amal and dissident Palestinian factions and the increasingly noticeable presence of Syrian agents in the camps themselves. After 2012, I stopped actively seeking to conduct new interviews about the War of the Camps and the Syrian occupation of Lebanon. By 2014, I had stopped talking about the

War of the Camps with all but my most trusted interlocutors. In a few cases, my interlocutors brought up my research on the War of the Camps with Palestinian friends from Syria, specifically in discussions of the siege of the Yarmouk Palestinian camp in Damascus with people who had fled.[14] Once, when my interlocutors explicitly mentioned one of my publications and its contents, the conversation became an opportunity to talk about the skill sets and knowledge base that Palestinians in Lebanon had prior to the War of the Camps, whereas Syrians living in Yarmouk "didn't even have Kalashnikovs" (author's field notes, January 2014). While I engaged in these conversations and occasionally offered historical observations, I was extraordinarily careful of what I said, in light of my positionality as a US-based researcher and the potential for anything I said to be misinterpreted by both Palestinians from Syria and intelligence services.

Moving across Political Lines: Ethical Considerations

Countless ethical considerations emerge as researchers embark on intensive research in fragile and violence-affected settings, many of which have been discussed extensively in other works.[15] In her work on the Rwandan genocide, for example, Lee Ann Fujii discusses what she terms the "insider-outsider" distinction. She describes how as a non-Rwandan, being an "obvious outsider allowed [her] to ask questions that might have seemed too obvious, and thus suspicious, if posed by a Rwandan" (Fujii 2010, 34). Yet in ethnographic and other participatory research, sources of "outsider" status are almost inevitably interpolated by relationally based proximity to specific interlocutors. Researchers' ethical commitments necessarily shift as a result. While "outsider" researchers (one of which I was, as a white woman who held a US passport) may be able to ask the "too obvious" questions initially, interlocutors' expectations change as relationships deepen. For example, over the months and then years, people with whom I had repeated interactions anticipated that I would change the type of questions that I asked. My not knowing someone in the camp's political affiliation was acceptable to my interlocutors for a few months; it later became a mark of either willful ignorance or dishonesty.

In the contexts where I conducted research, people tended to conceive of their position in society and their safety in terms of those immediately around them, like their families, as well as their formal political affiliations (and thus the protection they could mobilize). The inverse also applied; distance from other sorts of actors granted security. It was common to hear people refer to each other in terms of their organizational affiliations, their occupation (especially if it was associated with one of the parties), and their home camp. For example, in response to the question "Which Abir?" someone might answer: "Abir—she's married to the guy who owns the cell phone shop near Karaj Darwish, they live in Sabra, they're with the PFLP, but his mother is PCP. She works for a NGO." Most people to whom I spoke instinctively ordered their lives in a similar way; in social network terms, who people considered *close* to them was primarily a function of social ties based on kinship, factional affiliation, friendship, or co-membership in a social club such as a dance team. They also could articulate closeness in near-textbook social network measures.

Political neutrality was not a particularly legible position in these settings. People still read individuals who were unaffiliated with any faction or who professed political apathy—as many of my friends and interlocutors did—as being "close" to certain factions and hostile to or opposed to others. For example, a friend in his late twenties who had left al-Saʿiqa was still widely considered to be "close" to the Syrian-allied parties because he worked in a community organization run by former members of the PFLP. Other friends, despite their refusal to join the parties, or their departure from them, were associated with them via their parents' or children's affiliations. I met only one person to whom no one assigned a factional affiliation or proximity; he worked for UNRWA and sent his children to private school.

In this sort of relational setting, a researcher's attempt to perform neutrality or impartiality presents ethical questions because of the emotional and social stress those network positions can cause their interlocutors. For example, when one of my primary interlocutors, Sabah, became upset that I frequently visited Muna, the daughter of a former officer in a dissident faction,[16] she initially told me I visited Muna too much *given who my other friends were*. Sabah might speak to Muna once a month in a public place, to be polite. But when it came to Sabah's best friend in Fatah, she might visit her every day; a friend who was in another faction, like a former classmate, might get a visit once or twice a week. One of the ways that Sabah both measured and signaled closeness was in terms of the frequency of her social visits; Sabah and I saw each other almost every day. For me to visit Muna as frequently as Sabah was to imply that I had a dangerous degree of closeness with a radical, dissident faction (even if Muna wasn't aware of her father's politics and even if he was no longer an active cadre).

My interlocutors expected, not unreasonably given how their social circles operated, that I would adjust my behavior outside of my research with them according to the knowledge that I gained and the emotional bonds our interactions generated. As I became closer to individuals in several parties, they became comfortable scolding me as they would a family member or childhood friend, rather than keeping me at a professional distance. Occupying my specific network position after beginning research with the Women's Office increasingly came with a set of intense expectations. For example, my interlocutors in the Women's Office began using the title of "Sister" with me, indicating to others a particular level of trust and social expectation; it was also a discursive move to claim me as an affiliate (that is, someone whom they considered to be "with them" if not a formal party member).[17] Several pressured me to transfer my teaching position to a space under Fatah's control.[18] On top of representing an attempt at network closure, their move also reflected a desire to capitalize on the prestige that having a foreign scholar teaching in a faction-sponsored educational program would bring, a dynamic that surfaces across research contexts (Malejacq and Mukhopadhyay 2016, 1014).

I increasingly thought about how a "network sensibility" could inform my perspective on these social dynamics.[19] Specifically, I considered how social proximity—understood, for example, in terms of repeated interactions, increasingly complex relationships, incorporation into multiplex social networks, escalating emotional obligations, and growing trust—could either close or open potential research trajectories. Scholars have long contemplated the challenges and fallacies of maintaining neutrality, objectivity, and emotional distance, especially in conflict research (Robben 1995; Sluka 2007; Moser 2008). Romain Malejacq and Dipali Mukhopadhyay (2016, 1012) emphasize that regardless of scholars' epistemological or ontological commitments, fieldwork in contexts affected by violence is characterized by "unavoidable partiality" and shaped by the "social micro-systems" that researchers construct in order to collect data. However, rather than partiality's being portrayed as a negative, I want to emphasize that chosen proximity to one group—party, NGO, or sports team—is often essential to understanding aspects of organizational life such as cliques, boundaries, rivalries, and memory politics (see, e.g., chapter 1 as well as Parkinson 2016 and 2021a). Certain organizational behaviors, such as socialization into community norms or sharing organizational history, may not occur when a researcher divides her time and emotional investment among multiple groups—whether political factions, clans, or religious communities—or if they try to avoid becoming "too" embedded to start.[20] In terms of my own inclusion in these networks, my personal biography was less important than the way that I fit into a biographically defined role, especially in Fatah's organizational structure. I was in my mid-to-late twenties, I identify as a woman, I was unmarried,[21] and I was clearly politically active, so members often classified me much as they did potential recruits.

My friendship with Sabah became stronger and subtly politicized through my research activities with Fatah. As a result, the context in which Sabah saw my relationships with others evolved as well. In a continuation of the vignette above, she grew increasingly desperate to keep me from visiting Muna's father, Abu

Ghassan, who had been affiliated with Fatah-Revolutionary Council. It became clear that my continued interactions with him were upsetting her. But for months, she used gossip to communicate her concern, rather than telling me her underlying motivation. Sabah was initially trying to shield a new, outsider friend (me) while simultaneously protecting her community's image. After several months, during which our relationship deepened significantly, she eventually revealed that Abu Ghassan had tortured and killed people in Fatah—information that she would likely not share with an outsider (even a Lebanese friend, much less a foreigner), since it might have reinforced the camps' reputation among many Lebanese and foreigners as violent spaces.

But, when she shared this information, Sabah was telling me, in no uncertain terms, that my relationship with Abu Ghassan was unacceptable to her and her colleagues. The obligations accompanying my status in a web of social and political networks meant that once I knew the "real story," my professional *and personal* judgment would come into question if I continued treating Abu Ghassan as equivalent to other members of Fatah. Although I regularly interacted with people from multiple parties without Fatah (or any other organization) taking issue, interacting socially with someone who was as stigmatized as Abu Ghassan was unacceptable.

These interactions and similar ones increasingly revealed intimate and often emotional aspects of organizational membership and affiliation. While the head of the journalism NGO where I volunteered offered that Americans could never understand the exact mentality of factional affiliation, he still tried to explain it: "It's as if everyone is part of a family. If someone hurts someone from a family, the whole family will avenge them . . . people stand up for each other." A friend my age who had quit one of the factions later relayed similar sentiments when he explained the difficulty of leaving the group. He emphasized that without rule of law, Palestinians and Lebanese only had their relatives and their parties to protect them. People, he emphasized, needed to know where others stood. Indeed, when a Lebanese woman who worked in the camp where I volunteered attempted to falsely inform on me, members of the Women's Office stepped in to defend me, potentially saving me from interrogation, or worse.[22] The types of protection that factions offered—physical, psychological, economic, social, emotional, reputational—seeped into the practices of everyday life, expanding the domain of "political" work to the balcony, living room, and kitchen. Yet they also demonstrated how repeated micro-interactions—a snub there, a scowl there, a perceived threat there—worked to either positively or negatively reinforce social relationships, thus structuring broad social worlds (Parkinson 2018, 2021a).

As a researcher, I initially felt that I had an ethical obligation not to adjudicate claims between parties such as Sabah and her colleagues on one side and those such as Abu Ghassan and his family on the other. Mostly out of fear, I did eventually stop visiting Abu Ghassan's family. I made this choice after Abu Ghassan figured out that I knew his backstory—specifically about the torture and killings—and subtly threatened me.[23] When he called to inquire as to my whereabouts after several weeks, I told him that I was ill and couldn't come to the camp. I later started visiting his daughter, Muna, again, though with some trepidation. At first, I attempted to avoid Abu Ghassan by timing my visits against his work and prayer schedule, but the tactic started to become obvious. Instead, I started imitating the daughters of senior Fatah officers who I learned were neighborhood friends with Muna; I had never before realized that they strictly confined their social interactions to the highly public and observable space of the sandwich shop that Muna's family owned. Their behavior was certainly intentional—only one girl from a Fatah family ever visited Muna in her home, and her family was not from the camp—but the availability of discounted food and drinks in the restaurant conveniently masked their motivations. Sharing the girls' predicament revealed their subtle way of bridging a bitter and emotionally loaded divide and sensitized me to the ways that members of different factions negotiated historical animosities.

Research Assistance and Interpreters

I employed two Palestinian research assistants (RAs) in Lebanon as well as several US-based students for the archival element of my work (See Appendix B.) They did not engage in any of my participant observation or interviews. I deliberately chose RAs from different political backgrounds who lived in different cities. I paid them at an hourly rate commensurate with a graduate research assistant's pay at the American University of Beirut. Both came highly recommended, and in both instances the recommender made a point of telling me the individual's political loyalties. These were later confirmed—unprompted—by the RAs themselves.

With early exceptions in 2007 and 2008, I chose not to use an interpreter or fixer during my research. On the two occasions when someone accompanied me to interviews, one was in the summer of 2007 when I was not yet proficient in colloquial Arabic and accompanied a journalist friend to conduct interviews among militia leaders in Ain al-Hilweh (see chapter 2). Entry to the camp in South Lebanon required a military permit, which the fixer obtained; he then facilitated and translated a series of interviews with Palestinian organizational elites whom he knew from prior work with journalists. The following summer, I again used a fixer to obtain the necessary military permit to visit Ain al-Hilweh, but largely conducted my own interviews.

Given my advanced competence in Arabic, I decided to conduct my subsequent interviews without research assistance. On the one hand, Palestinian RAs might have allowed me to access a broader spectrum of people or helped to transcribe my unrecorded interviews more thoroughly in the moment (see, e.g., Fujii 2009). However, conducting my research without an interpreter or fixer carried several advantages that generalize to similar research sites. First, I felt that bringing an interpreter would have conveyed that I was a particular type of foreigner: the type that needs one (in the parlance of the camps, probably a journalist or someone doing government-sponsored research on violent extremism or refugee dignity, two much-maligned but commonly proposed projects in the spaces where I worked). I didn't want to obtain the organizations' carefully choreographed policy statements or their bluster about weapons that they provided as sound bites to many outsiders (which I witnessed firsthand during the 2007 interviews in Ain al-Hilweh). I recognized that bringing a RA would likely trigger this specific type of performance because I would likely be read, by many, as a journalist doing "one-shot" interviews, and provided with a practiced script.

Second, from an ethical perspective, I knew that people in many Palestinian communities felt that outsiders who used interpreters often bought access, rather than earning it. This system produced economic incentives for introducing any paying outsider to a camp community without that community's consent.[24] I was frequently present when Palestinian friends who were not my research participants scornfully joked about foreigners visiting the camps looking to meet "terrorists" or discussed their feeling that many foreigners treated Shatila, the site of an internationally known massacre, like a "zoo." I did not want to employ the subtle coercion that can accompany a family member's or friend's introduction of a foreigner who is paying them into their milieu; I wanted to be confident that people freely chose to talk to me, rather than their feeling obligated to do so out of fear of risking a loved one's or neighbor's job.

Third, I was concerned about both my interlocutors' and any potential RAs' security. My interlocutors often felt that "insiders" probably posed a greater threat to them than I did. On both early occasions when I used a fixer, my interviewees' vetting of them took a substantial amount of time; people obviously worried about what a fixer could do with any off-the-record or background information that they shared. In some settings, community leaders or politicians may question research brokers about the work they do with scholars or about who has been interviewed, placing the brokers in a vulnerable position and potentially compromising interlocutors' anonymity (Malejacq and Mukhopadhyay 2016, 1019). Indeed, Roman Malajacq has commented that in some contexts, the people whom scholars and journalists hire as interpreters often later go into politics themselves, typically with inside knowledge of their rivals gained from their prior work with media and researchers.[25] In the Lebanese context, Palestinian factions and various divisions of the Lebanese security apparatus (controlled, in turn, by various Lebanese parties) frequently approach Palestinian youth to act as informers. Because of Palestinians' precarious civil rights situation in Lebanon, refusal to serve in such a capacity could potentially place any RA in an uncomfortable position vis-à-vis their personal and family security.

Practical Notes on Confidentiality and Security

I took several additional precautions in order to ensure my interviewees' security and comfort. These efforts included the following:

1. I never recorded interviews; I felt that doing so posed an obvious security risk (having digital files with identifiable voices) as well as potentially making interviewees uncomfortable and consequently hesitant to speak freely.
2. I used verbal consent procedures both (a) to avoid a paper trail, thus helping to ensure confidentiality and (b) to avoid the discomfort, fear, and suspicion that can accompany the request for someone who is either legally marginalized or a member or former member of a semilegal armed organization to sign any kind of document.
3. With interviewees' permission, I took written notes both in colloquial Arabic (phonetically or using the alphanumeric system that people employed to write text messages, online instant messages, and posts on social networking sites) and in English. If I was confused by or didn't know a term in Arabic, I asked people about it. When it was impossible or impractical to take notes, I tried to jot down coded keywords in notebooks, on paper menus, or on old receipts and to reconstruct events later in my field notes. I transcribed these materials electronically, encrypted them, and destroyed the paper notes to ensure confidentiality/anonymity.
4. I kept my computer passworded and encrypted files in a vault on the hard drive and backed up on encrypted external drives. Most of my research took place before I could reliably upload from Lebanese internet via VPN to a secure cloud.
5. I took several precautions to ensure that the technology that I used could provide as little information as possible if inspected or confiscated. During the main period of research in 2009–2010 and again in 2011, I

deliberately chose not to use a smartphone because, first, the Global Positioning System (GPS) feature could have been used by government agencies to place or locate me in certain areas as opposed to proximate to certain cell phone towers, and second, because if my phone were lost or confiscated, someone could potentially gain access to my emails as well as my phone numbers. There was extreme suspicion surrounding mobile phones during the main period of my research because of their increasing use for Lebanese government and foreign state surveillance, so I often visibly shut down my phone and removed the battery during many interviews. However, given the increasing prevalence of messaging through apps such as WhatsApp, Facebook Messenger, and Viber (often because these services operate using data or WiFi rather than phone credit), this approach became practically infeasible by 2012, when I began using a smartphone.

6. I tried to schedule as many meetings as possible in person so that meeting information did not travel through and was not stored on my phone. When I was visiting militant organizations' or social associations' offices, I sat out of view of their doorways so that passerby could not easily note my presence. Interviewees always selected the time and location of our meetings; we frequently met at outdoor cafés or in private homes. Depending on the interview and the interviewee's preference, I met people both alone and in groups (usually families or organizational cohorts). I varied the pathways that I took through the camps to avoid passing particular offices and shops, and I took cabs from different intersections around my various homes so that I would not always encounter the same taxi drivers.

7. Interlocutors' names have all been changed. I invited all of them to contribute their own pseudonym. In a limited number of cases where I cite from my interlocutors in both the contemporary era and regarding their past experiences, I use separate names for each time period to further protect their identities. In some cases, I have also obscured potentially identifying details such as their precise professional position or exact migration journey. In consultation with several interlocutors who felt that a particular experience could be linked to them personally, I have worked with them to substitute particular details in a way that still preserves the story's core content.

Appendix B
ARCHIVAL MATERIALS AND METHODS

To develop a detailed representation of the repertoires of violence that shaped Palestinian militant organizations and communities in the 1980s, the organizational context, and the broader environment, I gathered archival materials such as primary source documents (published by militant organizations, the PLO, aid organizations, and the United Nations, among others); Arabic, English, and French newspaper reports; and surveys (published by political organizations, aid organizations, and the United Nations as well as by researchers). Aware of the fact that different sources often focus upon distinct aspects of violence and repression (Davenport and Ball 2002), I deliberately sought out materials that varied as broadly as possible in their authorship, political orientation, and institutional origins (e.g., militant faction, newspaper, civil society organization, think tank). I used these archival materials to build an understanding of localized repertoires of violence during the 1975–1990 Lebanese Civil War, the 1982–2000 Israeli occupation, and the 1976–2005 Syrian occupation. Archival materials deeply inform the historical narrative in chapter 2 and provide evidence of Palestinian interpretations of and reactions to the conflict throughout the book. Intensive archival work also provided key historical background that helped me to develop more meaningful interview questions and to competently participate in conversations about the past with both current and former members of Palestinian militant groups.

Publicly Accessible Archives

I consulted materials from and benefited from the research staff at five archival institutions over the years. In Beirut, I visited the American University of Beirut's (AUB) Jafet Library; the Institute for Palestine Studies; the *al-Safir* newspaper archives; and the Institut français du Proche Orient (IFPO). In the United States, the American Friends Service Committee (AFSC) archival collections in Philadelphia also provided invaluable documentation.

The contents of AUB's and *al-Safir*'s collections, combined later with material from *al-Nahar* available on microfiche in the US, allowed me to construct a collection of newspaper articles and other media reports on each of the camps and their broader environments from 1975 to 1990; in some cases, I extended my searches up to 2008. I relied heavily on AUB's digitized editions of *al-Safir*, a daily, left-leaning Arabic-language paper that is generally understood in Lebanon as trending toward the "pro-Syrian" side of contemporary Lebanese politics. I also consulted microfiche copies of *al-Nahar*, the other primary Arabic daily in Lebanon (which, in turn, has been described as trending toward the "pro-European and American" side of Lebanese politics). However, former journalists who had worked at *al-Nahar* informed me that the paper did not have reporters who covered the Palestinian refugee camps consistently during the 1980s, whereas *al-Safir* did.[1] Since I use the articles in order to help establish differences in localized repertoires of violence, I determined that *al-Safir* was more likely to cover the events of concern, so I focused my time in Lebanon on gathering those data. *Al-Safir* itself holds a topically and chronologically organized clippings archive that includes articles from major Arabic, English, and French publications in Lebanon dating back decades. I examined their extensive dossiers on the 1982 invasion, the Sabra-Shatila massacre, the War of the Camps, the Battle of Magdousheh, and postwar violence in the camps. After locating and skimming these articles, I organized these articles by year and by camp and had research assistants briefly annotate them. I then triangulated among interviews, memoirs, and secondary sources in order to present the most detailed version of events possible (particularly during the War of the Camps, when *al-Safir*'s coverage became noticeably more limited).

Though I do not consider these articles to represent the full scope of historical events, this technique allowed me to broadly understand distinctions in regionalized repertoires of violence and how they changed over time. Local newspapers told very different stories about each of the camps; initially planning to construct an events dataset, I spent months reading every digitized issue of *al-Safir*, starting in 1974, especially looking for news about the camps and local branches of the Palestinian factions. Accessing thousands of individually scanned page images representing thirty years of journalistic coverage gave me a feel for what types of incidents affected each camp over time; I came to identify local repertoires of violence (and also to recognize which types of events weren't commonly reported), to distinguish camp-specific organizations, and to identify recurring local characters. Yet these reports could not be treated as indisputable reflections of reality. Speaking to former journalists from *al-Safir* and *al-Nahar* clarified what might be expected: that media access issues, particularly in South Lebanon under the Israeli occupation, Syrian censorship, and the papers' own political leanings profoundly shaped what had been reported. For example, in 2014, one former journalist told me exactly where I could find a box of censored, never-published photographs he had taken during the 1985–1988 War of the Camps. When I contacted the newspaper, an employee confirmed that a storage room was full of such boxes related to a multitude of sensitive topics.[2]

At AUB's Jafet Library, I also made use of materials held by the Archives and Special Collections department. These include the Political Poster Archive, which comprises materials from the factions as well as UNRWA. The Palestinian Oral History Archive (POHA), now an open-access, annotated, online repository of video interviews related to Palestinian history and culture, was not yet public when I conducted the bulk of my research. In 2018, with the aid of AUB's Archives and Special Collections staff, I was able to access four interviews that are part of the archive's Ein al-Hilwet (Ain al-Hilweh) collection before they were publicly posted. I quote from them with permission from POHA and the copyright holders.

The library staff at IPS helped me to locate materials such as PLO camp studies (which described conditions in each refugee camp before the 1982 invasion), consultant reports on the PLO's and guerrilla factions' social institutions, and the nine copies of *Sawt al-Mukhayyam* that the book references extensively. In addition to the materials quoted in the book, I also read and took notes on other materials available at IPS—collections of local media reports, research institutions' and local scholars' studies of the camps, and hard-to-find almanacs, as well as back issues of the factions' and PLO's various journals (e.g., *al-Buraq, al-Hurriya, al-Quds,* and *Shu'un Falastiniyya*).These all provided crucial background, helped me to narrow my research questions and scope, aided my ability to contextualize other materials, and supported my general understanding of the political and social environment, both historically and in the context of my own research efforts.

The AFSC archives, which hold materials created and collected by the organization's humanitarian staff in Lebanon during the 1970s and 1980s, include public and internal reports, private letters, field notes, interviews, records of conversations, and related materials. After consulting with the archivist in charge to determine whether the collection held relevant items, I sent a graduate research assistant to Philadelphia to photograph the Lebanon materials, which included hundreds of pages in total.[3] These materials, some containing minute details of how collaborator organizations operated, dynamics in Ansar prison camp, and human rights conditions, became of particular importance for my chapters on South Lebanon. They often detailed less-visible modes of violence and repression from the perspective of foreign humanitarian workers who were embedded in the context. Because these individuals were frequently more mobile than many of the Palestinians and Lebanese who lived in the region, and also because they were in direct contact with a diverse array of actors, these materials present a uniquely comparative view of dynamics in Saida versus Sur, as well as within both cities. I quote from these materials with the permission of the AFSC.

Private Archives

Several people also granted me temporary access to smaller, private archives in Mar Elias, Shatila, Burj al-Barajneh, Burj al-Shamali, and al-Buss camps. Some of these materials had been relocated from other camps during the war; the joint PLO-LNM media archive that a Fatah officer gave to me (see Appendix A) had originally been housed in Rashidiyeh camp in South Lebanon. Officers in the PLO's Lebanon office provided me with materials from their internal archives, including digitized versions of the PLO's original film and video footage of the 1976 siege of Tel al-Zaʿtar, the 1982 Sabra and Shatila massacre, and the War of the Camps in Beirut. This film archive enabled me to view, literally through the lens of the PLO, what wartime violence in the 1970s and 1980s looked like to cadres on the ground. Two individuals who had lived in Tel al-Zaʿtar also provided me with copies of foreign documentaries that had been made on the 1976 siege and massacre; others from the community gave me books that locals had written about the events, while others permitted me to view their personal photo archives of the camp.[4] Other archives represented personal collections of materials tied to a relative, a camp, or a village community. Many contained copies of personal documents and correspondence related to people who disappeared or died during the civil war or occupation (e.g., during the Sabra and Shatila massacre). I used these materials to reconstruct and better understand the narratives and symbolic production that surrounded different, regionalized environments of violence during the 1980s as well as aspects of organizational decision-making and community mobilization.

An Archival Archipelago

Several limits to existing archival collections should be addressed. Much of the PLO's and the guerrilla organizations' archives have been destroyed or lost. Some materials never left Lebanon; Rashid Khalidi, for example, notes that officers did not have time to microfiche documents before they departed Beirut in 1982 (Khalidi 1985). Much of the material that did remain vanished when the PLO's Fakhani offices were raided and when the IDF destroyed the Institute for Palestine Studies as well as Palestinian and Lebanese intellectuals' private collections (Said 1983). Israeli forces took massive amounts of Palestinian documentation back to Israel, where much of it, to the best of my knowledge, remains in government archives that are largely inaccessible to researchers.

Even the documentation that made it out of Lebanon during the evacuation is not necessarily available today. Some of the materials that were salvaged by departing PLO personnel, such as the Chairman's Archive (later used extensively by Yezid Sayigh in his 1997 book), were taken to Tunis in 1982 and then to Gaza and Jericho following the Oslo Accords in 1993. I was told that the archives that the PLO deposited in Gaza upon its return were, for the most part, destroyed by Hamas in 2006.[5] People informed me that many of the Syrian-allied factions' archives were stored in facilities around Damascus; they were inaccessible to me for the duration of my research. Extant materials must therefore be treated as both informative windows onto the PLO's and guerrilla organizations' structures and behaviors in the early 1980s and the product of preservation efforts by archivists and private individuals in the face of the broader destruction, inaccessibility, denial of access to, or disappearance of historical documentation.

Research Assistants' Contributions

A series of superb research assistants supported much of this archival work. In Lebanon, Salah Hamzeh helped me to gather and photograph archival materials at IPS; he and a second research assistant, Rima, aided in the annotation of the media reports gathered at AUB, *al-Safir,* and IPS for later reference. While I was at the University of Minnesota, Thomas Vargas traveled to Philadelphia to photograph the 1970s and 1980s Lebanon files from the AFSC holdings, which he then catalogued and annotated for easy consultation. At the University of Minnesota, Sean Williams, Eslam Bedawy, and Kelsey Fogt collected and organized thousands of English-language news wire reports and *al-Nahar* articles into searchable datasets. Bedawy also helped to located and translate relevant material in Mahmoud al-Natour's (2014a, 2014b) Fatah histories and in DFLP commander Mamdouh Nofal's (2006) memoir of the Battle of Magdousheh. At Johns Hopkins University, Sofia J. Smith and Raied Haj Yahya assisted with the translations of *Sawt al-Mukhayyam* and of excerpts from Mahmoud Zeidan's (2017) memoir.

Appendix C

PALESTINIAN REFUGEE CAMPS IN LEBANON

TABLE C.1 Population of UNRWA-Administered Refugee Camps in Lebanon (1980 and 2011)

NAME	LOCATION (UNRWA REGION)	POPULATION IN 1979–1980 (PLO DEMOGRAPHIC STUDY/ UNRWA REGISTERED)	REGISTERED POPULATION IN 2011
Ain al-Hilweh	Saida (Saida)	20,021/24,340	50,309
Beddawi	Tripoli (North)	5,791/8194	7,866
Burj al-Barajneh	Beirut (Central)	8,886/9,466	16,888
Burj al-Shamali	Sour (Tyre)	None given/10,644	21,205
Al-Buss	Sour (Tyre)	None given/5,133	10,559
Dbayeh	Beirut (Central)	None given/2,834	4,237
Dikwaneh (Tel al-Za'tar)	Beirut (Central)	Destroyed 1976 (1972 population: 11,415)	N/A
Gourand	Bekaa	Closed 1963	N/A
Jisr al-Basha	Beirut (Central)	Destroyed 1976	N/A
Mar Elias	Beirut (Central)	466/472	627
Miyeh wa Miyeh	Saida (Saida)	1,933/2,347	4,958
Nabatiyeh	Saida (Saida)	None given/4,039	N/A
Nahr al-Bared	Tripoli (North)	11,455/15,205	36,338
Rashidiyeh	Sour (Tyre)	None given/14,628	29,363
Shatila	Beirut (Central)	8,278/5,435	9,154
Wavel (Jalil)	Bekaa	2,858	8,308

Notes:
1. 1979/1980 population numbers are drawn from the Palestine Liberation Organization's July 1981 Central Bureau of Statistics Report and from Sa'id Ibrahim (1983, 19). Refugees registered with UNRWA usually remain registered in their original host country, so Palestinians who moved from Jordan in 1970–1971 did not re-register in Lebanon and would not be counted in these numbers.
2. Approximately 50 percent of Palestinian refugees in Lebanon live outside the camps. Sa'id Ibrahim (1983, 19) puts the 1980 total registered population of Palestinian refugees in Lebanon at 226,554.
3. People have long moved into or out of the camps (e.g., due to marriage). UNRWA does not remove people who emigrate from its rolls.
4. Tel al-Za'tar numbers are from Faris (2007, 23). Berggren et al. (1996) place the 1976 population of the camp at approximately 30,000 people. When the camp was destroyed, survivors among its population moved to neighborhoods around West Beirut, to areas around the Sabra and Shatila districts, and to Damour.
5. 2011 registered refugees numbers are drawn from the UNRWA Public Information Office (2011).

Notes

INTRODUCTION

1. Padgett and Ansell (1993, 1263) refer to this trait as "multivocality," which they define as "the fact that single actions can be interpreted coherently from multiple perspectives simultaneously, the fact that single actions can be moves in many games at once, and the fact that public and private motivations cannot be parsed. Multivocal action leads to Rorschach blot identities, with all alters constructing their own distinctive attribution of the identity of ego."

2. In addition to al-Hout's (2004) foundational study of the massacre, see Ang (1989, chap. 6), Fisk (2002, chap. 11), Hanf (1994, 268–69), Y. Sayigh (1997, 539), and Schiff and Ya'ari (1984, chap. 13) as well as chapter 3.

3. The traditional period of mourning in Islam.

4. Conversations with Aisha and Ibrahim, author's field notes, June 2012.

5. I follow the terminology used in Palestinian history and politics by referring to individual parties that trained and fielded armed wings focused on irregular warfare as the "guerrilla parties" or "factions." These include Fatah, the Popular Front for the Liberation of Palestine, al-Saʿiqa, the Democratic Front for the Liberation of Palestine, Fatah al-Intifada, and so on. The Palestine Liberation Organization is a separate, umbrella entity that fielded its own armed divisions, including both security forces and the Palestine Liberation Army (PLA), a more conventionally trained force.

6. See Clemens (1999) on skill diffusion across activist networks over time.

7. Wood's use of the term "repertoire of violence" draws from Charles Tilly's concept of a "repertoire of contention" or a "repertoire of collective action" (See, e.g., Tilly 1978, 1986, 2008; della Porta 2013; Hoover Green 2016; Gutiérrez-Sanín and Wood 2017). Throughout the book, I reference both "repertoires of violence" and Francisco Gutiérrez-Sanín and Elisabeth Jean Wood's (2017) related concept of "patterns of violence," where said patterns are "comprised of the repertoire of violence in which the organization regularly engages and, for each element of the repertoire, its targeting, frequency, and technique" (23).

8. John Padgett and Christopher Ansell (1993, 1468–69) refer to these resource-based ties as "relational flows."

9. Repurposing and remapping closely resemble Padgett and Ansell's (1993, 1468) concepts of "transposition" and "recombination" of social ties across network domains—processes themselves modeled via a "perspectival" comparison (Schaffer 2018) between network transformation and biochemical processes. Individual, agentive actions play a greater role in repurposing and remapping than they do in Padgett and Ansell's approach, meaning that individual-level actors can also err, learn, and update in the process to a greater degree.

10. See, for example, Reno (1999), Nordstrom (2004), and Avant (2005).

11. This theory builds on Elisabeth Jean Wood's (2008) analysis of the transformative effects of war on social networks. Specifically, Wood emphasizes how processes that characterize wartime environments—such as mobilization and polarization—structurally alter everyday social relations by both creating new networks and destroying others.

12. Researchers have shared increasingly robust findings on the interaction of social networks with violence, demonstrating, for example, that it is interactions between violent

victimization and victims' presence within dense relational networks—rather than the attribute of victimization or dense social networks in and of themselves—that drive political outcomes (Dorff 2017).

13. The concept of social infrastructure builds on Roger Petersen's (2001) research, which demonstrates how various degrees of overlap between distinct, everyday social networks—for example, chambers of commerce and fraternities—shape and sustain mobilization. His work, in turn, draws from threshold models of mobilization (Granovetter 1978). By contrast, recent research on insurgency portrays "networked" insurgencies as distinct from "hierarchical" armed organizations (see, e.g., Serena 2014, 3–5, 30, 42–47), treating a "networked" organizational structure as an attribute and assigning intrinsic characteristics (such as adaptability) to "networked" versus "hierarchal" groups rather than examining patterns and degrees of social and organizational network overlap and their effects on outcomes.

14. Y. Sayigh (1997, 39).

15. On this point, see also Schulhofer-Wohl (2020).

16. Author's field notes, May and June 2012.

1. MEMORIES AND MYTHOLOGIES OF MILITANCY

1. Critics of structural ethnographies have noted the reductionism inherent to functionalist approaches (see, e.g., Kapferer 1972) by highlighting that they tend to gloss over meanings and subtleties and take responses to questions as providing face value "data" on ties (Wedeen 2010, 257–58; see also Pachucki and Breiger 2010, 207). Yet scholars have also highlighted how network analysis has been used to challenge structural-functionalist accounts, in particular by demonstrating "how idealized structural components stressed by the structural-functionalists—such as kinship, political, religious, and economic subgroups—are *ignored* [their emphasis] in the daily interactions of people" (Laumann et al. 1992, 62). Kate Meagher (2010, 23) presents an excellent critique of functionalist network and social capital approaches, emphasizing the need to move toward "an institutional problematic that reconnects networks with social and historical processes."

2. Research on conventional militaries emphasizes the role of logistical operations in shaping strategic options and efficacy (Van Creveld 1977).

3. In the words of Soss (2018), to iteratively "case" studies as opposed to studying preset cases.

4. I first visited Lebanon in the summer of 2007 for language training and initial research. I returned the next summer, stayed for a year from October 2009 to the following October, and visited again for May–June of 2011, May–June of 2012, January and May–June of 2014, and for a final two weeks of archival work in 2018. A fuller description of my research methods and ethical considerations is available in Appendix A.

5. "Fly-by research" occurs when researchers spend only a few days conducting interviews at a site and then leave (Sukarieh and Tannock 2013).

6. Many of my interlocutors perceived foreign researchers and journalists as conducting interviews in the camps only to reinforce stories they had already decided to tell. For cadres and former militants, adopting the language of "Christian versus Muslim" to describe the Lebanese Civil War was usually not a reflection of their lived experience or genuine political analysis; rather, it served as a stock narrative to "give outsiders what they wanted," when members of camp communities didn't feel people were genuinely interested in their reflections. See Parkinson (2022) for an analysis of related research dynamics in crisis-affected spaces.

7. Conversation with Nafisa, author's field notes, June 2012.

8. In Shatila, many of those who died during the siege were buried in the mosque in the center of the camp, where a memorial exists today.

9. I attended several large Fatah and PLO events in which politicians from Amal were featured on the program as being Lebanese supporters of the Palestinian cause. Their presence was a frequent source of tension within the organizations' memberships. On more than one occasion, I overheard people around me—and, in one case, the elderly woman next to me—muttering with disdain during these officials' speeches.

10. Conversation with Nafisa, author's field notes, June 2012.

11. Author's field notes, May 2010.

12. Similar events are detailed in Pauline Cutting's (1989) memoir of working in the camp hospital at this time.

13. Farouq had worked with women who were smugglers from his more protected location. His primary contact in the network, a woman who acted as a bridge between cells in several neighborhoods within Beirut, had been caught and executed. He had previously facilitated multiple productive introductions to male cadres.

14. See Parkinson (2016) on memory cultures associated with Old Fatah. See McLean (2016, 7 and 8) for a broader theory of how social networks produce culture and are produced by it.

15. They all spoke to friends and colleagues about the interview; there was nothing sensitive about our conversations.

2. BUILDING A SOCIAL INFRASTRUCTURE

1. Interview with Abu Bakr, Saida, summer 2010.

2. Interview with Giovanni, summer 2008.

3. Interviews with Ansar Allah commander in Ain al-Hilweh, Usbat al-Ansar's public affairs officer in Ain al-Hilweh (as told to and transcribed by a fixer), and a Fatah leader in Ain al-Hilweh, August 2007.

4. Interview with Ansar Allah commander in Ain al-Hilweh and head Ansar Allah checkpoint officer, August 2007.

5. See, e.g., Sogge (2016) for a recent example. The "imminent jihad in Ain al-Hilweh" story is a common early pitch for journalists arriving in Lebanon to the extent that it is a joke among long-term observers of Lebanese and Palestinian politics.

6. Author's field notes, summer 2012.

7. Interview with Abu Taha, al-Buss, August 2010.

8. For example, see the work of scholars such as Rosemary Sayigh (1979, 1994, 1995, 2007), Brynen (1990a, 1990b), Jaber Suleiman (1997, 1999), Bayan Nuwayhed al-Hout (2004), Diana Allan (2013), Laleh Khalili (2007a, 2005), and Nadya Hajj (2016), in addition to organizers of projects such as the Palestinian Oral History Archive at the American University of Beirut; community historians such as Hilana Abdullah (2008), Mahmud Abdullah Kallam (2008), and Ahmed Ali al-Hajali (2007); and documentary filmmakers such as Mai Masri (1998), Dahna Abourahmane (2010), and Mahdi Fleifel (2014).

9. Meaning "catastrophe" and referring to Palestinians' dispossession and expulsion from Mandate Palestine and the establishment of the contemporary state of Israel.

10. Rosemary Sayigh (1979, 65, 99) places the number of Palestinian refugees who arrived in Lebanon in 1948–49 at 104,000, a number close to the 106,500 that the UN published in 1951 following a census of registered refugees (al-Hout 2004, 21). Al-Hout (2004, 21) reports that the commonly held estimate of registered and unregistered Palestinian refugees at the time was 120,000. Picard (2002, 79) puts the number of refugees at 110,000; she also notes that the Lebanese government divided Christian refugees into particular camps, including Dbayeh and Jisr al-Pasha. Mar Elias (which was established

by an Orthodox convent) and al-Buss also housed large Christian populations. Approximately 87 percent of Palestinian refugees in Lebanon identify as Sunni, 10 percent as Christian, and less than 3 percent as Shi'a.

11. For local histories of Burj al-Shamali, Burj al-Barajneh, Shatila, and Tel al-Za'tar camps that cover this era, see Abdullah (2008), al-Hajali (2007), Kallam (2008), and Faris (2007). The October 1943 Lebanese National Pact was ostensibly intended to recognize the country's unique sectarian "balance" between Christians and Muslims; Lebanon experts repeatedly point to its more instrumentalist origins as "the winning formula for specific leaders to create a coalition government in a nominally independent Lebanon still controlled by the French" (Schulhofer-Wohl 2020, 63; see also el-Khazen 1991). Salloukh et al. (2015, 15–17) emphasize that the Pact was predominantly an "unwritten gentleman's agreement" between Maronite and Sunni elites; Schulhofer-Wohl (2020, 62–63) underscores that it "favored the interests of Maronite and Sunni businessmen and to a large extent excluded the interests of Druze, Shi'a, and other minority communities." Based on numbers from the 1932 census, the Pact institutionalized a 6:5 Christian-Muslim ratio in the state bureaucracy and parliament. Maronite Christians were allotted the powerful presidency as well as command of the army and control of both the General Security Directorate and the Military Intelligence Directorate (the *Deuxième Bureau*) (Salloukh et al. 2015, 17). The Sunni community was allocated the position of prime minister, the position of president of parliament went to the Shi'i community, and the position of vice president of parliament went to the Greek Orthodox community.

12. As a point of reference, the World Bank gives Lebanon's 1960 population (the first year for which data are listed) as approximately 1.8 million people, with a refugee population of 137,884 (World Bank, n.d.a, n.d.c). There have been two instances in Lebanese history when large groups of Palestinians in Lebanon have received nationality: up to 55,000 Christians in the 1950s (a number given to me by a Lebanese government source who requested anonymity due to the sensitivity of the topic, but also referenced in works such as Hermez 2017); and several thousand Sunnis and Shi'as in 1994, mostly from Burj al-Shamali camp (a number relayed to me by several of the camp's leaders, as well as five residents of the camp who could show me Lebanese identity cards, and the same Lebanese government source). Palestinian women who marry Lebanese men are granted Lebanese citizenship, which their children inherit; but neither Palestinian men who marry Lebanese women nor children of these marriages receive Lebanese citizenship. When I was in Lebanon, there was noteworthy Palestinian-Lebanese cooperation in lobbying the government to change this law, though it failed in parliament.

13. Lebanese bankers' 1966 collaboration to bring down the extremely successful and Palestinian-owned Intra Bank is only one example of how Palestinian professionals and businesses were targeted. See Picard (2002, 79).

14. Yezid Sayigh (1997, 31) and a guide published by the Palestinian Academic Society for the Study of International Affairs (PASSIA) both date the ANM's founding to 1951. Sayigh notes that the organization set up a specific Palestine committee in 1959; PASSIA says that Habash set up "Palestinian Chapters" in 1964 to carry out armed attacks; while Khaled (1973, 71), an early member, writes that activists established the Palestine "branch" in 1962. See Y. Sayigh (1997, 75–80) on the activities of the ANM, particularly its close relationship with Nasserist Egypt and Syria.

15. Yezid Sayigh (1997, 74) notes that the ANM sought to recruit teachers in the refugee camps in Lebanon, Syria, and Jordan.

16. See *al-Shahriyya* (2008) for a useful summary of this information.

17. Arafat, Khalaf, and al-Wazir all came from relatively middle-class families and received at least some university education in Cairo (Khalaf and al-Wazir after their families fled Palestine in 1948, Arafat because he had grown up in Cairo in a Gazan family).

Arafat and Khalaf were cofounders of the General Union of Palestinian Students in Cairo in 1952. See Palestinian Academic Society for the Study of International Affairs (PASSIA) (2012a, 2012b, 2012c). PASSIA differentiates between the date when the first Fatah cell was founded (1957 by Arafat and al-Wazir) and the date when the Fatah party was formally founded (1959). Yezid Sayigh (1997, 87) argues that the group did not truly coalesce into a party until 1962. Many early members of Fatah had deep ties to Gaza and the Palestinian Muslim Brotherhood. See Y. Sayigh (1997, 80–87).

18. Like the ANM, the PLF worked to recruit among UNRWA teachers.

19. By 1969 Fatah controlled the PLO's apparatus and worked to fill various positions with party members. The PLFP joined the Executive Committee (EC) in 1971, left it in 1974 in protest, and rejoined it in 1981.

20. Before Fatah opened training sites in Lebanon, its training occurred in Syria and Jordan. Fatah initially did not have its own training camps and instead used sites run by other factions. My interlocutors who had been early joiners traveled to train at these sites rather than receiving instruction in Lebanon. As a result, they were much more likely to have known people both across multiple parties and in the PLA (or had served in the PLA themselves). Later training sites were frequently differentiated by party, so there was less of a chance that trainees would develop cross-organization connections.

21. See Khalili 2007, 145 on Palestinian nationalists' deliberate decision to call their fighters "fida'iyyin" (redeemers, sing. "*fida'yi*") rather than "*mujahidin*" (holy warriors).

22. These suburban shanty districts became known as the "Belt of Misery."

23. Picard (2002, 81–82) places the number of Palestinians who left Jordan for Lebanon at over 100,000 people.

24. Interview with a member of the Lebanese Palestinian Dialogue Committee, summer 2008; interview with Abu Talib, an aid official who formerly worked in the Gulf, summer 2010.

25. Interview with Yunis (1), spring 2011.

26. The NLP was associated with the Tigers militia, which was led by Dany Chamoun, Camille's son.

27. See Cobban (1985, 156). The PFLP's early-1970s aircraft hijackings involved some militants from Lebanon (including Leila Khaled), though they had often trained in Jordan or in other countries.

28. One of the more spectacular acts of reprisal was the IDF's December 28, 1968, bombing of thirteen jets that belonged to Middle East Airlines (the Lebanese national carrier) at the Beirut airport in response to a PFLP operation against an El Al passenger plane in Athens on December 26, 1968. The event became notorious for the Lebanese military's inability to protect the airport.

29. The circumstances of the attack are highly disputed. For example, el-Khazen (2000, 286) argues that agreements between Palestinian factions and Lebanese authorities were supposed to prevent political convoys from traveling through Ain al-Rummaneh on that day, but that police directed the bus driver through the neighborhood anyway, implying a setup.

30. See Schulhofer-Wohl (2020, 96–101) for a brief summary of these events.

31. Hussein Faris (2007, 23) places the population of Tel al-Zaʿtar in 1972 at approximately 11,415 people. Anders Berggren et al. (1996) estimate the camp's 1976 population to have been around 30,000 people.

32. Tel al-Zaʿtar's politics and location encapsulated many of the contributing dynamics to the early stages of the Lebanese Civil War, including those related to class, ideology, migration, and sectarian cleavages. Nabʿa housed many displaced, working-class Lebanese from South Lebanon, many of whom benefited from Palestinian institutions in the absence of state social services. Palestinian organizations in the camps provided

both Palestinian and Lebanese workers support for collective action, for example by backing employee strikes. In 1972, for instance, tobacco workers led significant labor actions, and employees of the Ghandour chocolate factory went on strike. However, Palestinian factions were also illicitly levying taxes in the area; Christian politicians worried that the camps provided a potential location from which to stage politician kidnappings and other military operations. Interview with Abu Tariq (1), Beirut, fall 2010; interview with Hala, Beirut, summer 2012.

33. This chain of events was brutal; at one point, soon-to-be members of the FLA executed Muslim officers in their barracks. Interview with Mina, NGO worker and daughter of one of the executed officers, Saida, spring 2010.

34. Interview with Hala, Beirut, summer 2012.

35. In other words, her family's village in Palestine, a common means of identification in the camps.

36. Interview with Zahra, spring 2010.

37. While I did not inquire about interviewees' experiences of sexual violence, several women voluntarily identified themselves or family members as having survived sexual assault.

38. Sayigh also notes that around 3,000 civilians and 400 fighters had fled the camp on August 9 and 10. In sum, 4,280 people died during the siege; 450 were members of militant organizations and 750 were "armed volunteers."

39. There is considerable debate over Yasir Arafat's role in the siege and diplomacy surrounding it. The Palestinian leadership could have told the camp to surrender when the situation proved hopeless, but did not. Arafat also ordered fighters in the camp to break various ceasefires, prolonging hostilities and potentially provoking both reprisals and the media coverage they would invite. Arafat's deployment of moral hazard tactics became a bone of contention within Fatah and the PLO during the 1985–1988 War of the Camps.

40. Multiple accounts tell of this particular operation, known in Israel as the Coastal Road Massacre. Cobban records thirty-seven dead, including six Palestinian commandos, in an attack on a single passenger bus. Hugh Macleod (2008), a journalist who researched the incident on the occasion of a 2008 prisoner and body exchange between Israel and Lebanon, writes that the team hijacked two civilian buses, one of which later exploded during a gun battle with Israeli security forces. The cause of the explosion is disputed; Macleod notes that Israeli authorities maintain that al-Mughrabi used grenades to blow it up with the civilians on board, though Palestinian sources argue that gunfire from an Israeli helicopter ignited the bus.

41. In 1980 the FLA was rebranded the South Lebanon Army (SLA).

42. A crusader castle southeast of Nabatiyeh that overlooks the Lebanon–Israel border. Palestinian militants held the castle throughout the 1970s.

43. Interview with Hala, Beirut, summer 2012.

44. A standard US or NATO brigade comprises approximately 2,000–5,000 people. A battalion commonly includes 500–800 people.

45. By the World Bank's measures, Lebanon's population in 1980 was approximately 2.59 million Lebanese and 235,105 refugees (World Bank n.d.a; n.d.c). The refugee number, which the World Bank sources from UNRWA and United Nations High Commissioner for Refugees (UNHCR), almost certainly does not include Palestinians who left Jordan in 1970–1971; the World Bank numbers for refugees in Jordan consistently increase throughout the 1970s (World Bank n.d.b).

46. To this day, medical institutions are one of the favored forms of social service provision for the militant parties because they can employ high numbers of people through part- and full-time work. Conversation with Sabah, author's field notes, June 2010.

3. SOCIAL NETWORKS AND WARTIME VIOLENCE

1. See, e.g., Y. Sayigh (1983a, 1983b), Schiff and Ya'ari (1984), Khalidi (1985), Rabinovich (1985), and Fisk (2002).

2. Kalyvas (2006, 142) defines selective violence as occurring "when there is an intention to ascertain individual guilt" and indiscriminate violence as being when "the concept of individual guilt is replaced with the concept of guilt by association." While Balcells (2010, 2011, and 2017, 6–7, 21–24) uses the terms "direct violence" and "indirect violence," her conceptual distinction centers on the agents deploying violence, for example, either an armed group alone or an armed group with civilian collaborators, as well as on the level of intimacy involved in the tactics, such as "indirect" aerial bombardment versus "direct" small arms fire and other forms of face-to-face violence. Balcells's analytical focus is predominantly on pathways to direct violence behind the front lines of civil war, rather than on counterinsurgent success.

3. On the incentives associated with indiscriminate versus selective violence see Kalyvas (2006, 143–55).

4. The faction's armed wing from the 1960s through the 1980s.

5. Mazzeh is a neighborhood in Damascus that is home to the Mazzeh Military Airport and a Syrian Air Force Intelligence base that includes detention facilities. "Qism Falastin" was Kamal's term for the "Palestine Branch," a name that refers to Branch 235 of Syrian Military Intelligence, which has its own detention facilities in Mazzeh. Tadmor (previously located near the Palmyra ruins in eastern Syria) and Sadnaya (located just north of Damascus) are Syrian military prisons.

6. The majority of people with whom I conducted in-depth interviews or life histories moved at least once, if not several times, throughout the wars and occupations of the 1980s. Several, like Nader and Aisha, moved both within and between cities. Zahra, Nawal, Mahmud, Dalal, Abu Houli, Kamal, and Yusif moved from city to city for their military work, personal security, and family reasons. See also al-Hajali (2007, 66), Abdullah (2008, 49–56).

7. *Al-Safir,* July 6, 1982. Interview with Dalal, spring 2011. Most of the PLO's leadership doubted that the Israelis would reach Beirut, so few military arrangements were made for the city's defense.

8. Rubenberg (1986, 281) and the Advisory Committee on Human Rights in Lebanon (1983). The estimated number of registered Palestinians residing in South Lebanon—both inside and outside the camps—at this time was 106,023. This number would not have included either unregistered refugees or Palestinians who had been registered in Syria or Jordan before moving to Lebanon (e.g., those who arrived following Black September or when PLA units that had trained in Syria moved into Lebanon).

9. It is traditional to decorate the bride's and groom's cars with ribbons, tulle, and flowers, so this was a funny statement; they were escaping a war zone in a car ostensibly covered in flowers and pink and white fabric.

10. Interview with Abu Wissam, Sur, summer 2010.

11. The conflicting destruction estimates could reflect anything from varying measurement approaches (a house still standing is not necessarily inhabitable) to different reporting time frames (before or after bulldozing).

12. White phosphorous is used as an incendiary and as a marker, as well as to screen troop movements. It is not illegal to produce or deploy in combat. However, Protocol III of the Convention on Prohibition or Restrictions on the Use of Certain Conventional Weapons Which May be Deemed to be Excessively Injurious or to Have Indiscriminate Effects (CCW) "prohibits and restricts the use of incendiary weapons in civilian populations" (Federation of American Scientists, n.d.) as do the Geneva Conventions. The

previously named Convention itself, though authored in 1980, did not enter into force until December 1983. Israel has not consented to be bound by Protocol III. Lebanon, while a party to the Convention, did not consent by be bound by Protocol II, which restricts the use of mines and booby-traps. (*Convention on Prohibitions or Restrictions on the Use of Certain Conventional Weapons Which May Be Deemed to Be Excessively Injurious or to Have Indiscriminate Effects (with Protocols I, II, and III)*, n.d.)

13. Interview with Abu Riyad, summer 2012.

14. Interviews with Yahya and Khalid, Burj al-Shamali, June 2012. The Israeli air raids are also discussed in Abdullah (2008, 50).

15. Abdullah (2008, 50–52). This question was partially meant to assess my respect for the camp's community and history, in addition to sharing knowledge of the massacre with me as an outsider.

16. "US says Israelis lax in refugee efforts." *United Press International*. Wire report: Tel Aviv, Israel, October 8, 1982; Nadler, Gerald. "Tents for Homeless Refugees." *United Press International*. Wire report: Ein Hilwe-Israeli Occupied Lebanon, October 7, 1982.

17. According to Schiff and Ya'ari (1984), officers in the Kastel Brigade, the Yarmouk Brigade, the Jarmak Battalion, and the Karameh Brigade also abandoned their posts. Shuquair (1983) notes that Colonel Saied al-Muragha (Abu Musa), who served as Commander of the Yarmouk Brigade and who spearheaded the PLO's 1982 defense of Beirut, held one of Yasir Arafat's key supporters responsible for the rout in Saida. My Palestinian interlocutors repeatedly referenced Kastel Brigade Commander Colonel Haj Ismail's desertion as noteworthy because he was later the subject of an internal Fatah inquiry. Afterward, Arafat controversially reinstalled him in a high-ranking post in Lebanon, contributing to internal turmoil in Fatah that culminated in a 1983 mutiny that al-Muragha led (see chapter 6).

18. Yermiya (1984, 15) describes in detail the IDF's harsh treatment of Lebanese as well as Palestinian residents of Saida, emphasizing that the IDF made few plans to manage civilian communities' needs following the destruction of their homes.

19. Most authors agree that religious authorities contributed significantly to the defense of the camp. Schiff and Ya'ari (1984) reference an Iranian-inspired mullah by the name of Haj Ismail leading a group called the Soldiers of Allah. Khalidi (1985) cites "Muslim *shaykhs*" as helping to lead the defense of the camp. Rougier (2007) attributes Ain al-Hilweh's resistance efforts to "Islamist networks," on the basis that the PLO factions had "retreated north to defend Beirut." He contends that "The Islamist militants who provided the camp's principal defense were almost all students of the Palestinian shaykh Ibrahim Ghunaym, who was visiting Iran during the clashes but lost a son in the siege of the camp." Khalili (2007b) specifically disputes Rougier's account, arguing: "He writes that Islamist organizations in Ain al-Hilweh spearheaded the defense of the camp in 1982 (they did not)." The distinction pertains to the extent of specifically Islamic organizations' involvement and leadership in the camp's defense, rather than the participation of local religious authorities and students. My interviews indicated that local (non-Islamic) militias and camp-based cadres played more of a role than Rougier's account implies.

20. Civilians may or may not have initially known what different forms of ordnance were. Mahmoud Zeidan's memoir, which is based on his experience as a child in the camp during this time, simply mentions a nameless white drizzle or spray that covered surfaces following some air raids (Zeidan 2017, 254).

21. Conversations with Abu Houli, author's field notes, June 2012; conversations with Nader, author's field notes, June 2012; group interview with former Shatila defensemen, Beirut, summer 2012.

22. Advisory Committee on Human Rights in Lebanon (1983, 24). See also Denkner (1983), Schiff and Ya'ari (1984, chap. 8), Yermiya (1984), Khalidi (1985), Abourahme (2010).

23. Central Bureau of Statistics (1981) and Saʿid Ibrahim (1983).

24. Yermiya (1984, 28) notes that IDF officers quickly became aware that the collaborators (whom they referred to as "monkeys") had accused innocent people and protected their own acquaintances. He emphasizes that the practice was allowed to continue because Israeli officers believed it would warn innocent people of "what waits for terrorists."

25. Kalyvas (2006) extensively discusses denunciation of this sort. He notes the use of hooded informers, in multiple counterinsurgent repertoires, underscoring its deployment by invading and colonial forces such as the British in Kenya (p. 186), the Germans in Greece (p. 148), and Americans in Iraq (p. 187), summarizing: "The figure of the hooded informer fingering the people to be arrested (the infamous *encapuchado* in Latin America) is common across most civil wars" (193). See Balcells (2017) on the use of civilian collaborators.

26. Interview with Abu Haytham, Sur, summer 2010.

27. Advisory Committee on Human Rights in Lebanon (1983, 27).

28. Interviews with Yusif, who was held at the Safa facility, summer and fall 2010; Ziyad, a former inmate of Ansar, fall 2010; Abu Riyad, a former leader of an Ansar subcamp, summer 2012; Mahmud, former inmate of Ansar, spring 2011. Ziyad, Abu Riyad, and Mahmud spent several years in Ansar. A woman interviewed for this project spent a month in Ansar after being imprisoned at IDF headquarters (most likely the facility housed at Saida's St. Joseph's Convent) for over a week for displaying a Palestinian flag. According to her, the women's section of Ansar was much smaller (when she was there, about twenty-five other women were with her) and the women were generally held for about a year. Abourahme (2010) also discusses the transfer of high-level Lebanese and Palestinian female political prisoners to Israel. Also see Khalili (2008), and *al-Safir*, October 1 and 2, 1982, and March 16, 1983.

29. "Notes on Two Interviews with Dan Friesen, MCC staff, Sidon," September 23, 1983. Box "1983-Middle East-Lebanon-Relief/Reconstruction," Folder 10153. American Friends Service Committee Archive. Philadelphia, p. 2. In July 2008, Israel returned to Lebanon five living prisoners and the remains of 200 Lebanese and Palestinian soldiers who had been kept in Israel, in exchange for the remains of two Israeli soldiers held by Hizbullah. Many of the Lebanese and Palestinian bodies were people taken prisoner or killed during this period. The day when trucks drove through the border bearing prisoners and caskets was treated as a somber holiday in the camps but also understood as a significant symbolic victory over Israel.

30. Original data gathered by Ayesha Durrani for the author.

31. The Italian contingent was stationed around Mar Elias and Sabra-Shatila; the French patrolled northwest Beirut, while the Americans took up positions around the airport, close to Burj al-Barajneh.

32. Fisk (2002, 350) discusses several competing sources of the actual number of evacuees. He also notes that at least 10,000 fighters remained in northern and eastern Lebanon in the zones of Syrian control. Schiff and Ya'ari (1984, 228) place the number of evacuees at 14,398 fighters (both Palestinian and Syrian), plus 664 women and children. This number jibes with Mahmoud al-Natour's report that 14,000 Palestinian fighters battled the IDF's 170,000 (al-Natour 2014a, 1:659). Al-Hout (2004, 35–39) notes that there was considerable confusion over whether members of the PLO and guerrilla fighters who lived in Lebanon (rather than those who had transferred from Jordan in 1970 and 1971) were supposed to leave with the rest, given that they may have been permanently blocked from returning to their families.

33. Interview with Zahra (1), spring 2010. Y. Sayigh (1997, 541–42) notes that military leaders across organizations had not seriously expected—or planned for—the IDF to reach Beirut.

34. Interview with Aisha (1), spring 2010.

35. The assassination can be seen as a "triggering event," that is, "an event or part of a chain of events that initiated a sharp escalation in atrocity violence" (Straus 2015, 10). Straus (2015, 8) notes that such moments must be historically and contextually situated, as well as being closely examined for how "influential actors manipulate and use events," rather than being understood as singularly and independently causal.

36. Shatila has been an official—that is, UNRWA administered—refugee camp since 1949. The camp itself occupies only one square kilometer. Though the term is not technically accurate, many of my Palestinian and Lebanese interlocuters referred to Sabra, and sometimes al-Daouk, using the term *mukhayyam* ("camp"). See Appendix C.

37. Documents produced by the government-convened Kahan Commission demonstrated that Israeli leaders were well aware of the potential for their Lebanese allies to commit a massacre and did not work to prevent it. See Kahan Commission (1983); Anziska (2018); Khalidi (2018).

38. Interview with Abu Hassan, Summer 2012. *Watha'iq al-Harb al-Lubnaniyya*, a multi-volume collection that documents the war in detail, mentions raids and arrests occurred in mid-October in Burj al-Barajneh. The writing corroborates the detention site at the Ministry of Defense and puts the number of Palestinians, Lebanese, and other nationalities arrested at 1,441 people (al-Din 1985, 102–104).

4. BEYOND THE LINES

1. Author's field notes, May 2010.

2. Heavily militarized, often Syrian-trained guerrilla factions such as al-Sa'iqa and the PFLP-GC tended to be smaller overall, to focus less on social service provision, and to be more dominated by men in comparison to Fatah, the PLFP, and the DFLP. The large majority of the women I interviewed were in or had been in Fatah, the DFLP, or the PFLP. While I interviewed several women who were associated with the PFLP-GC and had participated in various roles, they had not previously been scouts, nor had they received military training.

3. The PSP is a predominantly Druze party, whereas Amal is a predominantly Shi'i party. Amal was initially founded in 1974 as *Harakat al-Mahrumin* (The Movement of the Deprived), to represent marginalized Shi'a and other populations' interests in Lebanon. Amal recruited heavily in neighborhoods in the "Belt of Misery" around Beirut where Shatila and Burj al-Barajneh are located (and where Tel al-Za'tar and Jisr al-Basha were also located). In the suburbs of East Beirut, Palestinian and poor Shi'a populations often engaged in labor and political organizing together. Hizbullah, a predominantly Shi'i militant party that follows an expressly Islamist ideology, coalesced in the 1980s with support from Iran and largely in response to the Israeli occupation. It attracted many of its members from Amal. Palestinians who had trained with Amal militants in the 1970s (see chapter 2), thus often knew people in both Amal and Hizbullah in the 1980s. I note throughout the book when people cited these connections to Lebanese parties as shaping network change in Palestinian groups.

4. Interview with Dalal, Saida, spring 2011.

5. Interview with Dalal, Saida, spring 2011.

6. Interview with Dalal, Saida, spring 2011.

7. Interview with Munadileh, Saida, spring 2011.

8. Al-Mughrabi, Bushra. 2009. Interviews with Umm Karim Abu Salim and Hala Abu Salim. Video. Palestinian Oral History Archive. https://n2t.net/ark:/86073/b3h05z. Copyright holder Al-Jana/AUB University Libraries, licensed under CC BY-NC-ND 4.0. m. 12:30–15:00.

9. Abourahme (2010) and author interview with Dalal, Saida, spring 2011.

10. Interview with Dalal, Saida, spring 2011.
11. Interview with Yusif (4), Beirut, autumn 2010.
12. Interview with Kamal, summer 2012.
13. Interview with Yusif (4), fall 2010.
14. These particular experience jibes with Finkel's (2015 and 2017) arguments about the role of past repression in activists' ability to acquire "toolkits" for rebellion.
15. In Paul Staniland's (2014, 25–28) terms, these organizations had been "integrated" prior to 1982, with strong horizontal and vertical ties between militants.
16. Interview with Hussam, fall 2010.
17. Interview with Yusif (4), fall 2010.
18. See, for example, *al-Safir*, on these dates in 1984: January 24, March 14, May 5 and 17, and December 9 and December 23.
19. Advisory Committee on Human Rights in Lebanon (1983, 24).
20. "Notes on Two Interviews with Dan Friesen, MCC staff, Sidon." September 23, 1983. Box "1983-Middle East-Lebanon-Relief/Reconstruction," Folder 10153. American Friends Service Committee Archive. Philadelphia. P. 1.
21. Interviews with Abu Riyad, former military officer from Sur, summer 2012; Ziyad, former fighter from Ain al-Hilweh, fall 2010; and Mahmud, spring 2011.
22. Interview with Ziyad, fall 2010.
23. Interview with Abu Riyad, summer 2012.
24. Interview with Rahaf, spring 2011. AFSC documents note that the IDF routinely threatened female prisoners with rape. See "Notes on Two Interviews with Dan Friesen, MCC staff, Sidon." September 23, 1983. Box "1983-Middle East-Lebanon-Relief/Reconstruction," Folder 10153. American Friends Service Committee Archive. Philadelphia. P. 1.
25. Conversation with Mahmud, author's field notes, June 2012.
26. Interview with Yusif (4), Beirut, autumn 2010.
27. Interview with Kamal, Beirut, summer 2012.
28. Interview with Dalal, Saida, spring 2011.
29. "According to the Messenger." *Sawt al-Mukhayyam* August 1984, Issue 2. P. 1.
30. I was able to fully access nine issues of *Sawt al-Mukhayyam* at the Institute for Palestine Studies in Beirut and also to interview one of its former editors.
31. At this juncture, repair contracts were tied to the company that sold the machine. Interview with Bassam (2), spring 2012.
32. Indeed, in my fieldwork, I frequently noticed that party officials would read their own newsletters as well as those of rival organizations, prompting me to ask people how they had previously interacted with publications such as *Sawt al-Mukhayyam*.
33. "According to the Messenger." *Sawt al-Mukhayyam*. August 1984, Issue 1. P. 1.
34. "Women's Role in the Success of the Vietnamese Revolution." *Sawt al-Mukhayyam*. August 1984, Issue 1. P. 4.
35. Giannou (1990, 41).
36. Interview with Munadileh, Saida, spring 2011.

5. CROSSING COLLABORATORS

1. Author's field notes, June 2012.
2. Issues related to collaboration, infiltration, and the presence of spies surfaced in most of my interviews with former militants, with varying degrees of detail. Multiple interlocutors identified accused collaborators by name in their conversations with me, both as historical information and as a personal warning. In the interest of confidentiality and safety, I do not identify living individuals whom my interviewees accused and do not otherwise reveal accused collaborators' names unless the material is directly quoted from a broadly

and publicly circulated source such as a national newspaper. I have provided pseudonyms for individuals identified in publicly accessible but not widely circulated archival materials, such as internal NGO reports and the POHA video archives. I never asked about specific individuals' histories of collaboration even if multiple others identified them as collaborators. I interviewed several people whom others had accused of collaboration. None of them revealed themselves as collaborators, but people did speak openly of having held leadership roles in Ansar. Other Ansar inmates strongly believed these positions were given to collaborators and associated them with collaboration (see chapter 3).

3. Interview with Dalal, spring 2011.

4. Al-Mughrabi, Bushra. 2009. Interview with Fatimah Yusuf, Zahrah al-Asadi, and Halimah Shanaʿah. Video. Palestinian Oral History Archive. https://n2t.net/ark:/86073/b3105m. Copyright holder Al-Jana/AUB University Libraries, licensed under CC BY-NC-ND 4.0. Around m. 30:00.

5. Al-Mughrabi, Bushra. 2009. Interview with Umm Karim Abu Salim and Hala Abu Salim. Video. Palestinian Oral History Archive. https://n2t.net/ark:/86073/b3h05z. Copyright holder Al-Jana/AUB University Libraries, licensed under CC BY-NC-ND 4.0. Around m. 28:00. The term *"zalama"* can be used to indicate "man" or, in more colloquial usage, is roughly equivalent to "the man."

6. Interview with Tala, Sur, summer 2012.

7. Interview with Dalal, Saida, spring 2011.

8. Al-Mughrabi, Bushra. 2009. Interview with Fatimah Yusuf, Zahrah al-Asadi, and Halimah Shanaʿah. Video. Palestinian Oral History Archive. https://n2t.net/ark:/86073/b3105m. Copyright holder Al-Jana/AUB University Libraries, licensed under CC BY-NC-ND 4.0.

9. *Al-Safir*, July 10, 1982. It was incredibly difficult for Lebanese and Palestinian journalists to travel across the front lines; many international outlets covered South Lebanon during this time via their Jerusalem correspondent.

10. "Notes on Two Interviews with Dan Friesen, MCC staff, Sidon." September 23, 1983. Box "1983-Middle East-Lebanon-Relief/Reconstruction," Folder 10153. American Friends Service Committee Archive. Philadelphia. P. 2.

11. *Al-Safir*, October 3, 1982.

12. Interview with Chantal, spring 2010.

13. "Eviction of Palestinian from their home in AL-Adusia (south of Sidon)." February 2, 1983. Box "1983-Middle East-Lebanon-Relief/Reconstruction," Folder 11551. American Friends Service Committee Archive. Philadelphia.

14. This tactic had been used from the early days of the Lebanese Civil War to request people's ID cards, which listed their confessional background and thus could be used to target people of a particular group.

15. Interview with Yusif (2). On denunciation and violence in civil war, see Kalyvas (1999, 2006).

16. *Sawt al-Mukhayyam*. "News from the Camps." August 1984. P. 7.

17. Interview with Dalal, Saida, spring 2011.

18. Fatah issued a statement directly on this point on September 30, 1982, that emphasized not only the presence in Saida of the same Lebanese Christian militias that had perpetrated the Sabra and Shatila massacre, but reported that thousands of men and youths were being held at Ansar, leaving the Palestinians in the region even more vulnerable. *Al-Safir*, September 30, 1982.

19. See Deborah Gould (2009) and Erica Simmons (2016) on the importance of collective meaning and emotion in mobilization.

20. "Raids on Ain al-Hilweh Camp ... Arrests and Assassination Attempts." *Sawt al-Mukhayyam* August 1984, Issue 2. P. 2.

21. See Doug McAdam (1986), Roger Gould (1995), and Charles Tilly and Sidney Tarrow (2015) on processes of network formation via narrative and claim-making.

22. See *al-Safir* November 7 and December 2, 1984.

23. See Abourahme (2010) for an in-depth documentary exploration of this era in Ain al-Hilweh.

24. Al-Mughrabi, Bushra. 2009. Interview with Fatimah Yusuf, Zahrah al-Asadi, and Halimah Shanaʿah. Video. Palestinian Oral History Archive. https://n2t.net/ark:/86073/b3105m. Copyright holder Al-Jana/AUB University Libraries, licensed under CC BY-NC-ND 4.0.

25. Al-Mughrabi, Bushra. 2009. Interview with Fatimah Yusuf, Zahrah al-Asadi, and Halimah Shanaʿah. Video. Palestinian Oral History Archive. https://n2t.net/ark:/86073/b3105m. Copyright holder Al-Jana/AUB University Libraries, licensed under CC BY-NC-ND 4.0. Around m. 1:53:00.

26. Interviews with Munadileh and Dalal, spring 2011; *al-Safir* October 4, 1982; March 15, 1983; March 1 and September 9, 1984. See also Abourahme 2010.

27. Al-Mughrabi, Bushra. 2009. Interview with Fatimah Yusuf, Zahrah al-Asadi, and Halimah Shanaʿah. Video. Palestinian Oral History Archive. https://n2t.net/ark:/86073/b3105m. Copyright holder Al-Jana/AUB University Libraries, licensed under CC BY-NC-ND 4.0. Around m. 41:00.

28. See *al-Safir* November 7 and December 2, 1984.

29. "Ain al-Hilweh Camp Announces their Anger in the Massacre Remembrance." *Sawt al-Mukhayyam*, October 1984, Issue 1. P. 2.

30. Interview with Yusif (2), fall 2010.

31. Abu Houli also chose to share this story with me after we had spent two hours drinking coffee and smoking cigarettes with the son as he shared his experiences from prison and from the Sur guerrilla underground in the latter half of the decade. His timing seemed designed to evoke the complexity of the son's position under the occupation, especially as a former prisoner; intimidated by the Israelis both in his personal life and as a member of a different political faction than his father, he made his choice not simply as a matter of either money or revenge (though it was one that Abu Houli deplored).

32. "Siblin Principal CONFIDENTIAL." April 25, 1983. Box "1983-Middle East-Lebanon-Relief/Reconstruction," Folder 11551. American Friends Service Committee Archive. Philadelphia. P. 1.

33. "Meeting with IDF Colonel Sami, Sidon, 2 Feb. 1983." February 2, 1983. Box "1983-Middle East-Lebanon-Relief/Reconstruction," Folder 11551. American Friends Service Committee Archive. Philadelphia. "TRANSLATION: Al-Safir Daily. Monday 15 November 1982. Page 5 Columns 7&8, left upper corner." November 15, 1982. Box "1982-Middle East-Lebanon-Relief/Reconstruction," Folder 2337. American Friends Service Committee Archive. Philadelphia. P. 2.

34. Al-Mughrabi, Bushra. 2009. Interview with Umm Karim Abu Salim and Hala Abu Salim. Video. Palestinian Oral History Archive. https://n2t.net/ark:/86073/b3h05z. Copyright holder Al-Jana/AUB University Libraries, licensed under CC BY-NC-ND 4.0. Around m. 38:45.

35. Zeidan uses the terms "*umalaʾa*" (informants) and "*jawasis*" (spies) to describe collaborators.

36. Given the determination and tactics of Ain al-Hilweh's defensive forces during the invasion, it is likely that the camp retained a reputation among IDF soldiers.

37. The implication was that the men were trying to act tough and exhibiting bravado.

38. Al-Mughrabi, Bushra. 2009. Interview with Umm Karim Abu Salim and Hala Abu Salim. Video. Palestinian Oral History Archive. https://n2t.net/ark:/86073/b3h05z. Copyright holder Al-Jana/AUB University Libraries, licensed under CC BY-NC-ND 4.0. Around

NOTES TO PAGES 106–114

m. 50:20. The word *"ytzaharu"* was transcribed phonetically from the original interview video; the author thanks Faten Ghosn for her assistance with precise translation.

39. Al-Mughrabi, Bushra. 2009. Interview with Fatimah Yusuf, Zahrah al-Asadi, and Halimah Shana'ah. Video. Palestinian Oral History Archive. https://n2t.net/ark:/86073/b3105m. Copyright holder Al-Jana/AUB University Libraries, licensed under CC BY-NC-ND 4.0.

40. See, for example, *al-Safir,* January 3 and May 11, 1984. Interview with Abu Houli, June 2012.

41. Interview with Fadi, fall 2010.

42. Al-Mughrabi, Bushra. 2009. Interview with Fatimah Yusuf, Zahrah al-Asadi, and Halimah Shana'ah. Video. Palestinian Oral History Archive. https://n2t.net/ark:/86073/b3105m. Copyright holder Al-Jana/AUB University Libraries, licensed under CC BY-NC-ND 4.0. Around m. 43.00.

43. Al-Mughrabi, Bushra. 2009. Interview with Fatimah Yusuf, Zahrah al-Asadi, and Halimah Shana'ah. Video. Palestinian Oral History Archive. https://n2t.net/ark:/86073/b3105m. Copyright holder Al-Jana/AUB University Libraries, licensed under CC BY-NC-ND 4.0. Around m. 43.00.

44. Al-Mughrabi, Bushra. 2009. Interview with Fatimah Yusuf, Zahrah al-Asadi, and Halimah Shana'ah. Video. Palestinian Oral History Archive. https://n2t.net/ark:/86073/b3105m. Copyright holder Al-Jana/AUB University Libraries, licensed under CC BY-NC-ND 4.0. Around m. 53:00.

45. On the National Guard see *al-Safir,* June 15 and June 16, 1983; March 10, May 6, May 8, May 17, October 20, and November 4, 1984; on targeting accused collaborators see *al-Safir* August 8, 1983; September 28, 1984; and *al-Safir,* January 5, 1985, on the murder of Abu Maher al-Hindawi and a member of the al-Issa family. The IDF had replaced many local goods with Israeli ones, meaning that even people who were not politically affiliated had economic incentives to engage in these activities.

46. For example, see *al-Safir,* December 30, 1983.

47. *Al-Safir,* October 28, 1984.

48. Author's field notes, July 2010.

49. "Rashidiye Camp Near Sour (Tyre)." March 21, 1983. Box "1983-Middle East-Lebanon-Relief/Reconstruction," Folder 11551. American Friends Service Committee Archive. Philadelphia. P. 1.

50. "Rashidiye Camp Near Sour (Tyre)." March 21, 1983. Box "1983-Middle East-Lebanon-Relief/Reconstruction," Folder 11551. American Friends Service Committee Archive. Philadelphia. What seems to be the man's real name is printed in the AFSC reports. I have chosen to give him a pseudonym in the event that printing a name contained in rarely quoted archives held in the US could cause harm to the man's family or community. The pseudonym I have given him cannot be mistaken for the name of a living person.

51. "Rashidiye Camp Near Sour (Tyre)." March 21, 1983. Box "1983-Middle East-Lebanon-Relief/Reconstruction," Folder 11551. American Friends Service Committee Archive. Philadelphia. P. 3.

52. Interview with Abu Haytham, Sour, summer 2010.

53. "Rashidiye Camp Near Sour (Tyre)." March 21, 1983. Box "1983-Middle East-Lebanon-Relief/Reconstruction," Folder 11551. American Friends Service Committee Archive. Philadelphia. P. 1.

54. I thank Jon Mercer for helping me to clarify this point.

6. THE FACE OF THE CAMPS

1. I met and interviewed several of the people who post on the page. I have thus been able to triangulate much of its content through primary and secondary sources. How-

ever, I am interested predominantly in how his former colleagues represent Abu Tawq, particularly with relation to the Fatah leadership and his status peers in other Palestinian organizations.

2. Disillusioned with the PLO and with Fatah's elite leadership and command style, military strategy, and changing stance toward Israel, as well as Arafat's nepotism in military appointments, al-Muragha had been building a dissident network since 1982. Following his submission of a dissenting memo to the January 1983 PLO Revolutionary Council meeting, al-Muragha led a Syrian-supported mutiny in summer 1983 against Arafat, splitting the Yarmouk Brigade, executing Fatah loyalist officers, and triggering intra-Palestinian fighting in the Bekaa and Trablous. He publicly justified the group's actions in an interview with *al-Kifah al-'Arabi,* a weekly Beirut-based publication, in part by referencing the events of June 1982: "Arafat insisted on giving the most sensitive posts to persons known for their moral, political, and military limitations. Such persons were directly responsible for the [1982] defeat. Arafat promoted them or assigned them to more sensitive jobs. This meant that Arafat was preparing for a new defeat, with the same persons. We had no choice but to act quickly in order to stop this deterioration" (Abu Musa and Abu Salih 1983, 180). For a summary of al-Muragha's stance and the mutiny's dynamics see, e.g., Shuquair (1983), Rouleau et al. (1983), Rouleau (1983), and Wright (1983).

3. Conversation with Aisha and Ibrahim, author's field notes, June 2012.

4. See Hundman and Parkinson (2019) on how multiplex network identifications spur disobedience in military organizations.

5. Interview with Aisha (1), spring 2010.

6. Interviews with Zahra (1, 2), Abu Umar, Aisha (1, 2), and Abu Tariq (2). Nader's family was from Tel al-Za'tar camp; his mother told me that their greatest fear during was being separated as they were following the camp's evacuation and the massacre of thousands of refugees. The experience of separation following the fall of Tel al-Za'tar was particularly trying for the women, who spent weeks trying to find news of the men. Their family consequently decided to live clustered in one camp; they were convinced that there would be more massacres and wanted to be able to find and protect each other. Conversation with Umm Nader, author's field notes, June 2012.

7. While the majority of my interviewees were born sometime in the 1960s (give or take a few years), earlier generations of militants (those who had been born in Palestine or born shortly after the Nakba) who joined groups such as the ANM had used cell-based organizational structures to operate underground on university campuses where political organizing was banned (see Khaled 1973, 63–64). By the early 1980s, many in this older generation had moved into leadership roles in organizations that originated from the ANM, including the PFLP, DFLP, ALF, and PFLP-GC. In the 1980s, high-ranking officers in these organizations were often based in Damascus.

8. Interview with Nader, fall 2010.

9. Abu Tawq replaced the former head of the clandestine apparatus in West Beirut. The former leader had refused to leave Lebanon with the leadership and guerrillas in 1982; he was killed in early 1985. Several of his cousins were key players in the underground cell network.

10. Interview with Abu Hassan, Beirut, summer 2012.

11. Interview with Abu Hassan, Beirut, summer 2012.

12. Conversation with Abu Majd, author's field notes, summer 2010.

13. Interview with Abu Hassan, Beirut, summer 2012.

14. Both in general and with specific regard to potential PLO negotiations with the Israeli government.

15. This comparison may have had even more salience at the time if Palestinians were then aware that the LAF's predominantly Christian Eighth Brigade was supporting the

predominantly Shi'i Sixth Brigade, that the LAF's command (also Christian dominated) had decided to supply the Sixth Brigade with extra ammunition, and that East Beirut hospitals had been expressly opened to wounded Amal militiamen (Aruri 1985, 8). However, none of my interlocutors ever mentioned this connection, so I was unable to empirically link knowledge of the Eighth Brigade's involvement to contemporaneous understandings of the War of the Camps.

16. Interview with Sami Ibrahim, former member of Beirut's building committee, June 2012.

17. Interview with Abu Tariq (2), spring 2011.

18. Interview with Sami Ibrahim, June 2012.

19. With inflation at the time, Abu Tariq noted, this amount was around US$500.

20. Interview with Abu Tariq (2), spring 2011.

21. Yezid Sayigh (1997, 583) places the number of defenders (militia members or guerrillas) in Sabra and Shatila at 250–300 and at 500–600 in Burj al-Barajneh. In the following nine months, Fatah, the PLO's leading organization, only sent 150 guerrilla reinforcements to the Beirut camps (Y. Sayigh 1997, 589). Chris Giannou (1990, 44–45), who was in the camp by fall of 1985, estimates that Fatah had about 1,000 members (90 percent of whom were camp residents) but that the majority of groups only fielded 90–120 members, though he notes a distinction between the PFLP members, who were from the camp, versus factions that brought in members from outside, including al-Sa'iqa, Fatah al-Intifada, and the PFLP-General Command.

22. One of the fighters drew a map of the system for me; it looked like a wagon wheel with spokes and no rim, with the camp in the center. Group interview with fighters from Shatila's defense, Beirut, summer 2012.

23. Conversation with Naji, author's field notes, May 2011.

24. Conversation with former resident of Shatila who was present for the siege; author's field notes, May 2012. Several families in Beirut, who were associated with multiple groups (including Fatah, the DFLP, and the PFLP), repeated this story to me (identifying the individual by name, which I do not do here); they all held the man in very high respect.

25. Conversation with Aisha and Ibtisam, author's field notes, May 2010.

26. Conversation with Murid, author's field notes, June 2012.

27. Conversation with Abu Husayn and Abu Jamal, author's field notes, June 2012.

28. Conversation with Aisha and Rawan, Beirut, May 2010.

29. Interview with Aisha (1), Beirut, summer 2010. See Giannou (1990, 37–40) for a doctor's account of treating a woman targeted by Amal militiamen with sexual violence near the camp.

30. Conversation with Aisha, author's field notes, June 2012.

31. "Declaration from health workers in Burj el-Barajneh Camp." January 23, 1987. Reproduced in Message #20, AFSERCO-PHA, 297761 BTIEQ G, Our Ref 6508 87-02-11 12:55. Box "1987-Middle East-Lebanon-Relief/Reconstruction," Folder 55487. American Friends Service Committee Archive. Philadelphia. P. 1.

32. "2nd Telex Received 8/2/87." February 8, 1987. Reproduced in Message #20, AFSERCO-PHA, 297761 BTIEQ G, Our Ref 6508 87-02-11 12:55. Box "1987-Middle East-Lebanon-Relief/Reconstruction," Folder 55487. American Friends Service Committee Archive. Philadelphia. Pp. 1–2.

33. Interview with Zahra (1), summer 2010.

34. Conversation with Ibrahim, author's field notes, May 2012.

35. Interview with Abu Hassan, Beirut, summer 2012.

36. Interview with Abu Tariq (2), spring 2011.

37. Interview with Abu Tariq (2), spring 2011.

38. Interview with Abu Tariq (2), spring 2011.
39. Interview with Abu Adnan, autumn 2010.
40. Interview with Aisha (1), spring 2010. Lines such as this often feed into a specific politics of memory that sees the past as a time when people were more supportive of each other. See Allan (2013, chap. 2). Yet, as Chapter 1 notes, people also contested this narrative, emphasizing that elite leaders had access to supplies and even luxury items such as chocolate. My goal here is less to adjudicate the truth claims (e.g., whether or not everyone actually shared) than to establish the presence of clearly shared narratives, norms, and expectations that constituted these networks.
41. Sami remembered salaries in Shatila being cut for several months during this time, but did not specify why.
42. The idea that certain political leaders did not "get their feet dirty" or "live the reality" of the camps was a recurring theme throughout my research. These accusations were repeatedly used to question leaders' moral right to make policy. Once I learned to recognize Ali Abu Tawq's picture, I started seeing it in small, carefully curated displays in the offices of leaders—but only those who had been present in Beirut during the 1980s.
43. Conversation with Aisha and Ibrahim, author's field notes, June 2012.
44. Author's field notes, September 2008.

7. "EVERY FACTION FOR ITSELF"

1. A bean-based dish eaten for breakfast.
2. "My dear," a common term of endearment used between both friends and romantic partners.
3. Adapted from the author's field notes, spring 2011. Names, titles, and other identifying details have been changed to protect confidentiality.
4. A significant number of Palestinians in Burj al-Shamali also identify as Shiʿa.
5. On the IDF shelling Ain al-Hilweh, see *al-Safir*, April 16, 1985, and April 4, 1986.
6. AFSC documents describe similar processes. See: "Letters and Reports from Barbara Pizacani, Lebanon." May 12, 1987. Box "1987-Middle East-Lebanon-Relief/Reconstruction," Folder 10067. American Friends Service Committee Archive. Philadelphia.
7. "Hawatmeh's Unity, What a Color, What a Taste." *Sawt al-Mukhayyam*. November 1984, Issue 1. P. 4. Diaries of the National Resistance in Palestine." *Sawt al-Mukhayyam*. December 1984. P. 6. "Treason Steps and the National Confrontation." *Sawt al-Mukhayyam*. December 1984. P. 6
8. "For a new start." *Sawt al-Mukhayyam*. January 1985. P. 12.
9. "The Massacre: Actions, Goals, Results." *Sawt al-Mukhayyam*. October 1984, Issue 1. P. 4.
10. Conversation with Abu Houli and Nader, author's field notes, summer 2012. Interview with high-level PLO intelligence officer who reinfiltrated through Jounieh, spring 2010. Interview with Yusif (4), fall 2010. Also see, for example, *al-Safir*, September 19 and September 21 1986, which describes clashes between members of rival groups within Fatah.
11. See, for example, *al-Safir*, May 5, 1986 on the murder of a Fatah commander in Ain al-Hilweh.
12. Nader was actually approached by groups of officers who were organizing against the returnees from Tunis, but refused to participate in their plans. Conversation with Nader and Abu Houli, summer 2012.
13. Interview with Yusif (4), fall 2010.
14. Abu Houli confirmed this practice of attributing blame for murders to Mossad as well. Conversation with Abu Houli, author's field notes, June 2012.
15. Interview with George, fall 2010.

16. Conversation with Abu Ali, author's field notes, spring 2010. This turn of events could be evaluated in the context of competition within organizational "domains" or "fields." See DiMaggio and Powell (1983).

17. See: *al-Safir,* September 22, 1987, "Celebrations of the Islamic Front in Ain al-Hilweh in memory of the massacres of Sabra and Shatila;" and *al-Safir,* August 7, 1987, "Islamic Cultural Center in Ain al-Hilweh."

18. Interview with Yusif (4), fall 2010.

19. Interviews with Yusif (2, 4), fall 2010.

20. Conversation with Abu Haytham, author's field notes, spring 2010; conversation with Abu Ghassan, author's field notes, spring 2010; conversation with Assad, author's field notes, summer 2010; conversation with Adnan, author's field notes, spring 2010; conversation with Sabah, spring 2010.

21. Conversation with former employee of a militant organization's recruitment office, author's field notes, June 2012.

22. *Al-Safir,* July 16, 1985.

23. *Al-Safir* January 13, 1986.

24. *Al-Safir,* January 13 and 27, 1986.

25. *Al-Safir,* February 10, 1986. A week later, the PNSF demanded the execution of individuals who fired shots during a wedding and wounded fourteen people. See *al-Safir,* February 17, 1986.

26. The newspaper was also heavily censored by Syrian authorities, so even if reporting was more balanced, stories that made pro-Arafat factions look good or PNSF factions look bad may not have been printed. Informal interview with a former *al-Safir* reporter for South Lebanon, summer 2014.

27. Interview with Yusif (4), fall 2010; interview with Dalal, spring 2011; conversation with Nawal and her husband, Hisham, author's field notes fall 2010.

28. Interview with Yusif (4), fall 2010; interview with Nawal, fall 2010.

29. Interview with Munadileh, spring 2011.

30. Nofal had been criticizing factionalism within the Palestinian military effort and advocating a joint military command and better interorganizational coordination since before the 1982 invasion. See Schiff and Ya'ari 1984 (84–85).

31. Interview with Yusif (4). See also Y. Sayigh (1997, 593–94)

32. Conversation with Yusif, author's field notes, May 2012.

33. Letter to Sally and Gail. March 30, 1987. Box "1987-Middle East-Lebanon-Relief/Reconstruction," Folder 10067. American Friends Service Committee Archive. Philadelphia. P. 3.

34. "Summary of political-military events up till Syrian entry into West Beirut." February 22, 1987. Box "1987-Middle East-Lebanon-Relief/Reconstruction," Folder 10067. American Friends Service Committee Archive. Philadelphia. P. 1.

35. "Summary of political-military events up till Syrian entry into West Beirut." February 22, 1987. Box "1987-Middle East-Lebanon-Relief/Reconstruction," Folder 10067. American Friends Service Committee Archive. Philadelphia. P. 1.

36. Author's field notes, June 2012.

37. See *al-Safir,* July 5, 1987: "Two statements accuse "Amal" for their continuous detention of Palestinians."

38. Interview with Abu Zaki, Saida, summer 2010.

39. Interview with Tala, Sur, summer 2012.

40. Interview with Nadia (2), spring 2011.

41. Interviews with Yahya and Khalid, Burj al-Shamali, June 2012. Also mentioned in Abdullah (2008, 56).

42. Conversation with Tala, her husband, and her brothers-in-law, author's field notes, June 2012.
43. Giannou (1990, 42–49); Khalili (2007a, chap. 7).
44. Interview with Abu Umar, Beirut, autumn 2010.
45. See *al-Safir*, July 5, 1987: "Graduation of first aid session in Ain al-Hilweh Camp"
46. See *al-Safir*, 12 March 1987: "Seminar on Women's Day in Ain al-Hilweh."
47. Interview with Munadileh, Saida, spring 2011.
48. Interview with Nawal, South Lebanon, autumn 2010.
49. Conversation with Hisham, author's field notes, autumn 2010.
50. Interview with Nawal, South Lebanon, autumn 2010.
51. This military campaign was expressly designed to put pressure on Amal in order to lift the sieges in Beirut and Sur camps.
52. Interview with Nawal, South Lebanon, autumn 2010.
53. See Padgett (2010) on social networks and shifting notions of eliteness.
54. Interview with Ziyad, fall 2010, and interview with Aisha (1), spring 2010.
55. Interview with Abu Taha, al-Buss, August 2010.

CONCLUSION

1. See also Mazur (2020, 484–86). J. Krause (2019) also centers neighborhood-level ties in her analysis of the role of gender and local networks in (dis)incentivizing ethno-religious violence in Jos, Nigeria. Scacco (2021) reports similar findings regarding the salience of grassroots networks, rather than group-level solidarities, in her work on communal riots in Nigeria.
2. An argument that complements Kalyvas's (2003) observation that civil war violence is generally the product of local politics rather than "master cleavages."

APPENDIX A

1. In 2007, I stayed on the American University of Beirut campus in Hamra. In 2008, I lived with a friend in the East Beirut neighborhood of Jeitawi, which is known for being a working-to-middle class, predominantly Lebanese Christian neighborhood that at the time was associated with the Kata'ib, because of the presence of a party office and several memorials.
2. Hamas, Islamic Jihad, the PFLP, the PFLP-GC, and Usbat al-Ansar were or are on the FTO list; at the time of my research, Fatah-Revolutionary Council (the Abu Nidal Organization) was also on the list; it was delisted in 2017. The DFLP was delisted in 1999.
3. See Yanow (2012) for a concise overview of organizational ethnography.
4. For a discussion of the advantages and challenges of conducting research in the Middle East as a Western woman, see Schwedler (2006).
5. See D. K. Cohen (2016, chap. 2), Kostovicova and Knott (2020), and Fujii (2010, 2017) for helpful discussions regarding historical interviews about political violence.
6. Per my IRB, I did not interview children under the age of 18 or include them in my research. I did observe youth events—events that included people whose ages ranged up to their mid-twenties—such as scout meetings and field trips.
7. *Nakba*, or "Catastrophe" Day, which falls on May 15, commemorates Palestinians' displacement and dispossession by Israeli forces in 1947–1948.
8. The Mavi Marmara was one of six ships in a joint Free Gaza Movement and (Turkish) Foundation for Human Rights and Freedoms and Humanitarian Relief flotilla that was trying to break the Israeli blockade of Gaza to deliver humanitarian and construction

supplies. The IDF raided the ship in international waters, killing nine activists. See al-Jazeera (2010) and Reynolds (2010).

9. I subsequently donated the binder to UMAM Documentation and Research, an archival and artistic space in South Beirut, so that the material would remain accessible to Palestinian and Lebanese researchers. UMAM digitized the material and holds the original binder.

10. A full Fatah cadre would not have been permitted to hold the position that I did because of my supervisor's leftist history; members were, however, allowed to participate in the classes and workshops that the association sponsored. I met several members of Fatah's political and media apparatus at the association's workshops and taught several in my class.

11. The PNSF included the PFLP, the PFLP-General Command, Fatah al-Intifada, the Palestinian Popular Struggle Front (PPSF), al-Saʿiqa, and a faction of the Palestine Liberation Front (PLF).

12. I thank Lee Ann Fujii for helping me to clarify these points

13. Disaster researchers consistently find evidence that people act in altruistic ways and build social cohesion in times of crisis, so these memories were often not entirely romanticized. See, e.g., Solnit (2010)

14. Pre-civil war, Yarmouk was a vibrant Damascus neighborhood and unofficial refugee camp that housed over 110,000 people. The Syrian regime and its allies besieged the district from 2013 to 2014 following battles in 2012, resulting in starvation conditions that in many ways replicated those that Palestinians in Lebanon experienced during the War of the Camps. Those initial battles reduced the camp's population to approximately 18,000. In 2015, ISIS entered the camp, prompting intense battles with the Syrian regime and the flight of the majority of remaining residents. For more details, see "The Crisis in Yarmouk Camp" n.d.; Sherwood 2014; Betere 2021.

15. See, e.g., Clark (2006); E. J. Wood (2006a; 2003, chap. 2); Blee (2007); Blee and Currier (2011); Brand (2014); Schwedler (2014); Campbell (2017); Clark and Cavatorta (2018); MacLean et al. (2018); Shesterinina (2018); Bond et al. (2020); J. Krause (2021).

16. See Parkinson (2021a) for a full account of these interactions.

17. I thank Lee Ann Fujii for helping me to clarify this point

18. The meeting set up to discuss this proposal was the first time I met the Beirut regional leadership (mostly men).

19. The term "network sensibility" is a riff on the term "ethnographic sensibility," coined by Pader (2006), and advanced by Schatz (2009) and Simmons and Smith (2017).

20. See, for example, Bringa (1995).

21. Unmarried and presumed heterosexual, to put a finer point on it.

22. I was told that she had hoped to get me fired from my volunteer position so that she could step into it.

23. See Shesterinina (2018) on power dynamics and threatening interlocutors in violence research.

24. Particularly during the 2006 July War, but also for reporting trips to locales such as the southern border zone, Ain al-Hilweh, or the Bekaa Valley, a good interpreter—known as a fixer in the media world—could make between US$150 and US$400 a day for facilitating interviews for a journalist. By contrast, a typical family in a camp might make that much money in a month. On the commodification of research assistance in Lebanon, see Sukarieh and Tannock (2019) and Parkinson (2019).

25. Conversation with Roman Malajacq, summer 2018. Cited with permission.

APPENDIX B

1. Author's field notes, December 2009.
2. Informal interview with a former reporter for South Lebanon, summer 2014.
3. Reading Ilana Feldman's (2007) work on Quaker humanitarianism in Gaza, which draws from the AFSC archives, inspired me to investigate whether the organization had also been present in Lebanon.
4. Books that focused on the camp communities themselves mimicked formats used by authors of Palestinian village books. See Davis (2010).
5. Personal conversation with Palestinian Interior Ministry official. Ramallah, June 2012.

References

ARABIC-LANGUAGE NEWSPAPERS
al-Nahar
al-Safir
Sawt al-Mukhayyam

ARCHIVES
American Friends Service Committee (AFSC) Archives, Philadelphia, United States
American University of Beirut (AUB), Jafet Library, Beirut, Lebanon
Institute for Palestine Studies (IPS), Beirut, Lebanon
Institut français du Proche Orient (IFPO), Beirut, Lebanon
al-Safir Archives, Beirut, Lebanon

DOCUMENTARIES AND FILM FOOTAGE
Abourahme, Dahna. 2010. *Mamlaka al-Nisaa 'Ayn al-Hilwa (The Kingdom of Women, Ein El Hilweh)*. Documentary. ARCPA/al-Jana.
Berggren, Anders, Carl Javer, and Peter Ostlund. 1996. *Tel al-Zaatar: Vagen tillbaka (Tel al-Za'tar: The Way Back)*. Documentary. GotaFilmAB.
Fleifel, Mahdi, dir.. 2014. *Alam laysa lana (A World Not Ours)*. PBS-POV.
Masri, Mai, dir. 1998. *Atfal Shatila (Children of Shatila)*. Honolulu: Asia Pacific Films.
Palestine Liberation Organization: Raw archival footage from Tel al-Za'tar, the 1982 Sabra and Shatila massacre, and the War of the Camps in Beirut.

ENGLISH-LANGUAGE MEDIA REPORTS AND INTERVIEWS
Abouzeid, Rania. 2013. "Syrian Opposition Groups Stop Pretending." *The New Yorker Blogs* (blog). September 26, 2013. http://www.newyorker.com/online/blogs/newsdesk/2013/09/fsa-assad-syrian-opposition-groups-leaders-in-exile.html.
Abu Musa and Abu Salih. 1983. "What the Opposition Says." *Journal of Palestine Studies* 13 (1): 180–83. https://doi.org/10.2307/2536936.
Al-Jazeera. 2010. "Israel Attacks Gaza Aid Fleet." *Al-Jazeera English*, May 31, 2010, sec. Middle East. http://www.aljazeera.com/news/middleeast/2010/05/201053133047995359.html.
Associated Press. 1983. April 8, 1983, sec. International News.
———. 1984. "Precede Tel Aviv," November 27, 1984, sec. International.
BBC. 2011. "Heroes of the Tripoli Underground," December 3, 2011, sec. Magazine. http://www.bbc.co.uk/news/magazine-16001247.
Black, Ian. 2014. "Evidence of 'Industrial-Scale Killing' by Syria Spurs Call for War Crimes Charges." *The Guardian*, January 20, 2014, sec. World news. http://www.theguardian.com/world/2014/jan/20/evidence-industrial-scale-killing-syria-war-crimes.
Chulov, Martin. 2014. "Isis: The Inside Story." *The Guardian*, December 11, 2014, sec. World news. http://www.theguardian.com/world/2014/dec/11/-sp-isis-the-inside-story.

Cobban, Helena. 1982. "Eyewitness: The Battle for South Lebanon. Interview with Dr. Chris Giannou." *Journal of Palestine Studies* 11/12 (July): 69–84. https://doi.org/10.2307/2538335.

The Economist. 2013. "The Country Formerly Known as Syria," March 23, 2013.

Faramarzi, Scherezade. 1983. "Palestinian Squatters Flee, Claiming Beatings." Associated Press, April 16, 1983, sec. International News.

Holmes, Oliver. 2012. "Syrian Women Risk Lives to Smuggle Aid to Dissidents." Reuters, April 25, 2012. http://www.reuters.com/article/2012/04/25/us-syria-smuggling-idUSBRE83O0TA20120425.

Macleod, Hugh. 2008. "Israel-Hizbullah Prisoner Exchange: Profiles." *The Guardian*, July 16, 2008. http://www.guardian.co.uk/world/2008/jul/16/lebanon.israelandthepalestinians1.

Moaveni, Azadeh. 2015. "ISIS Women and Enforcers in Syria Recount Collaboration, Anguish and Escape." *The New York Times*, November 21, 2015. http://www.nytimes.com/2015/11/22/world/middleeast/isis-wives-and-enforcers-in-syria-recount-collaboration-anguish-and-escape.html.

Nadler, Gerald. 1982. "Tents for Homeless Refugees." United Press International, October 7, 1982.

Ohlheiser, Abby. 2014. "The U.N. Has Stopped Counting the Deaths in Syria." *The Atlantic*, January 7, 2014. https://www.theatlantic.com/international/archive/2014/01/un-stopped-updating-its-syria-death-toll/356758/.

Pérez-Peña, Richard. 2008. "The War Endures, but Where's the Media?" *The New York Times*, March 24. http://www.nytimes.com/2008/03/24/business/media/24press.html.

Petti, Matthew. 2021. "Progressive Dems: Biden Needs to Move First on Iran Nuclear Deal." *Responsible Statecraft* (blog). March 31, 2021. https://responsiblestatecraft.org/2021/03/31/progressive-dems-biden-needs-to-move-first-on-iran-nuclear-deal/.

Reynolds, Paul. 2010. "Israeli Raid: What Went Wrong?" BBC, June 2, 2010, sec. Middle East. http://www.bbc.co.uk/news/10203333.

Safi, Michael. 2019. "Syrian Regime Inflicts 72 Forms of Torture on Prisoners, Report Finds." *The Guardian*, October 23, 2019, sec. World news. http://www.theguardian.com/world/2019/oct/23/syrian-regime-inflicts-72-forms-of-torture-on-prisoners-report-finds.

Sherwood, Harriet. 2014. "Queue for Food in Syria's Yarmouk Camp Shows Desperation of Refugees." *The Guardian*, February 26, 2014, sec. World news. https://www.theguardian.com/world/2014/feb/26/queue-food-syria-yarmouk-camp-desperation-refugees.

Taylor, Adam. 2016. "The Syrian War's Death Toll Is Absolutely Staggering. But No One Can Agree on the Number." *Washington Post*, March 15, 2016, sec. WorldViews. https://www.washingtonpost.com/news/worldviews/wp/2016/03/15/the-syrian-wars-death-toll-is-absolutely-staggering-but-no-one-can-agree-on-the-number/.

Torbati, Yeganeh. 2019. "How Mike Pence's Office Meddled in Foreign Aid to Reroute Money to Favored Christian Groups." *ProPublica*, November 6, 2019. https://www.propublica.org/article/how-mike-pences-office-meddled-in-foreign-aid-to-reroute-money-to-favored-christian-groups?token=y9NSvs1x_hAQvqoINpu6MLMPe1dBbBJ-.

Wainwright, Oliver. 2016. "'The Worst Place on Earth': Inside Assad's Brutal Saydnaya Prison." *The Guardian*, August 17, 2016. http://www.theguardian.com/artanddesign/2016/aug/18/saydnaya-prison-syria-assad-amnesty-reconstruction.

Wright, Robin. 1983. "Bekaa Mutiny May Leave Arafat a General without Any Troops." *Christian Science Monitor*, July 1, 1983. https://www.csmonitor.com/1983/0701/070151.html.

MEMOIRS

Abu Iyad and Eric Rouleau. 1981. *My Home, My Land: A Narrative of the Palestinian Struggle*. Translated by Linda Butler Koseoglu. New York: Times Books.
Ang, Swee Chai. 1989. *From Beirut to Jerusalem*. London: Grafton Books.
Cutting, Pauline. 1989. *Children of the Siege*. New York: St. Martin's Press.
Giannou, Chris. 1990. *Besieged: A Doctor's Story of Life and Death in Beirut*. Ithaca, NY: Olive Branch Press.
Khaled, Leila. 1973. *My People Shall Live: The Autobiography of a Revolutionary*. London: Hodder and Stoughton.
Nofal, Mamdouh. 2006. *Maghdusha: Qussat al-Harb ʿala al—Mukhayyamat fi Lubnan (Magdousheh: The Story of the War of the Camps in Lebanon)*. Ramallah, Palestine: Muwatin.
Yermiya, Dov. 1984. *My War Diary: Israel in Lebanon*. London: Pluto Press.
Zeidan, Mahmoud. 2017. "Nazuh fi Ghurbatayn: Yawmiat Min al-Ijtiyah al-Israʾili li Lubnan ʿam 1982 (An Exodus in Two Exiles: Diaries from the Israeli Invasion of Lebanon in 1982)." In *11: Hikayat min al-Lujuʾ al-Filastini (11: Stories from the Palestinian Exile)*, 254–301. Beirut, Lebanon: Institute for Palestine Studies.

REPORTS AND THESES

Advisory Committee on Human Rights in Lebanon. 1983. "Lebanon: Toward Legal Order and Respect for Human Rights." Philadelphia: American Friends Service Committee Middle East Program.
Central Bureau of Statistics. 1981. "Demographic Characteristics of the Palestinian Arabs in Libanon's Camps." 3. Statistical Surveys. Damascus, Syria: Palestine Liberation Organization, Economic Department.
Kahan Commission. 1983. "Report of the Commission of Inquiry into the Events at the Refugee Camps in Beirut." 104. Israel Ministry of Foreign Affairs. https://www.mfa.gov.il/mfa/foreignpolicy/mfadocuments/yearbook6/pages/104%20report%20of%20the%20commission%20of%20inquiry%20into%20the%20e.aspx
Saʿid Ibrahim, Fawziyya. 1983. "Al-Khasaʾis al-Dimughrafiyya wa-l-Ijtimaʿiyya wa-l-Iqtisadiyya lil-Falastiniyyin fi Mukhayyamat Lubnan wa Suriyya (Demographic, Social, and Economic Characteristics of the Palestinians in the Camps of Lebanon and Syria)." Thesis. Beirut: Lebanese University.
Team International Engineering and Management Consultants. 1981. "Appendix VI: PLO"s Affiliated Institutions. Progress Report II Presented to Economic Commission for Western Asia (ECWA)." 4.10–5.1. Beirut.

SECONDARY SOURCES

Abdullah, Hilana. 2008. *Mukhayyam al-Burj al-Shamali: Hithu yushikh alam (Burj al-Shamali Camp: Where the Sorrow Ages)*. Palestinian Camps Series. Sur (Lebanon): Palestinian Organization for Right of Return (Thabit).
Abu-Assad, Hany, dir. 2013. *Omar*. Kino Lorber.
Alison, Miranda. 2003. "Cogs in the Wheel? Women in the Liberation Tigers of Tamil Eelam." *Civil Wars* 6 (4): 37–54. https://doi.org/10.1080/13698240308402554.
———. 2004. *Women and Political Violence: Female Combatants in Ethno-National Conflict*. London and New York: Routledge.
Allam, Nermin. 2018. *Women and the Egyptian Revolution: Engagement and Activism during the 2011 Arab Uprisings*. Cambridge and New York: Cambridge University Press.

Allan, Diana. 2013. *Refugees of the Revolution: Experiences of Palestinian Exile*. Stanford: Stanford University Press.

Al-Shahriyya. 2008. "Al-Munazzamat wa-l-Ahzab fil-Mukhayyamat al-Falastiniyya fi Lubnan (The Organizations and the Parties in the Palestinian Camps in Lebanon)." *al-Shahriyya (The Monthly)*, February 2008. 8–13.

Amrane-Minne, Danièle Djamila. 1992. "Les Combattantes de La Guerre d'Algérie." *Matériaux Pour l'histoire de Notre Temps* 26 (1): 58–62. https://doi.org/10.3406/mat.1992.404867.

———. 2004. *Des Femmes dans la Guerre d'Algérie*. Algiers: Editions Dis. Ibn Khaldoun.

Andoni, Lamis. 1988. "Fracas in Fateh." *Journal of Palestine Studies* 17 (2): 198–99. https://doi.org/10.2307/2536887.

Andreas, Peter. 2008. *Blue Helmets and Black Markets: The Business of Survival in the Siege of Sarajevo*. Ithaca, NY: Cornell University Press.

Andreas, Peter, and Kelly M. Greenhill. 2010. *Sex, Drugs, and Body Counts: The Politics of Numbers in Global Crime and Conflict*. Ithaca, NY: Cornell University Press.

Anziska, Seth. 2018. "Sabra and Shatila: New Revelations." *The New York Review of Books*, September 17, 2018. https://www.nybooks.com/daily/2018/09/17/sabra-and-shatila-new-revelations/.

Arjona, Ana. 2014. "Wartime Institutions: A Research Agenda." *Journal of Conflict Resolution* 58 (8): 1360–89. https://doi.org/10.1177/0022002714547904.

———. 2015. "Civilian Resistance to Rebel Governance." In *Rebel Governance in Civil War*, 180–202. Cambridge and New York: Cambridge University Press. https://doi.org/10.1017/CBO9781316182468.009.

———. 2016. *Rebelocracy: Social Order in the Colombian Civil War*. Cambridge and New York: Cambridge University Press.

Arjona, Ana, Nelson Kasfir, and Zachariah Cherian Mampilly, eds. 2015. "Performing the Nation-State: Rebel Governance and Symbolic Processes." In *Rebel Governance in Civil War*. Cambridge: Cambridge University Press.

Arreguín-Toft, Ivan. 2001. "How the Weak Win Wars: A Theory of Asymmetric Conflict." *International Security* 26 (1): 93–128.

———. 2005. *How the Weak Win Wars: A Theory of Asymmetric Conflict*. New York: Cambridge University Press.

Aruri, Naseer H. 1985. "Pax-Syriana and the Palestinians in Lebanon." In *Amal and the Palestinians: Understanding the Battle of the Camps*, edited by Elaine C. Hagopian, 4–8. Arab World Issues. Belmont, MA: Association of Arab-American University Graduates.

Asal, Victor, Richard Legault, Ora Szekely, and Jonathan Wilkenfeld. 2013. "Gender Ideologies and Forms of Contentious Mobilization in the Middle East." *Journal of Peace Research* 50 (3): 305–18. https://doi.org/10.1177/0022343313476528.

Asociación Madres de Plaza de Mayo. n.d. "Asociación Madres de Plaza de Mayo." Historia de Las Madres de Plaza de Mayo. http://www.madres.org/navegar/nav.php?idsitio=5&idcat=906&idindex=76.

Auyero, Javier. 1999. "Re-Membering Peronism: An Ethnographic Account of the Relational Character of Political Memory." *Qualitative Sociology* 22 (4): 331–51. https://doi.org/10.1023/A:1022059705335.

Avant, Deborah D. 2005. *The Market for Force: The Consequences of Privatizing Security*. Cambridge and New York: Cambridge University Press.

Bakke, Kristin M., Kathleen Gallagher Cunningham, and Lee J. Seymour. 2012. "A Plague of Initials: Fragmentation, Cohesion, and Infighting in Civil Wars." *Perspectives on Politics* 10 (2): 265–83. https://doi.org/10.1017/S1537592712000667.

Balcells, Laia. 2010. "Rivalry and Revenge: Violence against Civilians in Conventional Civil Wars." *International Studies Quarterly* 54 (2): 291–313. https://doi.org/10.1111/j.1468-2478.2010.00588.x.
———. 2011. "Continuation of Politics by Two Means: Direct and Indirect Violence in Civil War." *Journal of Conflict Resolution* 55 (3): 397–422. https://doi.org/10.1177/0022002711400865.
———. 2012. "The Consequences of Victimization on Political Identities: Evidence from Spain." *Politics & Society* 40 (3): 311–47. https://doi.org/10.1177/0032329211424721.
———. 2017. *Rivalry and Revenge: The Politics of Violence during Civil War*. Reprint edition. Cambridge University Press.
Balcells, Laia, and Stathis N. Kalyvas. 2014. "Does Warfare Matter? Severity, Duration, and Outcomes of Civil Wars." *Journal of Conflict Resolution* 58 (8): 1390–1418. https://doi.org/10.1177/0022002714547903.
Bateson, Regina. 2017. "The Socialization of Civilians and Militia Members: Evidence from Guatemala." *Journal of Peace Research* 54 (5): 634–47. https://doi.org/10.1177/0022343317721812.
———. 2021. "The Politics of Vigilantism." *Comparative Political Studies* 54 (6): 923–55. https://doi.org/10.1177/0010414020957692.
Bayard de Volo, Lorraine, and Edward Schatz. 2004. "From the Inside Out: Ethnographic Methods in Political Research." *PS: Political Science & Politics* 37 (2): 267–71. https://doi.org/10.1017/S1049096504004214.
Beardsley, Kyle, and Brian McQuinn. 2009. "Rebel Groups as Predatory Organizations: The Political Effects of the 2004 Tsunami in Indonesia and Sri Lanka." *Journal of Conflict Resolution* 53 (4): 624–45. https://doi.org/10.1177/0022002709336460.
Beber, Bernd, and Christopher Blattman. 2013. "The Logic of Child Soldiering and Coercion." *International Organization* 67 (1): 65–104. https://doi.org/10.1017/S0020818312000409.
Bernal, Victoria. 2001. "From Warriors to Wives: Contradictions of Liberation and Development in Eritrea." *Northeast African Studies* 8 (3): 129–54.
Berry, Marie E. 2017. "Barriers to Women's Progress After Atrocity: Evidence from Rwanda and Bosnia-Herzegovina." *Gender & Society* 31 (6): 830–53. https://doi.org/10.1177/0891243217737060.
———. 2018. *War, Women, and Power: From Violence to Mobilization in Rwanda and Bosnia-Herzegovina*. New York: Cambridge University Press.
Betere, Nidal. 2021. "The Assad Dynasty Was Hatched at My Grandfather's Home. They Later Destroyed It." *Newlines Magazine*, March 16, 2021. https://newlinesmag.com/essays/the-assad-dynasty-was-hatched-at-my-grandfathers-home-they-later-destroyed-it/.
Blee, Kathleen M. 2007. "Ethnographies of the Far Right." *Journal of Contemporary Ethnography* 36 (2): 119–28. https://doi.org/10.1177/0891241606298815.
Blee, Kathleen M., and Ashley Currier. 2011. "Ethics Beyond the IRB: An Introductory Essay." *Qualitative Sociology* 34 (3): 401. https://doi.org/10.1007/s11133-011-9195-z.
Bond, Kanisha D., Kate Cronin-Furman, Meredith Loken, Milli Lake, Sarah E. Parkinson, and Anna Zelenz. 2019. "The West Needs to Take the Politics of Women in ISIS Seriously." *Foreign Policy* (blog). March 4, 2019. https://foreignpolicy.com/2019/03/04/the-west-needs-to-take-the-politics-of-women-in-isis-seriously/.
Bond, Kanisha D., Milli Lake, and Sarah E. Parkinson. 2020. "Lessons from Conflict Studies on Research during the Coronavirus Pandemic." *Items* (blog). July 2, 2020. https://items.ssrc.org/covid-19-and-the-social-sciences/social-research-and-insecurity/lessons-from-conflict-studies-on-research-during-the-coronavirus-pandemic/.

Borri, Francesca. 2013. "Woman's Work." *Columbia Journalism Review.* July 1, 2013. http://www.cjr.org/feature/womans_work.php.

Bourdieu, Pierre. 1977. *Outline of a Theory of Practice.* Translated by Richard Nice. 1st English edition. Cambridge: Cambridge University Press.

Branch, Adam, and Zachariah Cherian Mampilly. 2005. "Winning the War, but Losing the Peace? The Dilemma of SPLM/A Civil Administration and the Tasks Ahead." *The Journal of Modern African Studies* 43 (1): 1–20. https://doi.org/10.1017/S0022278X04000588.

Brand, Laurie A. 2014. "Of Power Relations and Responsibilities." POMEPS Studies 8. The Ethics of Research in the Middle East. Washington, DC: Project on Middle East Political Science. http://pomeps.org/wp-content/uploads/2014/07/POMEPS_Studies_8_Ethics.pdf.

Bringa, Tone. 1995. *Being Muslim the Bosnian Way: Identity and Community in a Central Bosnian Village.* Princeton, NJ: Princeton University Press.

Brynen, Rex. 1990a. *Sanctuary and Survival: The PLO in Lebanon.* Boulder, CO: Westview Press.

———. 1990b. "The Politics of Exile: The Palestinians in Lebanon." *Journal of Refugee Studies* 3 (3): 204–27. https://doi.org/10.1093/jrs/3.3.204.

Buford, Bill. 1993. *Among the Thugs.* New York: Vintage.

Bultmann, Daniel. 2018. "The Social Structure of Armed Groups. Reproduction and Change during and after Conflict." *Small Wars & Insurgencies* 29 (4): 607–28. https://doi.org/10.1080/09592318.2018.1488402.

Bulutgil, H. Zeynep. 2019. "Prewar Domestic Conditions and Civilians in War." *Journal of Global Security Studies* 5(3): 528–41. https://doi.org/10.1093/jogss/ogz039.

Burawoy, Michael. 1998. "The Extended Case Method." *Sociological Theory* 16 (1): 4–33. https://doi.org/10.1111/0735-2751.00040.

———. 2003. "Revisits: An Outline of a Theory of Reflexive Ethnography." *American Sociological Review* 68 (5): 645–79. https://doi.org/10.2307/1519757.

Burt, Ronald S. 2005. *Brokerage and Closure: An Introduction to Social Capital.* Oxford: Oxford University Press.

Cammett, Melani. 2014. *Compassionate Communalism: Welfare and Sectarianism in Lebanon.* Ithaca, NY: Cornell University Press.

Cammett, Melani, and Sukriti Issar. 2010. "Bricks and Mortar Clientelism: Sectarianism and the Logics of Welfare Allocation in Lebanon." *World Politics* 62 (3): 381–421. https://doi.org/10.1017/S0043887110000080.

Campbell, Susanna P. 2017. "Ethics of Research in Conflict Environments." *Journal of Global Security Studies* 2 (1): 89–101. https://doi.org/10.1093/jogss/ogw024.

Cederman, Lars-Erik, and Luc Girardin. 2007. "Beyond Fractionalization: Mapping Ethnicity onto Nationalist Insurgencies." *The American Political Science Review* 101 (1): 173–85.

Cederman, Lars-Erik, Andreas Wimmer, and Brian Min. 2010. "Why Do Ethnic Groups Rebel? New Data and Analysis." *World Politics* 62 (1): 87–119. https://doi.org/10.1017/S0043887109990219.

Chang, Han Il, and Leonid Peisakhin. 2019. "Building Cooperation among Groups in Conflict: An Experiment on Intersectarian Cooperation in Lebanon." *American Journal of Political Science* 63 (1): 146–62. https://doi.org/10.1111/ajps.12397.

Christia, Fotini. 2013. *Alliance Formation in Civil Wars.* Cambridge and New York: Cambridge University Press.

Clark, Janine A. 2006. "Field Research Methods in the Middle East." *PS: Political Science & Politics* 39(3): 417–24. https://doi.org/10.1017/S1049096506060707.

Clark, Janine A., and Francesco Cavatorta, eds. 2018. *Political Science Research in the Middle East and North Africa: Methodological and Ethical Challenges.* New York and Oxford: Oxford University Press.
Clark, Janine A., and Bassel F. Salloukh. 2013. "Elite Strategies, Civil Society, and Sectarian Identities in Postwar Lebanon." *International Journal of Middle East Studies* 45 (4): 731–49. https://doi.org/10.1017/S0020743813000883.
Clemens, Elisabeth. 1999. "Securing Political Returns to Social Capital: Women's Associations in the United States: 1880s–1920s." *Journal of Interdisciplinary History* 29 (4): 613–38.
Cobban, Helena. 1985. *The Palestinian Liberation Organisation: People, Power and Politics.* Cambridge: Cambridge University Press.
Cohen, Adam, and Elizabeth Taylor. 2001. *American Pharaoh: Mayor Richard J. Daley—His Battle for Chicago and the Nation.* Reprint. New York: Back Bay Books.
Cohen, Dara Kay. 2016. *Rape during Civil War.* Ithaca, NY: Cornell University Press.
Convention on Prohibitions or Restrictions on the Use of Certain Conventional Weapons Which May Be Deemed to Be Excessively Injurious or to Have Indiscriminate Effects (with Protocols I, II, and III). n.d. https://treaties.un.org/doc/Treaties/1983/12/19831202%2001-19%20AM/XXVI-2-revised.pdf.
Coulter, Chris. 2009. *Bush Wives and Girl Soldiers: Women's Lives through War and Peace in Sierra Leone.* Ithaca, NY: Cornell University Press.
"The Crisis in Yarmouk Camp." n.d. UNRWA. Accessed November 25, 2018. https://www.unrwa.org/crisis-in-yarmouk.
Cunningham, David E. 2006. "Veto Players and Civil War Duration." *American Journal of Political Science* 50 (4): 875–92.
Cyert, Richard M., and James G. March. 1992. *Behavioral Theory of the Firm.* Malden, MA, and Oxford: Wiley-Blackwell.
Daly, Sarah Zukerman. 2012. "Organizational Legacies of Violence: Conditions Favoring Insurgency Onset in Colombia, 1964–1984." *Journal of Peace Research* 49 (3): 473–91. https://doi.org/10.1177/0022343311435801.
———. 2014. "The Dark Side of Power-Sharing: Middle Managers and Civil War Recurrence." *Comparative Politics* 46 (3): 333–53. https://doi.org/10.5129/001041514810943027.
———. 2016. *Organized Violence after Civil War: The Geography of Recruitment in Latin America.* New York: Cambridge University Press.
Davenport, Christian. 2009. *Media Bias, Perspective, and State Repression: The Black Panther Party.* Cambridge and New York: Cambridge University Press.
Davenport, Christian, and Patrick Ball. 2002. "Views to a Kill: Exploring the Implications of Source Selection in the Case of Guatemalan State Terror, 1977–1995." *The Journal of Conflict Resolution* 46 (3): 427–50. https://doi.org/10.1177/0022002702046003005
Davis, Rochelle. 2010. *Palestinian Village Histories: Geographies of the Displaced.* Palo Alto, CA: Stanford University Press.
della Porta, Donatella. 1988. "Recruitment Processes in Clandestine Political Organizations: Italian Left-Wing Terrorism." *International Social Movement Research* 1 (1): 155–69.
———. 2013. "Repertoires of Contention." In *The Wiley-Blackwell Encyclopedia of Social and Political Movements,* edited by David A. Snow. Malden, MA: Wiley. https://doi.org/10.1002/9780470674871.wbespm178.
Denkner, Amnon. 1983. "Israel in Lebanon." *Journal of Palestine Studies* 12 (2): 179–82. https://doi.org/10.2307/2536425.

DiMaggio, Paul J., and Walter W. Powell. 1983. "The Iron Cage Revisited: Institutional Isomorphism and Collective Rationality in Organizational Fields." *American Sociological Review* 48 (2): 147–60. https://doi.org/10.2307/2095101.

Din, Raja Sari al-, ed. 1985. *Watha'iq al-Harb al-Lubnaniyya: 1982-1983-1984 (Documents of the Lebanon War 1982-1983-1984)*. Beirut: Al-Markaz al-Arabi lil-Bahath wal-Tawthiq (The Arab Center for Research and Documentation).

Dorff, Cassy. 2017. "Violence, Kinship Networks, and Political Resilience: Evidence from Mexico." *Journal of Peace Research* 54 (4): 558–73. https://doi.org/10.1177/0022343317691329.

Downes, Alexander B. 2007. "Draining the Sea by Filling the Graves: Investigating the Effectiveness of Indiscriminate Violence as a Counterinsurgency Strategy." *Civil Wars* 9 (4): 420–44. https://doi.org/10.1080/13698240701699631.

———. 2008. *Targeting Civilians in War*. Ithaca, NY: Cornell University Press.

Dupuy, Kendra, Scott Gates, Håvard Mokleiv Nygård, Ida Rudolfsen, Siri Aas Rustad, Håvard Strand, and Henrik Urdal. 2017. "Trends in Armed Conflict, 1946–2016." Oslo: Peace Research Institute Oslo. https://www.prio.org/utility/DownloadFile.ashx?id=1373&type=publicationfile.

Eck, Kristine. 2014. "Coercion in Rebel Recruitment." *Security Studies* 23 (2): 364–98. https://doi.org/10.1080/09636412.2014.905368.

Eggert, Jennifer Philippa. 2018. "Female Fighters and Militants during the Lebanese Civil War: Individual Profiles, Pathways, and Motivations." *Studies in Conflict & Terrorism*. https://doi.org/10.1080/1057610X.2018.1529353.

Electronic Disease Early Warning System. 2018. "Yemen Cholera Response: Weekly Epidemiological Bulletin Jan. 22–Jan. 28." Geneva: World Health Organization.

Ellis, Stephen. 2013. *External Mission: The ANC in Exile, 1960–1990*. Oxford and New York: Oxford University Press.

Emirbayer, Mustafa. 1997. "Manifesto for a Relational Sociology." *American Journal of Sociology* 103 (2): 281–317. https://doi.org/10.1086/231209.

Emirbayer, Mustafa, and Jeff Goodwin. 1994. "Network Analysis, Culture, and the Problem of Agency." *American Journal of Sociology* 99 (6): 1411–54.

———. 1996. "Symbols, Positions, Objects: Toward a New Theory of Revolutions and Collective Action." *History and Theory* 35 (3): 358–74. https://doi.org/10.2307/2505454.

Enloe, Cynthia. 2000. *Maneuvers: The International Politics of Militarizing Women's Lives*. Berkeley: University of California Press.

Eriksson Baaz, Maria, and Maria Stern. 2009. "Why Do Soldiers Rape? Masculinity, Violence, and Sexuality in the Armed Forces in the Congo (DRC)." *International Studies Quarterly* 53 (2): 495–518.

———. 2013. "Fearless Fighters and Submissive Wives: Negotiating Identity among Women Soldiers in the Congo (DRC)." *Armed Forces & Society* 39 (4): 711–39. https://doi.org/10.1177/0095327X12459715.

Faris, Hussein. 2007. *Tel al-Zaʿtar: Thakira Falastiniyya Khalida (Tel Zaʿtar: An Eternal Palestinian Memory)*. Beirut, Lebanon: Dar al-Nada.

Fazal, Tanisha M. 2014. "Dead Wrong?: Battle Deaths, Military Medicine, and Exaggerated Reports of War's Demise." *International Security* 39 (1): 95–125. https://doi.org/10.1162/ISEC_a_00166.

Fearon, James D. 2004. "Why Do Some Civil Wars Last So Much Longer than Others?" *Journal of Peace Research* 41 (3): 275–301. https://doi.org/10.1177/0022343304043770.

Federation of American Scientists. n.d. "White Phosphorus Fact Sheet." Accessed March 21, 2019. https://fas.org/programs/bio/factsheets/whitephosphorus.html.

Feldman, Ilana. 2007. "The Quaker Way: Ethical Labor and Humanitarian Relief." *American Ethnologist* 34 (4): 689–705. https://doi.org/10.1525/ae.2007.34.4.689.

Fielding-Smith, Abigail. 2015. "Assad Goes on Spinning as Syria Burns." *Foreign Policy* (blog). June 30, 2015. https://foreignpolicy.com/2015/06/30/assad-goes-on-spinning-as-syria-burns/.

Finkel, Evgeny. 2015. "The Phoenix Effect of State Repression: Jewish Resistance during the Holocaust." *American Political Science Review* 109 (2): 339–53. https://doi.org/10.1017/S000305541500009X.

———. 2017. *Ordinary Jews: Choice and Survival during the Holocaust*. Princeton, NJ, and Oxford: Princeton University Press.

Fisk, Robert. 2002. *Pity the Nation: The Abduction of Lebanon*. Fourth edition. New York: Thunder's Mouth Press/Nation Books.

Foster, Margaret J., and David A. Siegel. 2019. "Pink Slips from the Underground: Changes in Terror Leadership." *International Studies Quarterly* 63 (2): 231–43. https://doi.org/10.1093/isq/sqz017.

Freeman, Mark Philip. 2010. *Hindsight: The Promise and Peril of Looking Backward*. New York: Oxford University Press.

Fujii, Lee Ann. 2009. *Killing Neighbors: Webs of Violence in Rwanda*. Ithaca, NY: Cornell University Press.

———. 2010. "Shades of Truth and Lies: Interpreting Testimonies of War and Violence." *Journal of Peace Research* 47 (2): 231–41. https://doi.org/10.1177/0022343309353097.

———. 2017. *Interviewing in Social Science Research: A Relational Approach*. 1st edition. London: Routledge.

Gade, Emily Kalah. 2020. "Social Isolation and Repertoires of Resistance." *American Political Science Review* 114 (2): 309–25. https://doi.org/10.1017/S0003055420000015.

Gal, Reuven. 1985. "Commitment and Obedience in the Military: An Israeli Case Study." *Armed Forces & Society* 11 (4): 553–64. https://doi.org/10.1177/0095327X8501100405.

Gates, Scott. 2002. "Recruitment and Allegiance." *Journal of Conflict Resolution* 46 (1): 111–30. https://doi.org/10.1177/0022002702046001007.

Geiger, Mark W. 2010. *Financial Fraud and Guerrilla Violence in Missouri's Civil War, 1861–1865*. New Haven, CT: Yale University Press.

Gerner, Deborah J., and Phillip A. Schrodt. 1998. "The Effects of Media Coverage on Crisis Assessment and Early Warning in the Middle East." In *Early Warning and Early Response*, edited by Susanne Schmeidl and Howard Adelman. New York: Columbia University Press.

Ghosn, Faten, and Sarah E. Parkinson. 2019. "'Finding' Sectarianism and Strife in Lebanon." *PS: Political Science & Politics* 52 (3): 494–97. https://doi.org/10.1017/S1049096519000143.

Goodwin, Jeff. 1997. "The Libidinal Constitution of a High-Risk Social Movement: Affectual Ties and Solidarity in the Huk Rebellion, 1946 to 1954." *American Sociological Review* 62 (1): 53–69. https://doi.org/10.2307/2657452.

Gordon, Anna, and Sarah E. Parkinson. 2018. "How the Houthis Became 'Shiʻa.'" MERIP Online (January). https://merip.org/2018/01/how-the-houthis-became-shia/.

Gould, Deborah B. 2009. *Moving Politics: Emotion and ACT UP's Fight against AIDS*. Chicago: University of Chicago Press.

Gould, Roger V. 1995. *Insurgent Identities: Class, Community, and Protest in Paris from 1848 to the Commune*. Chicago: University of Chicago Press.

Gowrinathan, Nimmi. 2017. "The Committed Female Fighter: The Political Identities of Tamil Women in the Liberation Tigers of Tamil Eelam." *International Feminist Journal of Politics* 19 (3): 327–41. https://doi.org/10.1080/14616742.2017.1299369.

———. 2021. *Radicalizing Her: Why Women Choose Violence*. Boston: Beacon Press.

Granovetter, Mark. 1973. "The Strength of Weak Ties." *American Journal of Sociology* 78 (6): 1360–80.

———. 1978. "Threshold Models of Collective Behavior." *American Journal of Sociology* 83 (6): 1420–43.

———. 1985. "Economic Action and Social Structure: The Problem of Embeddedness." *American Journal of Sociology* 91 (3): 481–510.

Grossman, Lt Col Dave. 2014. *On Killing*. Revised edition. New York: Open Road Media.

Gutiérrez-Sanín, Francisco. 2018. "The FARC's Militaristic Blueprint." *Small Wars & Insurgencies* 29 (4): 629–53. https://doi.org/10.1080/09592318.2018.1497288.

Gutiérrez-Sanín, Francisco, and Antonio Giustozzi. 2010. "Networks and Armies: Structuring Rebellion in Colombia and Afghanistan." *Studies in Conflict & Terrorism* 33 (August): 836–53. https://doi.org/10.1080/1057610X.2010.501425.

Gutiérrez-Sanín, Francisco and Elisabeth Jean Wood. 2017. "What Should We Mean by 'Pattern of Political Violence'? Repertoire, Targeting, Frequency, and Technique." *Perspectives on Politics* 15 (1): 20–41. https://doi.org/10.1017/S1537592716004114.

Hajali, Ahmad Ali al-. 2007. *Mukhayyam Burj al-Barajna: Zulul al-Mawt wa al-Hayaa (Burj al-Barajna Camp: Shades of Death and Life)*. Palestinian Camps Series. Sur (Lebanon): Palestinian Organization for Right of Return (Thabit).

Hajj, Nadya. 2016. *Protection Amid Chaos: The Creation of Property Rights in Palestinian Refugee Camps*. New York: Columbia University Press.

Haklai, Oded. 2007. "Religious–Nationalist Mobilization and State Penetration." *Comparative Political Studies* 40 (6): 713–39. https://doi.org/10.1177/0010414006290109.

Hamid, Rashid. 1975. "What Is the PLO?" *Journal of Palestine Studies* 4 (4): 90–109. https://doi.org/10.2307/2535603.

Handelman, Stephen. 1997. *Comrade Criminal: Russia's New Mafiya*. New Haven, CT: Yale University Press.

Hanf, Theodor. 1994. *Co-Existence in Wartime Lebanon: Decline of a State and Rise of a Nation*. London: I.B. Tauris.

Harb, Jehad. 2009. "Al-Haris al-Jadid Dakhal Harakat Fatah (The New Guard in the Fatah Movement)." Awraq Siyasa. Ramallah: Palestinian Center for Policy and Survey Research.

Hardan, Anaheed al-. 2017. "Researching Palestinian Refugees: Who Sets the Agenda?" *Al-Shabaka* (blog). April 27, 2017. https://al-shabaka.org/commentaries/researching-palestinian-refugees-sets-agenda/.

Haugbolle, Sune. 2012. *War and Memory in Lebanon*. Cambridge and New York: Cambridge University Press.

Hazelton, Jacqueline L. 2021. *Bullets Not Ballots: Success in Counterinsurgency Warfare*. Ithaca, NY: Cornell University Press.

Hegre, Håvard. 2004. "The Duration and Termination of Civil War." *Journal of Peace Research* 41 (3): 243–52. https://doi.org/10.1177/0022343304043768.

Hermez, Sami. 2017. *War Is Coming: Between Past and Future Violence in Lebanon*. Philadelphia, PA: University of Pennsylvania Press.

Hoover Green, Amelia. 2016. "The Commander's Dilemma Creating and Controlling Armed Group Violence." *Journal of Peace Research* 53 (5): 619-32. https://doi.org/10.1177/0022343316653645.

———. 2017. "Armed Group Institutions and Combatant Socialization: Evidence from El Salvador." *Journal of Peace Research* 54 (5): 687–700. https://doi.org/10.1177/0022343317715300.

———. 2018. *The Commander's Dilemma: Violence and Restraint in Wartime*. Ithaca, NY: Cornell University Press.

Horowitz, Donald L. 2000. *Ethnic Groups in Conflict*. 2nd ed. Berkeley: University of California Press.

Hout, Bayan Nuwayhed al-. 2004. *Sabra and Shatila: September 1982*. London and Ann Arbor, MI: Pluto Press.
Howard, Philip N. 2002. "Network Ethnography and the Hypermedia Organization: New Media, New Organizations, New Methods." *New Media & Society* 4 (4): 550–74. https://doi.org/10.1177/146144402321466813.
Huang, Reyko. 2016a. "Rebel Diplomacy in Civil War." *International Security* 40 (4): 89–126. https://doi.org/10.1162/ISEC_a_00237.
———. 2016b. *The Wartime Origins of Democratization: Civil War, Rebel Governance, and Political Regimes*. Cambridge and New York: Cambridge University Press.
Humphreys, Macartan, and Jeremy M. Weinstein. 2006. "Handling and Manhandling Civilians in Civil War." *American Political Science Review* 100 (3): 429–47.
———. 2008. "Who Fights? The Determinants of Participation in Civil War." *American Journal of Political Science* 52 (2): 436–55. https://doi.org/10.1111/j.1540-5907.2008.00322.x.
Hundman, Eric, and Sarah E Parkinson. 2019. "Rogues, Degenerates, and Heroes: Disobedience as Politics in Military Organizations." *European Journal of International Relations* 25 (3): 645–71. https://doi.org/10.1177/1354066118823891.
Johnston, Patrick. 2008. "The Geography of Insurgent Organization and Its Consequences for Civil Wars: Evidence from Liberia and Sierra Leone." *Security Studies* 17 (1): 107–37. https://doi.org/10.1080/09636410801894191.
Kallam, Mahmud Abdullah. 2008. *Mukhayyam Shatila: Al-Jaraah wa-l-Kifaah (Shatila Camp: The Wounds and the Struggle)*. Palestinian Camps Series. Sur (Lebanon): Palestinian Organization for Right of Return (Thabit).
Kalyvas, Stathis N. 1999. "Wanton and Senseless? The Logic of Massacres in Algeria." *Rationality and Society* 11 (3): 243–85. https://doi.org/10.1177/104346399011003001.
———. 2003. "The Ontology of 'Political Violence': Action and Identity in Civil Wars." *Perspectives on Politics* 1 (3): 475–94.
———. 2006. *The Logic of Violence in Civil War*. Cambridge: Cambridge University Press.
Kalyvas, Stathis N., and Laia Balcells. 2010. "International System and Technologies of Rebellion: How the End of the Cold War Shaped Internal Conflict." *American Political Science Review* 104 (3): 415–29. https://doi.org/10.1017/S0003055410000286.
Kalyvas, Stathis N., and Matthew Adam Kocher. 2007. "How 'Free' Is Free Riding in Civil Wars?: Violence, Insurgency, and the Collective Action Problem." *World Politics* 59 (2): 177–216. https://doi.org/10.1353/wp.2007.0023.
Kapferer, Bruce. 1972. *Strategy and Transaction in an African Factory: African Workers and Indian Management in a Zambian Town*. Manchester, UK: Manchester University Press.
Kaplan, Oliver. 2013. "Protecting Civilians in Civil War: The Institution of the ATCC in Colombia." *Journal of Peace Research* 50 (3): 351–67. https://doi.org/10.1177/0022343313477884.
———. 2017. *Resisting War: How Communities Protect Themselves*. Cambridge and New York: Cambridge University Press.
Kawar, Amal. 1996. *Daughters of Palestine: Leading Women of the Palestinian National Movement*. Albany, NY: SUNY Press.
Khalidi, Rashid. 1985. *Under Siege: PLO Decisionmaking During the 1982 War*. New York: Columbia University Press.
———. 2018. "The Sabra and Shatila Massacre: New Evidence." *Institute for Palestine Studies* (blog). September 25, 2018. https://www.palestine-studies.org/en/node/232060.
Khalili, Laleh. 2005. "Places of Memory and Mourning: Palestinian Commemoration in the Refugee Camps of Lebanon." *Comparative Studies of South Asia, Africa and the Middle East* 25 (1): 30–45. https://doi.org/10.1215/1089201X-25-1-30.

———. 2007a. *Heroes and Martyrs of Palestine: The Politics of National Commemoration*. Cambridge: Cambridge University Press.

———. 2007b. "Everyday Orientalism." *Middle East Report*, no. 244 (October): 42–45.

———. 2008. "Incarceration and the State of Exception: Al-Ansar Mass Detention Camp in Lebanon." In *Thinking Palestine*, by Ronit Lentin, 101–15. London: Zed Books.

Khashan, Hilal. 1992. "The Despairing Palestinians." *Journal of South Asian and Middle Eastern Studies* 16 (1): 2–17.

el-Khazen, Farid. 1991. "The Communal Pact of National Identities: The Making and Politics of the 1943 National Pact." 12. Papers on Lebanon. Oxford: Centre for Lebanese Studies.

———. 2000. *The Breakdown of the State in Lebanon, 1967–1976*. Cambridge, MA: Harvard University Press.

Kinsella, Helen M. 2019. "Sex as the Secret: Counterinsurgency in Afghanistan." *International Theory* 11 (1): 26–47. https://doi.org/10.1017/S1752971918000210.

Klouzal, Linda A. 2008. *Women and Rebel Communities in the Cuban Insurgent Movement, 1952–1959*. Amherst, MA: Cambria Press.

Kocher, Matthew Adam, Thomas B. Pepinsky, and Stathis N. Kalyvas. 2011. "Aerial Bombing and Counterinsurgency in the Vietnam War." *American Journal of Political Science* 55 (2): 201–18. https://doi.org/10.1111/j.1540-5907.2010.00498.x.

Kostovicova, Denisa, and Eleanor Knott. 2020. "Harm, Change and Unpredictability: The Ethics of Interviews in Conflict Research." *Qualitative Research*, December. https://doi.org/10.1177/1468794120975657.

Krause, Jana. 2018. *Resilient Communities: Non-Violence and Civilian Agency in Communal War*. Cambridge and New York: Cambridge University Press.

———. 2019. "Gender Dimensions of (Non)Violence in Communal Conflict: The Case of Jos, Nigeria." *Comparative Political Studies* 52 (10): 1466–99. https://doi.org/10.1177/0010414019830722.

———. 2021. "The Ethics of Ethnographic Methods in Conflict Zones." *Journal of Peace Research*, February. https://doi.org/10.1177/0022343320971021.

Krause, Peter. 2017. *Rebel Power: Why National Movements Compete, Fight, and Win*. Ithaca, NY: Cornell University Press.

Kuran, Timur. 1991. "Now out of Never: The Element of Surprise in the East European Revolution of 1989." *World Politics* 44 (1): 7–48. https://doi.org/10.2307/2010422.

Lake, Milli. 2014. "Organizing Hypocrisy: Providing Legal Accountability for Human Rights Violations in Areas of Limited Statehood." *International Studies Quarterly* 58 (3): 515–26. https://doi.org/10.1111/isqu.12144.

Lake, Milli, and Marie Berry. 2017. "Women and Power after War." *Political Violence at a Glance* (blog). June 6, 2017. https://politicalviolenceataglance.org/2017/06/06/women-and-power-after-war/.

Larson, Jennifer M., and Janet I. Lewis. 2018. "Rumors, Kinship Networks, and Rebel Group Formation." *International Organization* 72 (4): 871–903. https://doi.org/10.1017/S0020818318000243.

Laumann, Edward O., Peter V. Marsden, and David Prensky. 1992. "The Boundary Specification Problem in Network Analysis." In *Research Methods in Social Network Analysis*, 61–88. New Brunswick, NJ: Transaction Publishers.

Lawrence, Adria. 2010. "Triggering Nationalist Violence: Competition and Conflict in Uprisings against Colonial Rule." *International Security* 35 (2): 88–122.

———. 2013. *Imperial Rule and the Politics of Nationalism: Anti-Colonial Protest in the French Empire*. New York: Cambridge University Press.

Leenders, Reinoud. 2012. *Spoils of Truce: Corruption and State-Building in Postwar Lebanon*. Ithaca, NY: Cornell University Press.

Lewis, Janet I. 2017. "How Does Ethnic Rebellion Start?" *Comparative Political Studies* 50 (10): 1420–50. https://doi.org/10.1177/0010414016672235.
———. 2020. *How Insurgency Begins*. Cambridge and New York: Cambridge University Press.
Lubkemann, Stephen C. 2008. *Culture in Chaos: An Anthropology of the Social Condition in War*. Chicago: University of Chicago Press.
Lyall, Jason. 2009. "Does Indiscriminate Violence Incite Insurgent Attacks? Evidence from Chechnya." *Journal of Conflict Resolution* 53 (3): 331–62. https://doi.org/10.1177/0022002708330881.
MacFarland, Susan. 1994. "Women and Revolution in Indonesia." In *Women and Revolution in Africa, Asia, and the New World*, edited by Mary Ann Tétreault, 192–210. Columbia: University of South Carolina Press.
MacLean, Lauren M., Elliot Posner, Susan Thomson, and Elisabeth Jean Wood. 2018. "Research Ethics and Human Subjects: A Reflexive Openness Approach." Qualitative Transparency Deliberations. https://papers.ssrn.com/sol3/papers.cfm?abstract_id=3332887.
Majed, Rima. 2016. "In the Arab World, Sectarianism Is Real, Sects Are Not." *Al-Jazeera* (blog). October 16, 2016. https://www.aljazeera.com/news/2016/10/16/in-the-arab-world-sectarianism-is-real-sects-are-not.
Makdisi, Ussama. 2000. *The Culture of Sectarianism: Community, History, and Violence in Nineteenth-Century Ottoman Lebanon*. Berkeley: University of California Press.
Malejacq, Romain, and Dipali Mukhopadhyay. 2016. "The 'Tribal Politics' of Field Research: A Reflection on Power and Partiality in 21st-Century Warzones." *Perspectives on Politics* 14 (4): 1011–28. https://doi.org/10.1017/S1537592716002899.
Mampilly, Zachariah Cherian. 2009. "A Marriage of Inconvenience: Tsunami Aid and the Unraveling of the LTTE and the GoSL's Complex Dependency." *Civil Wars* 11 (3): 302–20. https://doi.org/10.1080/13698240903157545.
———. 2011. *Rebel Rulers: Insurgent Governance and Civilian Life During War*. Ithaca, NY: Cornell University Press.
Mampilly, Zachariah, and Megan A. Stewart. 2020. "A Typology of Rebel Political Institutional Arrangements." *Journal of Conflict Resolution* 65 (1): 15–45. https://doi.org/10.1177/0022002720935642.
Manekin, Devorah. 2017. "The Limits of Socialization and the Underproduction of Military Violence: Evidence from the IDF." *Journal of Peace Research* 54 (5): 606–19. https://doi.org/10.1177/0022343317713558.
———. 2020. *Regular Soldiers, Irregular War: Violence and Restraint in the Second Intifada*. Ithaca, New York: Cornell University Press.
March, Andrew F., and Mara Revkin. 2015. "Caliphate of Law," December 16, 2015. https://www.foreignaffairs.com/articles/syria/2015-04-15/caliphate-law.
Mazur, Kevin. 2019. "State Networks and Intra-Ethnic Group Variation in the 2011 Syrian Uprising." *Comparative Political Studies* 52 (7): 995–1027. https://doi.org/10.1177/0010414018806536.
———. 2020. "Networks, Informal Governance, and Ethnic Violence in a Syrian City." *World Politics* 72 (3): 481–524.
———. 2021. *Revolution in Syria: Identity, Networks, and Repression*. Cambridge and New York: Cambridge University Press.
McAdam, Doug. 1986. "Recruitment to High-Risk Activism: The Case of Freedom Summer." *American Journal of Sociology* 92 (2): 64–90.
McGovern, Mike. 2011. *Making War in Côte d'Ivoire*. Chicago: University of Chicago Press.
McLauchlin, Theodore. 2020. *Desertion: Trust and Mistrust in Civil Wars*. Ithaca, NY: Cornell University Press.

McLean, Paul. 2016. *Culture in Networks*. Cambridge and Malden, MA: Polity.
Meagher, Kate. 2010. *Identity Economics: Social Networks and the Informal Economy in Nigeria*. Melton, UK: James Currey.
Mercer, Jonathan. 2010. "Emotional Beliefs." *International Organization* 64 (1): 1–31. https://doi.org/10.1017/S0020818309990221.
Metelits, Claire M. 2018. "Bourdieu's Capital and Insurgent Group Resilience: A Field-Theoretic Approach to the Polisario Front." *Small Wars & Insurgencies* 29 (4): 680–708. https://doi.org/10.1080/09592318.2018.1488407.
Metternich, Nils W., Cassy Dorff, Max Gallop, Simon Weschle, and Michael D. Ward. 2013. "Antigovernment Networks in Civil Conflicts: How Network Structures Affect Conflictual Behavior." *American Journal of Political Science* 57 (4): 892–911. https://doi.org/10.1111/ajps.12039.
Mikdashi, Maya. 2014. "Can Palestinian Men Be Victims? Gendering Israel's War on Gaza." *Jadaliyya* (blog). July 23, 2014. http://www.jadaliyya.com/Details/30991/Can-Palestinian-Men-be-Victims-Gendering-Israel%60s-War-on-Gaza.
Moaveni, Azadeh. 2019. *Guest House for Young Widows: Among the Women of ISIS*. New York: Random House.
Moore, Pauline. 2019. "When Do Ties Bind? Foreign Fighters, Social Embeddedness, and Violence against Civilians." *Journal of Peace Research* 56 (2): 279–94. https://doi.org/10.1177/0022343318804594.
Moser, Sarah. 2008. "Personality: A New Positionality?" *Area* 40 (3): 383–92. https://doi.org/10.1111/j.1475-4762.2008.00815.x.
al-Natour, Mahmoud. 2014a. *Harakat Fatah: Bayn al-Muqawama wa-l-Ghatialat (The Fatah Movement: Between Resistance and Assassinations): 1965–1982*. Vol. 1. Amman: al-Ahlia.
———. 2014b. *Harakat Fatah: Bayn al-Muqawama wa-l-Ghatialat (The Fatah Movement: Between Resistance and Assassinations): 1983–2004*. Vol. 2. Amman: al-Ahlia.
Nayel, Moe Ali. 2013. "Palestinian Refugees Are Not at Your Service." *The Electronic Intifada*. May 19, 2013. http://electronicintifada.net/content/palestinian-refugees-are-not-your-service/12464.
Nordstrom, Carolyn. 2004. *Shadows of War: Violence, Power, and International Profiteering in the Twenty-First Century*. Berkeley: University of California Press.
Obert, Jonathan. 2014. "The Six-Shooter Marketplace: 19th-Century Gunfighting as Violence Expertise." *Studies in American Political Development* 28 (1): 49–79. https://doi.org/10.1017/S0898588X13000187.
———. 2018. *The Six-Shooter State: Public and Private Violence in American Politics*. Reprint edition. Cambridge and New York: Cambridge University Press.
"Open Letter to the Public." 2021. *Jineoloji* (blog). May 10, 2021. http://jineoloji.org/en/2021/05/10/open-letter-to-the-public/.
Pachirat, Timothy. 2009. "The Political in Political Ethnography: Dispatches from the Kill Floor." In *Political Ethnography: What Immersion Contributes to the Study of Power*, edited by Edward Schatz, 143–62. Chicago: University of Chicago Press.
———. 2011. *Every Twelve Seconds: Industrialized Slaughter and the Politics of Sight*. New Haven, CT: Yale University Press.
Pachucki, Mark A., and Ronald L. Breiger. 2010. "Cultural Holes: Beyond Relationality in Social Networks and Culture." *Annual Review of Sociology* 36 (1): 205–24. https://doi.org/10.1146/annurev.soc.012809.102615.
Pader, Ellen. 2006. "Seeing with an Ethnographic Sensibility: Explorations Beneath the Surface of Public Policies." In *Interpretation And Method: Empirical Research Methods And the Interpretive Turn*, by Dvora Yanow and Peregrine Schwartz-Shea. New York: Routledge.

Padgett, John F. 2010. "Open Elite? Social Mobility, Marriage, and Family in Florence, 1282–1494." *Renaissance Quarterly* 63 (2): 357–411.
Padgett, John F., and Christopher K. Ansell. 1993. "Robust Action and the Rise of the Medici, 1400–1434." *American Journal of Sociology* 98 (6): 1259–1319.
Padgett, John F., and Paul D. McLean. 2006. "Organizational Invention and Elite Transformation: The Birth of Partnership Systems in Renaissance Florence." *American Journal of Sociology* 111 (5): 1463–1568.
Padgett, John F., and Walter W. Powell. 2012. *The Emergence of Organizations and Markets*. Princeton, NJ: Princeton University Press.
Palestinian Academic Society for the Study of International Affairs (PASSIA). 2012a. "Arafat, Yasser (Abu Amar) (1929–2004)." Palestinian Personalities-A. 2012. http://www.passia.org/palestine_facts/personalities/alpha_a.htm.
———. 2012b. "El-Wazir, Khalil (Abu Jihad) (1935–1988)." Palestinian Personalities-W. 2012. http://www.passia.org/palestine_facts/personalities/alpha_w.htm.
———. 2012c. "Khalaf, Salah (Abu Iyad) (1934–1991)." Palestinian Personalities-K. 2012. http://www.passia.org/palestine_facts/personalities/alpha_k.htm.
Papachristos, Andrew V. 2006. "Social Network Analysis and Gang Research: Theory and Methods." In *Studying Youth Gangs*, edited by James F. Short Jr. and Lorine A. Hughes, 99–116. Lanham, MD: Altamira Press.
———. 2009. "Murder by Structure: Dominance Relations and the Social Structure of Gang Homicide." *American Journal of Sociology* 115 (1): 74–128.
Parkinson, Sarah E. 2013. "Organizing Rebellion: Rethinking High-Risk Mobilization and Social Networks in War." *American Political Science Review* 107 (3): 418–32. https://doi.org/10.1017/S0003055413000208.
———. 2015. "Towards an Ethics of Sight: Violence Scholarship and the Arab Uprisings." *LSE Middle East Center Blog* (blog). August 26, 2015. http://blogs.lse.ac.uk/mec/2015/08/26/towards-an-ethics-of-sight-violence-scholarship-and-the-arab-uprisings/.
———. 2016. "Money Talks: Discourse, Networks, and Structure in Militant Organizations." *Perspectives on Politics* 14 (4): 976–94. https://doi.org/10.1017/S1537592716002875.
———. 2018. "Seeing Beyond the Spectacle: Research on and Adjacent to Violence." In *Political Science Research in the Middle East and North Africa: Methodological and Ethical Challenges*, edited by Janine A. Clark and Francesco Cavatorta, 73–82. New York: Oxford University Press.
———. 2019. "Humanitarian Crisis Research as Intervention." *Middle East Report* 290 (Spring 2019): 29–37.
———. 2021a. "Practical Ideology in Militant Organizations." *World Politics* 73 (1): 52–81. https://doi.org/10.1017/S0043887120000180.
———. 2021b. "Composing Comparisons: Relational Cases and Cases of Relations in Qualitative Research." In *Rethinking Comparison in the Social Sciences: Innovative Methods for Qualitative Political Inquiry*, edited by Erica Simmons and Nicholas Rush Smith. Cambridge and New York: Cambridge University Press.
———. 2022. "(Dis)Courtesy Bias: 'Methodological Cognates,' Data Validity, and Ethics in Violence-Adjacent Research." *Comparative Political Studies*. https://doi.org/10.1177/00104140211024309.
Parkinson, Sarah E., and Sherry Zaks. 2018. "Militant and Rebel Organization(s)." *Comparative Politics* 50 (2): 271–93. https://doi.org/info:doi/10.5129/001041518822263610.
Pearlman, Wendy. 2011. *Violence, Nonviolence, and the Palestinian National Movement*. Cambridge and New York: Cambridge University Press.

———. 2013. "Emotions and the Microfoundations of the Arab Uprisings." *Perspectives on Politics* 11 (2): 387–409. https://doi.org/10.1017/S1537592713001072.
Pedahzur, Ami, and Arie Perliger. 2006. "The Changing Nature of Suicide Attacks: A Social Network Perspective." *Social Forces* 84 (4): 1987–2008. https://doi.org/10.1353/sof.2006.0104.Peteet, Julie. 1991. *Gender in Crisis: Women and the Palestinian Resistance Movement*. New York: Columbia University Press.
Petersen, Roger D. 2001. *Resistance and Rebellion: Lessons from Eastern Europe*. Cambridge: Cambridge University Press.
Philbrick Yadav, Stacey. 2014. "The Limits of the 'Sectarian' Framing in Yemen." *Washington Post*, September 25, 2014, sec. Monkey Cage. https://www.washingtonpost.com/news/monkey-cage/wp/2014/09/25/the-limits-of-the-sectarian-framing-in-yemen/.
Picard, Elizabeth. 2002. *Lebanon: A Shattered Country*. New York and London: Holmes & Meier.
Pool, David. 2001. *From Guerrillas to Government: Eritrean People's Liberation Front*. Columbus: Ohio University Press.
Rabinovich, Itamar. 1985. *The War for Lebanon, 1970–1985*. Ithaca, NY: Cornell University Press.
Reno, William. 1999. *Warlord Politics and African States*. Boulder, CO: Lynne Rienner Publishers.
Revkin, Mara. 2016. "ISIS' Social Contract," February 25, 2016. https://www.foreignaffairs.com/articles/syria/2016-01-10/isis-social-contract.
———. 2019. "What Explains Taxation by Resource-Rich Rebels? Evidence from the Islamic State in Syria." *The Journal of Politics* 82 (2): 757–64. https://doi.org/10.1086/706597.
Robben, Antonious C.G.M. 1995. "The Politics of Truth and Emotion among Victims and Perpetrators of Violence." In *Fieldwork Under Fire*, by Carolyn Nordstrom and Antonius C. G. M. Robben, 81–103. Berkeley: University of California Press.
Rose, Elihu. 1982. "The Anatomy of Mutiny." *Armed Forces & Society* 8 (4): 561–74. https://doi.org/10.1177/0095327X8200800403.
Rougier, Bernard. 2004. "Religious Mobilization in Palestinian Refugee Camps in Lebanon: The Case of Ain al-Helweh." In *The Middle East and Palestine: Global Politics and Regional Conflict*, edited by Dietrich Jung, 151–81. New York: Palgrave Macmillan.
———. 2007. *Everyday Jihad: The Rise of Militant Islam Among Palestinians in Lebanon*. Cambridge, MA: Harvard University Press.
Rouleau, Eric. 1983. "The Future of the PLO." *Foreign Affairs* 62: 138–56.
Rouleau, Eric, Jim Paul, and Joe Stork. 1983. "The Mutiny against Arafat." MERIP Reports, no. 119 (November): 13–16. https://doi.org/10.2307/3010860.
Roy, Olivier. 1986. *Islam and Resistance in Afghanistan*. Cambridge UK: Cambridge University Press.
Royko, Mike. 1988. *Boss: Richard J. Daley of Chicago*. New York: Plume.
Rubenberg, Cheryl. 1983a. *Palestine Liberation Organization: Its Institutional Infrastructure*. Belmont, MA: Institute of Arab Studies.
———. 1983b. "The Civilian Infrastructure of the Palestine Liberation Organization: An Analysis of the PLO in Lebanon Until June 1982." *Journal of Palestine Studies* 12 (3): 54–78.
———. 1986. *Israel and the American National Interest: A Critical Examination*. Champaign: University of Illinois Press.
Rubin, Barnett R. 2002. *The Fragmentation of Afghanistan: State Formation and Collapse in the International System*. 2nd ed. New Haven, CT: Yale University Press.

Said, Edward W. 1983. "Palestinians in the Aftermath of Beirut." *Journal of Palestine Studies* 12 (2): 3–9.
Salah, Salah. 2008. *Al-Laji'un al-Falistiniun fi Lubnan (Palestinian Refugees in Lebanon)*. Palestinians in the Diaspora. Damascus, Syria: al-Ghad al-Arabi lil-Dirasat.
Salloukh, Bassel F., Rabie Barakat, and Jinan S. al-Habbal. 2015. *The Politics of Sectarianism in Postwar Lebanon*. London: Pluto Press.
Sayigh, Rosemary. 1979. *Palestinians: From Peasants to Revolutionaries*. London: Zed Books.
———. 1985. "The Mukhabarat State: A Palestinian Women's Testimony." *Journal of Palestine Studies* 14 (3): 18–31.
———. 1994. *Too Many Enemies: The Palestinian Experience in Lebanon*. London: Zed Books.
———. 1995. "Palestinians in Lebanon: Harsh Present, Uncertain Future." *Journal of Palestine Studies* 25 (1): 94–105.
———. 1998. "Gender, Sexuality, and Class in National Narratives: Palestinian Camp Women Tell Their Lives." *Frontiers: A Journal of Women Studies* 19 (2): 166–85.
———. 2007. "Product and Producer of Palestinian History: Stereotypes of 'Self' in Camp Women's Life Stories." *Journal of Middle East Women's Studies* 3 (1): 86–105. https://doi.org/10.2979/MEW.2007.3.1.86.
Sayigh, Yezid. 1983a. "Palestinian Military Performance in the 1982 War." *Journal of Palestine Studies* 12 (4): 3–24. https://doi.org/10.2307/2536242.
———. 1983b. "Israel's Military Performance in Lebanon, June 1982." *Journal of Palestine Studies* 13 (1): 24–65. https://doi.org/10.2307/2536925.
———. 1997. *Armed Struggle and the Search for State: The Palestinian National Movement, 1949–1993*. Oxford: Oxford University Press.
Scacco, Alexandra. 2021. "Anatomy of a Riot: Participation in Ethnic Violence in Nigeria." Book manuscript. WZB Berlin Social Science Center. https://www.wzb.eu/system/files/docs/ped/ipi/Scacco_Anatomy_of_a_Riot_Introduction.pdf.
Schaffer, Frederic Charles. 2018. "Two Ways to Compare." *Qualitative and Multi-Method Research* 16 (1): 15–20. https://doi.org/10.5281/zenodo.2562165.
Schatz, Edward. 2009. *Political Ethnography: What Immersion Contributes to the Study of Power*. Chicago: University of Chicago Press.
Schiff, Ze'ev, and Ehud Ya'ari. 1984. *Israel's Lebanon War*. New York: Simon and Schuster.
Schulhofer-Wohl, Jonah. 2020. *Quagmire in Civil War*. New York and Cambridge: Cambridge University Press.
Schwedler, Jillian. 2006. "The Third Gender: Western Female Researchers in the Middle East." *PS: Political Science & Politics* 39 (3): 425–28. https://doi.org/10.1017/S104909650606077X.
———. 2014. "Toward Transparency in the Ethics of Knowledge Production." POMEPS Studies 8. The Ethics of Research in the Middle East. Washington, DC: Project on Middle East Political Science. https://pomeps.org/2014/06/23/toward-transparency-in-the-ethics-of-knowledge-production/.
Scott, James C. 1987. *Weapons of the Weak: Everyday Forms of Peasant Resistance*. New Haven, CT: Yale University Press.
———. 1990. *Domination and the Arts of Resistance: Hidden Transcripts*. New Haven, CT: Yale University Press.
———. 2010. *The Art of Not Being Governed: An Anarchist History of Upland Southeast Asia*. New Haven, CT: Yale University Press.
Serena, Chad C. 2014. *It Takes More than a Network: The Iraqi Insurgency and Organizational Adaptation*. 1st edition. Stanford: Stanford Security Studies.

Shapiro, Jacob N. 2013. *The Terrorist's Dilemma: Managing Violent Covert Organizations.* Princeton, NJ, and Oxford UK: Princeton University Press.

Sheldon, Kathleen. 1994. "Women and Revolution in Mozambique: A Luta Continua." In *Women and Revolution in Africa, Asia, and the New World*, edited by Mary Ann Tétreault, 33–61. Columbia: University of South Carolina Press.

Shesterinina, Anastasia. 2016. "Collective Threat Framing and Mobilization in Civil War." *American Political Science Review* 110 (3): 411–27. https://doi.org/10.1017/S0003055416000277.

———. 2018. "Ethics, Empathy and Fear in Research on Violent Conflict." *Journal of Peace Research* 56 (2): 190–202. https://doi.org/10.1177/0022343318783246

———. 2021. *Mobilizing in Uncertainty: Collective Identities and War in Abkhazia.* Ithaca, NY: Cornell University Press.

Shibutani, Tamotsu. 1978. *The Derelicts of Company K: A Sociological Study of Demoralization.* Berkeley: University of California Press.

Shuquair, Muhammad. 1983. "The Fateh Split." *Journal of Palestine Studies* 13 (1): 169–80. https://doi.org/10.2307/2536935.

Simmel, Georg. 1964. *Conflict/The Web of Group Affiliations.* New York: Free Press.

Simmons, Erica S. 2016. *Meaningful Resistance: Market Reforms and the Roots of Social Protest in Latin America.* New York: Cambridge University Press.

Simmons, Erica S., and Nicholas Rush Smith. 2017. "Comparison with an Ethnographic Sensibility." *PS: Political Science & Politics* 50 (1): 126–30. https://doi.org/10.1017/S1049096516002286.

———. 2019. "The Case for Comparative Ethnography." Text. April 2019. https://doi.org/info:doi/10.5129/001041519X15647434969920.

Sinno, Abdulkader H. 2010. *Organizations at War in Afghanistan and Beyond.* Ithaca, NY: Cornell University Press.

Sito-Sucic, Daria. 2006. "Bosnia: Sarajevo's War Damage Totalled $18.5 Bln—Study." *ReliefWeb* (blog). December 12, 2006. https://reliefweb.int/report/bosnia-and-herzegovina/bosnia-sarajevos-war-damage-totalled-185-bln-study.

Sjoberg, Laura. 2013. *Gendering Global Conflict: Toward a Feminist Theory of War.* New York: Columbia University Press.

Sjoberg, Laura, and Caron E. Gentry. 2007. *Mothers, Monsters, Whores: Women's Violence in Global Politics.* London: Zed Books.

Sluka, Jeffrey A. 2007. "Reflections on Managing Danger in Fieldwork: Dangerous Anthropology in Belfast." In *Ethnographic Fieldwork: An Anthropological Reader.* Malden, MA, and Oxford: Wiley-Blackwell.

Small, Mario Luis. 2009. "'How Many Cases Do I Need?': On Science and the Logic of Case Selection in Field-Based Research." *Ethnography* 10 (1): 5–38. https://doi.org/10.1177/1466138108099586.

———. 2010. *Unanticipated Gains: Origins of Network Inequality in Everyday Life.* Oxford: Oxford University Press.

Smith, Nicholas Rush. 2015. "Rejecting Rights: Vigilantism and Violence in Post-Apartheid South Africa." *African Affairs* 114 (456): 341–60. https://doi.org/10.1093/afraf/adv023.

———. 2019. *Contradictions of Democracy: Vigilantism and Rights in Post-Apartheid South Africa.* New York: Oxford University Press.

Sogge, Erling. 2016. "Negotiating Jihad in Ain al-Hilweh." *Carnegie Endowment for International Peace* (blog). May 25, 2016. https://carnegieendowment.org/sada/63670.

Solnit, Rebecca. 2010. *A Paradise Built in Hell: The Extraordinary Communities That Arise in Disaster.* New York: Penguin.

Soss, Joe. 2018. "On Casing a Study versus Studying a Case." *Qualitative and Multi-Method Research* 16 (1): 21–27. https://doi.org/10.5281/zenodo.2562167.
Souleimanov, Emil Aslan, and David S. Siroky. 2016. "Random or Retributive?: Indiscriminate Violence in the Chechen Wars." *World Politics* 68 (4): 677–712. https://doi.org/10.1017/S0043887116000101.
Staniland, Paul. 2012. "Organizing Insurgency: Networks, Resources, and Rebellion in South Asia." *International Security* 37 (1): 142–77. https://doi.org/10.1162/ISEC_a_00091.
———. 2014. *Networks of Rebellion: Explaining Insurgent Cohesion and Collapse.* 1st edition. Ithaca, NY: Cornell University Press.
Stewart, Megan A. 2018. "Civil War as State-Making: Strategic Governance in Civil War." *International Organization* 72 (1): 205–26.
———. 2020. "Rebel Governance: Military Boon or Military Bust?" *Conflict Management and Peace Science* 37 (1): 16–38. https://doi.org/10.1177/0738894219881422
Straus, Scott. 2005. *The Order of Genocide: Race, Power, and War in Rwanda.* Ithaca, NY: Cornell University Press.
———. 2015. "Triggers of Mass Atrocities." *Politics and Governance* 3 (3): 5–15.
Sukarieh, Mayssoun, and Stuart Tannock. 2013. "On the Problem of Over-Researched Communities: The Case of the Shatila Palestinian Refugee Camp in Lebanon." *Sociology* 47 (3): 494–508. https://doi.org/10.1177/0038038512448567.
———. 2019. "Subcontracting Academia: Alienation, Exploitation and Disillusionment in the UK Overseas Syrian Refugee Research Industry." *Antipode* 51 (2): 664–80. https://doi.org/10.1111/anti.12502.
Suleiman, Jaber. 1997. "Palestinians in Lebanon and the Role of Non-Governmental Organizations." *Journal of Refugee Studies* 10 (3): 397–410. https://doi.org/10.1093/jrs/10.3.397.
———. 1999. "The Current Political, Organizational, and Security Situation in the Palestinian Refugee Camps of Lebanon." *Journal of Palestine Studies* 29 (1): 66–80.
Swidler, Ann. 1986. "Culture in Action: Symbols and Strategies." *American Sociological Review* 51 (2): 273–86. https://doi.org/10.2307/2095521.
Syrian Network for Human Rights. 2020. "The Ninth Annual Report on Enforced Disappearance in Syria on the International Day of the Victims of Enforced Disappearances: There Is No Political Solution without the Disappeared." Syrian Network for Human Rights. https://sn4hr.org/wp-content/pdf/english/The_Ninth_Annual_Report_on_Enforced_Disappearance_in_Syria_on_the_International_Day_of_the_Victims_of_Enforced_Disappearances_en.pdf.
Syrian Network for Human Rights. 2021. "At Least 3,364 Health Care Personal Still Arrested/Forcibly Disappeared, 98% by the Syrian Regime." Syrian Network for Human Rights. https://sn4hr.org/wp-content/pdf/english/At_Least_3364_Health_Care_Personnel_Still_Arrested_Forcibly_Disappeared_en.pdf.
Tétreault, Mary Ann. 1994. *Women and Revolution in Africa, Asia, and the New World.* Columbia: University of South Carolina Press.
Thomas, Jakana L., and Kanisha D. Bond. 2015. "Women's Participation in Violent Political Organizations." *American Political Science Review* 109 (3): 488–506. https://doi.org/10.1017/S0003055415000313.
Thomas, Jakana L., and Reed M. Wood. 2017. "The Social Origins of Female Combatants." *Conflict Management and Peace Science*, 35 (3): 215–32. https://doi.org/10.1177/0738894217695524.
Tilly, Charles. 1978. *From Mobilization to Revolution.* New York: Random House.
———. 1986. *The Contentious French.* Cambridge, MA: Harvard University Press.

——. 2008. *Contentious Performances*. Cambridge and New York: Cambridge University Press.
Tilly, Charles, and Sidney Tarrow. 2015. *Contentious Politics*. 2nd edition. New York: Oxford University Press.
Toft, Monica Duffy. 2005. *The Geography of Ethnic Violence: Identity, Interests, and the Indivisibility of Territory*. Princeton, NJ: Princeton University Press.
Traboulsi, Fawwaz. 2007. *A History of Modern Lebanon*. London and Ann Arbor, MI: Pluto Press.
Tripp, Aili Mari. 2015. *Women and Power in Postconflict Africa*. New York and Cambridge: Cambridge University Press.
Tsai, Lily L. 2007. *Accountability Without Democracy: Solidary Groups and Public Goods Provision in Rural China*. Cambridge and New York: Cambridge University Press.
Tse-tung, Mao. 2007. *On Guerilla Warfare*. Translated by Samuel B. Griffith. LaVergne, TN: BN Publishing.
Tsoukas, Haridimos. 2001. "Re-Viewing Organization." *Human Relations* 54 (1): 7–12. https://doi.org/10.1177/0018726701541002.
United Nations High Commissioner for Refugees. 2020. "Figures at a Glance." Statistical Yearbooks. Geneva: United Nations High Commissioner for Refugees. https://www.unhcr.org/figures-at-a-glance.html.
UNRWA. n.d. "UNRWA-Overview." About UNRWA: Overview. http://unrwa.org/etemplate.php?id=85.
UNRWA Public Information Office. 2011. "Palestine Refugees, UNRWA Lebanon: A Special Case." Beirut, Lebanon: UNRWA.
Van Creveld, Martin. 1977. *Supplying War: Logistics from Wallenstein to Patton*. Cambridge, UK: Cambridge University Press.
Verkaaik, Oskar. 2004. *Migrants and Militants: Fun and Urban Violence in Pakistan*. Princeton, NJ: Princeton University Press.
Villeneuve, Denis, dir. 2011. *Incendies*. Culver City, CA: Sony Pictures Home Entertainment.
Viterna, Jocelyn. 2006. "Pulled, Pushed, and Persuaded: Explaining Women's Mobilization into the Salvadoran Guerrilla Army." *American Journal of Sociology* 112 (1): 1–45. https://doi.org/10.1086/502690.
——. 2013. *Women in War: The Micro-Processes of Mobilization in El Salvador*. Oxford and New York: Oxford University Press.
Volkov, Vadim. 2002. *Violent Entrepreneurs: The Use of Force in the Making of Russian Capitalism*. Ithaca, NY: Cornell University Press.
Warrick, Joby. 2016. *Black Flags: The Rise of ISIS*. Reprint edition. New York: Anchor.
Wedeen, Lisa. 1999. *Ambiguities of Domination: Politics, Rhetoric, and Symbols in Contemporary Syria*. Chicago: University of Chicago Press.
——. 2008. *Peripheral Visions: Publics, Power, and Performance in Yemen*. Chicago: University of Chicago Press.
——. 2009. "Ethnography as Interpretive Enterprise." In *Political Ethnography: What Immersion Contributes to the Study of Power*, edited by Edward Schatz. Chicago: University of Chicago Press.
——. 2010. "Reflections on Ethnographic Work in Political Science." *Annual Review of Political Science* 13 (1): 255–72. https://doi.org/10.1146/annurev.polisci.11.052706.123951.
Weinstein, Jeremy M. 2005. "Resources and the Information Problem in Rebel Recruitment." *The Journal of Conflict Resolution* 49 (4): 598–624. https://doi.org/10.1177/0022002705277802

———. 2007. *Inside Rebellion: The Politics of Insurgent Violence*. Cambridge and New York: Cambridge University Press.
White, Harrison. 2008. *Identity and Control: How Social Formations Emerge*. Second edition. Princeton, NJ: Princeton University Press.
Wickham-Crowley, Timothy. 1992. *Guerrillas and Revolution in Latin America: A Comparative Study of Insurgents and Regimes Since 1956*. Princeton, NJ: Princeton University Press.
Wilson, Amrit. 1991. *The Challenge Road: Women and the Eritrean Revolution*. Trenton, NJ: The Red Sea Press.
Wood, Elisabeth Jean. 2003. *Insurgent Collective Action and Civil War in El Salvador*. Cambridge: Cambridge University Press.
———. 2006a. "The Ethical Challenges of Field Research in Conflict Zones." *Qualitative Sociology* 29 (June): 373–86. https://doi.org/10.1007/s11133-006-9027-8.
———. 2006b. "Variation in Sexual Violence during War." *Politics & Society* 34 (3): 307–42. https://doi.org/10.1177/0032329206290426.
———. 2008. "The Social Processes of Civil War: The Wartime Transformation of Social Networks." *Annual Review of Political Science* 11: 539–61. https://doi.org/10.1146/annurev.polisci.8.082103.104832.
———. 2009. "Armed Groups and Sexual Violence: When Is Wartime Rape Rare?" *Politics and Society* 37 (1): 131–61. https://doi.org/10.1177/0032329208329755.
Wood, Reed M., and Jakana L. Thomas. 2017. "Women on the Frontline: Rebel Group Ideology and Women's Participation in Violent Rebellion." *Journal of Peace Research* 54 (1): 31–46. https://doi.org/10.1177/0022343316675025.
World Bank. n.d.a. "Lebanon | Data." Data. Accessed July 21, 2021. https://data.worldbank.org/country/lebanon.
———. n.d.b. "Refugee Population by Country or Territory of Asylum—Jordan." Data. Accessed July 21, 2021. https://data.worldbank.org/indicator/SM.POP.REFG?locations=JO.
———. n.d.c. "Refugee Population by Country or Territory of Asylum—Lebanon." Data. Accessed July 21, 2021c. https://data.worldbank.org/indicator/SM.POP.REFG?locations=LB.
World Health Organization. 2017. "Yemen Humanitarian Response Plan 2017." Emergencies. http://www.who.int/emergencies/response-plans/2017/yemen/en/.
———. 2020. "Cholera Situation in Yemen." World Health Organization Office for the Eastern Mediterranean. https://reliefweb.int/sites/reliefweb.int/files/resources/Cholera%20situation%20in%20Yemen%2C%20December%202020.pdf.
Yanow, Dvora. 2012. "Organizational Ethnography between Toolbox and World-Making." *Journal of Organizational Ethnography* 1 (1): 31–42. https://doi.org/10.1108/20246674121122063.
Zerubavel, Eviatar. 1996. "Social Memories: Steps to a Sociology of the Past." *Qualitative Sociology* 19 (3): 283–99. https://doi.org/10.1007/BF02393273.

Index

Abu Mujahid (Abu Moujahed), 117, 130
Abu Tawq, Ali (Abu Toq, Ali), 114–17, 121, 123, 130–32
adaptability/flexibility, organizational, 6, 51, 78–79, 156, 158–59
advocacy, 13, 32, 92–93, 97, 98–102, 113, 147
aerial attacks. *See* bombing
affiliations: in cross-factional defensive fronts, 115–16, 117, 119, 121, 126–28, 129–31; and crossing political lines, 179–80, 181–83; in emergence of clandestine operations, 72, 78–79, 89–90; ethnic, 126–28, 162–63; experience of the Israeli invasion across, 58; factional, 121, 129, 142–43, 180, 181–83; organizational, 89–90, 129–31, 179–80; political, 13, 43, 58; during siege, 43
Afghan militant groups, 158–59
Ain al-Hilweh camp: collaboration in, 93, 100–102, 105–11; contemporary factions in, 30–32; emergence of advocacy and counterintelligence networks in, 93, 94–97, 98–102, 105–11; emergence of personalized militias in, 137–38, 143–46, 153; in the Israeli invasion, 56, 59–60, 64; militarized performances in, 30–33; religious authorities in defense of, 202n19. *See also* Saida
Ain al-Rummaneh bus attack, 41–42
ALF (Arab Liberation Front), 36–37, 48, 50–51
Amal (Shi'i Lebanese militia): foundation of, 204n3; and Palestinians in 1980s Lebanon, 11; in the War of the Camps, 117, 119–20, 121–23, 124, 126–28, 129, 137–39, 144, 145–47
American Friends Service Committee (AFSC), 34–35, 188, 189–90
ANM (Arab Nationalist Movement), 2, 33, 36–37, 198n14, 209n7. *See also* PFLP (Popular Front for the Liberation of Palestine)
Ansar prison camp, 60–64, 80–84, 90, 100–101, 203n28. *See also* imprisonment/incarceration, mass
Arafat, Yasir (Abu Ammar), 36–37, 114, 121–23, 145, 153, 200n39, 209n2

arrests: of children, 100–101, 108, 128–29; and collaborators, 96–97, 106–7; in collective activation, 147–48; in emergence of clandestine operations, 73, 77, 79–80, 81–82, 83–84; in the Israeli invasion, 60–64, 66–67, 68–69; in network disruption, 7. *See also* imprisonment/incarceration, mass
artillery attacks, 42, 52, 56–57, 65
Assad, Hafiz al-, 44, 122–23
assassinations, 53, 104, 107, 109–10, 112, 132, 140–41, 142
atrocities, 42, 68–69, 204n35

Beirut: collaboration in, 61–62; PLO and guerrilla organizations in, 38–39, 66; remapping of camp-level shared defense in, 116–17, 118–21; siege of, 12, 13, 54–55, 57, 64–66; War of the Camps in, 116–22, 124–25, 126–27, 131–32, 137–38, 146, 147, 148. *See also* Burj al-Barajneh camp; Shatila camp; Tel al-Za'tar camp
Black September, 1970, 38–39
bombing, 52, 55–58, 59–60, 64, 65, 121–22
brokerage roles: in clandestine operations, 73–74, 81–82, 89–90; between local militias and exiled leadership, 116–17, 142; and marriage, 128, 150–51, 158–60; in personalized militias, 142; in the War of the Camps, 116–17, 128; of women, 28, 73–79, 90, 119, 128, 149–50, 164–65
Burj al-Barajneh camp, 40, 65, 66–67, 117, 121–25, 128–33, 152–53, 156. *See also* Beirut
Burj al-Shamali camp, 56–58, 59, 60–61, 124–25, 137–38, 146–48, 152–53. *See also* Sur
al-Buss camp, 56–58, 60–61, 112, 137–38, 148. *See also* Sur

Cairo Agreement, 37–38
Chamoun, Dany, 43–44
children: arrests of, 100–101, 108, 128–29; in counterintelligence, 107–10; as information brokers, 164–65; in narrative networks, 97; in the Sabra and Shatila massacre, 68–69; in social infrastructure, 46–47

239

INDEX

civil defense and political committees, 122–24
cleavages: in emergence of camp-level shared defense, 129–30, 133–34, 160–61; between ground forces and exiled elites, 60, 82–83, 88, 133–34, 157–58, 160–61; during mass incarceration, 79, 82–83; PLO-PNSF, at the Magdousheh front, 143–44; political, in the Lebanese Civil War, 10–11
Coastal Road Massacre, 200n40
cohesion/fragmentation: of battle lines in Saida, 138–46; and collaboration, 101–2, 112–13; of factions, 153; and insider-outsider dynamics, 160–61; in social infrastructure, 50–51, 162
collaboration/collaborators: in advocacy narratives, 97–102; in Ansar prison camp, 82–83; in emergence of clandestine networks, 77; in emergence of personalized militias, 142; in the Israeli invasion, 60–64, 69–70; known identities of, 110–13; unmasking of, 92–93, 106, 107–8. *See also* infiltration of social networks; informants
combat units/forces: adaptation of, in Beirut, 118–21; capacity and training of, 47–49; during the Israeli invasion, 58–59, 64; local loyalty and disobedience in, 128–32; mixed-descent militants in, 126–28; reconstitution of, as organizational resilience, 86–87, 90–91; remapping of, 72–74, 77–79, 116–17, 132–34; remapping of women's work in support of, 72–73, 148–49, 150–51; unified command of, 121–28. *See also* militias
command/commanders: assassination of officers in, 142; in emergence of camp-level shared defense, 117, 119–20, 129–30, 131–32; in emergence of personalized militias, 137, 139, 140–41, 143–45, 152–53; independence of, 48; in insider-outsider dynamics, 160–61; intelligence and logistics apparatuses in, 84; meso-level, 13, 140–41, 143–45, 152–53, 160–61; reporting of sexual harassment to, 151–52; small unit independence from, 72–73, 77–78; unified, in the War of the Camps, 121–28
communications: collaboration in new modes of, 97; in emergence of clandestine operations, 77, 79, 80–81, 86–87, 90; in emergence of cross-factional defensive fronts, 121, 122–23; in the Siege of Beirut, 66; strategic center for, in al-Buss, 137–38
consolidation/reconsolidation of networks, 74–75, 77–79, 82–83, 90, 109–10, 111–12, 136–37

corruption, 37–38, 88, 119–20, 136–37, 139–40, 141
counterinsurgency: divergent outcomes of, 112–13; and emergence of clandestine operations, 72–74, 77, 79, 82, 90; gendered, 12–13, 82, 90, 94–97, 98–100; in the Israeli invasion, 53–54, 59, 60–61, 69–70; mass incarceration in, 8–9, 60–61, 79; in narrative networks and international advocacy, 97–102
counterintelligence networks, 13, 64, 102–3
couriers/courier networks, female, 69, 84–85, 116–17, 164
cross-factional defensive fronts. *See* defense, camp and community-based
culture clubs, Palestinian, 50–51, 109

Damour, 42
Dbayeh camp, 42
decision-making, organizational, 7–8, 117, 124, 159–60, 162–63, 167–68
defense, camp and community-based: disobedience and solidarity in, 128–32; independence of, 113; in militant adaptation in Beirut, 118–21; neighborhood-based, 60; organizational hybridity in, 124–26; remapping of, 116–17, 118–22, 123, 125–28, 129–30, 132–34; unified command in, 121–28
Defense of Palestinian Prisoners, Committee for, 147
detention, mass. *See* imprisonment/incarceration, mass
Deuxième Bureau, 33, 34–38
DFLP (Democratic Front for the Liberation of Palestine), 41, 48, 126–27, 133, 143–44, 148–49, 151–53
disappearances, 3, 6, 8–9, 67–68, 76–77, 94, 107, 165–67
discipline, military, 115–16, 140–41
disobedience. *See* obedience/disobedience
divisions, political, 24–25, 27, 128–29. *See also* factions/factionalism

education, 46–47, 74–75, 170
Ein el Hilweh/Ein Hilwe camp. *See* Ain al-Hilweh camp
elites, militant: in adapting logistics and intelligence networks, 84–85; corruption of, 88, 119–20; and emergence of camp-level shared defense, 117, 119–20, 129–30, 131, 132–34; in emergence of personalized militias, 137, 138, 140–41, 152–53; women as, 150–51

embeddedness, social: in building social infrastructure, 46, 47, 51; of collaborators, 104; of collective meanings of violence, 7, 16, 70; in emergence of clandestine operations, 73, 78–79; in ethnographic research, 21–22, 181; of local leaders, 131, 133; in relational plasticity, 158–59; in rethinking intrastate war, 157–60

emergence, organizational: of intelligence and logistics apparatuses, 84–86; and organizational adaptation, 5; and relational plasticity, 159–60; and repertoires of violence, 52, 60; in rethinking intrastate war, 157; and social infrastructure, 10, 51; and women's high-risk work, 148–52. *See also* advocacy; counterintelligence networks; defense, camp and community-based; militias: personalized; operations, clandestine

emotions: in civilian mobilization, 92–93, 96–97, 98–99, 101–2, 106–8, 113; in obligations, in the War of the Camps, 125–26

Eritrean People's Liberation Front, 158–59
evictions, 95–96
exile. *See* leaders/leadership, exiled

factions/factionalism: in building social infrastructure, 30–31, 32, 49; and camp-level shared defense, 116, 122–24, 125, 133–34; and collective activation and divergent outcomes, 146–48; and community-based counterintelligence, 109–10; and emergence of clandestine networks, 83–84, 97; and emergence of personalized militias, 138–46; insider-outsider dynamics in, 160–61; and memory, 23, 26–27; protection via membership in, 133, 142–43, 152–53, 182; women's high-risk work across, 148–52. *See also* divisions, political; militias: personalized

families/family ties: in clandestine operations, 74, 75–76, 80–82, 83, 86–87, 89–90, 148, 164–65; in community-based counterintelligence, 104, 106–7; effects of mass incarceration on, 60–61, 63–64, 82, 83; factions and protection of, 133, 142–43, 152–53; and gendered counterinsurgency, 94, 96, 98–99. *See also* kinship ties/networks

Fatah: and building social infrastructure, 46, 50–51; capacity and training of, 47–49; cooptation of small cells by, 19–20; in cross-factional defense of camps, 116, 119–20, 121, 122–23, 126–27, 129–30, 133; and factionalism in Saida, 143–46, 153; in insider-outsider dynamics, 160–61; rise of, in Lebanon, 37, 38–40; in the Siege of Beirut, 65–66; training in Syria and Jordan, 199n20; women in, 71–72, 84–85, 126–27, 150

Fatah al-Intifada, 126, 132, 176–77
Fatah Women's Office, 20–21, 25–27, 171–74, 180–81

feedback: complexity of, in intra-state war, 156–57; in emergence of clandestine operations, 76, 90; in emergence of united defensive fronts, 132–33; in organizational adaptation, 4–5, 7; from violence in Saida and Sur, 13; between women's roles and everyday relationships, 150–51

finances/financial networks, 72–74, 84–85, 89–90, 121–22, 131, 142–43
FLA (Free Lebanon Army), 45
Force 17, 40, 118–19
forgery of documentation, 85, 119–20
friendship ties, 50–51, 74, 90, 150, 181–82

Gemayel, Amin, 68–69
Gemayel, Bashir, 67–68
generations/generational cohorts, 13, 64, 92–93, 94, 97, 105–10, 112–13, 172
GUPW (General Union of Palestinian Women), 3–4, 38–39, 149–51

Habash, George, 36, 126
Habib, Philip, 66
Haddad, Saad, 44–45
Haddad, Wadi, 36
Hashemite Kingdom. *See* Jordan
healthcare and aid, 46–47, 49, 145–46
hierarchies: alternative, 12–13; collective insubordination to, 117; military, adaptation and remapping of, 73–74, 77, 121; and organizational memory, 22–29; and relational plasticity, 158–59
al-Hindi, Hani, 36
Hizbullah, 126, 204n3
holdover practices, 155–56
homes/housing, 56–58, 98–100, 112–13
hybridity, organizational, 117, 121, 124–26, 128, 132–33
hypo-plasticity, 158–59

ICRC (International Committee of the Red Cross), 34–35
ideology, 46–47, 129, 158–59, 162–63

INDEX

IDF (Israel Defense Forces): in 1980s Lebanon, 11–12; collaborators used by, 102, 104, 105–6, 110–11; Operation Litani, 44–45; role in Sabra and Shatila massacre, 68; in the Siege of Beirut, 55–58, 59–60, 64, 66; withdrawal from Saida, 139. *See also* Israeli invasion

imprisonment/incarceration, mass: in emergence of clandestine networks, 73–74, 79–84, 90; gendered effects of, 94–97; in the Israeli invasion, 57–58, 60–64, 69–70, 201n5, 203n24; in social infrastructure, 8–9; as violence, 60–64, 165–67

indiscriminate/selective violence, 52–54, 60–65, 69, 70, 82–83, 201n2

infiltration of social networks, 82–83, 93, 100–102, 103, 104, 113, 142. *See also* collaboration/collaborators

informants, 61–64, 77–78, 82–83, 100–102, 104–5, 107–8, 110–12. *See also* collaboration/collaborators

information networks, 12–13, 73–74, 77–79, 85, 88–90

insider-outsider dynamics, 160–61, 179–80, 184–85

institutionalization: of clandestine operations, 147–48; of collaboration, 102–3, 110–11; of cross-factional defensive fronts, 116; of logistics and intelligence roles, 84–86; in organizational adaptation and change, 5, 8

insubordination, 115–16, 117, 126, 131–33, 146, 152–53

intelligence: Israeli, 57–58, 102; Lebanese, 33, 34–38, 178; Syrian, 153, 176–77, 178–79, 201n5

intelligence, Palestinian: and camp-level shared defensive fronts, 121, 124–25; clandestine operations in, 12–13, 84–86, 90; remapping of, 12–13, 72–74; women in, 72–74, 75–76, 148–52, 163–65

Internment. *See* imprisonment/incarceration, mass

intrastate war, 3–5, 11–12, 156–65, 167–68

ISIS (Islamic State in Iraq and Syria), 155

isolation from social networks, 35, 74, 82, 83, 103, 104, 107–8, 111–12

Israel: incursions into from Lebanon, 37–40, 44–45; in the Lebanese Civil War, 45; retaliation on Palestinian forces in Lebanon by, 41

Israeli invasion: aerial bombardment and close combat in, 55–60; counterinsurgency in, 53–54, 59, 60–61, 69–70; and emergence of Palestinian personalized militias, 137–38; healthcare institutions targeted during, 49; mass imprisonment during, 57–58, 60–64, 69–70; "mopping-up" campaigns, 54–55, 66–67; repertoires of violence during, 12, 52–70; siege of Beirut and aftermath in, 64–69

Jisr al-Pasha camp, 42
Jordan, 38–39, 47

Kahan Commission, 65
Karameh, Battle of, 37
Kata'ib militia, 39–40, 41–42, 44, 66–68, 94–95, 100–101. *See also* Lebanese Christian militias; Phalange party
al-kifah al-mussalah, 137, 143–44
kinship ties/networks, 75–76, 90–91, 104, 116–17, 126–27, 132, 148, 150–51. *See also* families/family ties

LAF (Lebanese Armed Forces): in conflict with *fida'iyyin*, 34, 37–38, 40; in gendered counterinsurgency, 94–95; in the Lebanese Civil War, 34, 41, 42; in "mopping up" campaigns after the siege of Beirut, 66–67; in the War of the Camps, 121–22, 210–11n15

leaders/leadership: in building social infrastructure, 30–33; in emergence of camp-level shared defense, 114–17, 118, 121–32, 133–34; in emergence of clandestine operations, 82–83, 88, 89; in emergence of personalized militias, 139–40, 141, 142–43, 146, 157–58, 160–61; insider-outsider dynamics in schism of, 160–61; in the Israeli invasion, 60; recruitment of, as collaborators, 106

leaders/leadership, exiled: cleavages with ground forces, 60, 82–83, 88, 133–34, 157–58, 160–61; in emergence of camp-level shared defense, 115–17, 118, 128–32, 133–34; and personalized militias, 141, 142, 146, 157–58, 160–61

Lebanese Christian militias: in 1980s Beirut, 11; in counterinsurgency, 94–96; in the Israeli invasion, 67–68, 69–70; in the Lebanese Civil War, 18–19, 41, 42, 43–45, 196n6; in the Sabra and Shatila massacre, 66–69

Lebanese Civil War, 10–12, 34, 41–45, 47, 51, 199–200n32

Lebanese Front, 41, 43–44

INDEX   243

Lebanese government and state: collapse of, 41–42, 120–21; confessional power sharing in, 34; protest of IDF occupation by, 45; restrictions on refugees by, 34–38, 197–98n10
LF (Lebanese Forces), 41–42, 95–96. *See also* Lebanese Christian militias
LNM (Lebanese National Movement), 39–40, 41–42, 44, 65–66
logistics apparatuses/roles: as backstage labor, 2; in building social infrastructure, 49; in emergence of clandestine operations, 78, 84–86, 88–89, 90, 91; in the War of the Camps, 127–28, 137–38; women in, 127–28, 148–49, 163–64
loyalty, 89–90, 104, 117, 128–32, 137–38, 141, 143

Magdousheh, Battle of, 13, 137–38, 143–46, 150–51, 152–53
maintenance, organizational, 74, 86–87, 90, 120–21
Maronite Christians and militias, 42–43, 198n11. *See also* Lebanese Christian militias; militias
marriage, 9, 13, 72, 75–76, 116–17, 128, 132, 150–51, 158–60. *See also* families/family ties; kinship ties/networks
Maslakh-Karantina, 42
massacres, 7, 41–42, 58, 66–70, 101–2, 118–19, 122–24, 132, 200n40
Mavi Marmara incident, 173, 213–14n8
meanings, collective: in categorizing tactics, 53–54; in emergence of new organizations, 10, 137–38; of home raids, in civilian narrative networks, 98–99; in the Israeli invasion, 56–57, 70; of violence, 7–8, 10, 13, 16, 70
Melkart Protocol, 40
memory, 15–29, 57–58, 131–32, 137–38, 177–78, 211n40
metadata, organizational, 25–27, 31–32, 51
mihwar (intersection/axis) system, 124–25
militias: Lebanese, 42, 67–69, 85, 94–97, 102, 120; personalized, 137–46 (*see also* factions/factionalism). *See also* Amal; combat units/forces; Lebanese Christian militias; *name of militia*
MNF (Multi-National Forces), 66, 120–21
mobilization: civilian, 92–93, 95–96, 97–110, 113; in emergence of personalized militias, 143; gendered, 72–75, 85, 88–89, 90–91; insider-outsider dynamics in, 160–61; and social infrastructure, 9–10, 74–75

money: in emergence of personalized militias, 141, 142–43, 144–45; kinship and marriage ties in movement of, 116–17; in militant adaptation in Beirut, 119–21; in organizational resilience, 89–90; women in smuggling and transfer of, 25–26, 71–72, 75–76, 84–85, 148. *See also* salaries
"mopping-up" campaigns, 54–55, 66–67, 116–17
morality/moral obligation, 88, 117, 124, 125–26, 128–29, 130–32
Mossad, 57, 141. *See also* intelligence
al-Mughrabi, Dalal, 44–45, 200n40
mukhabarat (state intelligence services), 3–4, 122, 149, 153, 201n5. *See also* intelligence
multivocality, 195n1
al-Muragha, Saied, 47–48, 115, 202n17, 209n2
mutiny, 115, 140–41, 202n17, 209n2
mu'askarat (detention pens), 80–81

Nadi al-Houli massacre, 58
Nakba, 34
Nakba Day, 20–21, 172–75, 213n7
National Pact, Lebanese, 1943, 34, 198n11
networks: bridges, 8–10, 75–76, 90, 150–51, 161–62; civilian, 93–94, 97–100, 102–5; clandestine, 12–13, 84–85, 89–90, 125–26, 137–38, 146–48, 158–59; consequences of violence for, 7–8; discursive, 171–72; intra-organizational, 28; narrative, 97–102; network closure, 142, 180–81; overlap of, 8–10, 19, 21, 33, 85, 90
Nofal, Mamdouh, 138–39, 144–45
noncombatants: activism of, 163–64; collaborators in social relations of, 92–93; emergent intelligence and logistics operations of, 85; occupation in mobilization of, 97–102; in organizational resilience, 91

obedience/disobedience, 115–17, 125–26, 128–33, 143, 145–46, 157–58
occupation: effects of counterinsurgency during, 94–97, 112–13; in emergence of clandestine operations, 73, 77, 88–89, 90–91; experience of, 54–56, 69–70, 88; and gendered incarceration, 61–64; local collaboration and counterintelligence under, 102–13; narrative networks and internationalizing advocacy during, 93–94, 97–102, 113; in organizational adaptation and emergence, 60, 137–38

officers. *See* command/commanders; leaders/leadership
Operation Litani, 44–45
operations, clandestine: brokerage roles in, 73–79, 81–82; in camp-level shared defense, 116–17, 118–21, 123, 126–28; in countering collaboration, 99–100, 108, 109; cross-regional, 146, 147–48, 149; under the Deuxième Bureau, 35; family ties in, 148, 164–65; intelligence and logistics apparatuses in, 72–74, 75–76, 84–86, 90; and the Israeli invasion, 64; mass imprisonment and evolution of, 79–84; and personalized militias, 137–38, 147–52; socialization and indoctrination in, 87–91; supply networks, 12–13, 84–85, 125–26, 137–38, 147–48; women in, 24–28, 72–79, 82, 88–89, 90, 148–52, 163–65
outcomes, organizational, 7, 53–54, 70, 91–92, 112–13, 157–58, 162–63

Palestine Liberation Front-Path of Return, 37
Palestinian National Movement, 139–40, 160–61
Palestinian Social and Humanitarian Committee, 105
patronage, 142–43, 161–62
patterns of violence, 116–17, 137, 165–66, 167, 195n7
PCP (Palestinian Communist Party), 133
PDFLP (Popular Democratic Front for the Liberation of Palestine), 36–37
PFLP (Popular Front for the Liberation of Palestine), 36–37, 40–41, 48, 130, 145–46, 153. *See also* ANM (Arab Nationalist Movement)
PFLP-GC (Popular Front for the Liberation of Palestine-General Command), 40–41, 48, 125–26
Phalange party, 96. *See also* Kata'ib militia
PLA (Palestine Liberation Army), 37, 47–48
plasticity, relational, 9–10, 158–60
PLF (Palestine Liberation Front), 36–37
PLO (Palestine Liberation Organization): in building social infrastructure, 33–34, 36–41, 42, 43–45, 46–51; cooptation of small cells by, 116–17, 119–20, 132; and disobedience, 128–29, 130, 132–33; and emergence of clandestine operations, 75, 84–86, 88, 90; in emergence of personalized militias, 137, 139, 143–46, 149, 153; establishment of, 36–37; in insider-outsider dynamics, 160–61; in the Israeli invasion, 55, 58, 60, 65–67, 69; in the Lebanese Civil War, 42, 43–45; in unified command of camp-level shared defense, 121–24, 126; violent and nonviolent roles in, 4
PNC (Palestinian National Council), 37
PNG (Palestinian National Guard), 105–6
PNSF (Palestinian National Salvation Front), 116, 122–24, 125–27, 128–29, 143–45, 146–47, 153, 176–77
political parties, 36–37, 39–40, 49, 51, 159–60, 162–63. *See also* under *name of party*
Popular Committees, PLO, 38
PPSF (Palestinian Popular Struggle Front), 36–37, 145–46, 153
PRCS (Palestinian Red Crescent Society), 38–39, 49, 57, 123
protection: cross-factional defensive fronts in, 116, 119, 129, 133; factional membership in, 133, 142–43, 152–53, 182; gendered stereotypes as, 99–100; and mass imprisonment, 82–83; for mixed-descent militants, 126–27; as motive for collaboration, 104; personal relationships in, 86
PSP (Progressive Socialist Party), 79, 120, 144, 204n3

al-Quds magazine (Fatah), 71–72

Rashidiyeh camp, 56–57, 59, 110–12, 121–22, 137–38, 146–48, 152–53. *See also* Sur
recreational programs and sports clubs, 46–47, 50–51
recruitment: of collaborators, 102, 103–4, 105, 106, 110–11; in emergence of personalized militias, 142–43; and publications, 88–89; social connections in, 119, 159; social infrastructure in, 8, 47–49, 50–51; of women, 48–49, 74–75, 85, 88–89
refugee camps: destruction of, in the Israeli invasion, 55–58; under the Deuxième Bureau, 34–38; Palestinian, in Lebanon, 10–11, 34–38; population of, 193tC.1; in research methodology, 18–22, 169–70. *See also* under *name of camp*
refugees: in contemporary multiparty and intrastate conflict, 5–6; numbers of (Palestinian) in Lebanon, 34, 193tC.1, 197–98n9; Syrian, in Lebanon, 178
remapping: in emergence of camp-level shared defense, 116–17, 118–22, 123, 125–28, 129–30, 132–34; in emergence of clandestine networks, 72–75, 77–79, 84–86, 88–89, 90–91; in emergence of counterintelligence

INDEX 245

and advocacy networks, 92–93, 98–100, 105–6, 108, 111–12; in emergence of personalized militias, 138–47, 150, 152–53; in organizational adaptation, 5, 9–10, 12–13, 156; and relational plasticity, 159–60

repression: in emergence of advocacy and counterintelligence networks, 93, 97, 112–13; in evolution of clandestine operations, 78, 90–91; in the Israeli invasion, 50, 51, 54, 64, 69; in organizational change, 7–8; in professionalization of high-risk work, 149; and rethinking intrastate war, 157–58; and social infrastructure, 16, 35–36; measurement challenges in study of, 165–66. *See also* imprisonment/incarceration, mass

repurposing: agency in, 195n9; in emergence of camp-based defensive units, 116–17, 119–20, 121–22, 132; in emergence of clandestine operations, 75–76, 78, 148; during the Israeli invasion, 57–58; and organizational adaptation, 5, 7–8, 9–10; and relational plasticity, 159–60; in resisting collaboration, 99–100, 108–9

research methodology: confidentiality in, 185–86; consent procedures in, 170–71; ethics in, 179–83, 184–85; ethnographic approach, 17–29, 169–85; ethnohistorical interviews, 22–29, 175–79; "network sensibility," 181

resentment: of collaborators, 107–8; of the Deuxième Bureau, 35; of Israeli attacks and occupation, 45, 51, 65, 83–84, 92–93, 107–8; of returning exiled elites, 139, 140–41, 153

resilience, organizational, 5–10, 16, 59, 71–72, 74–91

return/reinfiltration of PLO fighters, 119–22, 137, 139, 140–41, 142

revenge, 62, 95–96, 101–2, 107, 142–43, 207n31

risks: in anticollaboration and advocacy, 93, 100–101, 103–4, 106, 113; in clandestine networks, 73, 76–77, 83–84, 87–88, 89–91, 119, 127–28; everyday, 6, 7; in factional membership, 142–43; in formation of cross-factional defensive fronts, 119, 127–28; in the Israeli invasion, 62–63; of women's work, 73, 76–77, 127–29, 148–52, 163–64

rivalries, 122–24, 132–33, 143–45

romantic ties, 158–59. *See also* marriage

Sabra and Shatila massacre, 7, 66–70, 101–2, 116–17, 118–19, 122–24, 132, 206n18

al-Safir newspaper, 143–44, 188–89

Saida: 1975 fishing dispute, 41; collaborators and counterintelligence in, 92–93, 95–96; emergence of advocacy and counterintelligence in, 102–13; emergence of clandestine networks in, 86; hospital bombing in, 1–2; lessons from Ain al-Hilweh in, 60; in the War of the Camps, 13, 138–46, 152–53. *See also* Ain al-Hilweh camp

salaries, 72, 75–76, 84–85, 89–90, 119–20, 127, 142–43. *See also* money

Sarajevo, Siege of, 6, 164–65

Sarkis, Elias, 66

Sawt al-Mukhayyam ("The Voice of the Camps"), 82, 87–90, 99, 139–40, 189

al-Saʿiqa, 10–11, 47–48, 176–77

scouting/scouts *(ashbal/kashafa/zaharat)*, 46, 50–51, 109, 150

sectarianism, 41–42, 128, 161–63, 198n11, 199–200n32

selective violence. *See* indiscriminate/selective violence

Shatila camp: cross-faction defensive fronts in, 13; Lebanese military attack on, 40; massacre in, 7, 66–70, 101–2, 116–17, 118–19, 122–24, 132, 206n18; in the War of the Camps, 116, 117, 121–26, 128–30, 132–33. *See also* Beirut

al-Shuqayri, Ahmad, 36–37

sieges: of Beirut, 12, 13, 54–55, 57, 64–69; blockades in, 64–65, 121–22, 123–24, 129, 130–31; of Burj al-Barajneh camp, 117, 121–25, 128–33; in emergence of camp-level shared defense, 117, 121–29, 133–34; in organizational adaptation and emergence, 137–38; of Rashidiyeh camp, 146–47; of Sarajevo, 6, 164–65; of Shatila camp, 117, 121–26, 128–30, 132–33; of Tel al-Zaʿtar camp, 43–45

smugglers, female: in movement of money, 25–26, 71–72, 75–76, 84–85, 148; in organizational memory, 27–28; in the War of the Camps, 126–28, 132–33, 137–38, 147–48

social change and social infrastructure, 46–47, 48–49, 90

socialization/resocialization, 83, 86–91, 108–9, 115–16, 117, 132

solidarity, 65, 112, 128–32, 161–62

South Lebanon Army, 95–96

starvation, 44, 128–29, 165–66

structures/restructuring, organizational, 38–41, 77–79, 81–82, 118–19, 138–39, 156

supplies/supply networks, 12–13, 79, 84–85, 125–26, 130–31, 137–38

Sur: collaborators and counterintelligence in, 92–93, 102–13; in the Israeli invasion, 56, 58, 60; in the Lebanese Civil War, 45; personalized militias in, 137–38, 146–48; violent repertoires used in, 11; War of the Camps in, 13, 146–48. *See also* Burj al-Shamali camp; al-Buss camp; Rashidiyeh camp

surveillance, 35–36, 80–81, 86, 111–12, 142

suspicion, 82–83, 86, 93, 95–96, 102–3, 108–10, 113, 140–41

Syria: disappearances in, 166–67; incarcerations and torture during civil war in, 6, 166–67; in the Lebanese Civil War, 43–44; occupation of northern and eastern Lebanon by, 11–12; responses to emergent noncombat apparatuses by, 85; in the War of the Camps, 54, 121–22, 126

tactics: in camp-level shared defensive fronts, 124–25, 130–31, 132–34; categorization of, 53–55; in contemporary conflict, 6; and emergence of advocacy and counterintelligence networks, 92–93, 97, 99–100, 101–3, 104, 105–6, 111–13; and emergence of clandestine networks, 73, 78, 82–83; and emergence of factional militias, 138–39, 146, 148–49; in gendered counterinsurgency, 12–13; in the Israeli invasion, 56–58, 59; in the Lebanese civil war, 200n39; moral hazard, 200n39; network effects of, 7–8; in reshaping social networks, 92–93, 156. *See also* violence, repertoires of

Tel al-Zaʻtar camp, 3, 8–9, 41–42, 43–45, 199–200n32

threat, perception of: in emergence of advocacy and counterintelligence networks, 93, 95–97, 105–6, 113; in emergence of camp-level shared defense, 117, 118, 126–28, 132, 133–34; in emergence of clandestine operations, 76, 82–83, 91, 147–48; in emergence of private militias, 137–38, 152–53; during Israeli invasion, 61–63, 67; in organizational change, 10

Tigers, 43–44

torture, 4, 6, 67–68, 96–97, 138–39, 181–83

training, military, 47–49, 50, 65, 73, 78

trust/distrust: collaboration in, 61–62, 102, 103–4, 105–6; in counterintelligence, 108–9; in mobilization, 161–62; in organizational ethnography, 174–75; in organizational resilience, 90; of returning elites, 140–41; ties of, in women's smuggling, 75–76

unconventional warfare, 2–3

underground networks. *See* operations, clandestine

UNIFIL (United Nations Interim Force in Lebanon), 45

UNRWA (United Nations Relief and Works Agency), 33, 34–35, 105, 106, 110–11

Village Leagues, 105

violence, repertoires of: in adaptive trajectories, 156; in bridging networks, 162; direct/indirect, 12, 53, 70, 94–95, 201n2; and emergence of advocacy and counterintelligence networks, 92–93, 94–95, 98–100, 112–13; and emergence of camp-level shared defense, 116–17, 122, 128–29, 133–34; and emergence of clandestine networks, 72–73, 74–75, 77–78, 90–91; and emergence of personalized militias, 138, 147–48, 152–53; gendered incarceration in, 60–64; gender in analysis of, 164–65; in intrastate warfare, 156, 157–58, 161, 162; in the invasion of South Lebanon, 55–60; nonlethal and indirect aspects of, 167; and organizational adaptation, 4–5, 6–8, 11, 12–14; regionalized, 12, 54–55; in reshaping social networks, 69–70, 92–93, 156; in the siege of Beirut, 64–69; use of term, 195n7. *See also* imprisonment/incarceration, mass; sieges; tactics

vulnerability, 66–67, 68–69, 77, 79, 92–93, 99–100, 103, 118

War of the Camps: in Beirut, 116–22, 124–25, 126–27, 131–32, 137–38, 146, 147, 148; consequences of, 153–54; defensive models in, 60; disobedience in, 115–17, 125–26, 128–33; memories of, 22–29; organizational hybridity in, 124–26; regional comparisons of, 54–55; role of mixed-descent militants in, 126–28; in Saida, 13, 138–46, 152–53; in Sur, 13, 146–48; unified command in, 121–28; women's high-risk work in, 148–52

al-Wazzan, Shafiq, 66

white phosphorous, 57–58, 65, 201–2n12

Yarmouk Brigade, 47–48

youth: in anticollaborator networks, 106; in community-based counterintelligence, 109–10; gendered violence in mobilization of, 72–73

www.ingramcontent.com/pod-product-compliance
Lightning Source LLC
Chambersburg PA
CBHW021853230426
43671CB00006B/368